The Rural Foundation for Urbanism

The Rural Foundation for Urbanism

Economic and Stylistic Interaction between Rural
and Urban Communities in Eighth-Century Peru

WILLIAM HARRIS ISBELL

 ILLINOIS STUDIES IN ANTHROPOLOGY NO. 10

UNIVERSITY OF ILLINOIS PRESS   URBANA, CHICAGO, LONDON

Library of Congress Cataloging in Publication Data

Isbell, William Harris, 1943–
    The rural foundation for urbanism.

    (Illinois studies in anthropology ; no. 10)
    Bibliography: p.
    Includes index.
    1. Jargampata site, Peru. 2. Wari site, Peru.
3. Indians of South America—Peru—Pottery.
4. Urbanization—Peru. I. Title. II. Series.
F3429.1.A9I82   985'.004'98   77-1255
ISBN 0-252-00600-3

Acknowledgments

The fieldwork on which this study is based was conducted between June 15 and November 15, 1969, under Resolución Suprema No. 0754 issued by the Ministerio de Educación Pública upon the recommendation of the Patronato Nacional de Arqueología and the Dirección General de Cultura. The research, including a continued stay in Peru until August, 1970, during which the archaeological collections were studied, was made possible by grant GS-2542 for doctoral dissertation research in anthropology by the National Science Foundation and by grant agreement No. OEG 9-230215-068 as provided for by the Fulbright-Hays Mutual Educational and Cultural Exchange Act. I gratefully acknowledge this support.

I wish to express my thanks to many participants in the circle of Andean scholars who have provided stimuli during my research, but particularly I wish to thank Donald W. Lathrap, R. Tom Zuidema, Thomas Patterson, John H. Rowe, Dorothy Menzel, Rogger Ravines, and Luis G. Lumbreras.

This research was carried out in the San Miguel valley, along a tributary of the Pampas River. I want to express my gratitude to all of the people of San Miguel, whose hospitality made my work possible. Alvino Añaños, on whose land I excavated and in whose home I lived, provided not only living and working facilities but also a warm friendship and a fountain of information about the area. Alvino and his wife, Barbara, and other residents of the valley—Alberto Luis Fernández, Pepe and Arturo Carrasco, Umberto Moor, and the fine people of the community of Illaura—made my stay in the valley both intellectually profitable and pleasant. J. Scott Raymond participated with me in the initial site survey of various areas in the Pampas River valley, and Edmundo Pinto R., anthropologist from the Universidad San Cristobal de Huamanga, acted as my field assistant. For their excellent assistance I remain most grateful.

I wish to thank Rogger Ravines, Julie Espejo, Duccio Bonavia, and the late Jorge Muelle for their assistance with numerous problems, for stimulating conversations, and for access to ceramic collections at the Museo Nacional de Antropología y Arqueología. Deep gratitude is due to Luis G. Lumbreras and Félix Caycho of the Museo de Arqueología y Etnología of the Universidad de San Marcos for providing research and storage space for my collections as well as helpful encouragement and advice during many months of analysis.

Intellectual guidance was provided by the archaeologists who have directed the investigation into the Andean Middle Horizon. Chief among these are Luis G. Lumbreras, Dorothy Menzel, Gary S. Vescelius, Rogger Ravines, William Conklin, Allison Paulsen, and David Browman. Luis Lumbreras provided me with unpublished data from his excavations at Conchopata, Rogger Ravines gave me free access to his collections from Ayapata, Allison Paulsen provided unpublished manuscripts on late Early Intermediate styles of the South Coast, and both Conklin and Browman have helped me clarify my ideas about the Middle Horizon through long conversations. Dorothy Menzel provided the guiding chronological framework and freely gave of her time to discuss the elite pottery of the Middle Horizon and that which I recovered at Jargampata.

I wish to thank the Department of Anthropology of the University of Illinois for providing me with essential support, research space, and a stimulating environment during the analysis of Jargampata pottery. To the Archaeology Laboratory and the Department of Anthropology of the State University of New York at Binghamton I express gratitude for the many facilities provided me while writing and preparing illustrations. To my colleagues in the department and laboratory, particularly John Stank, Fred Plog, and Gene Sterud, I am grateful for numerous suggestions and stimulating discussions. Several volunteers also gave their time in coding pottery and preparing calculations, illustrations, and charts. I wish to thank Jane Vandament, Amy Harlib, and Carol Ricketts. Many of the finished illustrations were prepared by Barbara Richards.

Contents

Plates

Figures

Tables

Introduction

Urbanism in prehistory has become an important and popular topic of research which has had a great deal of impact upon the recent reevaluation of settlement patterns in the ancient Andes. Where scholars of several decades ago saw virtually empty ceremonial centers, researchers now see densely populated cities (Rowe 1963; Hardoy 1968; Parsons 1968; Ponce 1969a). However, these studies have tended to focus attention upon the study of urbanism in terms of the total population residing at a single site at any one time and the relative density of the arrangement of the inhabitants. This kind of research will lead to the definition of typologies of cities which may be arranged in different orders to create an evolutionary sequence, but it is very likely that such type concepts will obscure the study of the prehistoric process, or processes, which supported urbanism.

More meaningful research on the prehistoric city must go beyond a study of the size of the resident population and must focus on the degree and kinds of professional specialization within the city, urban facilities for the redistribution of produce and industrial products, and systems of importing raw materials for conversion into manufactured goods. Eric Wolf (1955: 452–55) has pointed out that the modern peasant cannot be distinguished or understood in terms of a particular culture content. Rather, "peasant" is a structural concept, and a peasantry exists only in opposition to a larger and dominant social unit. So also, the modern or prehistoric city is a structural concept existing in reality only as a partial society, albeit usually the dominant one. It exists in an economic, political, and religio-intellectual symbiosis with rural producer communities which provide the basic energy essential to the operation of the city. To understand any synchronic or diachronic process upon which the city is founded, we must understand the structural relationship between the urban center and its rural producer communities as well as the internal structure of the city itself.

It is the study of this rural-urban relationship which has motivated the problem-oriented research reported in this volume. Two problems have been studied; both are ultimately closely related in the study of urban processes in the Andes. First I have suggested what some of the salient features of the organization of the prehistoric Andean Wari polity may have been. This very generalized reconstruction is based primarily upon a progressive un-

derstanding of the Andean pattern of organizing ecologically contrastive environmental zones into a single economic system. The most comprehensive discussion of this multizonal integration is in a recent article by John V. Murra (1972), although many of his earlier works are based upon an implicit recognition of the system. A similar organization of cosmological zones is reported by Zuidema and Quispe (1968), and I have already indicated the utility of their model for interpreting prehistoric remains (W. Isbell 1968). The intensively studied site of Jargampata in the Central Highlands of Peru is described and interpreted in terms of the multizonal model, demonstrating a probability that the model applies to prehistoric Andean peoples as well as those described since the Spanish conquest.

The second problem discussed is the provision of a detailed description of a rural ceramic style which can be placed in time relative to fancy, elite ceramics and in space relative to other prehistoric ceramic styles in similar and contrasting ecological zones. The intensive study of such artifactual material permits the definition of a system of rules in terms of which a material cultural complex was produced. In turn, definition of such a system allows the archaeologist to identify a group of people who shared the same rule system and presumably shared a much larger cultural configuration which was less overtly manifested in the material culture. Once a series of rural styles has been adequately described, it will be possible to discover the distribution of groups sharing the same rule systems and cultural configurations and to observe specialization of activities, the extent of the urban hinterland, and the interaction between distinct groups. It may also be possible to identify the members of rural groups in the city and to study their progressive response to the urban milieu. Evidence from modern Andean cities indicates that migrants to urban zones often live in nucleated subcommunities composed of persons from a single village and that these urbanites maintain their village identity for generations (B. J. Isbell 1972). An active transaction goes on between the village and city, and it is largely mediated through a nucleated migrant community or a specially maintained "receiving house" within the city which is owned and operated by the rural community or kin alliance (Carter 1968: 260-61, nn. 5, 22). It is my conviction that to comprehend the processes which produced and maintained preindustrial cities we must be able to recognize

1

individual rural groups. The amount of research required is immense, but a step has been taken toward the identification of one Wari group with the description of Jargampata ceramics. This detailed description, which may appear absurd to some, is motivated by my belief that someday we will be able to identify the people of Jargampata in the urban center of Wari and will then be able to complete our study of the structural relations between urban and rural sites.

The spatial and temporal setting for this study and the selection of the Jargampata site were carefully made. First, it was necessary to consider a political unit which covered sufficient territory to include obviously distinct ecological areas within a centralized political system. Next, I wanted to study a prehistoric polity which was not so ancient that ethnohistorical models would seem inapplicable. Finally, it was necessary to deal with a case which had already been studied enough so that it would not be necessary to begin with the basic concerns of regional chronologies and their correlation.

The time period selected for study was the Middle Horizon, and the area was the Central Highlands of Peru in the rural hinterland of the Wari center. "Middle Horizon" is the name given to the prehistoric period which witnessed the first total political unification of the Central Andes (Rowe 1962: 49). Most Andeanists now believe that the unification took place as a result of political and military conquests beginning about 600 A.D. (Menzel 1964: 66-73; Menzel 1968a: 90-94; Lumbreras 1969: 233-70). The empire forged by these conquests endured only briefly, and by about 800 A.D. it disappeared as a centralized entity, leaving only independent subtraditions which descended from the great tradition expressed in the earlier unified style.

The iconographic and stylistic conventions which identify the Middle Horizon constituted the first pre-Inca cultural horizon to be recognized in the Central Andes. Furthermore, Wari—the ruins of a great city which may have been the Middle Horizon empire capital—was among the first archaeological remains in the Andes to be recognized as pre-Inca and described in print.

The early recognition of the Middle Horizon and its important role in deciphering the prehistoric sequences of nuclear South America would suggest to most scholars that research and knowledge concerning the period should be extensive and relatively complete. However, grave uncertainties exist about the mechanisms of expansion, the existence of urbanism, the urban-rural interaction system, the identification of political centers, and the economic base upon which the empire was founded.

Wari, which is only assumed to have been the urban Middle Horizon capital, was visited in about 1548 by Pedro de Cieza de Leon as he traveled through Guamanga (Ayacucho). In his famous chronicle of Peru (Cieza de Leon

n.d.: 416), he observed that the square ground plans at this site on the Vinaque River contrasted with the elongated enclosures characteristic of the Incas and that the condition of the walls indicated great age. Attributing the center to builders who predated the reign of the Incas, Cieza (n.d.: 458) went on with almost prophetic intuition to propose that both Tiahuanaco and Wari might represent the remains of a single pre-Inca people—light-skinned and bearded, according to local oral traditions—who had become absorbed into the larger population and lost in the obscurity of prehistory. Although the light-skinned and bearded folk of the sixteenth-century tales remain as obscure today as they did in Cieza's time (Lumbreras 1960: 132-34), generations of investigators have finally proved Cieza to have been generally correct in his association of Wari and Tiahuanaco. This raises a question concerning the basis and validity of the oral traditions which led Cieza to associate the peoples of Lake Titicaca with those of Ayacucho and to propose the existence of a single prehistoric group of people responsible for both sites. Was the Middle Horizon unification truly lost in obscurity, or did its structure and traditions continue to exercise an influence upon the organization and mythology of the Inca world?

Almost 350 years after Cieza's visit, Max Uhle recognized the existence of a widely spread Tiahuanaco-period style stretching from its proposed hearth on the Bolivian shores of Lake Titicaca to far northern Peru (Uhle 1903a: 784-85). Using a concept essentially identical with the "horizon style" (Willey and Phillips 1958: 31-33), Uhle identified a ceramic assemblage at Pachacamac which was related to that of Tiahuanaco. He realized that the earliest ceramics he found were very similar to those of Tiahuanaco except for differences in vessel shape. In addition, he isolated another inferior but related style which was named Epigone (Uhle 1903b: 26-34).

On the basis of both his archaeologically revealed Tiahuanaco period and the historically described Inca conquest, Uhle was able to correlate diverse local sequences from the Andes. He formulated a six-period scheme in which a "Tiahuanaco Period" formed the second and the "Inca Period" the sixth of a long stylistic succession (Uhle 1903a).

Later, Uhle abandoned the six-period scheme of Andean prehistory, but the Tiahuanaco horizon he had recognized continued to play a major role in chronological schemes of other Andean scholars. Alfred Kroeber and William Duncan Strong (1924: 53) recognized four successive periods which were later formalized by O'Neal and Kroeber (1930: 42-44, Table 1). The Tiahuanaco period was named the Middle Period since other styles were dated as earlier or later than the Tiahuanaco materials, or as Inca (Kroeber 1930: 108-14).

Wari played no role in the early twentieth-century discovery of the Tiahuanaco period, and it was not

recognized as related to this early pan-Andean horizon. Not until 1931, when Julio C. Tello made an expedition to the Mantaro valley and to Wari itself, did archaeologists begin to recognize the importance of this center. In a newspaper article in 1931, Tello compared the Wari remains with both Tiahuanaco and Chavín and asserted that the peoples of the Mantaro had exercised a decisive influence upon the peoples of the coast (Lumbreras 1960: 220-21). By 1939, Tello (1970) believed that the population at Wari had played the dominant role in originating and disseminating cultural manifestations of the coast which were generally ascribed to the Tiahuanaco period. In 1942, Tello again returned to the Mantaro River area and extended his investigations at Wari, but the results of his work were not published. Not until recently, when Luis G. Lumbreras (1960) published a detailed description of Tello's collections, did these materials become available to help solve the problem of the relationship between various Tiahuanaco-period centers.

Meanwhile, although Wari was perhaps recognized in Peru, it was virtually unknown in the North American literature. In 1942, Kroeber (1944: 29-31, 99, Pl. 39) published photographs of fifteen sherds of Wari pottery, which had been collected by Lila O'Neal when she accompanied Tello to the site in 1931, and a discussion of their stylistic characteristics and probable relationships to other known ceramic styles. Kroeber recognized both Nazca and Tiahuanaco features present in this pottery, but certainly did not ascribe a particularly important role to the Wari site—which appears by name only in his explanation of the plates (Kroeber 1944: 149). However, Kroeber did recognize the complex nature of the Tiahuanaco cultural horizon and, yielding to Tello's claims about the age of Chavín, he abandoned his term "Middle Period."

The growing recognition of the importance of Wari among Peruvian scholars culminated in the renaming of coastal Tiahuanaco styles about the same time that Wari made its first real appearance in archaeological literature in North America. Rafael Larco Hoyle (1948: 37-49) stated that the similarities between ceramics from the North Coast and those in collections from Ayacucho, Huancayo, Huanta, and Chincheros could only indicate a conquest of the North Coast from the Wari region. He named these local North Coast styles "Huari Norteño." Richard Schaedel (1948: 72) published the first photographs and brief descriptions of Wari in English about that same time. In 1946 the site was visited by John H. Rowe, Donald Collier, and Gordon Willey; in an excellent article published in 1950 they give a detailed history of research at Wari and describe its architecture, statuary, and ceramics. A penetrating analysis of surface collections and illustrated vessels allowed the authors to identify a blend of Tiahuanaco and Nazca features in Wari pottery and to show that this highland style was contemporary with, and most like, Coast Tiahuanaco pottery (Rowe, Collier, and Willey 1950: 129-33).

In the summer of 1950, Wendell Bennett (1953) undertook a systematic study which involved stratigraphic excavation at the Wari site. His research and detailed description of Wari architecture and pottery proved the association with Tiahuanaco but finally put to rest the belief that the Tiahuanaco styles of the Peruvian South and Central Highlands represented a gradual transition between the Bolivian Tiahuanaco styles of the Altiplano and the Coast Tiahuanaco styles of Peru. The Wari pottery definitely belongs with Peruvian coastal ceramics, which Bennett (1953: 110) proposed to combine as Peruvian Tiahuanaco. He believed the similarities between Peruvian and Bolivian Tiahuanaco indicated some form of direct contact, probably from the Altiplano site to the Mantaro basin, since there was a long developmental sequence represented at Tiahuanaco and little antecedent in the Mantaro (this is true in spite of Bennett's inversion of the Wari sequence). Finally, Bennett (1953: 114-18) suggested that Wari and the Mantaro basin comprised the center from which the Peruvian Tiahuanaco styles spread. He called for more research—including the study of local ceramic styles and of habitation sites—to clarify the nature of the Tiahuanaco Horizon.

Following the death of Wendell Bennett, the burden of investigating the Middle Horizon fell to John H. Rowe (1956) and his students Dwight T. Wallace (1957) and Dorothy Menzel (1964, 1968a, 1968b). Rowe (1956: 144) demonstrated that Wari ceramic styles have a wide distribution through the Central and South Highlands of Peru. The spheres of influence from Wari on the one hand and Tiahuanaco on the other must have intersected somewhere between Sicuani in southern Cuzco and Juliaca in Puno.

In Peru, Luis G. Lumbreras (1959, 1960, 1969) and his students Mario Benavides (1965) and J. Enrique Gonzáles (1966) became the principal investigators of the Tiahuanaco Horizon in the Central Highlands around Wari. Lumbreras (1960: 191-200) made particularly important contributions by correcting the succession of ceramic styles and occupations of major sites relevant to the rise of Wari. Ever since Bennett had inverted the sequence at Wari, the relationships between Wari and the coastal areas had been a matter of extreme confusion.

On the basis of detailed study of South Coast ceramic sequences from Ica, Menzel (1964, 1968b) defined regional styles within the Middle Horizon. She was able to distinguish several brief stylistic periods within the evolution of each regional variant and observe the interaction between these styles. Further research on the Middle Horizon, and particularly the work of Rogger Ravines (1968), enabled Menzel (1968a) to refine her description of Middle Horizon Epoch 2, especially for the Central Highlands.

The relationship between Middle Horizon Tiahuanaco

and Wari is now generally accepted. These ruins probably represent centers of separate but largely contemporary polities with the boundary which partitioned their spheres of political and economic interaction running between Sicuani and Juliaca in the highlands through Arequipa to the coast perhaps between the Majes and Sihuas valleys (Rowe 1956: 144; Kroeber 1944: 11-22; Schaedel 1957: 5-42). Their boundary remains to be identified in the eastern Andes, and there is still a question as to why this frontier seems to have been largely impenetrable to the exchange of stylistically identifiable materials such as ceramics. The presence of Cajamarca pottery at Wari provides evidence for the north-and-south movement of objects or people in the northern portion of the Wari sphere of influence, but the lack of flow of material between the Wari and Tiahuanaco zones suggests that in the south commerce must have been almost exclusively trans-Andean—east and west.

Over the past few decades the important role of Wari in Andean cultural development has become increasingly clear. Ethnohistory and archaeology have begun to provide a new understanding of the organizational basis of the Inca state and some insight into settlement systems and developing urbanization. However, much of the Inca organization seems to be based on older Andean patterns already manifest in smaller pre-Inca polities. The recognition of these patterns obliges the study of process to turn to still longer periods of time and to examine earlier examples of unified polities.

Wari appears to be the first great unity of nearly Inca scale. Although archaeologists have not yet provided convincing proof that Wari was a centralized state, the exceptional unification of iconographic expression throughout the Andes reveals a centralized phenomenon which enables us to work, at least provisionally, with the hypothesis that it was a political state. The existence of cities has not been proved either, but Wari and its influence are associated with the early appearance of some criteria of urbanism in so many Andean areas (Schaedel 1951: 234; Willey 1953: 412-13; Rowe 1963: 14; Menzel 1964: 66; Lumbreras 1969: 236) that it seems worthwhile to accept as a working hypothesis that Wari and some of its satellites were cities.

Wari provides an excellent subject for research into the development of cities and states. Although it is completely prehistoric, the 600 or 700 years which separate Wari from contact-period documentation do not stretch the search for ethnohistoric analogy nor for origins of Inca-period organizational patterns. Simultaneously, its history covers an adequate period of time to recognize organizational patterns with long-term adaptive advantages compared with those which were less successful. Finally, much information has already been accumulated about Wari. The temporal chronology has been outlined, some spheres of influence defined, and many important centers identified. Moreover, the great Wari centers are not buried under tells as are many early Middle Eastern cities, nor are they beneath the buildings of modern cities as in the case of the best-known contact-period American capitals of Cuzco and Tenochtitlán. The Andean cities of the Wari period may provide one of the best opportunities for studying the rise of urbanism within a regional context while considering the urban and the rural sectors simultaneously.

1
Jargampata and Wari Economic Organization

Prehistoric events in the central Andean highlands are considered to have centered in a series of intermountain basins which, relatively isolated one from the next, supported large populations and developed distinctive cultures. Only during periods of conquest did the cultures or peoples of one valley come into intensive contact with those of another (Bushnell 1957: 14; Bennett and Bird 1964:69-70). From north to south, the most important basins include Cajamarca, the Callejón de Huaylas, Huánuco, the Mantaro valley, Cuzco, the Titicaca basin, and the Cochabamba basin. Most of these valleys are so small that today they contain only one population center—usually with the same name as the basin. Cajamarca, Cuzco, Huánuco, and Cochabamba are the best examples. These valleys have long and complex prehistoric sequences, but evidence suggests that their population at any one moment was reasonably homogeneous. However, the larger multicenter basins are today, and have been in the past, far more heterogeneous. The large Callejón de Huaylas and the Titicaca basin were often occupied by radically different peoples at the same time.

Nowhere is the diversity within a single valley system more developed than in the Mantaro valley. Today there are three provincial capitals on the banks of the Mantaro, each established in a center of prehistoric population density. The northern headwaters of the Mantaro lie near the city of Huancayo in the fertile valleys of Junín. In the west, Huancavelica is located on a tributary system of the Mantaro. The major southern confluent of the Mantaro is the Huarpa River, which flows past the city of Ayacucho through the valley of the same name.

Ayacucho is the valley in which the sprawling ruins of Wari are found. It has often seemed appropriate to ask why such an important center was located in a relatively small and dry valley with low productive potential. Underlying such a question is the assumption that a site of human activity is a response to the immediate resources. It seems likely to me that the Mantaro valley does not provide for a single population located on vast, productive, and easily watered land. Rather, a center such as Wari can probably be better understood in terms of the coordination of production from diverse, small microenvironments.

The central section of the Mantaro River valley is a narrow, steep gorge which supports only a subtropical thorn forest or thorn forest–grassland phytoassemblage

(Tosi 1960). Consequently, occupation of the valley has concentrated in the headwaters of three main tributary systems. Although the archaeology of these areas is not known in detail (Lumbreras 1959; Ravines 1970a, 1970b; Matos Mendieta 1970; W. Isbell 1970a, 1970b; Thompson 1970a, 1970b), there can be little doubt that the local sequences are distinctive and that the cultures represented were not a homogeneous unit. They were separated by the sparsely populated central section of the river system. Conversely, these three local areas show greater continuity and cultural exchange than the cultures of the Mantaro do with the neighboring basins of Cuzco or Huánuco.

The relatively high headwater valleys of the Mantaro tributaries provide access to areas beyond the large basin systems. The headwaters of the Mantaro lie adjacent to the Pampa de Junín, while the western tributaries of Huancavelica interlace with the upper reaches of the coastal Pisco and Chincha rivers. Finally, the Rio Huarpa and the Ayacucho valley are surrounded by a minor valley, the Rio Pampas.

It is not surprising that early in the Middle Horizon, when the peoples of the Ayacucho valley apparently captured a dominant role in this entire interaction sphere, Wari styles and centers appeared in many strategic localities. In the northern zone, Wari centers were established near Huancayo at Wari-Willca (Flores Espinoza 1959) and Calpish (David Browman, personal communication). A major center near Lircay (Tello 1970), on a western tributary of the Rio Huarpa, probably relates to Wari occupations located around Huancavelica (Rogger Ravines, personal communication). These in turn may have been responsible for highland influence at Cerro del Oro in the Cañete valley (Menzel 1964: 34-35).

Rowe (1963: 14) revealed the presence of a Wari site in the headwaters of the Rio Pampas in the south. My survey of this site in Lucanas, next to the modern village of Cabana, confirms the presence of earlier relationships with the South Coast in late Early Horizon times, and the establishment of a center by the Wari peoples so near the headwaters of the south coast Nazca and Acari rivers may relate to renewed coast-highland interaction. In fact, this center may have been involved in the highland intrusion into the Nazca valley demonstrated by the elaborate ceramic offerings at Pacheco, Nazca (Menzel 1964: 23-28).

The location of Wari appears to relate to the control of a

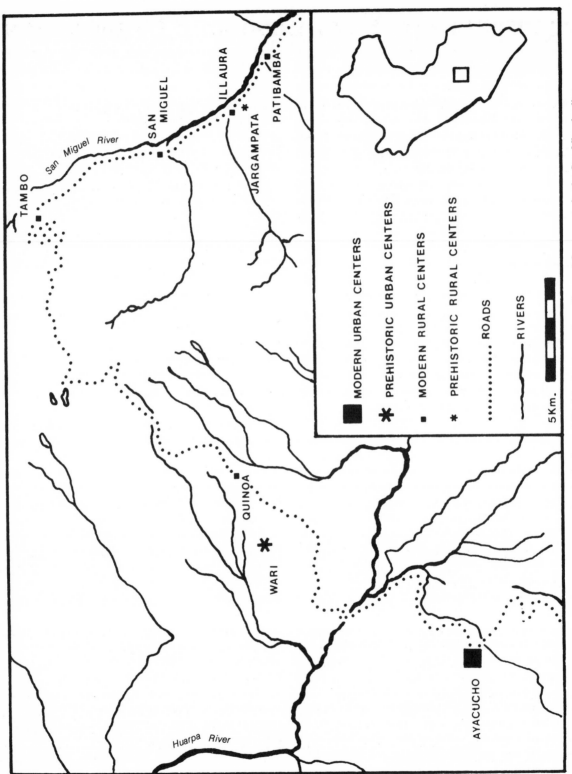

Figure 1. Map of Ayacucho area showing Ayacucho and Wari in the Ayacucho valley and Jargampata in the San Miguel valley.

series of different areas rather than the Ayacucho valley alone. The empire was probably organized around a complex system of redistribution of specialized products and goods from a large number of small, specialized zones.

The Rio Pampas valley drains the areas east and south of the Ayacucho valley. The San Miguel River flows south into the Pampas and runs parallel to the Ayacucho valley about 30 kilometers to the east. Wari is located on the eastern side of the Ayacucho valley and is therefore closer to the San Miguel section of the Pampas than any other valley system except that of Ayacucho itself. Although the San Miguel valley is small, it should provide evidence of Wari control if the Wari polity was indeed organized around a system of multizonal control and redistribution.

The ecological diversity found in the Ayacucho and San Miguel valleys is a product primarily of altitude and the effect of exposure to moisture-bearing winds. The deepest sections of both valleys, from about 2,100 to 2,400 meters above sea level, are subtropical deserts. From about 2,400 to 2,600 meters, a thorn forest grassland is usual, while the zone between 2,600 and 3,000 meters is characteristically a dry thorn forest. Above 3,000 meters, there is an increase in precipitation, and a humid scrub forest extends to an elevation of perhaps 3,700 meters. At greater altitudes a tundra, or puna, formation is typical (Tosi 1960; McNeish 1971). As one moves up from the Ayacucho valley bottom, all of these zones are crossed. The ancient Wari center and the modern city of Ayacucho both lie at an altitude between the dry valley bottom where irrigated agriculture is practiced and the high, wetter sections where hardy tubers are farmed and herd animals—including llamas and alpacas —are grazed. Both cities were established in the dry thorn forest, where some irrigation and some dry farming is done and where residents have the easiest access to all of the zones within the valley.

In the San Miguel valley, a preliminary archaeological survey revealed two large occupation sites of Middle Horizon date. One of these sites, Ayaurqo, lies on the east side of the San Miguel River, opposite the village of San Miguel, on a high bluff at an altitude of about 2,800 meters in dry thorn forest. Like the modern and ancient centers in the Ayacucho valley, it was probably located to provide best access to a series of microzones. If so, it seems unlikely that Ayaurqo represents a specialized station, and it was not intensively investigated. However, the second large Middle Horizon site lies near the valley bottom at an altitude of about 2,500 meters in subtropical desert to thorn forest grassland. This site, Jargampata, does not seem to be oriented to generalized exploitation but rather to the exploitation of a specific niche on the valley bottom. In consequence, it was the object of prolonged investigation.

Jargampata is on a sandy ridge and alluvial fan located 5 kilometers by road below the modern town of San Miguel, capital of the province of La Mar, in the modern depart-

ment of Ayacucho. The site lies between the community of Illaura, an independent and dispersed settlement, and the Hacienda Patibamba, on the land of the hacienda. Ruins are scattered along the west side of the valley for a kilometer, and sherd refuse can be found on both sides of the road, although the larger part of the site is located above the road. Almost the entire area of the site is now dry and uncultivated. However, Jargampata lies at the point where the valley of the San Miguel River begins to widen, and an extensive, relatively flat plain runs for 6 kilometers along the west side of the valley until the river again goes into a gorge below the Hacienda Macnopampa before joining the main stream of the Pampas River. This broad area of the valley contains the most productive land which can be easily irrigated. As calculated from measurements of aerial photographs and estimates by local hacienda owners, there are between 400 and 500 hectares of irrigated land from Patibamba to Macnopampa. Modern irrigation is by major canals up to five kilometers long, which collect water from the San Miguel River itself. By employing a gradient less than that of the river, the canals divert water to the sides of the valley where it can be distributed by gravity flow to numerous fields below. Smaller canals originate in the deep canyons of streams which feed the river, but these are generally dry around July and August and still may not carry adequate water by planting time in October and November. Furthermore, these streams are deeply incised into the mountainside so that the water they carry often cannot be elevated to the fields where it is needed until the streams approach their mouths. With few exceptions, only springs or streams diverted from the high punas are dependable sources of irrigation waters above the main course of the river. Most of the water must therefore be brought over long distances and can be raised only slightly above the valley bottom.

Contemporary cultivation of the bottomland belonging to the haciendas depends almost entirely on canal irrigation. Primary crops include oranges and other citrus fruits, sugarcane (which has traditionally been manufactured into alcohol for sale at local markets), wheat, barley, corn, beans, peas, alfalfa, cattle, avocados, cherimoyas, and tunas. The land is irrigated by channeling water from the main canal to the field and allowing sheets of water to run across the soil. Tree crops and other perennials reduce erosion, but even on the relatively flat land along the river erosion can become a problem with annual plowings.

With the exception of a small area of irrigated fields immediately below the major concentration of ruins of the Jargampata site, there is almost no Middle Horizon refuse in the modern fields. A general pattern emerges from the reconnaissance of three sample areas: the fields within a kilometer of the excavation site, the fields surrounding the hacienda house at Patibamba, and the land for a kilometer above the Hacienda Macnopampa. These irrigated lands

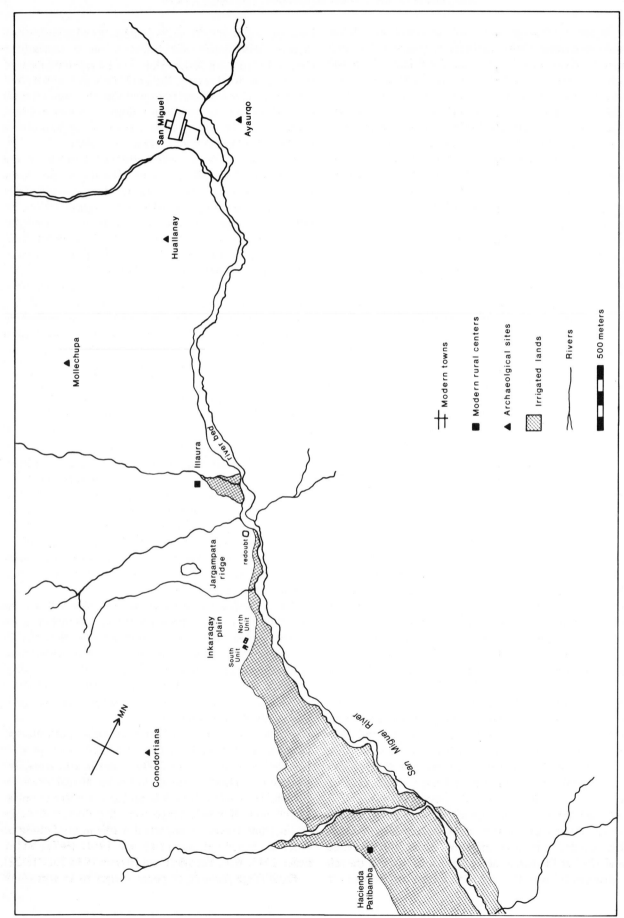

Figure 2. Map of San Miguel valley showing extent and position of Jargampata site, other important archaeological sites, and irrigated sector of the valley.

now under cultivation were not occupied by Middle Horizon residences. Only a single scattering of refuse with sherds like those from Jargampata was found. About 400 meters northeast of the Hacienda Patibamba house, there are the remains of a deteriorated and overgrown stone structure, which may be a long wall following the natural contours of the plain. Smaller retaining walls are in evidence in the fields immediately below the larger rubble concentration, suggesting an attempt to level the plain into a series of broad, flat terraces. The ceramics on the surface are scarce and not particularly diagnostic. However, Alvino Añaños, the owner of the Hacienda Patibamba, made a small excavation at the site and still had a few decorated sherds in his possession which he claimed had been found in the excavation. These sherds belong to the same style as those at Jargampata, most probably to that of the Early Patibamba Phase.

On the basis of the partial survey, I feel the evidence indicates that the alluvial plain along the river was not heavily settled in Middle Horizon times, but was rather utilized for intensive agricultural exploitation. The presence of retaining walls in close proximity to ruins, with some evidence of Middle Horizon pottery, favors an interpretation of extremely intensive agricultural exploitation at that time. Local informants recount that when tractors were first used to plow the fields of the irrigated plain the remains of numerous walls were struck. This prehistoric leveling effort can still be detected on the surface in various fields and appears in aerial photographs as well. It would seem that the prehistoric leveling was related to an irrigation system and was probably used to check erosion in Middle Horizon times. With the Wari collapse which followed Middle Horizon 2B (Menzel 1964: 72), the irrigation canals and terraces may both have fallen into disuse. Most other sites located by my preliminary survey, which probably date to the Late Intermediate Period or the Late Horizon, are located on high hilltops. The selection of the upper lip of the valley and the humid scrub forest zone for occupation suggests a rather different economic orientation in post-Wari times. There is evidence of only a small occupation, with ceramics of Jargampata style, on the site after the Epoch 2B abandonment.

The San Miguel valley eventually became part of the Jesuit hacienda of Ninabamba, and detailed documents probably exist on the sale of this land following the Jesuit expulsion. However, long-term occupants of the valley state that in the time of their grandfathers much of the land now under irrigation was covered by a heavy growth of thorn forest which had not been cleared for cultivation.

At least three or four generations ago, the valley was gradually cleared and converted to sugarcane production, which required extensive irrigation. Cane was processed into alcohol at Patibamba and other haciendas, and the sale of aguardiente was the primary source of income. In consequence, it is difficult to estimate to what degree the modern field system and irrigation canals represent a continuity from the Middle Horizon or a redevelopment of the same lands. However, the available water sources and the topographic configurations probably have not changed since Wari times, so that even though there may not be a continuity of use of the canal system the modern plan is probably very similar to any prehistoric system.

Jargampata is located where the valley opens up and an extensive flood plain is found. The site overlooks the mouth of the major irrigation canal, which provides water to the uppermost irrigated fields for 5 kilometers down the valley. The Jargampata ridge itself is the topographic feature which, because of its height above the valley floor, prevents the use of canals still farther upstream to irrigate fields at higher elevations on the valley side.

The altitude of the nearly level valley bottom between Jargampata and Macnopampa varies between 2,200 and 2,500 meters above sea level. The major indigenous American crops which are likely to have been found under cultivation at that altitude in pre-Columbian times are the following:

Maize (*Zea mays*) ranges in altitude from sea level to 3,200 or 3,500 meters, depending on exposure and on the variety planted (Weberbauer 1945: 626). Maize is still one of the major products of the San Miguel valley and ranges up to the slopes below Tambo at 3,300 meters.

Bean (*Phaseolus vulgaris*), or *poroto*, ranges to slightly above 3,000 meters in the Central Highlands of the Andes, where it is often interplanted with maize. The age of the species as a crop in the San Miguel valley is attested to by an indigenous place-name, Purutujata.

Lima bean (*Phaseolus lunatus*), or *pallar*, probably has an altitudinal range slightly more limited than or comparable to that of *poroto* and is found in the San Miguel-Pampas area to about 3,000 meters.

Tarwi (Lupinus matucanicus), also known as *chocho*, has an altitudinal range of from 1,800 to 2,400 meters in the western Andes. Although I have no ethnographic data for this cultigen in the San Miguel area, it is likely it was grown by prehistoric agriculturists.

Squash (*Cucurbita maxima* and *moschata*), or *zapallo*, is found from nearly sea level to 3,000 meters or slightly more in the Andean valleys.

Cactus (*Cactus* sp., *Cereus* sp., *Lobivia* sp., *Opuntia* sp.) compose a little-studied group of plants which produce fruits at altitudes of up to 3,000 meters in arid areas. The most common modern species in the San Miguel area is the *Opuntia ficus indica*, which is probably a post-Columbian introduction. However, it is probable that the various native cactus fruits played as important a role in pre-Columbian times as they do at present (Towle 1961: 69-71; Weberbauer 1945: 620; Yacovleff and Herrera 1934-35: 318-22).

Pacae (Inga feuillei), or *pacay*, ranges to an altitude of

2,700 to 2,800 meters in the Central Highlands.

Cherimoya (*Anona chirimolia*) is found to an altitude of 2,600 or 2,700 meters.

Sweet potato (*Impomoea batatas*) is not present in the San Miguel valley ethnographically, but ranges to an altitude of 2,500 meters in the Central Highlands, according to Weberbauer (1945: 625).

Avocado (*Persea gratissima*), or *palta*, is currently grown in the San Miguel valley to an altitude of 2,600 meters.

Cultigens which thrive at a lower altitude than the San Miguel valley are produced in the deeper and larger valley of the Apurímac River to the east. These include manioc, achira, coca, peppers, peanuts, pineapple, and *ciruela del fraile*. High, cold-resistant crops are produced in the upper end of the San Miguel valley around the town of Tambo as well as in the stretches of humid scrub forest which border the valley on the east and west. These include potatoes, ocas, *ullucos, mashua,* and quinoa. Potatoes have also been produced in the low valley with considerable success, but Alvino Añaños, the owner of the Hacienda Patibamba, states that it is necessary to bring in new seed each year from the puna or production will drop.

It is obvious that the San Miguel valley produced a number of crops in prehistoric times, of which only the most important have been listed above. However, the subtropical desert to dry thorn forest around Jargampata definitely belongs to a low valley, or quechua, zone of production, of which the most important single crop has been maize (Murra 1956). Because of this and the immense importance of maize cultivated ethnographically in San Miguel, I assume that the irrigated area of the valley was primarily developed in response to demands for maize production. Beans may have played an important role as a crop interplanted with maize, but it seems doubtful that any of the tree crops or the extreme xerophytes would have required the amount of terracing or irrigation which is indicated.

Assuming that corn was the principal product of the valley in Middle Horizon times, we can make some general estimates of the production capacity. Today one can recognize two radically different systems of maize production. Almost all the land on the flat plain is owned and farmed by the haciendas in the valley. On this land, plowed furrows are laid out in straight rows. When the corn stalks are about a foot high, small mounds of earth are thrown up around them and troughs are left separating the rows. The fields of corn are irrigated every two weeks. At the Hacienda Patibamba, the production from this method is between 2,000 and 3,000 kilograms of maize from a quarter of a hectare, an area 50 by 50 meters, without the aid of fertilizers. The other pattern is that practiced by the majority of the peasants and hacienda peons in their own fields outside the prime area of irrigation on the valley bottom. Maize is planted in November and depends

primarily on the rains for water. If there is irrigation available, the field will be watered for two days prior to planting, but once it is planted the owner will irrigate again only it threatened by imminent loss of the crop. If the year is dry, the field may be thoroughly soaked again in December before the time to *aporcar* (to mound earth around the base of the plants). However, once the mounds have been heaped up, there are no longer any rows or troughs through which the water can run, which makes further irrigation very difficult. One family of peasants, although cultivating on the flat bottom land, continued to follow their traditional pattern in spite of the fact that water was available for regular irrigation and the neighboring fields of the hacienda provided a model to copy. Most of the fields which are dry farmed are on the steeper sides of the valley, and particularly on the east side, where, although there are few sources of irrigation water, the annual rainfall is sufficient for a fairly dependable crop. Production estimates for this kind of agriculture vary from 400 to 1,000 kilograms per quarter of a hectare. Beans are generally planted along with the corn and are also harvested in April or May.

Considering now the problem of double crops, I believe that it is unlikely that two crops of maize were produced annually in the San Miguel valley in prehistoric times. There are a number of pests and diseases which attack the corn plants before they reach maturity. During the rainy season, these pests are not extreme and cause only a minor amount of damage. However, during the dry season they become so extreme that, in spite of controlled spraying, the harvest is often so small that the investment in labor is uneconomical. If these conditions prevailed in prehistoric times when insecticides were not in use, I suspect that no attempt would have been made to harvest a dry-season crop of corn in spite of the available water supply. In higher altitudes of 2,800 to 3,000 meters, the threat of pests is greatly reduced, but the maturation time is longer and the probability of frost much greater. The slower development at these altitudes prevents double cropping, but permits anyone who controls property in a number of altitudinal zones to stagger his harvests.

Discounting the probability that more than a single annual crop of maize was produced in the valley, and estimating the production as intermediate between that of the modern hacienda and peasant production, or at about 1,600 kilograms of maize to a quarter of a hectare, the prehistoric production of the lower valley can be estimated. There are roughly 450 hectares easily available for intensive irrigation in the valley now, and it is possible that a similar area was under irrigation in the past. Thus the valley bottom adjacent to the Jargampata site could have produced about 2,880,000 kilograms of maize annually. This estimate does not take into consideration products grown in the same fields with the maize, such as beans, and it

makes no effort to estimate the amount of land outside the irrigated valley bottom which might have been under cultivation during the Middle Horizon. Terraces are evident along some portions of the east side of the valley and appear to have been for dry farming. Although these cannot be dated, their existence strengthens the assumption that the valley sides were not totally neglected. I feel, therefore, that the production estimate above is an absolute minimum and that the actual output of the valley in various crops could easily have been double that calculated.

The unit of one quarter of a hectare, which is used so commonly in the Andes, is based on the average amount of land a single man can plow in one day. This estimate is based on the use of the Spanish plow drawn by oxen. In pre-Columbian times, however, the land was prepared with the *chaquitaclla*, or foot plow, by teams of one man and one woman working together, as is seen today where draft animals are not available or on terraces where the plow and team cannot be turned. I have no notes concerning the efficiency of the foot plow, but Mishkin (1963: 418) states that a single furrow 50 meters long can be plowed in about 22 minutes. Estimating two furrows to the meter, a quarter of a hectare could be prepared in 33 hours, or about four days of actual work.

Considering that the heavy work of plowing is the major bottleneck in the agricultural cycle, it is possible to estimate approximately the work force required to cultivate an area of some 450 hectares. Plowing begins in August and planting is delayed until September or October, although this is less rigidly dictated on irrigated lands. We can assume that there are at least forty working days during which plowing can be conducted, which means that each family of one man and one woman could prepare 10 quarter-hectare sections, or 2.5 hectares, during this time. Therefore, 180 family units could have cultivated the entire irrigated bottom of the San Miguel valley adjacent to Jargampata.

Families in the Andes are often large, but marriage and participation in the agricultural work begin early, so I feel that I am justified in estimating no more than three dependents for each working unit of an adult man and woman. This brings the minimum population dependent on the valley land to 900 persons. Estimating that 2 kilograms of maize per person per day was required by the working families for personal consumption, only 657,000 kilograms of maize would be required annually by the 900 persons composing the work force and families. This leaves a surplus of 2,223,000 kilograms, or enough maize to supply some 3,000 additional persons with the same ration of 2 kilograms per day through the year, discounting the requirement of seed for the coming year.

My calculations are not meant to correspond to an exact reconstruction for the San Miguel valley or the Central Highlands during the Middle Horizon. I wish only to demonstrate the productive potential of the valley and its

utility within a system of support for the city of Wari. Jargampata lies adjacent to the best lands on the western edge of the valley bottom, only 25 kilometers from the ruins of Wari. Trails still cross the divide between the drainage of the San Miguel River and the Rio Huarpa, providing easy access to the eastern edge of the Ayacucho valley where Wari is located. These trails are still in use by contemporary traders, who move potatoes, coca, and other products from areas beyond the reach of the roads into the markets of Ayacucho via llama caravan. Similar llama caravans could have linked Wari with Jargampata, and other such sites, in prehistoric times. Surplus from intensive cultivation of specialized zones such as the irrigated bottoms of the lower San Miguel valley could have been channeled into the city to support full-time specialists engaged in administrative, religious, military, or craft arts. In turn, the specialized products—redistribution, access to religion, protection, and crafts—were supplied to the rural producers.

The most surprising fact which emerges from the calculations outlined above is that as few as ten to twenty centers of production like Jargampata could have supported a population of about 30,000 non-agriculturalists!

As explained above, the Mantaro basin is characterized by numerous small and highly diversified environmental zones. Furthermore, it is not a well-defined and circumscribed zone but, rather, fragmented and in many cases almost as closely associated with neighboring basins and areas as with other parts of the same drainage. These data suggest that Wari should be understood as a center which coordinated and integrated many restricted and contrastive production areas rather than developing through progressive population growth and nucleation in a circumscribed but highly productive basin. Centralized administration of redistribution among complementary productive zones is hypothesized as the economic and political foundation of the Wari "city" and "state."

To test this hypothesis, a specialized production center in a neighboring valley was selected. It was assumed that sites located in intermediate areas along the valley sides were more likely to be involved in coordinating activities in several environmental zones than those located at one extreme, such as Jargampata on the valley floor, which were more likely the foci of specialized exploitation in a single microzone.

Produce typical of the San Miguel valley and the specialized products of the valley floor have been listed. Production facilities and potential agricultural output of the extensive zone apparently controlled by Jargampata have been reviewed and estimated to show the importance which the site should have had for a Wari redistributive administration. If Wari was based upon such an administration, we should find it, and its interests, clearly represented at Jargampata.

Plate 1. View of Jargampata and the San Miguel valley looking southeast from Mollechupa. In the foreground is the Mollechupa ridge, and next is the Illaura ridge, where harvested fields surrounded by trees may be seen. The Jargampata ridge and Inkaraqay plain occupy the center of the photo and can be distinguished by their complex wall patterns and sparse vegetation. At the left extreme of the Jargampata ridge, on a bluff overlooking the river, a small redoubt is visible. Down the valley in the upper center are the irrigated lands of the Hacienda Patibamba.

2
Jargampata Site

The Jargampata site can be conveniently divided into two areas on the basis of geomorphology (plate 1). The southeastern part of the site is composed of a large alluvial fan about 700 meters wide across its bottom and about 800 meters long. This area of the site is part of the zone of the Hacienda Patibamba known as Inkaraqay, a Quechua term translating roughly as "ruined enclosures of the Incas." The geological regime in this part of the site has been primarily deposition, and the old structures, although deeply buried in several cases, are quite well preserved. Some standing walls still reach the height of almost three meters, and it is from these remains that the name Inkaraqay is derived. The other portion of the site is a high ridge, which is probably a remnant of an ancient river terrace. This section, which is called Jargampata, is about 600 meters wide and at least as long. It is separated by a steep *quebrada* from a similar ridge which belongs to the community of Illaura. In some of the fields of Illaura there are sherds, and features which appear to be prehistoric walls on the surface at Jargampata can occasionally be traced for a short distance into Illaura on the other side of the *quebrada*. However, the high surface at Jargampata has been subjected to excessive erosion. Several test cuts were made on the ridge area, but the material recovered was scant, badly eroded, and without firm stratigraphic association. In consequence, almost all the excavations were conducted on the alluvial fan within the area called Inkaraqay. Were it not for the potential confusion which could result between this site and others of the same name (e.g., Lara 1967) and the possible assumption that any site named "ruined enclosures of the Incas" ought to belong to the Late Horizon, the name Inkaraqay would be most appropriate. However, the name Jargampata is interesting in itself and may be a more ancient name than that derived from the ruins. Informants could not translate the name, but the closest word in Ayacucho Quechua (Parker 1969: 133) is *harka*, to impede, stop, detain, or tie up (animals). *Jarga* or *harqa* may be alternate pronunciations in which a Spanish-loan voiced stop velar *g* is often substituted for a more ancient voiceless spirant post-velar *q*. The voiceless stop velar *k* may be a product of the forward shift of the sound under Spanish influence. If *jarga* does derive from the same form as *harka*, then Jargampata could be glossed as "place where animals are corralled." The suggestion made above that Jargampata may have been a center of production from which surplus produce was shipped to Wari, perhaps by llama caravan, is entirely consistent with the idea that a section of the site was devoted to animals and, perhaps, to the herders or traders responsible for the movement of the products.

Ayacucho has a barrio named Carmen Alto, or Carmenca, which overlooks the city and is the residence of many traders and transport specialists—including modern truckers. The barrio also has a plaza where the major market for livestock is conducted. Zuidema (personal communication) has argued that Cuzco had a similar barrio and that the residential separation of a specialist group who engaged in the transportation of products is a very ancient Andean tradition. It may be that it dates to Middle Horizon times as well.

The Jargampata ridge contains the remains of numerous stone walls, which appear to be rubble constructions without definite plan or layout. However, one such wall isolates a large semicircular area at the north end of the site. On a slight prominence within this area, and overlooking the mouth of the main modern irrigation canal, are the remains of an architectural unit which was probably several concentric circles terraced so that each interior circle rose above the level of the one below. The maximum diameter of the outer enclosure is about 50 meters. The highest circular terrace is clear of surface rubble, and foundations of rectangular rooms less than 3 meters square are visible in what may have been a straight-line layout. However, excavations showed that there was no refuse and that the foundation remains are very shallow. This circular construction probably represents a small redoubt placed where defense was easiest. However, the position above the mouth of the main modern irrigation canal suggests that the fortifications may have been associated with the control of water distributed by a similar prehistoric canal.

Much of the southern portion of the Jargampata ridge shows evidence of having been terraced into broad parallel sections across its rolling surface. These terraces occasionally show the remains of stone retaining walls, and in a few cases stone room foundations can be seen on their surfaces. One such room was test-excavated in hopes of finding evidence for dating as well as for function, but as elsewhere the erosion had not left any significant deposit. The room was almost rectangular, about 5 meters to a side.

No excavations were conducted on the terraces of Jargampata, but I suspect that the primary purpose of these

Plate 2. View of the Inkaraqay plain looking north from Condortiana. Walls and excavations in the North Unit and South Unit are visible in the center of the photo. Between the Inkaraqay plain and the river are irrigated fields. The route of the main canal is traced by the line of trees growing on the canal bank. To the left of the plain rises the Jargampata ridge.

was to level land for the construction of rooms. The occasional room foundations on the terraces and the extreme aridity of the site argue against an interpretation of the features as being agricultural.

Rubble walls wander over the surface at Jargampata and in several cases cross areas which had been terraced. In one case, we cut one of these walls to demonstrate the superposition of the wall over the terrace. We found that the wall had been over a meter thick, with two outside faces of fieldstone apparently laid up dry and then filled with rubble. The wall crossed over an eroded terrace face, proving our suspicion that the terracing predated the walls. However, the wall contained no sherd material. Another similar wall contained a fair quantity of sherds of both Huarpa and Middle Horizon styles.

Scattered about the unmodified surface of Jargampata are visible remains of irregularly shaped enclosures. Some of these may be recent, but it seems likely that most are contemporary with the major occupation of the site. These vary from nearly circular to triangular to rectangular and rarely exceed 3 meters in diameter. They are not frequent on the site and only seventeen were recorded in our survey of Jargampata, but none had any depth of deposit around them and it may be assumed that many such structures have disappeared because of erosion. It is possible that these units represent temporary residences on the site.

Along the south edge of the Jargampata ridge is a steep slope which drops to the Inkaraqay plain some 20 meters below. This slope has been terraced into a series of surfaces which appear too narrow to have served as house platforms. The lack of any architectural remains on their surfaces leads me to suspect that they may have had an agricultural function, although the problem of aridity makes this questionable.

At one spot in the eastern part of the slope, I encountered the remains of a structure rather high up on the slope where the terrace formations were not in evidence. This unit consisted of three small rooms joined in a line following the contour of the slope. Although the structure had been recently excavated and largely destroyed by a *huaquero*, some aspects of the architecture were still obvious. The unit had been laid out with two parallel walls which turned to meet one another in bonded and rounded ends. Then two interior partitions were built across the short axis, creating three interior rooms. The rooms were almost square and averaged 110 to 150 cm. to a side. The wall facing the uphill slope was in very poor condition, but it is possible that there were three entrances on the uphill

side. It was not until I had left the field that the comparison between these units at Jargampata and the Inca storage system at Huánaco Viejo described by Morris and Thompson (1970: 340-62) became apparent to me. Regrettably, I made no effort to investigate the possibility that the narrow terraces at Jargampata may have carried similar small structures. This investigation will have to wait for future field research.

The deep alluvial deposit which constitutes the Inkaraqay section of the site has thoroughly buried all but the largest structures. Surface collection yields very little ceramic or other refuse, although occasional visible walls indicate a substantial settlement. During excavations, it was possible to demonstrate that there are between one and two meters of alluvium deposited over the living surface of Middle Horizon times. It is possible that many small structures are preserved under the outwash, but it would require moving immense quantities of soil to investigate the settlement system.

Excavations were limited to areas showing evidence of architecture on the surface. Two distinct architectural units, those best preserved in terms of surface indications, were investigated. I shall refer to these as the South Unit and the North Unit through the remainder of this volume.

Remains of rubble walls wander in nonsensical directions across the surface of the Inkaraqay section. These walls are more superficial than the Middle Horizon constructions, and, like their counterparts on the Jargampata ridge, show no evidence of mortar. They most closely resemble old walls built around cultivated fields to remove rocks from the fields; they grow progressively in size and lack an ordered form. There can be little doubt that they postdate the major, Middle Horizon occupation of the site.

The condition of the site makes it difficult to evaluate the form of settlement and its density. The Jargampata ridge seems to include a redoubt and scattered irregular enclosures. The Inkaraqay section surface remains are more baffling because of the deep alluvial cover. However, there is at least one concentrated occupation area surrounced by a wide, relatively unoccupied zone, and there are probably several others. Sparse surface refuse suggests a low density of inhabitants for the large site, even though residences seem to have become agglutinated into crowded units. The scattered and contrastive architectural remains may relate to localized specialization within the settlement, perhaps including defense of the irrigation canal intake, a trader-herder section, permanent residences, agricultural areas, and possibly even small structures for storage.

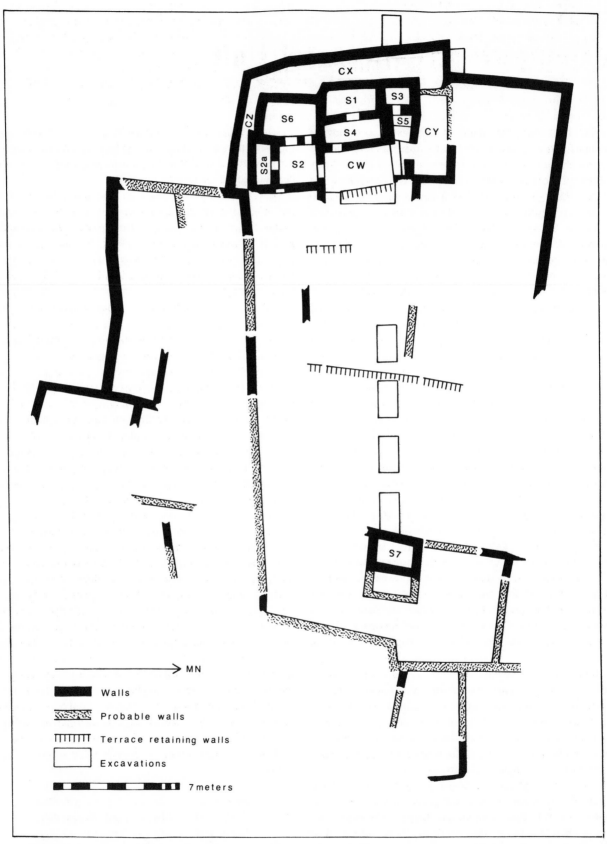

Figure 3. Floor plan of architectural remains of the Jargampata South Unit showing rooms and corridors excavated and the position of the House Group within the unit.

3

A Domestic Architectural Unit

Prior to excavation, the South Unit appeared as a roughly rectangular area of about 25 by 35 meters, more densely overgrown than the adjacent areas and with a heavy cover of stone rubble. Several sections of walls were visible on the surface, although none attained a height of more than 10 cm. In the southwest part of the unit, a *huaquero*'s clandestine excavation had caused some destruction but demonstrated the presence of well-preserved walls. Excavations were begun here within a grid system with a zero point in the North Unit, but it soon became apparent that it would be necessary to modify the grid, which was laid out in meter squares, to accommodate the architectural structure. As walls appeared, we adjusted our excavation units to correspond to individual rooms or sections of rooms, recording the positions of important finds within each room. All excavations in this unit were conducted by natural stratigraphic control. However, the stratigraphy in much of the South Unit had been badly disturbed, and very few of the stratigraphic associations can be relied upon.

The South Unit is a large enclosure of irregular form and undefined extent (fig. 3). The entire eastern part is poorly preserved, and the north and south extensions were not defined. It appears that the unit has an irregular rectangular perimeter with extensive architectural remains within, but I cannot discount the possibility that it extended over a very large area expanding to both the north and south along the lower, or east, end. The section excavated consists of an open plaza or courtyard constructed in three terraced levels with an east-west dimension of between 18 and 19 meters. One section of what appeared to be an east-west wall was detected in the plaza, but no other building was in evidence, suggesting that the north-south dimension of the open area was 12 to 13 meters. The irregularity of these walls and the presence of sections within a single wall which are built up against one another rather than bonded together indicate that the South Unit was probably constructed over a number of minor building periods rather than laid out and constructed at one time according to a single building plan. At Wari there are frequent cases of massive walls which appear to have been built in successive efforts within a single architectural scheme, as one can detect both vertical and horizontal unbonded joints. This is particularly obvious in the Ushpajoto section and the terraces between Robles Moqo and Bennett's triangulation point 2 (Bennett 1953: 19). However, these walls at Wari follow a straight layout and careful plan in spite of the

sections, while the walls of the South Unit at Jargampata take slightly different directional courses with each section. Furthermore, excavations demonstrate differences in foundation depth from section to section.

The westernmost extreme of the South Unit contains the ruin of a House Group which was totally excavated (plate 3). In its final configuration, this group consisted of four large rooms, three small rooms or enclosures, a front porch, and three narrow corridors which enclosed the entire group on the north, west, and south. The only apparent access was from the plaza or central court on the east. It is obvious that this group is the product of multiple constructions and was not originally laid out in this format. During excavation the rooms were numbered consecutively as they appeared, each with the prefix S for *sala*. Consequently, the numbering does not correspond to the construction sequence. The corridors were assigned letters from the end of the alphabet with the prefix C for *corredor*.

The initial structure of the House Group was S6, which is a rectangular room with bonded corners, a door, and a window opening to the east. The walls are between 40 and 50 cm. thick and are built of fieldstone laid in a clay mortar. The masons tended to select flat, fairly large stones, some of which span the entire thickness of the wall. However, most of the wall is composed of double-coursed masonry with a larger stone forming one wall face and several smaller rocks laid side by side to form the other face. The larger stones are alternated from one face to the other to create a well-bonded unit. These walls were then covered with a layer of clay averaging 6 to 8 cm. in thickness which was finished with a thin layer of white plaster. In the northwest corner of the room, where the plaster is thick and well preserved, there are visible finger marks left by the prehistoric mason as he smeared the plaster onto the wall (plate 4). A white plaster floor was also laid down to form a single unit with the plaster facing on the walls. However, the floor was rapidly worn away, except in the corners, which suggests considerable traffic in the room (fig. 4).

The inside dimensions at floor level of room S6 are as follows:

East wall	— 284 cm. long, 42 cm. thick
West wall	— 279 cm. long, 52 cm. thick
South wall	— 178 cm. long, 39 cm. thick
North wall	— 172 cm. long, 51 cm. thick

The entrance is located at the center of the east wall and

Plate 3. View of the excavated House Group from the east.

Plate 4. White plaster finish showing impressions of prehistoric mason's fingers where the plaster was thickly applied in the northwest corner of room S6. Remnants of a white plaster floor are also preserved at the base of the stadia rod. This finish was characteristic of the House Group but was best preserved in rooms S6 and S1.

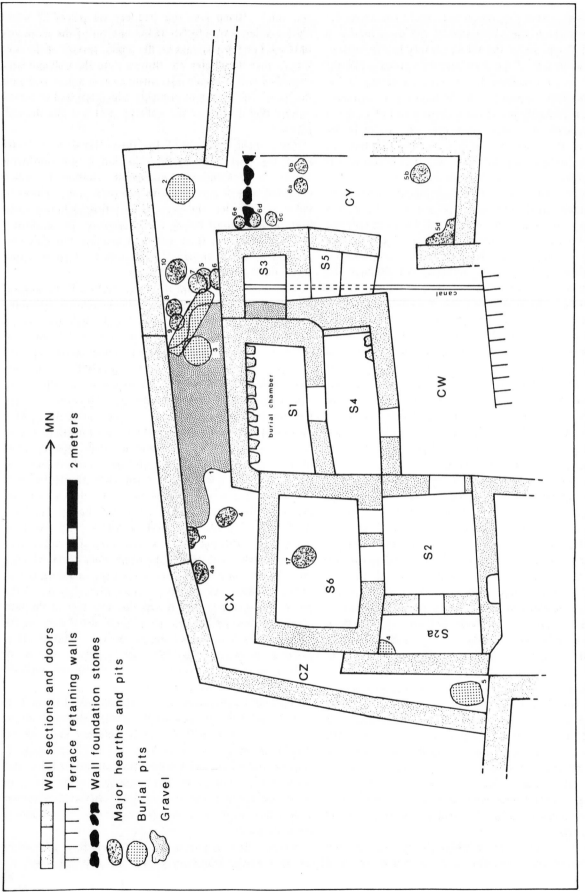

Figure 4. South Unit House Group floor plan demonstrating the relative construction sequence as indicated by bonded and unbonded sections of walls. The positions of burials 1 through 5 are indicated. Important features are represented with their element number. Projecting stones preserved in the west wall of room S1 and the east wall of S4 are indicated. The canal which originates under the foundation of room S3 is indicated, with the part covered by architecture represented by dotted lines. Feature element 1 or 11 received both labels during excavation but has been labeled by the former number only on this illustration. This gravel feature also underlies some parts of room S1, but since its extent was not defined the gravel has not been indicated.

is 62 cm. wide across the base, which lies 15 cm. above the floor. The wall on the south side of the door reaches a height of 107 cm. above the sill and is very nearly vertical, while the north side of the door reaches a preserved height of only 92 cm. but inclines slightly into the passage space. This creates the impression of a trapezoidal entrance, although it is probably fortuitous and the result of a general lack of emphasis on straight lines and right angles in the architecture. There was no visible indication of a lintel or other means of spanning the door, which indicates that it reached a greater height than that preserved.

In the east wall of S6 is a small rectangular opening or window which has dimensions of 35 cm. by 43 cm. It is located between 24 and 59 cm. south of the north wall and between 74 and 117 cm. above the floor. A single stone lintel caps the window. In the rest of the excavations, no other window openings were observed, and although the matrix surrounding the window contained many stones fallen from the walls, it appeared that the window had been filled with stones before the unit was abandoned. When room S6 was constructed, it was the only structure of the House Group, so the window offered a view of the hills rising on the opposite side of the valley as well as the irrigated bottom lands adjacent to the site. With the later construction of room S2, the window would only have opened into that room. One might suggest that the lack of windows in later rooms indicates a change in ideas through time: perhaps as more residents moved into the unit it was no longer desirable to have window openings.

The base of the walls of room S6 are cut into stratum 8, which is a yellowish-brown alluvial soil composed of clay, sand, fine gravel, and small rocks. This deposit was actively accumulating at the time of construction, and toward its top it contains cultural material. The foundations for the room were probably cut slightly into the existing surface, although no evidence of a trench excavated for the foundation was detected. For some other walls it was obvious that the bases were built on the surface and that no foundation excavations were made. In these cases, the floor level corresponded to the base of the walls and often constituted the break between one stratum and another. In the case of room S6, the walls penetrated between 10 and 12 cm. below the interior floor. If shallow excavations were made, the foundation trench must have been a slit trench exactly the width of the wall, which was then filled with rocks laid in clay mortar. Or it is possible that the foundation was built on the surface and that earth was then mounded around the base of the structure. The stratigraphic profiles make this very unlikely, although a comparable condition was encountered by McCown (1945: 324) in Excavation 3 at the Middle Horizon site of Viracochapampa.

The floor of room S6 is white plaster. It lies on a prepared bed of fine gravel and dusty gray soil about 5 to 6 cm. thick. Mixed into this bedding are pieces of white plaster which probably fell as the interior of the room was finished. Long drip streaks on the plaster surface of the wall suggest that the plaster was thrown onto the wall and later smoothed with a simple instrument such as a stick and with the hand. The floor was probably added last and is curved upward slightly toward the walls to meet and join the wall plaster.

Only small segments of the floor plaster were intact along the north and south walls and in the southwest corner. In consequence, excavation stratum 6, which consisted of soft gray soil with few rocks, many pieces of fallen wall plaster, and occupation refuse including some pottery and animal bones, lay in contact with stratum 7 and 7a, the plaster floor and floor bedding, but also with stratum 8, the essentially sterile surface of construction where these others were worn away.

Five circular pits were dug into stratum 8. Because of the absence of the floor, it was impossible to determine whether these features had been dug through the floor or whether they represent features present on the surface at the time of construction. However, several contained small fragments of wall plaster, which suggests that these pits were open during the occupation of the room. All but one contained only an earth fill with no occupation material, but the largest—which was oval in horizontal profile, with a maximum diameter of about 60 cm. and a depth of almost 50 cm.—contained animal bones of small rodents, most likely guinea pigs, and larger herbivores, probably llamas or deer, as well as a few sherds, small pieces of marine shell, and flecks of charcoal. No comparable features were found in any of the other rooms, which makes the interpretation of this pit particularly interesting. The feature was numbered El-17, with the prefix for *elemento*. If it represents a feature which was a part of the room, then it may be a fire pit with the remains of meals in the form of animal bones. However, there was no ash and very little charcoal in the pit. If this was a hearth, it was the only one in the unit inside a room. At this and later times, there were hearth areas located outside the rooms in the corridors. It is possible, however, that this first room served as an all-purpose living area until the House Group was enlarged and became functionally specialized.

Associated with the period of construction of room S6 is a pit located 50 cm. west of the northwest corner of the room and outside it. This feature, number El-4, is oval shaped, measures 35 by 51 cm., and is 35 cm. deep. It contained white ash and a little carbon, as well as bones and teeth of a large herbivore. The osteological remains were so poorly preserved that they disintegrated when exposed even with a fine brush. However, the teeth were of a llama or related camelid.

Feature El-1 is also broadly contemporary with room S6. It is a large irregularly shaped lens of gravel about 3.5

meters in length north to south, which disappears under rooms S1 and S3 in the east and under the west wall of corridor CX in the west. The function of this feature is unknown, although it did contain a small sample of ceramics which are related to but not identical with the pottery found elsewhere on the site, and it is possible that the feature represents an early occupation (fig. 37). It may be that El-1 was a surface feature already present on the site when the construction of room S1 was undertaken. There was evidence that the gravel feature was surrounded by a low stone wall on the north end.

Two rooms were added to room S6, each using an existing wall as a side for the new room. Both rooms were added directly to S6, but it is difficult to tell which was built first. The stratigraphic position of the foundations suggests that first room S1 was added to the north side of S6 and somewhat later room S2 was built against the east side (fig. 4).

The foundation of room S1 lies in stratum 8. In the south end it lies level with the upper surface of the gravel-filled El-1. The stratum and El-1 rise slightly toward the north so that in the north end of the room the foundation of the west wall cuts through the gravel, and one of our excavations cut in the interior northwest corner of room S1 showed that the gravel feature underlies the floor of the room.

The inside dimensions of room S1 are as follows:

    East wall   — 267 cm. long, 44 cm. thick
    West wall   — 258 cm. long, 39 cm. thick
    South wall — 132 cm. long, 51 cm. thick
    North wall — 130 cm. long, 43 cm. thick

The entrance is located near the center of the east wall, 103 cm. north of the south wall and 94 cm. south of the north wall, and is 72 cm. across its sill. The base of the door lies 6 cm. above the floor level. The south side of the door has a vertical wall standing to a preserved height of 91 cm., while the north wall has a sag which causes the north side, which is preserved to only 50 cm., to protrude slightly into the opening. The walls of room S1 received a clay and white plaster covering, like those of room S6, and the remains of a white plaster floor were also preserved. The floor was underlaid by a layer of fine gravel and powdery gray soil 6 to 8 cm. thick which rested on the coarser gravel fill of El-1. The plaster floor was preserved in only a small part of the room; but unlike room S6 it was well preserved in front of the door and a few areas of the center of the room, while some of the corners, such as the southeast corner, had no indication of the white plaster at all. From the mixed and jumbled condition of the fill of this room, it was obvious that it had been excavated in the past by *huaqueros*. Since there were no surface indications of the excavations and the upper two strata were intact, it is likely that this represents grave robbing in prehistoric times after the abandonment of the site by the Wari people.

Room S1 served as a mausoleum during some period of the occupation at Jargampata, and I suspect this may have been its primary purpose in the South Unit House Group. During excavation, we encountered the remains of at least six adult burials on, or near, the floor in S1. Great confusion was caused by the previous excavation and partial refill of the room. The fill in much of the room was an ashy white, fine, sandy soil containing many large stones, some as much as a meter long, chunks of clay and plaster which came from both the walls and the floor, and a scattering of variously crushed and broken human bones. Few sherds were encountered above the floor level, while on the floor there was not a single vessel or burial intact. Sherds found on the floor fit into partially reconstructible vessels, the other fragments of which came from disturbed fills, especially from strata 3 and 4 in room S4 and from corridors CX and CW. Fragments of human bone were also found in these disturbed fills, demonstrating that they represent materials thrown out of S1 during its excavation.

The fact that the floor of room S1 was intact in front of the door where traffic would have been heaviest suggests that the room was not used frequently. Breaks in the floor may have resulted from the *huaquero* excavations. The presence of the adult skeletons is an indication that the room served as a repository for mummy bundles, which may have been the venerated ancestors of a group resident in the housing unit. Most of the fine ceramics from the House Group came either from the mixed fill in the adjacent enclosures or from the floor of S1, and it is possible that the fancy ceramics recovered in the House Group were grave offerings which were disturbed and redeposited during the grave-robbing operation. No infant bones were found in the fill of S1, and three adult burials without pottery offerings were found interred in the corridors—a possible indication of social differences in burial custom. The mechanical destruction combined with the very poor preservation of the osteological material makes it impossible to draw field conclusions concerning the age and sex of the cadavers placed in S1 other than that two skulls were of young adults, probably not over 35, and one mandible had lost all of its teeth and had undergone considerable bone reabsorption, suggesting a person of advanced age. There was no evidence of skull deformation among the preserved specimens. One occiput with a long narrow perforation and no bone regrowth might indicate a violent death.

The best preserved of the walls of room S1 is the west wall, which still rises to a height of 2.15 meters above the level of the plaster floor. Along the east side, or interior side, is a row of nine stones which project from 17 to 25 cm. into the room at a height from the floor of from 155 to 162 cm. (plate 3). Unfortunately, the east wall of the room is not preserved to this height, but it seems likely that the projecting stones served as some sort of support, probably

for a second floor. This would have allowed a room little more than 1.6 meters high, which seems rather low, but I have reports of late preconquest structures in the mountains around Huarochirí where second floors are preserved which leave even less space than this for the ground floor. By ethnographic analogy, it seems likely that the house structures of the rural folk rarely served as places for social gatherings or for work. The more common pattern in the contemporary villages of Ayacucho is for the peasant to keep his house almost continually locked, using it as a place for storage of food, tools, and other possessions. A paved porch enclosed on three sides with the front opening onto a yard is used for sleeping and meetings, and for most work. If this pattern derives from prehistoric times as early as the Middle Horizon, then it is not surprising to find multi-floored structures with the height between each floor insufficient to stand up comfortably. Also, the evidence indicates that room S1 served as a mummy repository and may never have been intended for occupation by the living.

By the time room S1 was built, the fire pit El-4 and gravel feature El-1 had been abandoned and covered. At this time a new fire pit, El-3, was in use only 50 cm. west of the old one and partly overlying the gravel feature. There can be little doubt about the domestic function of this hearth, as it contained the charred remains of maize.

Room S1 was built on the surface and cut slightly into stratum 8. It was probably constructed shortly after room S6. A concentration of large chunks of burned wood and what looked like burned hair was found under the foundation of the west wall, running between 137 and 175 cm. from the exterior northwest corner of the room. This could represent a hearth which was abandoned before building, but the ash in the upper portion was in contact with the stones and clay mortar of the wall, suggesting that the shallow lens depression of a maximum of 11 cm. deep was open and filled with carbonized material at the time of construction. A more likely interpretation is that the pit contained an offering which was burned in place at the initiation of construction. A similar offering was found under the wall of room S4.

Shortly after the completion of room S1, the construction of the central segment of the west wall of corridor CX was undertaken. This wall segment is 5 meters long and parallels the west walls of rooms S6 and S1, creating a narrow passage running north to south, with the north end even with the north wall of S1 and the south end in front of the middle of S6.

The old hearth, El-3, was located within the corridor and was abandoned for a new site at the south opening. This fire was numbered El-4a, and corresponds to a new deposit, stratum 7a. The hearth contained numerous animal bones. The movement of the kitchen fire a few centimeters to the south to avoid locating it within the newly built corridor suggests that the narrow hallway was roofed over and that the placement of cooking hearths at the opening may have been to avoid excessive smoke within.

The next building effort in the South Unit House Group was the addition of another room, S2, on the east side of room S6 (fig. 4). None of the walls of this room are bonded to one another, and it is likely that the east wall of the room was already in place as part of a construction not belonging to the House Group but rather to another group within the South Unit. The west wall of S2 is the east wall of the earlier room S6, while the south wall is constructed against the ends of the east and west walls. The north wall closes the room by spanning the opening at that end and is built flush against the other two walls.

The inside dimensions of room S2 are as follows:

East wall	– 345 cm. long, 41 cm. thick
West wall	– 340 cm. long, 42 cm. thick
South wall	– 230 cm. long, 41 cm. thick
North wall	– 209 cm. long, 48 cm. thick

There are two entrances to room S2; one is the old entrance to room S6, so that now S6 can be entered only via S2, and the other is an entrance in the north wall. This doorway is 77 cm. wide and is located 112 cm. east of the west wall and 20 cm. west of the east wall. The floor of the room was totally worn out and only occasional white stains indicated its depth. However, the sill of the door opening to the north was at floor level, while the sill of the opening into S6 lay between 30 and 34 cm. above the floor level. The floor of S2 was about 20 cm. lower than that of S6, and no gravel fill was found underlying the S2 floor.

The walls of room S2 were covered with the same white plaster used in other rooms, but it is poorly preserved. At some time after the initial construction, room S2 was divided by an east-west wall which created a large room and a small elongated room numbered S2a (plate 5). This dividing wall is constructed of a masonry unique in the site. Broad flat fieldstone slabs were selected and laid in a clay mortar to form a single course of stonework. Each slab is as wide as the wall is thick. This interior dividing wall is from 49 to 52 cm. thick. It was built so that it ends are flush with the east and west walls of the room, but the clay and white plaster coatings placed on the walls are visible between the two constructions, showing that the dividing wall was built after the completion of the room. The partition wall was also given a plaster finish.

The partition wall foundation penetrates to 25 cm. below the level of the floor in room S2. There is no indication from the stratigraphy in the room about the relative date of construction of the partition other than that it is later than the initial construction of the room. There is a small entrance in the partiion wall which gives access to room S2a. In its original form, it was an opening about 65 by 65 cm. with its sill about 18 cm. above the floor, and it was spanned by a single stone lintel which is 116 cm. long, 16 cm. thick in the center, and 48 cm. wide

Plate 5. Late-addition wall which partitions room S2 into rooms S2 and S2a, viewed from the north. The original floor level is visible on the right, while the center area has been excavated to 25 cm. below the wall foundation. The lintel which spans the opening between S2 and S2a is still in place, although the stones in the left side and bottom of the opening have fallen out of the wall, giving the impression that the space was larger than its 65cm. x 65cm.

(plate 5). The small height of the opening suggests that S2a was for storage and that it was not regularly entered. In the excavation of S2a we found no evidence for a floor, and there were almost no cultural materials. However, in the southwest corner in a small pit below the south wall were the bones of an adolescent child. The remains included an occipital, a fragmentary frontal, part of a temporal, and a complete mandible lying over fragmentary long bones and ribs. The pit extended 20 cm. below the south wall but seems to be a feature disturbed by the wall construction rather than an offering made at the time of construction.

The final interior dimensions of the rooms of S2 are as follows:

Room S2

East wall   – 214 cm. long
West wall   – 201 cm. long
South wall   – 210 cm. long
North wall   – 209 cm. long

Room S2a

East wall   – 75 cm. long
West wall   – 87 cm. long
South wall   – 228 cm. long
North wall   – 215 cm. long

The foundations of room S2 rest at the base of a stratum termed 7a, as do the south wall of corridor CZ and the southernmost portion of the west wall of corridor CX. These walls form a single unit bonded in their southwest corner and must have been constructed at about the same time as room S2. This building addition completed the south end of the House Group, closing corridor CZ by building against a wall in the east end. The surface of the ground in the south and west ends sloped up markedly in prehistoric times, so that the absolute depth of the foundations in this portion is less than in other parts of the House Group, and the deep fills present in most of corridor CX were lacking in corridor CZ. Corridor CZ is very narrow, never more than 70 cm. across and at its narrowest point only 40 cm. wide. The difficulties we encountered in its excavation would suggest that the closed passage never served as a work area, and it appeared to have been used for dumping trash. We found the stratigraphy to be composed of numerous small localized lenses containing refuse.

With the completion of the south end of the corridor around the House Group, the kitchen area west of S6 was no longer located in the mouth of the passageway and was moved to the other end of the central section of corridor CX. In the area in front of the north end of the corridor, six fire pits or hearths were found superimposed one upon the other. Numbered El-5 through El-10, these hearths were dug into stratum 7a from a surface corresponding to that from which El-4a was excavated. Hearths El-5, El-6, and El-7 overlap one another and were probably in use in that order. Similarly, El-8 and El-9 were probably used in that order, while El-10 is located apart and can only be said to

be broadly contemporary. All of these hearths contained ash, charcoal fragments, and burned animal bone, while El-9 also contained two maize grains and carbonized cobs.

Gravel-filled El-1 was identified at this end of corridor CX and labeled El-11 until we realized that it formed part of the same feature identified in the southern portion of the passage. The surface of the gravel fill rises to the base of stratum 7a and was supported by a small retaining wall. Although the function of this element is obscure, the maintenance of a supporting wall suggests that it may have continued to fulfill some purpose.

The next construction phase represents the maximum extension of the House Group and probably the climax of the occupation at Jargampata. Stratum 7a probably corresponds to the construction of rooms S4 and, slightly later, S3 and S5. This stratum was then capped by a plaster floor which ran through at least corridors CX and CY and corresponded to a stone-paved floor in CW.

Room S4 was built onto the east side of S1 and also used the north side of S2 as its south wall (fig. 4). Consequently, only an L-shaped wall was built, with one rounded and bonded corner in the northeast. It was not possible to identify the sub-7 stratum in room S4, and its foundation lay on the surface of stratum 8. The construction was unique in its use of broad, flat stones wider than the wall as a foundation platform on which to build the wall. However, the walls were identical to those of the other rooms; and, although there was no wall plaster in position, a plaster floor was identified and chunks of fallen plaster lay above the floor demonstrating the prehistoric presence of the plaster finish. Two door openings give access to the room, one the old entrance to S1, so that room S1 could be entered only from room S4, and another opening to the east. The latter door is 54 cm. wide at its base and is located 47 cm. north of the south wall and 221 cm. south of the north wall. The sides of the door are nearly vertical and the sill is level with the floor. The sill of the entrance to S1 is 15 to 16 cm. above the floor.

The inside dimensions of room S4 are as follows:

East wall   – 323 cm. long, 50 cm. thick
West wall   – 311 cm. long, 52 cm. thick
South wall   – 107 cm. long, 48 cm. thick
North wall   – 106 cm. long, 39 cm. thick

The north end of the east wall is preserved to a greater height than other parts of the room, and a row of projecting stones which protruded as much as 20 cm. into the room is still in place (plate 6). Only two stones are still in position, with their upper surfaces 122 cm. above the floor level. A shelf is present in the north wall at the same height; it was produced by reducing the total thickness of the wall some 12 to 18 cm. There is no evidence of projections in the portion of the east wall preserved to the proper height, but it must be remembered that this wall was originally the exterior of room S1. The shelf arrangement in

Plate 6. Room S4 viewed from the south. The plaster floor is visible in front of the stadia rod. A shelf on the north wall and projecting stones on the east wall about 122 cm. above the floor may have supported a second floor level. A burned textile was found beneath the northeast corner of the room.

the north end may have aided in the support of a second floor. The position of the projecting stones indicates that if a second floor existed it would have been some 39 cm. below the second floor level of room S1.

At the time of construction of the L-shaped wall which formed room S4, an offering was made under the north wall where it joins the east wall. A small oval pit 39 cm. long and about 23 cm. deep was excavated. A textile was folded into a bundle 25 cm. long, placed into the pit, and burned in position. We recovered small fragments of the charred textile along with three shell disk beads and two sherds of a large open bowl from the pit. Overlying the offering was a layer of hard brown clay, which is the mortar into which the foundation stones were set. This stratigraphy demonstrates that this burned offering was related to the construction of the room.

In room S4 another offering or cache was made near the northeast corner, at 13 cm. south of the north wall and 23 cm. west of the east wall, below the plaster floor. This offering was made after the plaster floor was laid, as a small crack was visible in the floor 27 cm. from the north wall indicating that the floor had been broken and then repaired. The stratum overlying the floor was intact, however. The offering consisted of two miniature vessels of coarse manufacture and fragments of a third (plate 15K and L). They lay in a matrix of dusty soil with white flecks intruded into a rocky fill 16 cm. thick between the construction surface and the floor of S4.

Two small perforations or pits were found in the surface of stratum 8 in the south end under the floor of S4. These contained only an earth fill and probably correspond to a period prior to the construction of S4. It seems likely that they are contemporary with the initial construction of S6 and S1 but before S2 was built. However, the lack of a stratum 7a capping the pits makes this interpretation problematic. It is possible that this stratum did not accumulate in this area and that the pits were excavated after the construction of S2 and the transfer of the hearth area to the north end of corridor CX, even though the surface is that of stratum 8. Unfortunately, the contents of S4 had been disturbed by excavation and refilling, probably at the same time as the excavation of room S1.

The construction of S4 was followed by the apparently simultaneous construction of rooms S3 and S5, the termination of corridors CY and CW (fig. 4), and the laying of a plaster floor in CX and CY, while CW received a stone paving. All of these floors constitute the same stratum, number 7, and are flush with the base of the walls of the rooms added at this time.

The large west perimeter wall which joins the House Group where CY and CX intersect represents an earlier construction with foundations set into stratum 8. A row of stones in stratum 8, about 40 cm. east of the line of this wall but at the same depth, suggests that the wall may have jogged and continued into the area of the House Group at an early date but was removed by the time of the construction of rooms S3 and S5. What relation, if any, this wall may have had with the gravel fill feature El-1 was erased by the late constructions.

Room S3 was built onto the north side of room S1 so that only the northeast and northwest corners are bonded, forming rounded corners, while the southeast and southwest corners are built against the north walls of S1 and S4. Remains of a plaster floor and one remnant of wall plaster were found.

The inside dimensions of room S3 are as follows:

East wall	— 165 cm. long, 43 cm. thick
West wall	— 161 cm. long, 48 cm. thick
South wall	— 117 cm. long, 43 cm. thick
North wall	— 114 cm. long, 57 cm. thick

An entrance in the east wall gave access to the room from S5. The doorway was 57 cm. wide and was located 28 cm. north of the south wall and 80 cm. south of the north wall. The sill is 93 cm. above the floor. Taken together, the small size of the room and the small entrance suggest that this room may have been for storage. Room S5 was added to the east side of S3, probably in the same building period. It is unlikely that room S5 is a separate room; most likely it represents a stairway to give access to the opening in the east wall of S3. The entrance to S3 was located about one meter above the living surface at the time of construction. A single wall built on the east side of S3, continuing the line of the north wall and parallel to the north wall of S4, provided a structure closed on three sides. A long stone laid across the east opening provided a step about 30 cm. high, while a north-south retaining wall across the room provided another step of about 40 cm. so the surface of the upper step lay only 40 cm. below the base of the door. The east end of S5 was open to corridor CW. It seems most probable that room S5 was used only for storage and that the small, high door opening and stairway approach facilitated this function. The excavation of the room uncovered only a few sherds, mostly from upper strata, which are probably secondary associations. Consequently, it is impossible to draw any inferences about the association of ceramic shapes with storage in the room, and it seems likely that ceramics were not an important part of the storage arrangement of room S3. In the massive state storage at Huánuco Viejo described by Morris and Thompson (1970: 356-58), *colcas* without pottery were generally associated with the storage of root crops. The storehouses of Huánuco also included drains in their floors to insure against excess moisture and to prevent decay. Room S3, which appears to have been utilized exclusively for storage, also has a drain beneath its floor, but the stratigraphy is vague and it could be preserved from some earlier construction.

Room S3 contains a narrow canal 12 to 13 cm. wide and about 6 cm. deep which runs in an east-west direction with

a low downward gradient to the east. However, the canal is between 38 and 23 cm. below the irregular base of the wall foundation and level with the bottom of the walled and gravel-filled feature El-1, which passes under the south end of the west wall of the room. The plaster floor of S3 was poorly preserved, so it gives little clue to whether the drain was an intentional feature of the room or not. The floor lay 40 cm. above the drain and between 1 and 15 cm. above the room foundation. The drain lies in stratum 8, but we were not able to detect a differentiation in soil between the floor and the drain which could correspond to the depositional break between strata 8 and 7 or one of its subunits.

The drainage canal of room S3 appears against the west wall but 23 cm. below its base. It runs east across the center of the room to disappear under the east wall base, where it was carefully capped with small lintels so that the drain passed under the steps of S5, and then crosses the stone paving of CW to disappear in the wall of our excavation. The canal was till clear enough under S5 so that once it had been exposed in S3 a steel measuring tape could be passed into the covered drain for 90 cm.

Two alternative interpretations seem most likely, although it will be shown that one of these fits the data with greater consistency. First, it is possible that the drain was a surface feature constructed at the same time as the walled and gravel-filled feature El-1, which underlies and predates the construction of the earliest rooms. Favoring this interpretation is the fact that both features lie in the same stratum and at the same absolute depth. The alternative, and more attractive, hypothesis is that the drain was built as a part of the construction of rooms S3 and S5. Prior to construction, an excavation the size of the planned rooms but deeper in the center must have been made. Here in the deepest part the drain was constructed with a slight downward gradient. The drain was covered in the section to become room S5 and then the excavation was filled prior to construction. In the area to become room S3, it appears that a partial fill of stone was set in and the walls constructed. Later, a plaster floor may have covered the entire area, or perhaps only part of it, as the plaster was preserved best along the walls on the two sides of the room parallel with the drain. Favoring this interpretation is the correspondence of the west end of the drain with a plumb elongation of the west wall and the fact that the feature does not pass under the wall and was not identified in corridor CX. Even more conclusive is the stratigraphic association of the east end of the drain where it crosses the floor of CW as part of the paving which corresponds to stratum 7. It seems probable that the masons who constructed the rooms excavated for the drain to a greater depth in the west end and that the east end lies at the original construction surface, providing a gradient of about 20 cm. in 3 meters.

The continuation of the early west perimeter wall into corridor CY, which was identified only from the row of foundation stones, may have run farther south into the area occupied by room S3. It is possible that these stones were removed when excavations for the construction of the drain were made.

After completion of the two rooms, S3 and S5, a plaster floor was laid in a large part of corridor CX and CY. This was stratum 7, which was traced through parts of both corridors. However, some sections had been disturbed by grave robbing or other activities which required extrapolation across these sections. The remainder of the west wall of CX was constructed as well as the north wall, with a bonded corner in the northwest. This was probably done at the same time as the floors were laid, although the foundations lie in stratum 7a or 8. This again indicates the use of a narrow trench for a foundation base. The bases of rooms S3, S4, and S5 correspond to this floor and lie only 5 to 10 cm. below it, indicating that these walls were built on the surface or in a very shallow trench.

The plaster floor could be followed throughout much of corridors CX and CY but was not identified in CZ. It appears that this narrow section never received the white floor paving and was not intended as a work area. In corridor CW there was no evidence for a plaster floor, but there were remains of a paved stone floor at the same level. This corridor or porch was maintained in the east by a retaining wall about 50 cm. high, indicating that the level of the plaza to the east was half a meter below the level of the House Group. The work space on the paved area of CW was just over 200 cm. wide.

It was impossible to trace the plaster floor of stratum 7 into the east end of CY, but the visible stratigraphy and the correspondence in absolute depth between the north wall of S5 and the north and east walls of CY suggest that these must be contemporaneous constructions. A central segment of the north wall of CY was never clearly identified. The east end of the wall is well preserved, but from 180 cm. west of the corner to 420 cm. west, where the wall would have met the old west perimeter wall, we found only a line of stones, indicative perhaps of the foundation of the wall which probably enclosed the House Group on the north side. Since this corridor was within the perimeter wall, perhaps the north wall was not built up to a height great enough for roofing, as was postulated for CX. The idea that corridor CY was not roofed is supported by the movement of the kitchen area from CX, where hearths had been located in the area just west of room S3 prior to its construction when CX was open at that end. With the completion of rooms S3 and S5 and the closing of corridor CX to join CY, we find hearths in CY (fig. 4).

The plaster floor in corridor CY was often badly worn and difficult to identify. Three circular hearths were found between 105 and 195 cm. east of the northwest corner of

S3 in corridor CY. They have diameters of slightly over 30 cm. It was not clear whether these hearths cut through the plaster floor or were constructed slightly prior to the laying of the floor, but stratigraphically they are cut into a stratum corresponding to either stratum 7 or 7a. This means that they must postdate the hearths in the north end of corridor CX and leaves open only the question of whether the transfer was prior to the laying of the floor or immediately after it.

With the completion of the corridors, the final configuration of the House Group, the form which it maintained until abandonment, was reached. After the laying of the plaster floor in the corridors, two burials were interred in circular pits about 60 cm. in diameter. Both of these burials were seated and tightly flexed, but settling has made it impossible to identify a direction of orientation. Burial 3 was located between 220 and 285 cm. south of the northwest corner of room S3 in the middle of corridor CX. It lay in a pit 89 cm. deep, which had been carefully capped with three large, flat stone slabs. No grave goods were associated. Burial 2 was also located in CX between 25 and 75 cm. south of the north wall of the corridor. The upper part of the pit had been partially ringed with fieldstones, but no stone cap was placed over the pit. No artifacts were associated.

A third burial pit was found in the extreme east end of corridor CZ, but due to the complexity of the stratigraphy in this area it is impossible to be sure that it is contemporary with the other pit burials. The pit was 50 cm. across and somewhat subrectangular due to the narrow space into which it was accommodated. Stone slabs lined two sides of the pit. The long bones were so poorly preserved that many could not be identified, but two round stone beads and fifteen whole or fragmentary shell beads were found among the splinters of bone. These objects probably represent an offering or perhaps the personal adornment which accompanied the body.

Apparently, after the laying of the plaster floor the south end of corridor CX began to be used for dumping or filling activity. Stratum 6 was deposited only in the east side of the south end of CX and in several areas has a capping of whitish plaster which may represent a second floor or, more likely, a collection of wall plaster fallen from the exterior walls of the rooms. Stratum 6 is lacking in the north end of CX and in CY and CW. Stratum 5 appears to represent a continued occupation of the House Group. During the accumulation of stratum 5, which in most of the House Group lies on the stratum 7 floor, corridor CY continued to function as the kitchen area. Two hearths, which must have been excavated after the accumulation of stratum 5 since they intrude from the surface of the layer, were found in the east end of CY. Also intruded into stratum 5 from the surface of the stratum is a shallow fire pit dug against the exterior north wall of room S3 in

corridor CY, 80 cm. east of the northwest corner of S3. This pit was only 25 cm. by 28 cm. and 9 cm. deep. It contained remains of what appeared to be burned gourd rinds, bones which included those of guinea pigs, and burned hair. Fifteen cm. to the west lay another pit of similar size also dug from the surface of stratum 5 against the wall of S3. This pit contained a complete bowl of Late Patibamba I style inverted over unburned animal bones (plate 7, plate 13A1, A2, fig. 21I). It is possible that the bowl represents an offering, but the proximity to what I interpret as a kitchen hearth and the contents of the inverted bowl lead me to suspect that this was a kitchen in which meat had been temporarily stored in a shallow pit—perhaps one lined with grass or some other perishable material—and covered with a serving bowl inverted over the mouth of the pit. This must represent one of the final acts during the occupation of the House Group, for in the following accumulations there is evidence of progressive deterioration of the constructions within the group.

Stratum 4 contains many large stones which apparently fell from the walls, indicating that the House Group was abandoned at this time. However, with the accumulation of stratum 3 there again appears to be activity—though not occupation—in the House Group. At this time, room S1 was excavated and robbed. Pieces of pottery from the floor of S1 were found to fit sherds, particularly from stratum 3 of corridor CX and strata 3 and 4 of corridor CW. It appears from the stratigraphy that at least rooms S1 and S4 and corridors CX and CW were heavily affected by treasure-hunting operations. Excavations were made into all these enclosures and they were then refilled one from another so that the contents of the units were probably little affected but became extremely mixed. In corridor CW and in room S1 it was particularly obvious that we were digging in disturbed fill, while in some other areas the disturbances were less visible (plate 8).

Apparently, following the treasure hunting by those who reoccupied the Jargampata site, the rooms and corridors of the House Group were filled with gravel and rock, probably scraped together from the surface. Before this filling, however, an extended burial lying with the head to the north and the feet to the south was placed in corridor CX. This skull is the only obvious case of frontal-occipital skull deformation noted during the excavations. This burial, numbered burial 1, lay on the surface of stratum 4 and was capped by strata 3, 2, and 1. No intrusive pit could be detected, so it seems that the skeleton represents an original inclusion prior to filling.

Strata 3 and 2 are composed primarily of gravel with very little soil matrix. The filling operation must have been conducted quite rapidly so that dirt did not have time to infiltrate the spaces around the stones. A similar fill was found elsewhere in the site and will be described below. This leads me to suspect that there was reoccupation and a

Plate 7. Late Patibamba I bowl in situ in feature El-6e, excavated from the surface of stratum 5. This inverted bowl (fig. 21I, plate 13A1, A2) covered animal bones. To the left, or east, may be seen another shallow pit, feature El-6d, which contained burned hair, gourd rinds, and animal bones. Also visible on the left are the tops of stones which may constitute the remains of an earlier wall foundation.

Plate 8. Excavation of disturbed strata in corridor CW. This corridor, as well as corridor CX, room S4, and some other areas of the House Group, contained a mixed deposit with stones from the walls, fragmentary human bones, and pottery from room S6 mixed with the original refuse.

general effort to clear away rubble and gravel collected on the surface of the site—perhaps for agricultural purposes. Once the rubble was scraped together, it was thrown into empty rooms or raked up against larger walls. It seems that this clearing effort might also account for the dry-laid fieldstone walls which wander about the surface of the Inkaraqay section and the Jargampata ridge where they cross earlier terraces.

The gravel fill of strata 3 and 2, which was best defined in the north end of corridor CX, contained many sherds which were heavily eroded. Included in this material were examples of pottery typical of the Early Patibamba ceramic style. Stratum 1 is the active ground surface and the soil cementing the immediately underlying gravel into a solid matrix.

Within the South Unit, we excavated a single room at the east side of the small plaza or patio onto which the House Group opened. Numbered room S7, the enclosure of 205 cm. by 127 cm. lies 18.5 meters to the east of the House Group (fig. 3). It is possible that S7 represents one room of another cluster of rooms similar to the house group excavated, but time limitations prevented more extensive exploratory excavations.

Room S7 was not affected by the gravel fill which constituted the upper strata in the House Group. In consequence, erosion has caused much more destruction, and we found only 90 cm. of the walls even in the best-preserved parts of the room. Construction was carried out on the surface of stratum 5, which probably corresponds to stratum 8 of the House Group, judging from the appearance and texture of the soil. There is no means of correlating strata directly from the House Group to room S7 since there are at least two retaining walls which substantially alter the relationships of strata between the two units. Furthermore, there are no architectural features which can be traced over the intervening space to furnish a relative date based on construction sequence. However, it seems likely that the room was built on the same surface as the House Group. In the northwest corner, the remains of an ash lens lay on the bedding between strata 5 and 4, apparently underlying the wall. On this basis, I would suggest that the room was constructed after the site had been occupied for some time. The construction of S7 may be broadly contemporary with the later building in the House Group—the construction of rooms S4, S3, and S5. This dating is supported by ceramic comparisons which demonstrate that the pottery of S7 belongs to the Late Patibamba I Phase.

Two strata containing refuse were found in S7. The lower of these, stratum 4, contained the largest amount of pottery and corresponds to the main occupation following the construction. Stratum 3 overlay 4 and contained some sherds which fit reconstructable vessels from stratum 4. Consequently, there seems to be no valid temporal differ-ence between the contents of the two soil horizons, and they were combined for the ceramic analysis. Strata 2 and 1 contain very little occupation material and an abundance of stones fallen from the walls, indicating the post-abandonment nature of these accumulations.

There was no indication of a door opening in any of the walls of room S7. However, both the south and east walls were only preserved to heights of 30 cm. above the base of the foundation, so it is entirely possible that an opening did exist in one or both of these walls.

Examination of figure 3 shows that the South Unit was a large and complex construction. The House Group excavated in the west end was well preserved, primarily due to the gravel fill overlying stratum 4 in corridor CX. This provided a substantial backing to the upslope-facing west wall of the corridor, and erosion from wash coming down the alluvial fan had little effect on the group. Other sections of the unit did not fare so well. To the south of the last walls mapped on figure 3, erosion had been severe. Some 30 meters to the south, other foundation walls and retaining walls could be detected; it is possible that they are part of the same South Unit, although we could not demonstrate this by following intervening structures. It seems appropriate to assign to the South Unit the term "irregular agglutinated" unit (Willey 1953: 237), but I have some reservations as to whether we should employ the term "village" at Jargampata.

I suspect that large-scale stripping of the post–Middle Horizon alluvium on the Jargampata site would reveal a number of units similar to the South Unit, each containing various house groups. Corners of such enclosures and large rocks, which indicate the presence of walls, are visible at three other places on the Inkaraqay section.

It is unfortunate that temporally diagnostic sherds were not found among the eroded terraces interpreted as possible house platforms and among the small irregular enclosures on the Jargampata ridge. If these represent Middle Horizon living units, then there is a marked contrast in patterns of dwelling arrangement and construction within the Jargampata site. The diagnostic ceramics from the House Group of the South Unit indicate a Middle Horizon 2 occupation. Features of the local pottery style indicate that occupation had begun by 2A times and continued through 2B. Some sherds from the ridge area probably belong to the very poorly defined Early Intermediate Period Huarpa style, while most are probably Middle Horizon. However, ceramics from the late Illaura Phase, which will be described below, are very difficult to distinguish from the Middle Horizon 2 wares, and the superficial nature of the refuse on the ridge results in the mixing of any samples. Until more work is conducted on domestic architecture in the Central Highlands, it will be impossible to demonstrate the nature of the temporal and social significance of alternative housing patterns during the Wari Empire at Jargampata.

Although most of the building undertaken by Andean peoples during the time included within the Middle Horizon was probably for family living and domestic purposes, such remains have simply not yet been investigated by archaeologists. Excavations have focused on cemeteries, tombs, offering caches, and other features to the exclusion of simple dwelling units.

Lacking comparisons from other sites, it is impossible to demonstrate whether the House Group of the South Unit is typical of Central Highlands dwelling complexes or even what social level resided there. It is possible that the complex is associated with the North Unit and was occupied by reasonably important state officials, although I doubt it. If this were the case, the isolated structures on Jargampata could be peasant dwellings. It seems more likely that the South Unit represents living quarters for peasant farmers and the Jargampata structures belong to another group or class, perhaps herders. The South Unit appears to follow a general plan which may underlie the organization of late Early Intermediate and Middle Horizon communities in the Central Highlands upon which Wari architects developed their massive public architecture.

The House Group shows a pattern which permits addition of multiple rooms within a limited space, maintaining narrow access ways or corridors which appear to have functioned as work areas. The compound was enclosed on at least three sides from other possible house groups and organized within a much larger unit of construction—perhaps something like the barrio found elsewhere in Peru and developed to such an extreme at other sites. Perhaps kin or other social units are represented in these architectural subunits.

The narrow corridors which surrounded the House Group and functioned as work and cooking areas have some evidence for time depth and distribution in the Central Highlands. Lumbreras (1969: 223) notes the presence of narrow passages in constructions at Conchopata which date to the earliest building activity on the site. Although no data are provided concerning ceramics associated with the structures, vessels illustrated as pertaining to this and the preceding time period date to terminal Early Intermediate and Middle Horizon 1 (Lumbreras 1969: 223). Furthermore, the fieldstone walls of the rooms partially excavated by Lumbreras and Benavides were plastered with a thin coat of clay, which in a later construction may have been painted. These probable housing units were distributed within large plazas, again suggesting the barrio arrangement (Lumbreras 1969: 225).

Aerial photographs of Conchopata indicate the presence of rather large enclosures and complex wall patterns. It is difficult without more excavation to know whether these represent housing units or some kind of public structures. However, the famous Conchopata ceramic offerings excavated by Tello in 1942 (Menzel 1964: 6) suggest that the site was a center of ceremonial activity and that it should include public structures. Perhaps at Conchopata a style of architecture was developing for ceremonial and administrative buildings which was based upon agglutinated housing units built by the people.

It is interesting that there are general similarities in site location, agglutination, and to some degree even architectural layout between Jargampata and Middle Horizon sites of the Tomaval Period in the Virú valley (Willey 1953: 234-95). However, comparison of floor plans of agglutinated dwelling units from Virú with those of Jargampata is not any more striking than comparison with selected units from pre-Tomaval constructions. It is not until we deal with administrative architecture that more detailed comparisons can be made.

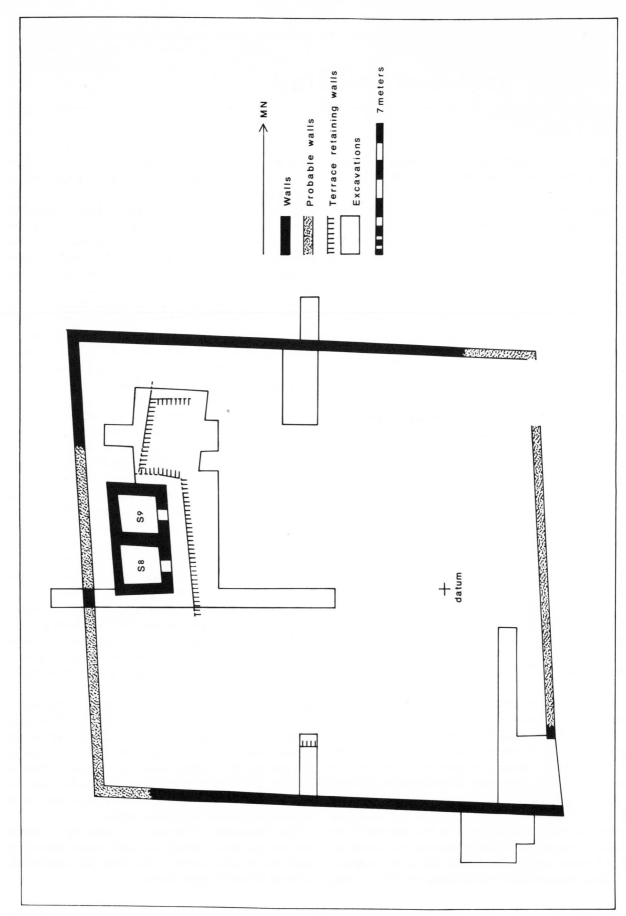

Figure 5. Floor plan of the North Unit during Middle Horizon 2A in the Middle Patibamba Phase. This building represents a single construction period.

4
A Public Architectural Unit

Excavations in the North Unit at Jargampata were conducted by following natural stratigraphy. Most of the individual excavation units were single meter squares keyed into a grid system with the datum point near the center of the architectural remains (fig. 5). Each meter unit was designated by the number of meters it lay in two cardinal directions from the datum, so any unit was referred to with a binomial abbreviation such as S5 x W4 (south 5 meters by west 4 meters). When rooms were found which did not correspond to the arbitrary grid, room numbers were assigned and the excavations were based upon the architectural unities. The positions of important artifacts were recorded in relation to the walls of the structures.

Morphologically, the North Unit is a slightly rhomboidal square of between 25 and 25.5 meters to a side. Added to this is what I shall refer to as the North Extension, which is a rectangular enclosure added to the north side. This addition measures 15 by 25 meters and it appears to have been constructed after the initial building of the North Unit (fig. 6).

Prior to excavation, the north and south walls of the North Unit were preserved in some areas to a height of 3 meters. In contrast, the east and west walls, which parallel the contour lines of the alluvial fan and offer direct resistance to water drainage, were almost totally invisible on the surface and in some areas could not be detected at all. It is possible that the walls of the unit were laid out in relation to cardinal points, as the well-preserved south and north walls lie between 2 and 4 degrees northwest-southeast of a perpendicular to magnetic north. However, no great effort seems to have been invested in the construction of straight walls, and it is equally likely that the walls were simply aligned with the contours of the surface of the alluvial fan.

The major building phases in the construction of the North Unit were detected by excavation. Initially, probably late in the Early Patibamba Phase, the unit was laid out as a large square 25 by 25 meters. In the south end of the east wall, there was an opening or entrance 3.5 meters wide which gave access to the interior of the enclosure. Although we did not excavate the north end of the east wall, the general symmetry of the building suggests that there may have been a similar opening there. In the west end of the enclosure, a rectangular building containing two rooms was built 1.5 meters north of the central axis of the enclosure. The outside dimensions of this structure are 620 cm. along

the west side, 593 cm. along the east wall, 325 cm. along the south wall, and 340 cm. along the north side (fig. 5). The foundations of the rectangular building and the enclosing wall rest on, or in, stratum F, which is a yellowish deposit of ungraded sand, clay, and gravel. The surface of this stratum should be broadly contemporary with, and probably corresponds to, stratum 8 in the South Unit, and the construction of both units must have begun about the same time.

From the appearance of the walls, the layout and construction of the North Unit was undertaken in a single effort. The large enclosing walls are continuous with no indication of unbonded sections, while the exterior walls and interior partition of the small rectangular building also form a single unit with all corners bonded.

Portions of a low retaining wall were found in the west end of the North Unit. The base of this wall lies in stratum F, and its construction probably followed the completion of the enclosure. This low wall of a single course of fieldstones supported an earth terrace 40 to 60 cm. high, which surrounded the rectangular building, raising the level of the west end of the courtyard. The internal stratigraphy of the terrace indicates that it was constructed with fill after the erection of the rectangular building so that the terrace lies around the deep foundation of the structure rather than supporting it. The raised terrace may also have run along part or all of the north and south walls of the enclosure, producing benches slightly more than 2 meters across. If this was the case, an essentially sunken courtyard of about 19 by 19 meters occupied the east center of the enclosure.

The primary feature of the North Unit appears to be the Rectangular Structure in the west end of the enclosure (plate 9). The masonry of this building is the most skillful in terms of the selection of materials and the laying of the stone, although it is built of fieldstone laid in a clay mortar and is not unlike the remainder of the building. These walls average about 60 cm. in thickness and are among the thickest observed at Jargampata. The base of the foundation averages 10 to 20 cm. below the level of the floor of the plaza and was cut into stratum F. However, with the surrounding low terraces the foundations were between 60 and 80 cm. below the occupation surface.

The Rectangular Structure is divided by a central east-west partition creating two small rooms, one on the south and the other on the north, which will be referred to as rooms S8 and S9, respectively.

Plate 9. Rectangular Structure of the North Unit viewed from the east. The stadia rod in room S8 rests on the subfloor level 3 cm. to 5 cm. below the final occupation floor, which contained the fragments of a black decorated bowl (fig. 42E, plate 19A). In the lower right may be seen the original level of the terrace east of the structure, and to the left the surface of a lower fill (fig. 47). A row of projecting stones may be seen in the west walls of rooms S8 and S9.

The inside dimensions of room S8 are as follows:

East wall   – 210 cm. long
West wall   – 200 cm. long
South wall   – 210 cm. long
North wall   – 210 cm. long

The west wall of S8 has a row of six stones tenoned into the wall and projecting between 25 and 30 cm. into the room. This row lies between 100 and 110 cm. above the clay floor of the room. An additional surface was found 3 to 5 cm. below the floor and may represent an earlier floor or perhaps simply a base for the last floor. Both of these surfaces are made of hard clay, and there was no evidence of white plaster on these or any other walls within the North Unit.

Below the surface of the floor, to a depth of 36 cm., there is a relatively homogeneous fill of light red-brown color, almost pink, containing some very fine gravel inclusions. Underlying this, to the base of the foundation and below it, is a stratum of yellow-brown soil which is part of stratum F. This stratigraphy closely parallels that of the low terrace with retaining wall found in front of the Rectangular Structure. Here also two layers of clay floors overlie a pinkish soil about 30 cm. thick. This pinkish fill lies on the yellow-brown stratum F, which represents the original surface at the time of construction. A thin courtyard floor lies in front of, and 25 cm. below, the surface of stratum F, where it is maintained by the terrace retaining wall. However, the floor also lies on stratum F, showing that the central area of the enclosure which was destined to become the courtyard was scraped and leveled, lowering the western end by at least 25 cm. at the time of the building.

A door in the east wall of room S8 opens onto the terrace and overlooks the plaza area. This entrance is 66 cm. wide and is located 77 cm. from the north wall and 67 cm. from the south wall. The sill is 24 cm. above the floor inside the room and about 40 cm. above the surface of the terrace on the outside. The position of this door must have been planned when the foundation was laid, as a single large stone forms the base of the foundation below the door.

Room S9 is similar to S8 in every respect. Across the inside of the west wall there is a row of seven projecting stones, which intrude into the room some 18 to 22 cm. at a height of 99 cm. above the floor. As in S8, there is evidence of a hard clay floor in the room, with another floor, or perhaps a floor bedding, between 10 and 11 cm. below it. These clay caps lie on a relatively homogeneous fill of red-brown color about 22 cm. deep, which in turn lies on the sterile stratum F.

The inside dimensions of room S9 are as follows:

East wall   – 205 cm. long
West wall   – 205 cm. long
South wall   – 207 cm. long
North wall   – 208 cm. long

A door or opening in the east wall of S9 gives access to the terrace and to the plaza area beyond. This opening is 65 cm. wide and is located 63 cm. south of the north wall and 77 cm. north of the south wall. The sill of the door lies about 30 cm. above the inside floor and about 45 to 50 cm. above the level of the terrace on the outside.

The floors of both rooms in the Rectangular Structure showed little or no wear—in sharp contrast to the plastered floors in the rooms of the House Group.

The deep foundations and thickness of the structure suggest that these walls may have been quite high. The maximum standing height of any wall at present is in the northwest corner of S9, where 230 cm. of masonry is preserved above the level of the floor and 80 to 85 cm. of foundation underlies the level of the floor. The row of projecting stones in each of the rooms suggests that there were several stories in the structure. Unfortunately, there is not sufficient preservation of the east wall of either room to demonstrate whether these walls had a similar row of projecting stones at the same height. Consequently, it is impossible to prove the existence of upper floor levels; an argument against multiple stories can be made on the basis of the very low height of the ceiling above the floor. The row of supports in room S8 is only 100 to 110 cm. above the floor, so the ceiling could not have been very much higher, while in S9 the supports lie only 99 cm. above the floor.

Nevertheless, the preserved height of the walls, the strength of the masonry, the depth of the foundation, and the rows of projecting stones all argue that the Rectangular Structure in the North Unit was a multistoried construction. It is necessary to assume that the ceilings of the individual levels were extremely low, but it is also probable, given the well-preserved nature of the floors, that the rooms suffered relatively little traffic. The interpretation of the function of these two rooms is particularly interesting, but the associated material from their excavation is of little help. The fill within the rooms was composed of large rocks which had fallen from the originally much higher walls, making it impossible to define or follow natural stratigraphic divisions. Artifact content of the fill was very low, and such materials were limited to the surface of the floors.

Room S8 produced virtually no material in the fill. Lying on the floor were the fragments of a flat-bottomed bowl of black ware painted on the interior with designs in semitransparent red paint (plate 19A; fig. 42E). No other materials were found on this floor. Room S9 contained more ceramics, all within 20 cm. of the floor. A large tubular pottery spout from a side-spout jar, a neck from a narrow-collar jar, and a small flaring-neck jar with a broken bottom were found near the south wall close to the center of the room only about 10 cm. above the floor. This suggests that these vessels were also on the floor at the time of abandonment, although in the case of S9 the association

of the ceramics and the last floor is not as certain as in the case of S8. It is interesting to note that the only pottery on the floor of room S8 was a decorated bowl of a ware probably imported to Jargampata, while S9 contained no decorated pottery but fragments of three utility vessels.

A metal shawl pin, or *tupo*, was also found in room S9 at a depth of 15 cm. below the row of projecting stones. It was lying against the west wall 27 cm. north of the south wall (plate 19L). This is within the fill of fallen stones and has little if any stratigraphic significance.

Considering the cultural remains recovered from both rooms S8 and S9, it seems obvious that the rooms do not contain habitation refuse, and it is unlikely that either was used as a living area. The well-preserved condition of the floors supports this belief. The most reasonable interpretation would be that these possibly multifloored, low-ceilinged, and not regularly occupied rooms were used for storage, ceremonial, or perhaps administrative activities.

The symmetric and planned appearance of the North Unit as a 25-meter square, walling off a plaza area with an elevated terrace in the west end which supported a tall tower-like structure divided into two rooms with multiple stories, favors an interpretation which associates the unit with state rather than family or village affairs. The stratigraphic associations indicate that the entire unit was constructed in accord with a master plan in one building epoch—in marked contrast to the room-by-room additions which typify the House Group of the South Unit.

After its initial construction, the North Unit did undergo a second construction phase. Over most of the plaza floor there was no evidence of stratified deposits, the ceramics lying on the floor apparently representing the final Late Patibamba II occupation refuse. This indicates that the plaza floor was kept clean. However, in rooms S10 and S11 (fig. 6), three strata were identified—Middle Patibamba, Late Patibamba I, and Late Patibamba II—which correspond to successive periods within the history of the North Unit. Close examination of excavation cuts at the edge of the plaza and a new test cut at E5-6 x S9-10 showed that it was possible to differentiate stratigraphically a Late Patibamba I and a Late Patibamba II ceramic sample which probably postdate the rebuilding in the North Unit.

These excavations in the southeast section of the North Unit also demonstrated the superposition of walls from the second building period upon those of the first. The entrance in the southeast part of the enclosure was closed with a wall which lies upon, but is not perfectly aligned with, the east wall of the first construction. Where the enclosure wall was open, the later wall lies 60 cm. above the foundation of the first construction. The base of the foundation of the new addition closing the entrance correlates with a floor and refuse deposition labeled stratum 4. It overlies stratum 5, which in this area contained few ceramics or other artifacts but which probably corresponds to the first construction.

At the same time the entrance was closed, a long east-west wall was built paralleling the south wall of the enclosure but just under 2 meters to the inside of the earlier wall. This produced a long gallery. On the north side of the courtyard, a similar wall was built to form a second gallery of comparable dimensions (fig. 6). Another part of the second building phase was the construction of rooms S10 and S11 in the northwest part of the enclosure. As originally laid out these two rooms were one, and at a later time they were divided to form the two smaller units. However, since they were excavated as two rooms, I shall continue to use the two designations in spite of the unit they originally comprised.

The low retaining wall supporting the terrace around the Rectangular Structure dates to the first period of construction. This wall ran across the west end of the enclosure and turned west at the north end of the Rectangular Structure. The west wall of rooms S10 and S11 abuts against the north wall of the Rectangular Structure; and its foundation rises 45 cm. as it approaches within 50 cm. of the Rectangular Structure, demonstrating that the west wall of S10 and S11 was built upon a floor level and over the surface of the low terrace without excavating for its foundation. The east wall of S10 and S11 curves west to abut against the northeast corner of the Rectangular Structure and also crosses the terrace, but in this case the terrace was removed so that the base of the foundation of the east wall is nearly level and lies only about 15 cm. above the foundation of the Rectangular Structure.

On its north end, the east wall of rooms S10 and S11 forms a bonded unit with the long east-west wall which forms the North Gallery. The gallery wall was also built on a terrace supported by a low stone wall, the remains of which appear some 40 cm. to the south and within the confines of S10. In finished format, S10 and S11 constituted a rather large enclosure with a low terrace from an earlier construction period running around three of its sides like a bench. The west terrace is the least securely dated and may actually have been added at this time. A door provided access to the room from the terrace in front of the Rectangular Structure. A step down of 15 cm. was required to enter the room. The door opening is 78 cm. wide, while the wall and the door sill are 45 cm. thick. A much larger opening is present in the west wall, 220 cm. wide, lying 58 cm. south of the north wall and 265 cm. north of the south wall. Only a single meter test unit was excavated within the room into which this passage opens. The room was labeled S12, but its dimensions were not defined, and it may be a continuation of the North Gallery.

The inside dimensions of rooms S10 and S11 combined are as follows:

East wall — 530 cm. long
West wall — 538 cm. long
South wall — 253 cm. long
North wall — 311 cm. long

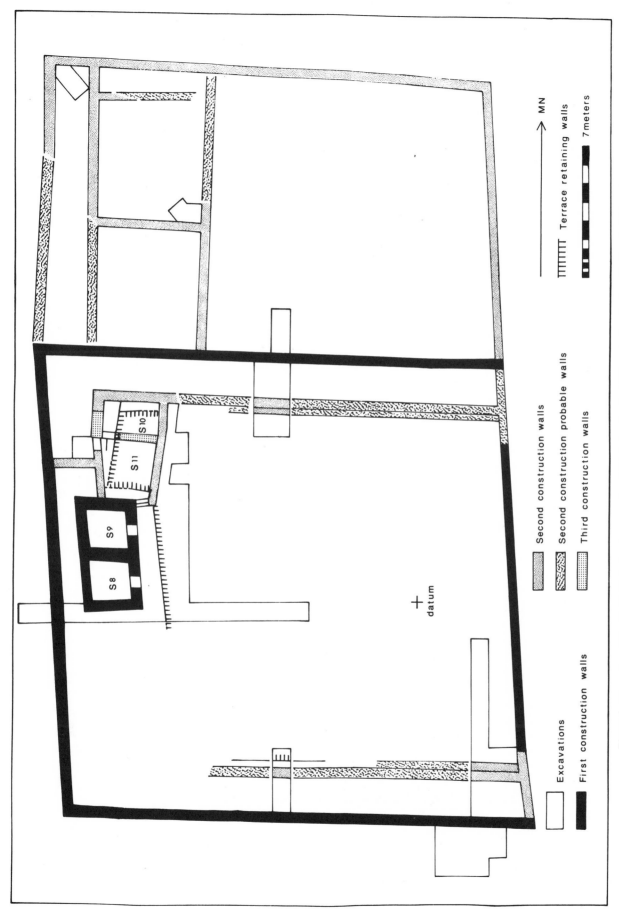

Figure 6. Floor plan of the North Unit showing second and third structural additions during the Late Patibamba I Phase in Middle Horizon 2B and during the Illaura Phase reoccupation in the Late Intermediate Period.

Excavations

First construction walls

Second construction walls

Second construction probable walls

Third construction walls

Terrace retaining walls

7 meters

MN

datum

S8 S9 S10 S11

Plate 10. Rooms S10 and S11 of the North Unit viewed from the north. Excavator with stadia rod stands on the north wall of room S9. Room S10 can be seen in the lower part of the photo, while room S11 is above it. Between the two is a third construction period wall resting on stratum C1 (fig. 44) which contained pottery of the Illaura Phase. In the upper left of room S11 is a remnant of the first construction period terrace retaining wall which is also visible across the center left of the photo east of the Rectangular Structure. The original height of the terrace may be seen to the left of the entrance to room S9 of the Rectangular Unit. The original plaza floor lies to the left of the terrace retaining wall.

A wall runs west from the west wall of S11, joining the exterior wall of the enclosure. This wall forms the south end of room S12, into which the large entrance in the west wall of S10 and S11 opened. The construction is contemporaneous with the other walls of S10 and S11, as the joint of the two walls is bonded, while there is no bonding between this wall and the outside wall of the enclosure against which it abuts.

The long east-west walls of the second construction period, which formed the narrow galleries, had low benches or terraces built against their courtyard faces. These benches are most frequently about 40 cm. high and about as wide. The example attached to the South Galley was well exposed at its east end. It is a low, flat-topped wall built against the gallery wall and is composed of stones laid in a clay mortar. Lying on a stone-and-clay platform raised 25 cm. above the rest of the bench is a grinding stone, or *batan*, roughly 50 cm. in diameter, located 135 cm. west of the east wall of the enclosure. This *batan* shows very little wear, but a rocker grinder made of a naturally crescent-shaped stone lay near the surface of the bench beside the *batan*.

The bench does not run the full length of the South Gallery wall. A trench 1 meter by 3.5 meters was cut across the gallery at W7 x S8-11, exposing the gallery wall, but the bench described above was not present. Instead, a low wall of a single course of stones supported a low terrace of dimensions essentially similar to those of the bench. The soil fill of the terrace was excavated and found to contain a single sherd from a flaring-neck jar. In all probability, the low terrace composed of retaining wall and earth fill served the same function as the stone bench, but it seems likely that this feature may be part of the first constuction rather than the second building period. The low retaining wall and terrace may be a part of the terrace which originally surrounded the Rectangular Structure and raised much of the west end of the interior of the North Unit. In this case, the terrace would have run along the south side of the enclosure and perhaps the north side as well. With the construction of S10 and S11, the terrace east of the room may have been eliminated. An excavation of 2 meters by 4 meters at W7-8 x N9-13 cut the North Gallery, revealing a wall forming the gallery wall and a low stone-and-clay bench. No evidence was found in this area for the earlier terrace and retaining wall. However, the trench which was excavated outside the east wall of rooms S10 and S11, at W14 x N11, showed that the terrace running along the north side of room S10 does not continue beyond the east wall. No bench structure was found at this point along the exterior of the gallery. The earlier terrace may therefore have been removed, in part, at the time the North Gallery and rooms S10 and S11 were constructed. The bench on the north side of the plaza did not run the entire length of the gallery wall; it was present only in the center and

probably in the east end of the enclosure.

If this interpretation is correct, and the raised terrace ran along part or all of the north and south sides of the enclosure, the construction of the galleries with floors at essentially the same level as the plaza floor would have required the excavation and removal of a large part of the terrace fill. This would account for the lack of refuse deposits corresponding to the first construction period in the cuts made across the center of the North and South galleries.

The galleries appear to have been long enclosed halls with no internal partitions. In the east end of the South Gallery, we opened an area 3 meters long, while 10 meters to the west we cut across the gallery with a 1-meter trench without finding any evidence for partitions forming individual rooms. In the North Gallery, we opened only a length of 2 meters, but again without evidence of internal divisions. However, the possibility must not be dismissed that rooms more than 3 meters long may have existed within the galleries.

One possible indication of a door or entrance from the plaza area into the South Gallery was found. The trench at W7 x S8-11 cut across the inner wall, revealing it to be in poor repair. The stones protruding from the west wall of the trench form a vertical line suggestive of a door jamb. However, no comparable evidence existed for a second jamb. If an entrance was present, it was about 60 cm. wide and was located 13 meters west of the east end of the gallery. Trenches W7-8 x N9-13 failed to reveal a comparable opening into the North Gallery, although the presence of rooms S10 and S11 on the north side of the Rectangular Structure, with no room on the south side, demonstrates that the interior of the enclosure was not laid out in a totally symmetrical pattern during the second construction period.

The presence of the *batan* grinding stone and the *mano* noted on the bench of the south side of the plaza area suggests that this bench may have functioned as a work area. There were more ceramic refuse and stratified deposits lying in front of the grinding stone at the foot of the bench than elsewhere on the plaza floor—with the exception of the floor area covered by the collapse of the terrace retaining wall in front of the Rectangular Structure. Although the *batan* shows little indication of use, the quantity of ceramic vessels suggests that the southeast corner of the plaza was used for preparation or serving of food or other material. No hearths were found and, although there was ash and an occasional fleck of charcoal on the floor of the plaza, we found no evidence of cooking activities. Ashy soil from this area was subjected to flotation in water with the hope of recovering botanical remains, but nothing was found. Animal bone was also absent, suggesting that perhaps the activities were centered around ceremonial undertakings or that organic refuse was

carried away but pottery sherds were not.

In excavating S1 x W20, we did recover a large quantity of animal bones lying in a pocket against the inside of the west wall of the enclosure. The stratigraphic association is somewhat problematic, as the bones may have been dumped into the original trench excavation for the wall just after construction. If this is the case, they represent the first construction period. More likely, however, is that the bones were deposited in a pit excavated after the second construction epoch, and they are therefore broadly contemporary with the *mano* and *batan* on the bench in the southeast corner of the enclosure. Bones recovered included fragmentary long bones of large quadrupeds and fairly complete sections of skulls and mandibles of grazing animals which must be from llamas or related camelids. There were only three sherds, all from utility vessels, associated with these bones, and there was insufficient charcoal to indicate that the area served as a hearth. The low frequency of animal bones elsewhere in the North Unit contrasts sharply with this cache along the west wall. Since no other excavations crossed the west wall, we must not discard the possibility that the west side of the enclosure served as a refuse area in which the remains of meals were interred. A more likely hypothesis is that these bones represent the remains of an offering or ceremonial meal rather than day-to-day refuse.

The North Extension on the North Unit was not extensively investigated. The enclosing wall of this rectangle was built up against the southwest corner of the North Unit, indicating that it represents a late addition. Given the constructional modifications within the North Unit which correspond to a second building epoch, I believe that the northward addition represents the same building expansion.

One final and later modification made within the North Unit seems to have affected only rooms S10 and S11. This large room was divided into two smaller rooms by filling in part of the western opening to S12 and constructing an east-west wall. The opening in the west wall, which had been 220 cm. long, was filled in at the north end, leaving an opening only 70 cm. wide. The east-west wall, which separates S10 and S11, was built against the south end of this addition to the west wall, is 320 cm. long, and abuts against the east wall (fig. 6). The bases of both of these additions rest on stratum C1, which is an easily defined floor from which ceramic refuse of the Illaura Phase was recovered. This demonstrates that no excavations were made for these walls and that they were constructed at the same time as the formation of the floor. An opening in the dividing wall provided access from S11 on the south into S10 to the north. This door was 96 cm. wide and its stone sill lay about 30 cm. above the stratum C1 floor. Room S11 could be entered from the terrace which lay in front of the Rectangular Structure, the same entrance which gave access to the room in earlier times. Also, a narrow door gave access to the area to the west, labeled S12.

Stratum C1, upon which the dividing wall separating S11 from S10 was built, is a living floor. It overlies stratum D, which contains Late Patibamba II pottery. The eroded ceramics from stratum D, the stone fallen from the walls, and the general appearance of the matrix suggest a period of disoccupation. No other floors were found in the North Unit which correlate with the C1 floor of room S10 and room S11. The North Unit was apparently abandoned shortly after the construction of the galleries. The terrace retaining wall in front of the Rectangular Structure collapsed onto the plaza floor, and stones from the walls fell into the living area. Room S10 and S11 was reoccupied later and divided into two smaller rooms. However, other rooms in the site which were examined seem not to have been reoccupied, suggesting that the population was low during the reoccupation and that the residents were doing little more than squatting in the ruins.

The North Unit is separated from the South Unit by only 25 meters of unoccupied space. However, the two are remarkably different in form and construction and presumably in function as well. The larger size of the enclosure, substantial single-period constructions, and the overall plan of the North Unit associate it with a much higher level of organization than the South Unit.

The South Unit may represent a continuous development of architectural form from the first stone dwellings of coresident social groups of the Ayacucho region. As such, it is a likely example of the kind of agglutinated groupings which served as models for architectural patterns in urban centers. The North Unit is more sophisticated and probably functionally specialized. It may be an example of one of the architectural forms which evolved from more generalized irregular agglutinated dwellings under the influence of urban residential and state organizational requirements. Indeed, it shows important evolution of form within itself when the original layout is compared with the later form including the narrow galleries, added rooms, and exterior extensions. Once the North Unit can be placed within its appropriate sequential context and compared with remains of public architecture from other Middle Horizon centers, it will contribute substantially to our understanding of the developing cultural responses which were part of the process of city and state formation during the Middle Horizon.

5
Dating the Occupation at Jargampata

The architectural sequence at Jargampata demonstrates that the site was occupied for some time. The House Group in the South Unit was constructed in a series of minor building efforts which consisted of room additions. This suggests gradual growth in the size of a social group. The North Unit, on the other hand, shows signs of two major construction periods and a late reoccupation.

Ceramics from the North Unit and the South Unit belong to the same style and time periods. However, with the exception of the floor in room S7, the ceramic associations from the South Unit are poor. The House Group was partially excavated at some time, and materials it contained were redistributed within the rooms. In consequence, the most reliable data for precise dating at Jargampata must come from elsewhere.

It is likely that Jargampata was already occupied during the Early Intermediate Period, since several sherds which resemble Huarpa ceramics from the Ayacucho valley (Rowe, Collier, and Willey 1950: 120-37; Bennett 1953: 80-82; Lumbreras 1960: 187-88; Menzel 1964: 8-10; Gonzáles 1967) were collected on the surface. However, since Huarpa has never been adequately defined and described for Ayacucho, it is difficult to make a comparison with the ceramics of Jargampata. Only a small number of black-on-white sherds with thickened rims from constricted-mouth jars and flaring-mouth jars indicate the presence of a diffuse Early Intermediate component.

A sample of sherds, which includes a distinctive "frying pan handle" not found in the rest of the Jargampata ceramic collection, comes from element El-11 of the House Group (fig. 37). These sherds cannot be seriated stylistically, although they are probably of Middle Horizon date but earlier than other ceramics in the House Group.

The earliest stylistic sample with firm stratigraphic association from Jargampata comes from excavations against the outside of the south wall of the North Unit (fig. 43). This sample, from strata 4 through 9, has been assigned to the Early Patibamba Phase. Although the temporal relationship with the construction of the North Unit perimeter wall is not totally clear, these ceramics probably represent the local Jargampata style before and during the initial construction of the North Unit. Early Patibamba ceramics were not found inside the enclosure, and stylistically more advanced pottery is very rarely found outside the wall. Taken together, these facts suggest, but do not prove, that the stylistic separation is temporal rather than social.

A single rim sherd from an open bowl, found with Early Patibamba ceramics, was identified as an exotic or imported vessel on the basis of its paste (fig. 39J). It strongly resembles bowls from a ceremonial offering of vessels from Ayapata (Ravines 1968: fig. 31) and may therefore date to Middle Horizon 2A.

It is probable that only one of the strata included in the Early Patibamba Phase represents a primary deposit. Stratum 9 is a primary deposition of refuse, while strata 4 through 8 contain materials carried by slope wash from above. However, they contain the same pottery found in stratum 9.

A feature composed of gravel, rock, and sherds lies against the enclosure wall between strata 4 and 3. Labeled El-1, this feature probably corresponds both temporally and functionally to strata 3 and 2, which covered burial 1 in corridor CX of the House Group. In spite of the late date of the formation of this feature, it appears that the gravel and sherds were raked together from the surface of stratum 4 and are primarily—or perhaps exclusively—Early Patibamba refuse.

Five sherds from the same fancy vessel were found scattered through El-1. These show differential degrees of erosion—in some cases rather extreme—confirming that the vessel had been broken and had been on the surface for some time prior to its inclusion in El-1. This vessel (plate 16C, fig. 39K) is a spherical bowl with a round base and incurving sides. It is decorated with a feline-headed angel with a human body, which can be dated by the stylistic seriation for fancy pottery developed by Menzel (1968a: 79-84). The theme is derived from a feline-headed angel which first appears in Ayacucho on Conchopata ceremonial offering vessels in Middle Horizon 1A. On these oversize vessels, the angel appears in association with a front-face deity, but the appearance of the angel alone as the major theme on lay elite pottery such as this example from Jargampata is limited to Middle Horizon 2A and 2B. Menzel (1968a: 81-82) has discussed conservative 2A and progressive 2B features of this angel for the Atarco style of the South Coast. Progressive features found on the Jargampata example include the form of the rear of the mouth, the short and thick proportions of the body, and the squared feet. However, a conservative 2A specimen from the Casma

valley has a mouth like that of the Jargampata angel (Menzel 1968a: fig. 42). The nose of the Jargampata specimen is like that of a profile feline head in Atarco style, also dated Middle Horizon 2A or early 2B (Menzel 1968a: fig. 45). More conservative features include the red-outlined and divided eye and the expanded base of the feather tuft on the staff. The absence of a skeletal structure within the limbs may be a progressive feature or may be simply stylistic. The Jargampata angel has both progressive and conservative features, but seems best dated as Middle Horizon 2A. It must be remembered that the Central Highlands Viñaque style was exercising considerable influence on the South Coast Atarco style and that contemporary pieces from the Ayacucho area are likely to appear slightly more progressive.

The stylistically earliest ceramic sample from within the North Unit comes from the northwest part and was isolated in stratum E of rooms S10 and S11 (fig. 44). The time unit represented by this style was named the Middle Patibamba Phase. The sample includes two exotic or imported sherds (plate 17B, E; fig. 39G, L). Neither of these can be stylistically dated, but a fragment of a flask with flattened side seam (fig. 17C) indicates that the Middle Patibamba Phase also belongs to Middle Horizon 2A. The flask with flat side seam has its origin in the Chakipampa B style of Middle Horizon 1B and continues on conservative specimens into Epoch 2A. The more progressive specimens of Middle Horizon 2A and those of Epoch 2B have tightly curved side seams (Menzel 1968a: 76). This would suggest that the Middle Patibamba Phase and the initial occupation of the North Unit date to Middle Horizon 2A.

A radioactive age determination made on small pieces of charcoal collected from stratum E within room S10 yielded an age of 1250±110 (GX-1932), based upon the Libby half-life of 5,570 years. The date of A.D. 700±110 is entirely consistent with the stylistic placement of the phase in Middle Horizon 2A. There are three dates from vicuña wool and feather hangings which are believed to have been inside large ceramic vessels from Ocoña on the South Coast. These vessels belong stylistically to Middle Horizon 2A (Menzel 1968a: 68-69), but the textiles provided dates of A.D. 645±120, A.D. 738±120, and A.D. 785±120, for an average of A.D. 723 (Rowe 1967: 27-28). The slightly later coastal date may reflect a stylistic lag between the highlands and coast. If this date is adjusted by adding about 40 years to its age for the more accurate C^{14} half-life of 5,730 years but subtracting nearly the same number of years for the Suess correction as published by Berger (1970: 31), it is apparent that Middle Patibamba deposits began about A.D. 700.

The second construction period in the North Unit correlates with the next stratum deposited in room S10 and S11 (fig. 44). This stratum, D1, was probably deposited immediately after the construction of the North Gallery and the South Gallery. The ceramics from stratum D1 compose the nucleus of the sample upon which the Late Patibamba I Phase is based. Other stratigraphic units which contain ceramics of the same phase are stratum 4 of E5-6 x S9-10 and strata 3 and 4 of room S7 in the South Unit.

During the Early Patibamba I Phase, interaction between Jargampata and other Wari sites was probably at its peak. The frequency of exotic or imported pottery is highest, and a number of pieces are very similar to ceramics from Wari. There are several pieces from this phase which can be dated as Viñaque or Middle Horizon 2 (plate 17D, fig. 39E; plate 17F, fig. 39I), by Menzel's seriation (Menzel 1964: 42-43). A fragmentary lyre-shaped cup, with a front-face deity head, represents a shape and a design theme which were widely dispersed in Middle Horizon 2 (Menzel 1968a: 89), but it appears to be a progressive Epoch 2B specimen. This piece from Early Patibamba I (plate 16A; fig. 39C) seems to be identical to another example from mixed strata of the House Group, which appears to have been grave furniture on the floor of room S1 (plate 16B1, B2; fig. 39D1, D2). Both pieces lack the conservative maize-ear element which is replaced by a simple feather design. The more complete piece from the House Group shows other progressive features, including simple eyes composed of a white disk and a black dot—which lack the red outline and vertical division—and a simple white mouth with a horizontal black line—which lacks the crossed canines (Menzel 1968a: 76).

I feel reasonably secure in assigning a date of Middle Horizon 2B to the Late Patibamba I Phase and to the second construction period in the North Unit. A radiocarbon age determination on fragments of charcoal from stratum D1 of room S10 produced an age of 1185±90 (GX-1933). This provides a date of A.D. 765±90 for the late Patibamba I Phase and for Middle Horizon 2B generally. Although this is fully acceptable in view of the dates for Middle Horizon 2A, it does give the impression that Epoch 2A was very short indeed. Examination of the Suess correlation chart published by Berger (1970: 31) shows that this date would be best interpreted as about A.D. 800, providing for the possibility that Epoch 2A may have had a greater duration than the uncorrected dates would indicate.

Following the Late Patibamba I Phase, the North Unit and the South Unit were abandoned. However, several areas within the site, including floors upon which rubble fell and strata indicating progressive deterioration of the constructions, contained a ceramic sample which was distinguished as Late Patibamba II. These ceramics are stylistically nearly identical to those of Late Patibamba I and must belong to late Middle Horizon 2B. However, it is noteworthy that the frequency of exotic or imported ceramics dropped radically between Late Patibamba I and Late Patibamba II. These data confirm Menzel's conclusion that Wari fell at the end of Middle Horizon 2B (Menzel 1964: 72) and indicate that

the breakup of the redistribution network which included pottery and the abandonment of Jargampata—a site dedicated to agricultural production—took place simultaneously.

No radiocarbon dates were obtained on materials from the Late Patibamba II Phase since the only stratum which contained sufficient carbon showed possible evidence of contamination by tree roots. However, the date is probably only slightly later than that of the Late Patibamba I Phase.

A reoccupation at Jargampata is indicated in room S10 and S11 in the North Unit. A wall was built to separate S10 from room S11 (fig. 6), and a floor was laid at the same level as the foundation of the new wall (fig. 44). The floor and pottery lying directly upon the floor were included in stratum C1, while the refuse deposited in the few centimeters above the floor was excavated as stratum C. However, because no stylistic difference could be detected between these two samples and because both samples contained fragments of the same vessels, both samples from room S10 and those from room S11 were handled together as the Illaura Phase.

There is no doubt that the Illaura ceramics represent the same Patibamba tradition present at Jargampata during the earlier phases. It was my original impression that the Illaura people were survivors of the Jargampata abandonment who remained or who returned to live and farm among the ruins. On the basis of the striking similarities between Late Patibamba I or II and Illaura, I supposed that the Illaura pottery must belong to Middle Horizon 3 or possibly 4. However, a radiocarbon age determination on charcoal flakes collected throughout strata C and C1 of room S10 provided a Late Intermediate Period date of 730±120 (GX-1934). This date of A.D. 1220±120 may be the result of contamination by roots, resulting in a figure too recent, or it may correctly indicate that the Jargampata site lay in ruins three to five centuries before reoccupation. Until confirmation is obtained from elsewhere at Jargampata or other sites, it is impossible to establish the date of the Illaura reoccupation. Provisionally, I accept the late date of thirteenth century, although the limited stylistic change between Late Patibamba and Illaura ceramics indicates four centuries of extreme stylistic conservatism.

It is worth noting that the interpretation that the Illaura

Phase was late is consistent with the proposition by Menzel (1964: 72) that after the Middle Horizon 2B collapse of Wari there were extreme economic depression and depopulation in the region around the capital. The Illaura ceramics should also demonstrate the error in the idea that the Wari disintegration was produced by foreign population intrusion. If the Illaura Phase is interpreted as late Middle Horizon, we must visualize a small group of stragglers gradually abandoning the progressively deteriorating structures. If the Illaura ceramics are 400 years later, we must reconstruct a relocation and contraction of local populations—and probably an abandonment of the valley bottoms—for several centuries. In this reconstruction, it would seem that about A.D. 1200 populations began to expand after a long period of isolation and conservatism. This interpretation is intersting in light of a series of population movements in the Central Highlands, which must have begun about A.D. 1200 and terminated with the Inca triumph over the Chancas in the fifteenth century.

In summary, Jargampata was probably sparsely occupied in the Early Intermediate Period by peoples who produced pottery similar to Huarpa ceramics of Ayacucho. The Middle Horizon began about A.D. 550, and Epoch 1A lasted until A.D. 600. By Epoch 1B, there may have been Wari influence at Jargampata, but the ceramic sample is very small. Epoch 1B drew to a close about A.D. 675 and was followed by Epoch 2A, during which the North Unit was constructed and there were walls and rooms in the South Unit. Epoch 2B can be considered to have begun about A.D. 750 and to have lasted until A.D. 825. During this period, the South Unit reached its final form and the North Unit was modified. However, at the end of Epoch 2B, Jargampata was totally abandoned for four centuries. The site deteriorated, and the entire San Miguel valley may have been virtually empty until reoccupied by peoples who manufactured closely related ceramics. These people cleared the site and built small rooms in the ruins and probably left a burial with deformed skull in extended position in the upper strata of Corridor CX of the House Group. However, this reoccupation in the Late Intermediate Period shows no indication of interaction with the Ayacucho valley or of a dense population in the valley.

6
The Great Enclosure in Wari City Planning

The sequence of construction indicated in the North Unit contrasts with that of the South Unit. The South Unit lacks a clearly defined plan and grew by progressive addition of rooms, while the North Unit was laid out as a square enclosure in one period. Later, in a second unified effort, the North Unit was altered and added to. These differences reflect not only the distinct functions fulfilled by the two units, but also the contrastive forms of labor used for their construction.

The South Unit was built in a series of minor additions which probably could have been carried out by single families working with reciprocal obligations of labor. However, the large enclosure walls and the Rectangular Structure of the North Unit—at least 300 cubic meters of stone masonry—were laid out and constructed in one effort and according to a formal plan. It seems likely that a large labor pool was drawn upon and that a well-defined administrative and authority structure are represented by the building.

The general configurations of the South Unit, and particularly the House Group, are consistent with a multifamily residential structure, while the North Unit gives the impression of public architecture. Unfortunately, the research on archaeological remains from the Middle Horizon is limited, and there is little comparative information. No excavations have been conducted in residential structures, and only limited data are available for public architecture. However, the small sample of material definitely provides an insight into the development of Wari city planning and the nature of the North Unit.

Large stone enclosures do not seem to appear in the Ayacucho area until late in the Early Intermediate Period or early in the Middle Horizon. There are stone features associated with such Early Horizon sites as Quichka Pata or Chupas (Casfranca 1960: 328-33) and Wichqana (Vescelius, personal communication), but these are small and unlike the enclosures of the Middle Horizon.

Extensive stone-wall enclosures or compounds might have been constructed during the Early Intermediate Period. Lumbreras (1969: 221) states that at the site of Kumun Senga there are rectangular walled areas. He also states that Ñawin Pukyu has large fieldstone enclosures on a part of the site which should correspond to an exclusively Huarpa occupation. This contrasts with the interpretation of Menzel (1964: 7), which questions whether the Ñawin Pukyu walls belong to the Early Intermediate Period or, more likely, to Middle Horizon 1.

The problem of whether the construction of great compounds began in the Late Intermediate Period is made more acute by the absence of any indications of walls on the site of Acuchimay. This site, on a hill overlooking Ayacucho and Conchopata, appears to have been occupied exclusively at the end of the Early Intermediate Period and in Middle Horizon 1A (Menzel 1964: 6).

The site of Conchopata or Chakipampa was occupied in Middle Horizon Epoch 1A and 1B (Menzel 1964: 6-7) and includes rather extensive architectural remains. Since Acuchimay and Conchopata are within sight of one another and are separated by less than an hour's walk, it is reasonable to suggest that the earliest construction of large stone enclosures may postdate the abandonment of Acuchimay in Middle Horizon 1A. This would indicate that the stone enclosures appeared rather suddenly—perhaps intrusively—in Ayacucho about the same time that Tiahuanacoid themes appeared in the Conchopata ceramic offerings.

Studying the development of the large walled enclosure is particularly important for understanding early urban patterns in the Central Highlands of Peru. Enclosures at Conchopata are perhaps the earliest of Middle Horizon date, and Lumbreras (1969: 223) states that the constructions at Conchopata have fieldstone walls built on the natural surface. Like the walls at Jargampata, they were finished with a mud plaster. Rooms are rectangular and, as in the House Group at Jargampata, there are narrow corridors. Field survey and aerial photographs reveal a number of large walled enclosures of irregular, to rectangular, to almost square form. Several of the enclosures are trapezoidal. Benavides (1965: Plan de Excavaciones) provides a diagram of walls found in excavations at Conchopata which shows acute and obtuse angles as well as right angles in the corners of enclosures.

Wari has never been well mapped, but survey and aerial photographs indicate that in the southeastern part of the site there are large square and rectangular enclosures. However, the northern sector of Wari, including Capilla Pata, Sullu Cruz, and on to the Robles Moqo hill, has primarily irregular trapezoidal or long, narrow rectangular enclosures. Square forms are very rare. Menzel (1964: 7) has pointed out that Early Intermediate Huarpa pottery and Middle Horizon 1 sherds are more densely distributed

in the northern part of Wari than elsewhere. This leads me to conclude that the elongated and trapezoidal enclosures, which usually lack a consistent orientation, found in Conchopata and the northern sector of Wari represent an early form of architecture associated with the first urbanism in Ayacucho.

The early Wari enclosures are often huge but were laid out in relation to natural topographic features and lack an overall plan. During Middle Horizon 1, it seems that Wari was growing by gradually filling in the space around great enclosure units and natural features including Capilla Pata, Sullu Cruz, Ushpajoto, and perhaps the Robles Moqo hill. Conchopata is not as well preserved, but as in the early section of Wari the enclosures are situated in a linear arrangement along the edge of a very deep and narrow valley, the Quebrada de Totora in the case of Conchopata and the Quebrada de Pacaicasa in the case of Wari.

It is possible that in Middle Horizon 1 there may have been more than a single group on the plateau of Wari. Along the southern edge of the site, Tello found large concentrations of Ocros pottery, which Menzel (1964: 7, 17-18) considers to represent a distinct local ceramic development from the Early Intermediate Huarpa base. Ocros pottery has particularly strong influences from the Nazca 9 style and developed through Middle Horizon 1. It seems that there is no large-scale architecture associated with the early Ocros refuse at Wari, and similar ceramics are found on Acuchimay, which also lacks stone enclosures. Conchopata, which has stone enclosures, has the same ceramic styles as Acuchimay, except for the Tiahuanacoid-influenced Conchopata style. These associations strengthen the interpretation that the urban architectural style of the Ayacucho valley was introduced at Conchopata along with the ceramic influences and that perhaps the occupants of this site were already, or were progressively becoming, socially differentiated from other local peoples.

There are no finds of Conchopata pottery among the early structures at Wari (Menzel 1964: 7), which calls into question the association of this ceramic style with walled enclosures. Until Wari is studied in detail, the absence of Conchopata-style ceramics may be interpreted as an indication that the transfer of compound builders to Wari dates just after the transition from the Conchopata style to the Robles Moqo style of offering pottery. Conversely, it may be that the lack of Conchopata pottery is due to sampling error, or perhaps the architectural tradition at Wari is a local development which was contemporary and competitive with that at the Conchopata site. Whether the great walled enclosures of Middle Horizon Ayacucho were introduced or developed from a local antecedent can only be settled by future research. However, there is no doubt that the architectural pattern underwent rapid transformation in the hands of Wari city planners.

By Middle Horizon 1B, there were highlanders from the Ayacucho area on the coast, as demonstrated by the Pacheco offering deposit in the Nazca valley. At the same time, the Central Coast was also under highland influence, and the new ceramic style which Menzel (1964: 31-33) calls Nieveria made its appearance. This new style has many pure Ayacucho loans and is found in the ruins and cemeteries of Cajamarquilla, often mixed with locally derived Lima-style ceramics (Menzel 1964: 31; Sestieri 1964).

Excavations at Cajamarquilla have not been extensive and are reported in summary form only. However, in some sections of the site three or four successive occupation periods are in evidence (Sestieri 1964), and the earlier layers appear to be associated with Early Intermediate Period pottery of the Lima style. Later excavations by the Italian archaeological mission on the Huaca Tello suggest that Nieveria pottery is found in tombs from the final occupation periods. It appears that Cajamarquilla was first occupied in the Early Intermediate Period but was rather extensively rebuilt early in the Middle Horizon, probably in Epoch 1B. There is no evidence that residence continued into Epoch 2, and the well-preserved surface remains may provide the best example of Wari city planning of Epoch 1B anywhere in the Andes.

Cajamarquilla has not been mapped, but Kosok (1965: 36-37) has published an excellent aerial photograph which shows the general configuration of the site. Examination of this photograph leads me to conclude that the Epoch 1B city was probably laid out as a series of great rectangular and trapezoidal enclosures, all of which maintain a generally similar orientation. At the upper right of Kosok's photograph, which is the northeastern extreme of the site, is the largest single enclosure, which may be one of the first in the Middle Horizon city. It is trapezoidal, with some internal partitions which isolate large rectangular enclosures and huge courtyards. With the exception of some large pyramid complexes also surrounded by enclosures, most of the remainder of the site is composed of little rooms within smaller enclosure compounds and rooms which seem to have filled the spaces between the compounds.

Cajamarquilla of Middle Horizon 1B must be considered only a partially planned city. It maintains a fairly consistent orientation of structural units and, unlike Wari, gives the impression of an overall plan. However, the aerial photograph reveals that many separate enclosures of square, rectangular, or trapezoidal form must have constituted the original layout. Later buildings appear to belong to the original plan only because of the observance of general directions of orientation. The lower center of Kosok's photograph, or south section of the site, is densely built up but lacks well-defined enclosures. This area probably represents a progressively built residential area not provided for by the original architects.

Following the occupation of the coast and the construction of Cajamarquilla, the Wari Empire may have suffered

something of a crisis, perhaps sparked by religious and political separatism on the Central Coast itself (Menzel 1964: 69; 1968a: 94). However, it appears to have become important for the Wari administrators to consolidate their strength in their own heartland, for Middle Horizon 2A is the time when Jargampata and other Central Highland sites were built.

The architectural data from Jargampata suggest it was laid out in much the same fashion as Cajamarquilla. The North Unit was planned and built as a large, self-contained square enclosure. It may have been one among a number of similar enclosures upon the site. The South Unit may also have been laid out as an enclosure compound in its original form, since there is some indication of early exterior perimeter walls. However, the entire area was slowly modified by the progressive addition of rooms. In the House Group, rooms were grouped into complexes, which were surrounded by walls forming irregular enclosures accommodated to the available space.

Pikillaqta, in the Lucre basin near Cuzco, was apparently begun in very late Middle Horison 1B or in Epoch 2A (Menzel 1968a: 93), so it is contemporary with Jargampata. This huge site, almost a kilometer square, has an overall plan considerably more developed than earlier Wari sites. Emilio Harth-Terre (1959) has published a small-scale map, but it does not help one determine whether the site represents a single, preplanned unit or several additions following the same basic plan. There are sections along the northeastern and northwestern parts of the great unit which depart from an otherwise rectangular, nearly square, perimeter. However, Harth-Terre's map shows that the finished format of Pikillaqta was a huge, irregular rectangular enclosure surrounded by high walls. The interior is divided into rectangular or square compounds and courtyards with a great rectangular terraced plaza in the southern corner. If the site did experience any gradual growth, the additions followed a rigid master plan.

In one very significant way, Pikillaqta differs from Conchopata, Wari, Cajamarquilla, and Jargampata. There is virtually no occupation refuse anywhere on the site. John Rowe has located an extensive Middle Horizon 2A occupation elsewhere in the Lucre basin, which probably represents the habitation associated with Pikillaqta (Menzel 1968a: 93). This contrasts with the other Middle Horizon sites, some of which probably became true cities which grew spontaneously around a series of planned rectangular enclosures.

Pikillaqta may represent a separation of the functions carried out within the same center in earlier Wari sites. The planned great enclosure complex, with its associated activities, is separated from the residential center and its associated activities. This may be responsible for an illusion of much greater organization at Pikillaqta than at Cajamarquilla. Another feature which differentiates Pikillaqta from Cajamarquilla and Wari is the virtual absence of trapezoidal enclosures at Pikillaqta and the development of a rigid grid pattern which produces only rectangular or square compounds. This is probably a feature of the regularization of city planning in the Middle Horizon.

Viracochapampa, in the North Highlands near Huamachuco, is the last great Wari construction about which we have published information. It is probably a Wari administrative center constructed after the overthrow of the fortified Huamachuco towns in Middle Horizon 2B (Menzel 1964: 70; Lanning 1967: 138-39). McCown (1945: 267) believed that the site was built by the Incas, but recognized that it was the product of a formal master plan. It is almost a square, with 580 meters and 565 meters respectively to the east-west and north-south sides of the perimeter, which is formed by a great wall with nearly perfect right-angle corners. The map of the site (McCown 1945: fig. 13) shows that almost without exception the corners of the internal constructions are right angles as well. The giant enclosure is divided into a series of smaller square or rectangular enclosures.

There is a problem about the nature of the refuse at Viracochapampa and whether it indicates a normal residential occupation. This will be dealt with in more detail below, but the infrequency of sherd material encountered by McCown (1945: 321-26), both on the surface and in excavations, makes it unlikely that the site served as a residential zone. Viracochapampa gives the impression of being the most rigorously planned Wari "city." It shares with Pikillaqta the exclusive use of square and retangular compounds and, apparently, the separation of the residential zone from the planned great enclosures. There are also changes in the internal organization of rectangular enclosures which follow, and therefore tend to confirm, the trends in site planning outlined above. Unfortunately, there is little information concerning the enclosures of Middle Horizon 1. Excavations at Conchopata and in the northern section of Wari have not been oriented to the definition of architectural features.

There is evidence from the Nazca valley that the Middle Horizon Epoch 1B offering at Pacheco was associated with a circular ceremonial structure, which is probably functionally contrastive with rectangular and trapezoidal enclosures. Similar circular units are found with Early Intermediate 7 and 8 pottery in the Nazca valley at Huaca del Loro and Huaca Tres Palos II (Paulsen 1965: 52-54) and are probably present at Conchopata, Wari, Pikillaqta, and other Central Highlands sites.

Rectangular units are not mentioned with the Pacheco offerings, but they are depicted upon the large urns which were ceremonially smashed at the site. One set of oversized urns has illustrations of deities, while a second and third series have plant representations on the upper half of the vessel exteriors (Ravines 1968: lam. 84; fig. 7A). The

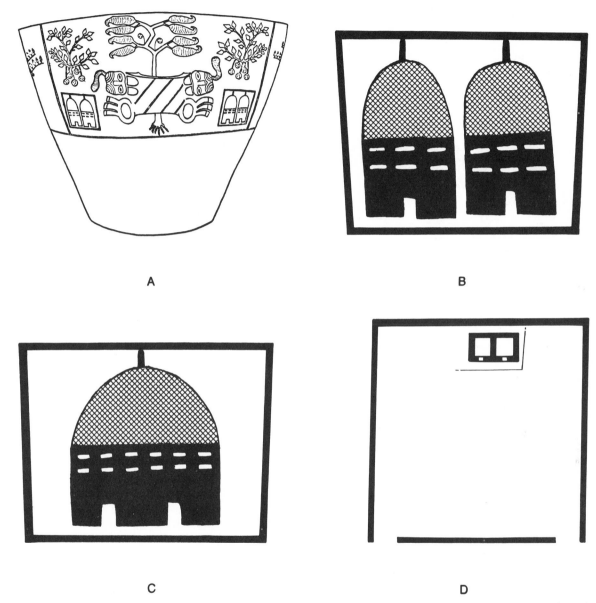

A

B

C

D

Figure 7. Rectangular Enclosures in the Middle Horizon

A Middle Horizon Epoch 1B oversize Robles Moqo urn from Pacheco, Nazca. This urn has painted representations of potato, ullucu, anu, and *tarwi*. On either side of the horizontal handles, which are modeled and painted to represent intertwined felinoid snakes, is a painted rectangle which encloses two buildings. (After Ravines 1968: lam. 85).

B Sketch of rectangular enclosure containing two buildings, from oversize Robles Moqo urn. (Based on sketches and notes made in the Museo Nacional and information provided by Rogger Ravines.)

C Sketch of alternative rectangular enclosure containing a single building with two entrances. (Based on sketches and notes made in the Museo Nacional.)

D Jargampata North Unit rectangular enclosure containing a single building with two entrances in Middle Horizon Epoch 2A.

Robles Moqo urns (Menzel 1964: 21-28), also with plant representations, depict rectangular or slightly trapezoidal enclosures which probably represent architectural units as seen from above. Furthermore, each enclosure includes two tall towers or buildings which are viewed in elevation (fig. 7B).

The buildings within the enclosures have small entrances or doors at their bases. Near their tops are two rows of three rectangles, which probably represent windows within these seemingly multistoried constructions. Each building has a steeply pitched conical or dome-shaped roof supported by a center pole. The steep roofs indicate that the buildings depicted are of highland origin since the roofs are designed to shed water and contrast with the flat or only slightly pitched roofs of most coastal buildings.

One of the Pacheco urns with phytomorphic representations on display in the Museo Nacional de Antropología y Arqueología in Lima depicts a rectangular enclosure with one rather than two buildings inside. The pot has been partially reconstructed and the drawing includes sherds from other vessels. Two roof peaks and center poles are shown, but the base of the building shows a single broad construction with two entrances. I would reconstruct this representation, like the others, with two rows of windows and a single steeply pitched roof (fig. 7C). It seems likely that because the structure required two doors it was divided into two rooms on the interior. In Middle Horizon 1B, then, artists painted rectangular or trapezoidal enclosures which contained pairs of multistoried buildings. Rarely, the artists depicted a single multistoried building with two doors which may have contained two interior rooms.

In Middle Horizon 2A, the North Unit was laid out and built at Jargampata. It was laid out as a nearly square enclosure, which probably had two openings to the east. Inside the enclosure stood a single building with an internal partition and two entrances opening onto the courtyard. It is likely that the building was tall and multistoried (fig. 7D). The North Unit, then, is similar to the units painted on the oversized offering urns from Pacheco.

In Middle Horizon 2B, the North Unit at Jargampata was altered by the addition of two long, narrow galleries on the north and south sides of the enclosure. Furthermore, the Rectangular Structure with double entrance was attached to one of the galleries by a new room (fig. 8A).

Viracochapampa was also constructed in Middle Horizon 2B as a giant square which included a series of interior enclosures. At least eight of the smaller enclosures are variations on the theme of long, narrow galleries which surround a courtyard on three sides, while on the fourth side there is a broader room which is often joined at one end to the enclosure wall (McCown 1945: 269, fig. 13; fig. 8B).

Epoch 1B Cajamarquilla has a great enclosure in the northeast which includes smaller enclosures not filled with rooms (Kosok 1965: 36-37). These may be the architectural equivalents of the contemporary depictions on the Pacheco urns. Unfortunately, there is almost no detailed information on the earlier constuctions at Conchopata and Wari. However, a sequence is indicated by the information available. In Middle Horizon 1, there were large trapezoidal and rectangular enclosures constructed in the Ayacucho area. By Epoch 1B, some rectangular enclosures had two tall multistoried buildings in them. Epoch 2A saw a rigidification of square and rectangular enclosure forms, and the pair of buildings was replaced by a single multistoried building with two interior rooms. During Epoch 2B, the free-standing building within the enclosure seems to have been replaced by a room attached to the exterior wall and, more significantly, by long, narrow galleries.

A number of architectural units can be identified as Wari constructions or as heavily influenced by the Wari patterns by comparison with the description above. For example, the distinctive architectural characteristics of Epoch 2B can be identified in the Virú valley at site V-297 (Willey 1953: 257-58; fig. 8C) and to a lesser degree at V-123 (Willey 1953: 261-62; fig. 8D) in the same valley. Tello (1956: fig. 2) provides a map of ruins in the Casma valley which leads me to believe that some of the structures on the Pampa de las Llamas are Middle Horizon enclosures. Rowe (1963: 14) has made this same observation, and although the ceramic associations do not support the date (Collier, personal communication), there are four rectangular units at the foot of Cerro San Francisco which appear to include long, narrow galleries and larger rooms at one end of the enclosure.

It is worth pointing out that the large double-walled rectangular enclosures typical of Chan Chan may also be the end product of the development of the Wari enclosure on the North Coast. These enclosures share a number of features with Pikillaqta and Viracochapampa and could have evolved from such planned units after the collapse of Wari control.

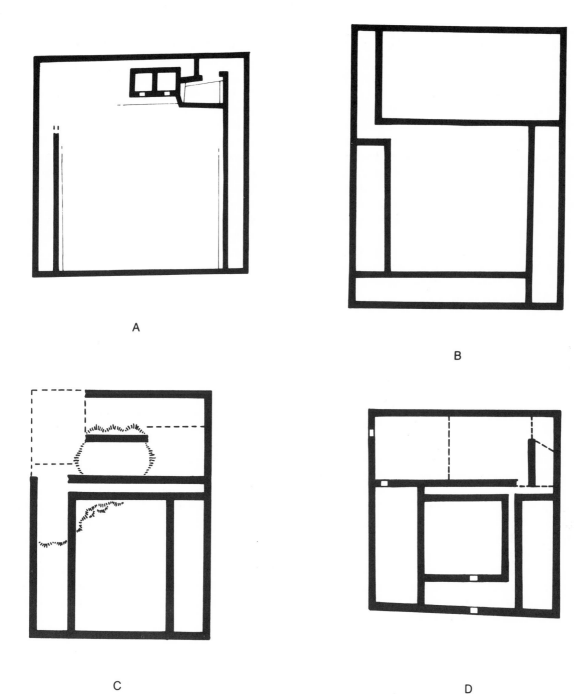

A

B

C

D

Figure 8. Variants of Middle Horizon 2B Rectangular Enclosures

A   Jargampata North Unit rectangular enclosure containing long, narrow galleries and a building joined to one gallery, as modified in Middle Horizon Epoch 2B.

B   Viracochapampa rectangular enclosure with long, narrow galleries and a large room joined to the enclosure wall, as constructed in Middle Horizon Epoch 2B. (After McCown 1945: fig. 13, construction form b.)

C   Rectangular enclosure with rooms and galleries resembling those of Middle Horizon Epoch 2B, from the Virú valley. (After Willey 1953: fig. 57, V-297.)

D   Rectangular enclosure with rooms and galleries reminiscent of those of Middle Horizon Epoch 2B, from the Virú valley. (After Willey 1953: fig. 59, V-123.)

7
Architecture and Economic Organization

I have suggested that Wari was an administrative center which coordinated the production and redistribution of goods from a number of contrasting environments. Wari controlled a large area, in which, it is likely, distinct ethnic groups were obliged to produce for the empire within their own ecological zones.

To test this hypothesis, we have examined a rural site in the San Miguel valley as a probable center of specialized production on an irrigated valley bottom. It is now possible to date the constructions at the site of Jargampata and to evaluate them with a chronological perspective on the development of great enclosures and their role in city planning during the Wari Empire. The North Unit at Jargampata is hardly an isolated phenomenon. It represents a variation on a long tradition of rectangular enclosures, one of the main components of Wari centers. The level of planning represented in these units demonstrates that they were of primary concern to the state administration.

If the proposal concerning the nature of Wari organization is correct, there should be evidence that produce from Jargampata was shipped to Wari and that the local peoples were under the control of the political center. Jargampata must have been one of a set of specialized production centers.

Inca storage and redistribution have become the subject of archaeological and ethnohistorical investigation, and the information available is slowly providing a picture of this essential feature of empire organization (Cieza de Leon n.d.: 419-20; Morris and Thompson 1970: 352-58). However, little research has been directed specifically toward the study of similar Wari institutions, and investigation of them must depend entirely upon the archaeological record.

It is generally recognized that if the Wari polity was a conquest-oriented empire, government storage facilities to provide for bureaucrats and troops must have existed. John Rowe (1963: 14-15) has argued that a number of large Wari constructions, including Capilla Pata at Wari, Pikillaqta, Viracochapampa, and Pampa de las Llamas, were government installations never intended to house people. Rather, they were storage facilities. The North Unit at Jargampata belongs to the same class of enclosures as those Rowe listed and will be considered along with others for which there are data.

If these centers were storage and redistribution units, it should be possible to demonstrate that they were not regular habitation sites where the activities of daily life were carried out. Second, these centers must have been constructed in strategic places. Finally, there must be independent lines of evidence which support the interpretation that the great enclosures were associated with agricultural produce or manufactured goods rather than some other activities.

At Jargampata, there is an obvious difference between the South Unit and the North Unit. In the South Unit House Group there are remains of hearths and culinary activities, including remains of plants and animals. Excavations in the North Unit failed to reveal a single hearth, and, with the exception of a dense concentration of animal bones against the west wall, almost nothing was found which would indicate the preparation, consumption, or disposal of food. The differences in design and construction sequence also identify the South Unit as a semiplanned housing facility distinct from the North Unit, which served another purpose.

McCown (1945: 269) proposed that at least part of Viracochapampa, specifically the narrow galleries, was intended for regular occupation. However, it is significant that in McCown's excavations only a single hearth was found (McCown 1945: 322). Even in the case of this one hearth, there is reason to question the stratigraphic association. All of the cuts at Viracochapampa revealed a very thin occupation stratum, with the exception of excavations 9 through 12 which probably include materials from a later reoccupation. Only excavations 1, 2, and 6 were within a large rectangular enclosure similar to the North Unit at Jargampata. Excavations 1 and 2 were in the same narrow gallery. Cut 1, near a corner where refuse might accumulate, produced only 389 sherds from an area 4.5 x 1.6 meters and 1 meter deep. Cut 2 produced only 20 sherds from an area 3 x 1.5 meters and 1 meter deep. Excavation 2 yielded a sterile red clay, which was probably a floor, with a thin refuse deposit of 5 cm. lying upon it. The stratigraphic condition of excavation 1 is less clear, but the deposit was deeper. However, the single hearth was located at a greater absolute depth than the living surface in cut 2, which raises some doubt about the validity of the association of all the materials from excavation 2.

Excavation 6, in a corner of the plaza of the same enclosure, was a test 2 x 1.8 meters and 1 meter deep. It produced only eleven plain sherds (McCown 1945: 322-26,

table 1). In summary, there was not only very sparse evidence of occupation on the surface at Viracochapampa, but excavations tend to confirm the conviction that little of the site was intended to house people or carry on the activities associated with daily life.

Pikillaqta has not been systematically discussed in the literature, but it is common knowledge that the frequency of pottery and other refuse is so slight that for years it has been very difficult to establish even a stylistic date for the site.

These data tend to confirm the belief that the great planned rectangular enclosures which have been studied were not regular habitations. What data are there for these units having been associated with storage or redistribution?

The study of Pikillaqta by Harth-Terre (1959) indicates that within the great rectangular perimeter there is a total of 137 large enclosures which may have narrow galleries within them. There is a highway which leads into the walled area and opens into a huge plaza which rises in a series of terraces to a small platform overlooking the area. From the plaza, access is provided to the inner enclosures (Rowe 1944: plate VII, 4). Although this great plaza may have served ceremonial purposes, it also might have served as a center for shipping and receiving materials—perhaps for the arrival and departure of caravans of llamas. More indicative of a storage facility is the presence of 618 to 620 small rectangular rooms which measure 3.75 to 4 meters by 7.7 to 8 meters. Harth-Terre (1959: 52-53) notes that the preserved height of these rooms ranges between 1.7 and 2 meters; from this he estimates the potential storage volume at 32,000 cubic meters.

It is useless to speculate about the position of Pikillaqta within a redistribution system until we know more about the Middle Horizon occupation of the Cuzco area. However, it seems likely that the construction of this most ambitious Wari architectural undertaking may be related to the frontier to the south of Cuzco, which separated the Wari and Tiahuanaco spheres of influence. It seems likely that any trade between the two polities would have been channeled between the Altiplano and Cuzco. In addition, any military movements would probably have followed the same route, so the location of a large storage and redistribution center on this crucial artery of communication undoubtedly fulfilled several functions.

Viracochapampa is also located in an important position near the northern frontier of the Wari political sphere. Wari control probably extended at least to the Chicama valley on the coast and to the Huamachuco and Cajamarca areas in the highlands (Menzel 1964: 70-72; Ravines 1968: 32-33; Donnan 1968: 15-18; Donnan 1972). Viracochapampa lies on a main artery of communication from Cajamarca to the south and may have been important in controlling the distribution of northern products—perhaps including ceramics—to the south. The ancient trade in *Spondylus* shell from Ecuador to the Peruvian Andes attests to the long importance of a north-south flow of goods (Paulsen 1974). Furthermore, Viracochapampa lies close to the continental divide and could have managed redistribution between the radically different highland and coastal environments.

Jargampata is located in the San Miguel valley near 400 to 500 hectares of easily irrigated land. As indicated above, the valley could have produced a substantial surplus in prehistoric times. Jargampata is only one day on foot from Wari and is in a particularly good position to act as a center of food production for specialists resident at Wari.

The strategic location of all these centers within a possible redistributional network favors the interpretation that the great enclosures were planned and constructed by a central political authority which controlled economic exchange and the storage of products. The strongest support of this hypothesis, however, does not come from site location, but from Middle Horizon iconography on offering ceramics.

It appears that ceremonial destruction of oversized urns was part of a widespread, centralized religion, probably organized at the state level. This is indicated by the discovery of highly standardized offerings at such widely separated places as Conchopata (Menzel 1964: 6), Pacheco (Menzel 1964: 23-26), and Ayapata (Ravines 1968), as well as of other such deposits found by nonarchaeologists and never properly recorded. The Pacheco offering was probably made by some of the first Wari colonists on the South Coast, and the iconography seems to emphasize features introduced to the coast, including highland deities, large modeled llamas, and vessels with highland plants (Menzel 1964: 26-27; Yacovleff and Herrera 1934-35: 258, fig. 4r, 306, fig. 27, 308, fig. 28). The plant representations include maize, potato, oca, ullucu, anu, *tarwi*, and perhaps quinoa. This group of plants is virtually identical to the prehistoric cultigens listed by Central Highland villagers of Huánuco as the major crops produced for the state on local Inca lands. Their lists run in formal order and include maize, potato, oca, ullucu, *mashua* (anu), quinoa, *taures* (*tarwi*), and beans (Bird 1967: 365-67; Murra 1967: 399-406).

One group of oversized vessels from Pacheco which is on display in the Museo Nacional de Antropología y Arqueología in Lima has maize represented in association with deities which Menzel (1964: 26) calls the Male Deity and the Female Deity. No other plants are depicted on these vessels. This is interesting because of the ceremonial importance which maize had in the Andes in Inca times (Murra 1960) and also because maize is the only crop depicted on the offering vessels which was almost equally important on the coast and in the highlands.

A second group of oversized vessels has representations of a deity face on one side. Below the face is a polychrome checkerboard pattern with pairs of dots in the squares. Above the face are drawings of plants, including maize,

tarwi, oca, and quinoa (Menzel 1964: 27). The checker-board with dots is strikingly reminiscent of a similar checkerboard of four-by-five squares with columns of five, three, two, and single dots which was drawn by an Indian, Felipe Guaman Poma de Ayala (1936: 360), about the year 1600. Poma's checkerboard must have been some sort of counting device and is included in a drawing of a non-Inca who is holding a string quipu. According to Poma, he is the major accountant or treasurer for the Inca Empire. The Inca accountants must have tallied produce—including maize, potatoes, oca, ullucu, anu, *tarwi*, and probably quinoa—produced on state lands for redistribution by the state. The oversized tumblers with checkerboards and plant depictions may represent an accounting system by which crops were tallied for redistribution by an accountant of the Wari state.

The third group of oversized urns from Pacheco has only plant representations—potatoes, ullucu, anu, and *tarwi* —associated with rectangular enclosures with two buildings inside (fig. 7A). These steep-roofed buildings are reminiscent of buildings drawn by Poma de Ayala (1936: 335) in an illustration which shows an Inca standing among the structures speaking with a non-Inca who holds a quipu and wears a head ornament like that of the major accountant. Poma explains that the drawing depicts the storehouses of the Inca.

It seems very likely, then, that the rectangular enclosures consistently associated with plant representations on the Pacheco urns are depictions of storage and redistribution centers managed by Wari administrators. It has already been pointed out that the enclosures from Pacheco are like the North Unit at Jargampata, which compare, with modifications, with enclosure units at Viracochapampa and perhaps Pikillaqta. Finally, by extension, the same functions were probably fulfilled by some of the earlier trapezoidal units at Conchopata and Cajamarquilla and perhaps the Capilla Pata sector of Wari.

The strategic location of the great planned enclosure units built by the Wari people and the iconographic associations of these enclosures on the offering vessels from Pacheco indicate that they functioned within a complex system of redistribution of goods which was managed by a centralized political authority composed of administrative specialists.

Although the origin of the specialized trapezoidal or rectangular enclosure remains obscure, it is likely that it appeared along with true state administration. The present information suggests that this occurred late in Middle Horizon 1A or early 1B at Conchopata at the same time as a South Highland Tiahuanacoid impact. Wari may have been a contemporary competitive center, but it became the single political center when Conchopata was eclipsed and abandoned by the end of Epoch 1B.

Although there is evidence for interaction between the Ayacucho area and the South Coast late in the Early Horizon, and the ceramic parallels show an intensification of the relationship at the end of the Early Intermediate Period, it is only after the appearance of the rectangular structures that we have evidence for highland colonies on the coast. There is also some indication of ethnic diversity —or at least ceramic diversity—in the Ayacucho valley, and perhaps much more if we include the San Miguel and Pampas valleys, which may have been under Wari control by the end of Middle Horizon 1A.

Large, nucleated sites were present in Ayacucho prior to the appearance of the rectangular redistribution units, but with the appearance of these units and centralized author-ity it seems that not only the various ethnic groups of Ayacucho but also the peoples of the coast were brought into a single, integrated economic group. In Middle Horizon 2, the peoples of Wari succeeded in integrating most of the peoples of the Central Andes within a single political and economic system. Planned enclosure complexes were con-structed in the North Highlands and South Highlands, and it is likely that populations were moved about within the empire. Not only were Wari colonies established elsewhere, but foreigners, such as people from Cajamarca, were moved to the heart of the empire.

Wari organization undoubtedly had a great impact on Andean society. For perhaps the first time, many pre-viously autonomous groups lost their independence and became integrated into a political and economic structure over which they had little or no control. It is likely that in the Middle Horizon a peasantry emerged in the Andes for the first time.

Peasants cannot be identified by any specific culture content, but must be recognized in terms of structural criteria (Wolf 1955: 452-55) within economic, political, and intellectual dimensions (Fallers 1967: 37-39). Within the economic dimension, peasants exist in an asymmetric relationship with a larger society composed of specialists. The peasant produces for his own subsistence, but his surplus is systematically extracted from him to support non-food producers. The mechanisms of extraction vary from renting land and sharecropping to a market exchange system, but their common element is that the peasant lacks control over the system.

Politically, the peasant community is at best semi-autonomous. Community leadership is truncated and the state imposes control at the intervillage level (Fallers 1967: 38). The peasant community maintains its own ceremonial system, which provides strong internal integration based upon customary law, but in extracommunity relations the peasant village stands in opposition to the outside world. The hierarchical structure which links communities does not exist within the villages but is the domain of adminis-trative specialists.

In the intellectual sphere, the peasant stands in opposi-

tion to the elite tradition of administrative and craft specialists. If the peasant accepts participation in a super-village system, he also accepts the elite judgment of him as ignorant and rustic. The peasant's status and self-image are achieved within his community, and he is denied full participation in, and identification with, the elite tradition. Frequently, features of the peasant tradition are archaic and outmoded adaptations from the elite tradition (Fallers 1967: 39).

Essentially, peasants exist only within a larger system which includes a controlling elite, from which the peasant is separated but which he is obliged to support. No people can be thought of as peasants in the absence of the elite tradition, which maintains economic, political, and intellectual domination over various communities.

Jargampata is near highly productive land which could have provided food for the administrative elite. The site is located close to Wari and has what is identified as a storage or redistributional architectural unit. The residents of Jargampata were apparently producing not only for their own consumption but for the support of populations outside the site—probably for specialists of Wari. In some way, the elite specialists controlled a portion of the agricultural production of the San Miguel valley.

The fact that the North Unit at Jargampata can be compared with similar units from as far away as the South Coast and the North Highlands suggests that this is a standardized state installation. Economic exchange, and probably most interaction, between Jargampata and other residential centers was not controlled by the local people but was in the hands of elite specialists of the state. The representation of architectural units similar to the Jargampata North Unit on offering urns which were part of an elaborate and widespread religious ritual strengthens the association of such units with state political authority. The presence of the North Unit at Jargampata indicates a systematic extraction of the local surplus by the state and undoubtedly the truncation of local political autonomy, at least at the intervillage level.

In both the economic and political dimensions, the people of Jargampata appear to meet the criteria for peasants. The intellectual dimension, however, is the most difficult area of analysis when dealing with prehistoric peoples. How can we determine whether the residents of the South Unit House Group were outside the elite tradition? Were these people ignorant rustics who turned inward to their community for social identity and integration? To try to answer these questions we can look at several archaeological features of the site.

First, the fancy elite ceramics of Wari style, which became progressively secularized during the Middle Horizon, are very rare at Jargampata. This fancy pottery was probably imported and accounts for less than 1% of the vessels in the Early Patibamba Phase. By Late Patibamba I,

external interaction had reached its maximum, and the elite pottery represents 6.4% of the identifiable vessels. If the frequency were calculated on the basis of all sherds recovered from each phase, the elite pottery would never reach a frequency of even 1%. Bennett (1953: 28-35, tables 1, 2) shows that the frequency of elite pottery at Wari is much higher. He calculated frequencies on the basis of sherds, not individual vessels, and it is impossible to establish phases. However, his elite types—Wari Polychrome, Wari Polychrome Fine, Ayacucho Polychrome, and Conchopata Polychrome—occur with a frequency of 3.8% for the materials from Pit 1, 13.1% for Pit 2, 16.6% for Pit 3, 13.4% for Pit 4, 9% for Pit 5, 11.1% for Pits 6 and 7, 8% for Pit 8, 13.8% for Pit 9, 10.6% for Pit 10, 6.4% for Pit 13, and 4.5% for Pit 14. This is a mean frequency of 11% fancy elite sherds at Wari, which is very much higher than at Jargampata.

Second, the House Group included a room with skeletal remains which had probably served as a repository for ancestral mummies of the residents. Although keeping the remains of ancestors within the home does not preclude participation in state religion and ceremony, it suggests a local, family-level religion and ceremonialism typical of peasant communities.

Third, the gradually built multiunit dwellings in the South Unit suggest that the residential group was an extended family or kin group rather than individual nuclear families. In addition, the dwelling units appear to be clustered into fairly large agglomerations, which may indicate larger nucleations of kin. This sort of residence is consistent with a situation in which there is a low proportion of full-time specialized labor and a wide range of part-time specializations within the cooperative kin group. This is a common pattern for peasants (Wolf 1966: 72).

Finally, there is some indication that ceramic styles were introduced to Jargampata from more prestigious centers in Ayacucho. Some of the local ceramic features, including black bands outlined in white, white circle elements, painted decoration on unpigmented surfaces, and open bowl shapes, may be rustic features which survive into Middle Horizon 2B at Jargampata but were typical of the Epoch 1 Chakipampa A and B style of Ayacucho (Menzel 1964: 12-16).

These features support the belief that within the intellectual dimension, as well as the economic and political dimensions, the residents of Jargampata were oriented to their community while being controlled by a distinct elite which did not participate in local community life. They meet the criteria generally expected of peasants.

I suspect that the presence of state collection and redistribution sites such as Jargampata indicates that the Wari centers were occupied largely by nonagricultural specialists who depended upon surplus production from a

rural peasantry for their livelihood. The presence of the state and its collection installations at the local level where primary production was carried out suggests a strong supervisory role by the state, and it may indicate that land was held under some form of prebendal domain (Wolf 1966: 51-52). Such tenure systems are generally associated with highly centralized bureaucratic states in which the ruler and his officials are ritual figures drawing sanctions from the supernatural realm through claimed descent from, or appointed stewardship of, a divine being. Land frequently belongs to the state and is not inherited; rather, privileges of land use are granted by the central authority and peasants become servants of the state. These generalizations, which Eric Wolf (1966: 51-52) has made for the prebendal state, apply to the Inca Empire and fit the data available for the Wari state as well.

It is likely that Jargampata was occupied by peasant agriculturalists under the supervision of state officials. They produced both for their own consumption and for state specialists, perhaps on state-owned lands. That protection was provided—perhaps by the state—is indicated by a small redoubt on the ridge section of the site. However, the little fort is in a better location to protect the mouth of the main irrigation canal than to defend the residences of the people. It could be that it was designed to protect state resources from the local people.

Finally, there is indirect evidence that the distinctive and irregular small enclosures on the Jargampata ridge may have been residences and perhaps corrals for animal herders. These people may have been members of the community or a specialized group of transporters responsible for conveying local produce to the Wari center and shipping specialized products from manufacturing and trade centers at Wari to the state officials and peasants of Jargampata.

Jargampata undoubtedly represents only one of a great many local populations under the control of the Wari administration. These communities were not linked directly to one another but to the state administration. The presence of Ecuadorian shells or Cajamarca spoons or copper pins from an unknown source does not indicate trade relations between Jargampata and distant centers. *Spondylus* shells and copper pins have both been found at Wari, but even more indicative are bowls and other pottery of the imported Cajamarca ware. Jargampata received only small and portable spoons while larger and more valuable Cajamarca vessels were apparently destined for consumption in the administrative center. Conversely, produce and probably labor flowed into the center in return for the luxury articles.

8

Ceramics and Artifacts from Jargampata

ANALYTICAL GOALS

Field work at Jargampata was designed primarily to provide information about the process of urbanization and state formation in the Andes. The research was problem-oriented and intended to test the hypothesis that an urban state was based upon politically or militarily integrated populations exploiting specialized environments within a dominant and centralized redistributional system during the Middle Horizon. This and other hypotheses are derived from ethnographic and ethnohistoric data (Isbell 1968; Murra 1972; Zuidema and Quispe 1968). My research program was problem- rather than process-oriented because of the complexity and magnitude of the sampling required to test for variation and transformation within an urban interaction sphere without introducing the bias of the investigator or sample. However, this exercise in problem-oriented archaeology should facilitate more elaborate tests of more specific hypotheses as well as indicate the importance of the Wari phenomenon for broader process-oriented investigation.

The second goal of the research was similarly problem-oriented, but it should also have application for process studies. The problem was to provide a detailed description of rural Jargampata pottery and to establish a temporal chronology of variation which can be dated in terms of seriations of fancy, elite pottery from prestigious urban centers (Menzel 1964, 1968a). It seems premature to attempt to account for the variation found in rural and urban pottery or other artifacts of the Middle Horizon until a wide range of cultural debris representing different activities has been sampled. Jargampata was selected for investigation because of my problem orientation, and the site was very selectively sampled. Since it represents the first Middle Horizon hinterland site to be investigated and since research in larger centers has the bias of limited tests in refuse and excavation of cemeteries, it is premature to attempt to account for variation in sociocultural terms. There are significant differences in the frequencies of certain vessel shape categories within the ceramic samples from Jargampata which must reflect intrasite and extrasite social relations and economic activities. My goal is to describe these differences and to place the vessels within a Middle Horizon temporal scheme and in association with architectural features. The description will thus provide a well-documented sample of known bias for comparison with yet unexcavated materials and will help to define the range of variation and activity which characterized Wari.

This chapter and the five that follow provide a detailed description of Jargampata pottery in stylistic and temporal terms. The ceramic samples were subjected to a modal analysis and qualitative seriation (Deetz 1965; Lathrap 1962; Menzel 1964, 1968a; Menzel, Rowe, and Dawson 1964; Rouse 1939; Rowe 1961) similar to that elaborated by Dorothy Menzel for other Middle Horizon ceramics. I want these results to be comparable to hers, but my approach differs from that of Menzel, Rowe, and other University of California Andeanists. I share with Lathrap (personal communications, 1962, 1964, 1966, 1970) the conviction that vessel shapes provide the best description of a ceramic tradition because shape categories are subject to elaborate functional constraints and are less free to vary than decorative attributes. Continuity of shape categories is maintained by culturally determined patterns of preferred foods and their modes of preparation, food service, storage, status, and ritual activities, and the acquired motor patterns associated with each.

The ceramics of Jargampata have been described in terms of the range of shapes present in each of the phases defined and the combinations of shape and decorative attributes of each phase. The treatment is primarily stylistic, although the implications of some attributes which are known to be shared with other sites and the importance and dating of diagnostic specimens will be discussed within the text of each chapter.

VESSEL SAMPLE AND ANALYTICAL APPROACH

All ceramic and nonceramic artifacts from excavations at Jargampata were washed, labeled, and transported to the laboratory for analysis. However, since most excavations were designed to reveal architectural features, their deposits varied from wash or fill with very little material to clearly stratified refuse with large quantities of sherds. Eleven ceramic samples from five excavation areas were finally selected for the description and seriation. These were selected on the basis of the reliability of the stratigraphy and the quantity of materials in the sample.

Two samples come from an area of six square meters outside the south wall of the North Unit at E2-3 x S13-15 (figs. 5, 6, 43). Materials from strata 1, 2, and 3 as well as feature El-1 were excluded because of the probability of mixing. Strata 4 through 8 were combined in one sample and the second represents stratum 9.

Four samples come from different strata of rooms S10 and S11 (figs. 5, 6, 44). Strata A and B were excluded because of their recent formation, while strata C and C1 comprise a single sample and strata D, D1, and E each constitute one.

Three samples come from a four-square-meter area at E5-6 x S9-10 in the North Unit (figs. 5, 6, 45). Strata 1 and 1a were exluded because of their mixed appearance and recent formation. Strata 2, 3, and 4 each constitute a ceramic sample subjected to analysis.

A single sample of pottery comes from room S7 in the South Unit (figs. 3, 46). Strata 1 and 2 were excluded, and materials from 3 and 4 were combined into a single sample.

The last sample comes from an area of about six square meters at W14 x N1-6, immediately in front of the retaining wall east of the Rectangular Structure (figs. 5, 6, 47). Recently deposited strata 1, 2, and 3 were excluded. The sample includes pottery from lower stratum 4 and the surface of the stratum 5 floor where it was covered by rock fallen from the retaining wall.

Pottery of these eleven samples was laid out in the laboratory, and all sherds which could be assembled to form complete or partially complete vessels were glued together. Materials from excavation units adjacent to the selected samples were also insepcted for fragments of the vessels which were being reconstructed from the eleven samples. Once it became clear that no more sherds could be reassembled, the samples were separated into individual vessels or vessel fragments. Most vessels were represented by a section of the rim, but any fragment with a diagnostic feature such as a base, a handle, or decoration which was not part of another pot was counted as a vessel. The remaining plain body sherds were excluded from further analysis.

This procedure yielded a total of 895 more or less complete vessels from the eleven selected samples. Twenty-three vessels from other units were also reconstructed to help amplify data on vessel shape and design theme which remained unclear from the pottery in the selected samples. The ceramic materials from the House Group in the South Unit were similarly treated, adding 277 vessels for a total inventory of 1,195 vessels studied. Because of the mixture of the contents of the House Group, this pottery was not included as a sample for seriation. However, the restorable pots facilitated the definition of vessel shape categories, and in the future the House Group materials will provide important information for the study and explanation of variation on Middle Horizon sites.

Inspection of the total sample of vessels revealed that there were two major categories of shapes represented. One of these includes necked jars and the other is composed of open bowl forms. The separation is partially supported by paste and surface finish characteristic of Jargampata pottery. However, the presence of two modes in these dimensions is not clearly defined, and they were not used in classification.

Jargampata pots have a hard, light-colored paste which ranges from buff to light brown to dull orange, with the latter most characteristic. Sherds generally show thorough oxidation, although there are occasional examples with gray cores. The paste contains a moderate amount of angular white sand as well as occasional particles of other colors, including shiny flecks of what may be mica. The inclusions are fairly well distributed within the matrix, and breaks are irregular and do not follow old coils.

There is much variation in the pots, and open bowls and necked jars tend to differ significantly. Small quantities of small inclusions are more characteristic of open bowl forms. Furthermore, the paste is more frequently light orange and thoroughly oxidized. Necked jars often have coarser particles included in larger quantities. The bases of jars may have coarser and more numerous inclusions than upper sections of the body or neck of the same vessels. The paste of jars is more frequently brown or buff, although the light orange of open bowl forms is also common.

Surface finish also distributes continuously but shows extremes which tend to be associated with the two main vessel shape categories. All Jargampata pots have dull, matte finishes. However, open bowl forms are usually coarsely polished. The surfaces remain irregular, with striations and pits not totally obliterated by the light polishing, which although it removes the rough surface does not leave clear polishing marks. The coarsely polished surface was often slipped with a light red pigment. When applied thickly, this ranges from streaky red-brown to dull red. However, the slip was frequently used as a very thin coating and can hardly be distinguished from the light orange natural surface. On other bowls, the slip is visible on some parts of the vessel but not on others. It seems that the potters may have distinguished two modes of surface color, since bowls which are decorated only on one surface frequently have a fairly thickly applied red on the undecorated surface and a nearly natural base color on the decorated side. However, since the red slip ranges from indistinguishable from the natural light orange (and possibly absent) to a streaky but obvious light red, and any such surface may be decorated, I have referred to all these light red and natural light orange surfaces as "natural" (fig.9).

Necked jars often have a rough surface finish which lacks the coarse polishing characteristic of bowls. Temper particles are frequently visible on the surface, and striations from scraping are obvious. Some jars and other rough-surfaced vessels were probably wiped with a wet cloth after they were scraped. This failed to erase the deep striations completely and left a second set of finer striations. Some vessels appear to have received a thin slip of the same color as the paste, but it may have been unintentionally applied in the wiping process. A small number of rough-finished surfaces have a red slip, which is usually darker and thicker than that found on bowls.

In order to develop a stylistic seriation, all vessel fragments were classified and coded within five major areas of variation:

1. vessel shape
2. decorative technique
3. design themes
4. design elements
5. selected combinations of design elements in themes

Vessel shapes were established on the basis of intuition guided by handling the materials. Where adequate quantities of a particular shape were present, subdivisions were created within the categories by using scattergrams which compared co-occurrence of modes within two dimensions. Further subcategories were constructed by discovering size groups with histograms based on mouth diameters. Other body dimensions were rarely preserved on enough vessel fragments to permit the use of histograms.

Dimensions of variation within the area of shape include the following:

1. Mouth diamater measured in 1 cm. intervals.
2. Wall angle measured in 5° intervals. Figure 9 shows how rim sherds were measured, although for convenience the illustration shows only 10° intervals.
3. Wall profile mode. Eleven modes were established (see fig. 9).
4. Lip treatment mode. Ten modes were established (see fig. 9).
5. Rim modification mode. Ten modes were established (see fig. 9).

6. Neck or wall thickness 2 cm. below the rim.
7. Vessel height, composed of both neck and body height in the case of composite shapes.
8. Shape of bottom.
9. Union of base and vessel walls.
10. Handle form and placement.
11. Form and placement of supports.
12. Spout form and placement.
13. Any other characteristics of shape.

The second area of variation considered was decorative technique. Since slip painting is by far the most common, it has been elaborated (fig. 9), while modeling and other plastic decoration are handled only briefly. The modes established are as follows:

2.1 slip painting
  2.1.1 single color
    2.1.1.1 dark red
    2.1.1.2 white
    2.1.1.3 black
    2.1.1.4 brown
  2.1.2 two colors
    2.1.2.1 dark red and white
    2.1.2.2 dark red and black
    2.1.2.3 dark red and gray
    2.1.2.4 dark red and light red
    2.1.2.5 white and black
    2.1.2.6 white and light red
    2.1.2.7 white and brown
    2.1.2.8 black and light red
    2.1.2.9 black and gray
    2.1.2.10 black and yellow
    2.1.2.11 black and brown
    2.1.2.12 gray and light red
    2.1.2.13 gray and brown
    2.1.2.14 gray and white
  2.1.3 three colors
    2.1.3.1 dark red, white, black
    2.1.3.2 dark red, white, gray
    2.1.3.3 dark red, white, light red
    2.1.3.4 dark red, white, orange
    2.1.3.5 dark red, white, yellow
    2.1.3.6 dark red, white, brown
    2.1.3.7 black, dark red, yellow
    2.1.3.8 black, dark red, gray
    2.1.3.9 black, dark red, orange
    2.1.3.10 black, white, yellow
    2.1.3.11 black, white, light red
    2.1.3.12 black, white, brown
    2.1.3.13 dark red, yellow, gray
    2.1.3.14 dark red, gray, brown
    2.1.3.15 dark red, yellow, orange
    2.1.3.16 white, brown, gray
    2.1.3.17 light red, dark red, white
  2.1.4 four colors
    2.1.4.1 black, white, dark red, gray
    2.1.4.2 black, white, dark red, yellow
    2.1.4.3 black, white, dark red, light red
    2.1.4.4 dark red, brown, orange, gray
    2.1.4.5 white, dark red, orange, gray
    2.1.4.6 black, white, dark red, orange
    2.1.4.7 black, white, dark red, crusty black
    2.1.4.8 black, dark red, brown, orange

    2.1.4.9 white, black, orange, gray
  2.1.5 five colors
    2.1.5.1 black, white, dark red, light red, crusty black
    2.1.5.2 black, white, dark red, brown, yellow
2.2 black ware
  2.2.1 black with red paint
  2.2.2 black with red paint and plastic decoration
2.3 plastic decoration
  2.3.1 incised
  2.3.2 press molded
  2.3.3 incised appliqué
  2.3.4 modeled adorno
  2.3.5 plain appliqué

The third area of variation consists of design themes or major design layouts. All are painted themes since plastic decoration is very rare. The intention was to set up a hierarchy of features and themes which actually occur in the collection, not all logical possibilities, which would include numerous empty categories. The highest order categories contain the least information and are particularly important for the classification of fragmentary or eroded materials on which only the most general aspects of design theme can be distinguished. Subcategories represent variations on the higher order theme, not necessarily logical subsets. The structure of the hierarchy departed even farther from ordering in terms of logical subsets to give lower subcategory status to exceedingly rare variants, even though these rare classes were sometimes logically more powerful than the popular class of which they were considered a lower order variant.

Themes recognized are as follows:

3.1 solid-colored disks arranged in quadrants of vessel
  3.1.1 solid-colored disk
    3.1.1.1 same, with contrastive dots
  3.1.2 solid-colored disk with contrastive Saint Andrew's cross
    3.1.2.1 same, with circles in quadrants
    3.1.2.2 same, with circles in quadrants and dots on cross
    3.1.2.3 same, with dots in quadrants
    3.1.2.4 same, with circles and dots in quadrants
  3.1.3 solid-colored disk with vertical cross
    3.1.3.1 same, with circles with central dot in quadrants
    3.1.3.2 same, with dots in quadrants
  3.1.4 colored line connecting colored disks
    3.1.4.1 same, with contrastive dots on line
3.2 vertical bands
  3.2.1 single vertical band
  3.2.2 groups of vertical bands
  3.2.3 isolated vertical bands arranged around vessel
  3.2.4 vertical bands and horizontal lines
3.3 decorated panels
  3.3.1 outlined panel with geometric design elements
    3.3.1.1 same, with geometric elements arranged in horizontal rows
  3.3.2 colored bands defining rectangles

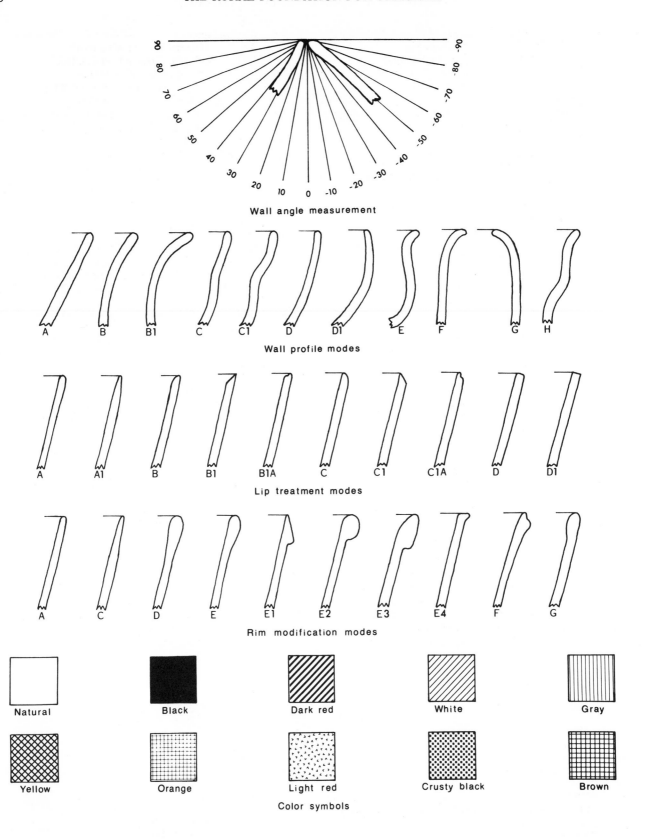

Wall angle measurement

Wall profile modes

Lip treatment modes

Rim modification modes

Color symbols

Fig. 9

3.3.2.1   same, but diagonal rectangle (diamond)
3.3.2.2   nested rectangles
    3.3.3   zigzag band confined to panel
3.4   vertical band and panel combination
    3.4.1   same, panel in horizontal divisions
    3.4.2   same, panel divided into upper and lower panels
3.5   horizontal bands
    3.5.1   single horizontal band just below rim
       3.5.1.1   same, white
          3.5.1.1.1   same, segmented
          3.5.1.1.2   same, but located well below rim
       3.5.1.2   same, dark red
          3.5.1.2.1   same, but located well below rim
       3.5.1.3   same, natural color
       3.5.1.4   same, black
       3.5.1.5   black band around middle of vessel
       3.5.1.6   same, gray
    3.5.2   two parallel horizontal bands
       3.5.2.1   same, dark red over black
       3.5.2.2   same, black over yellow
       3.5.2.3   same, black over dark red
       3.5.2.4   same, gray over dark red
       3.5.2.5   same, black over black
       3.5.2.6   same, dark red over yellow
       3.5.2.7   same, dark red over white
       3.5.2.8   same, white over orange
    3.5.3   three parallel horizontal bands
       3.5.3.1   same, black over dark red over black
       3.5.3.2   same, dark red over black over dark red
       3.5.3.3   same, gray over dark red over gray
       3.5.3.4   same, gray over dark red over dark red

3.6   diagonal lines
    3.6.1   diagonal lines in wing motif
    3.6.2   diagonal lines and vertical lines
3.7   row of diagonal crosses and dots
    3.7.1   row of diagonal crosses, no dots
3.8   wavy line below rim, not on a band
    3.8.1   same, with dots between crests of waves
    3.8.2   same, but multiple wavy lines
3.9   representational figures
3.10   white field with contrastive dots
    3.10.1   same, but field of different color (usually black)
3.11   row of vertical crosses
3.12   chain design
3.13   pendent triangles
3.14   grid with dots in squares
3.15   band with contrastive outline and dots

The fourth area of variation consists of painted design elements which were generally used in combination with one of the design themes listed above. The elements distinguished are as follows:

4.1   loop, spiral, or cursive triangular form
4.2   hook or crescent
4.3   vertical cross, solid or composed of dashes
4.4   ring or circle
    4.4.1   ring as part of complex design
       4.4.1.1   ring on colored disk
       4.4.1.2   rings on horizontal band
       4.4.1.3   rings on vertical band
       4.4.1.4   rings on rectangle, diamond, or zigzag band
4.5   wavy line
    4.5.1   horizontal wavy line
       4.5.1.1   same, single dot of same color between crests
       4.5.1.2   same, multiple dots of contrasting colors between crests
          4.5.1.2.1   same, but dots of same color between crests

---

Figure 9. Vessel Shape Attributes and Color Code Symbols

Wall angle measurement shows how vessel wall angles were measured. The sherd to the left has a wall angle of 35°, while that on the right has a wall angle of -50°.

Wall profile modes distinguished on Jargampata pottery:

A	straight	D	incurving convex
B	outcurving concave	D1	incurving convex, marked
B1	outcurving concave, marked	E	recurved
C	irregular curve	F	lip flare
C1	irregular curve, marked	G	lip constriction
		H	complex recurve

Lip treatment modes distinguished on Jargampata pottery:

A	rounded	C	exterior curve
A1	sharp rounded	C1	exterior bevel
B	interior curve	C1A	exterior step
B1	interior bevel	D	flattened
B1A	interior step	D1	flat

Rim modification modes distinguished on Jargampata pottery:

A	unmodified	E2	exterior thickened, rounded
C	thinned	E3	exterior thickened, straightened
D	interior and exterior thickened	E4	exterior thickened, flanged
E	exterior thickened	F	exterior thickened, stepped
E1	exterior thickened, angular	G	interior thickened

Color symbols used to indicate colors used on Jargampata pottery.

4.5.2 pairs of horizontal wavy lines of same color
    4.5.2.1 same, with contrasting color dots
4.5.3 multiple horizontal wavy lines and contrasting dots
    4.5.3.1 multiple wavy lines in different colors with dots
    4.5.3.2 multiple wavy lines, same color, no dots
4.5.4 single vertical wavy line
    4.5.4.1 same, with dot between crests
    4.5.4.2 same, with multiple dots between crests
4.5.5 multiple vertical wavy lines
4.6 circle with dot in center
    4.6.1 same, repeated in rows
    4.6.2 same, on quadrants of colored disk
4.7 no apparent pattern of lines, dots, and circles on undivided vessel surface
4.8 N shape
4.9 Z shape
4.10 irregular squiggles in panel
4.13 dots
    4.13.1 dots of one color as isolated space fillers
    4.13.2 dots of multiple colors as space fillers in geometric designs
    4.13.3 multiple dots of same color on defined field
    4.13.4 row of dots of contrasting color on wide line
    4.13.5 row of dots paralleling a line

Finally, the fifth area considered for seriational purposes includes certain popular themes with characteristic space-filling elements. They are as follows:

5.1 single wavy line with single dot between crests painted parallel to and slightly below vessel rim
5.2 single wavy line with single dots between crests painted on a single colored band
5.3 groups of vertical bands of alternating colors with alternating vertical wavy lines and vertical rows of circles on bands
5.4 groups of vertical bands of alternating colors with single vertical wavy line with dots between crests on each band
5.5 three horizontal bands, black over dark red over black, decorated with wavy lines, wavy lines and dots, or rows of circles
5.6 two horizontal bands decorated with wavy lines or wavy lines and dots
5.7 panel design divided into horizontal sections with horizontal rows of circles and/or horizontal wavy lines or horizontal wavy lines and dots

All of this information was then plotted on a series of charts by frequency within each ceramic sample. The eleven ceramic samples were then arranged into the best temporal order, primarily on the basis of simple presence or absence of particular attributes within a sample, but also considering the relative frequency of the attributes. Ceramic samples which shared the greatest similarity were combined in single temporal phases. The seriation of samples was then checked against the stratigraphic position of each sample and was found to be in agreement (tables 1, 2).

Five phases were established which belong to a single ceramic tradition, which I propose to call the Patibamba tradition. This name was selected since both sites which produce ceramics in this style—Jargampata and a small zone near the Hacienda Patibamba house—are on the lands of the Hacienda Patibamba. The phases are as follows:

Early Patibamba—Samples: E2-3 x S13-15 stratum 9; E2-3 x S13-15 strata 4-8

Middle Patibamba—Sample: Rooms S10 and S11 stratum E

Late Patibamba I—Samples: E5-6 x S9-10 stratum 4; rooms S10 and S11 stratum D1; room S7 strata 3 and 4

Late Patibamba II—Samples: W14 x N1-6 on the plaza floor; E5-6 x S9-10 stratum 3; rooms S10 and S11 stratum D; E5-6 x S9-10 stratum 2

Illaura—Sample: Rooms S10 and S11 strata C and C1

The remainder of this chapter consists of a description of all vessel shape categories found in Patibamba ceramics at Jargampata and a discussion of the variation within the categories in terms of the five-phase sequence established. A seriation chart which illustrates the distribution of vessel shapes (table 1) and one illustrating the distribution of decorative techniques, design themes, design elements, and combinations (table 2) are also provided. Finally, a discussion of exotic or imported vessels and nonceramic artifacts finishes the chapter. Chapters 9 through 13

Figure 10. Narrow-Collar Jars 1.1.1.1　　　(A: Scale = 1:1; B–Z: Scale = ½)

A   Middle Patibamba or Late Patibamba I; House Group, S4 stratum 2; solid miniature vessel; D=.8 cm.; plate 15I
B   Late Patibamba I or II; North Unit, S9 floor; D=12 cm.
C   Late Patibamba I; South Unit, S7 stratum 4; D=11 cm.
D   Early Patibamba; E2 x S15 stratum 8; D=12 cm.
E   Early Patibamba; E2 x S15 stratum 9; D=12 cm.
F   Early Patibamba; E2 x S14 stratum 9; D=12 cm.
G   Late Patibamba; South Unit, S7 stratum 4; D=9 cm.
H   Early Patibamba; E3 x S13-15 stratum 9; D=12 cm.
I   Early Patibamba; E2 x S14 stratum 9; D=8 cm.
J   Early Patibamba; E2 x S15 stratum 8; D=7 cm.
K   Illaura; North Unit, S11 stratum C1; D=12 cm.
L   Late Patibamba I; North Unit, S10 stratum D1; D=10 cm.
M   Illaura; North Unit, S11 stratum C; D=11 cm.
N   Late Patibamba I; North Unit, S10 stratum D1; D=10 cm.
O   Middle Patibamba; North Unit, S11 stratum E; D=9 cm.
P   Early Patibamba; E3 x S13-15 stratum 9; D=10 cm.
Q   Late Patibamba I; South Unit, S7 stratum 4; D=11 cm.

R   Middle Patibamba; North Unit, S11 stratum E; D=10 cm.
S   Late Patibamba I; North Unit, E5 x S10 stratum 4; D=7 cm.; 2.1.3.10 on natural
T   Early Patibamba (?); North Unit, E5 x S9 stratum 5; D=8 cm.; 2.1.1.3 on natural; 4.3
U   Early Patibamba; E2 x S15 stratum 9; D=9 cm.; 2.1.1.3 on natural; 4.3
V   Late Patibamba I; North Unit, E5 x S9 stratum 4; D=9 cm.; 2.1.2.5 on red; 4.3, 4.6
W   Late Patibamba II; North Unit, plaza floor; D=8 cm.; 2.1.1.3 on natural
X   Late Patibamba II; North Unit, E5 x S9 stratum 2; D=6 cm.; 2.1.3.1 on natural; 3.5.2.3
Y   Early Patibamba; E2 x S15 stratum 8; D=9 cm.; 2.1.1.3 on red; 3.13
Z   Late Patibamba II; North Unit, plaza floor; D=6 cm.; 2.1.1.3 on red; 3.5.1.4

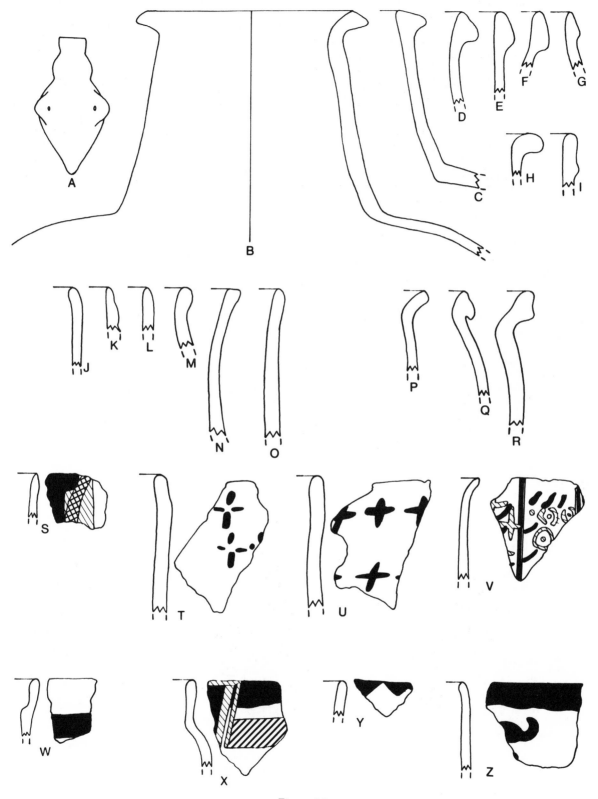

Fig. 10

Plate 11. Necked Jars 1.1.1   (Scale = ½)

A   Face-Neck Jar; 1.1.1.2; Figure 11E   D   Bilobed Jar; 1.1.1.3; Figure 12G

B   Bilobed Jar; 1.1.1.3; Figure 12A   E   Bottle; 1.2.1; Figure 17E

C   Side-Spout Jar; 1.1.2 (miniature vessel); Figure 13C   F   Bottle; 1.2.1; Figure 17D

contain more detailed descriptions of the ceramics of each phase.

NECKED JARS 1.1

This general category includes jars with necks (figs. 10-16). All have circular horizontal profiles, but most bodies are somewhat elongated (figs. 14A, C, D, G, H, 15A). In the Early Patibamba Phase there is evidence only for conical bottoms, but both rounded and flat bottoms—occasionally with sharp basal angles—gradually increase in frequency until by the Illaura Phase 75% of the necked jars have flat or slightly curved bottoms. There is a broad range in size of necked jars, from less than 10 cm. to over 40 cm. in mouth diameter, and it seems that most jars and certainly all of the flaring-neck jars were supplied with strap handles placed in either vertical or horizontal positions (figs. 10A, 12A, D, G, 13C, D, 14A-G, 15A).

It is interesting that plastic decoration, other than the facial features of face-neck jars, is nearly absent on Jargampata jars. An appliqué and incised fillet at the base of the jar neck is very common on many hilltop sites in the Rio Pampas drainage, but is paralleled by only one rather unique example from Jargampata (fig. 16X). Also, jar necks are short, ranging from 2 cm. or 3 cm. on the small jars to about 10 cm. or 12 cm. on medium and large jars. These short necks do not have the sharply everted or flaring rims characteristic of the ceramics from hilltop sites.

As described above, necked jars generally have rather coarse antiplastic inclusions and rough, unslipped surface finishes. Some bases, particularly the conical forms, show evidence of soot stains from exposure to fire. These bases often have very coarse inclusions, suggesting that the jars were culinary vessels. Others show no trace of exposure to fire and were probably storage jars, brewing urns, serving pitchers, and the like.

Necked jars constitute the second most popular gross shape category, but they undergo considerable change in frequency through time. In the Early Patibamba Phase, necked jars account for about 45% of the vessels, but they steadily lose popularity until they drop to just over 25% of the Late Patibamba II pottery. The reoccupation of Jargampata during the Illaura Phase includes 49% necked jars, a frequency almost identical to that of Early Patibamba. It seems likely that both the Early Patibamba and the Illaura samples do not relate to the state-instituted North Unit, while the lower frequency of jars from Middle Patibamba, Late Patibamba I, and Late Patibamba II probably does reflect activities associated with the North Unit enclosure.

The category of necked jars includes three subcategories, constricted-neck jars, side-spout jars, and flaring-neck jars, which are described in more detail below.

Constricted-Neck Jars 1.1.1

Jars with constricted necks differ from other necked jars in that their collars are nearly vertical or even inclined slightly inward with wall angles ranging from -15° to about 10°. The mouth diameter is small, but unlike the smallest flaring-neck jars these have no handles attached to the collars and the necks appear to have been rather tall for such small mouth openings. Constricted-neck jars are also distinctive in being the only jars which are decorated.

Painted decoration was added to the collars and perhaps the vessel bodies, and these jars frequently also had elaborate rim modifications (fig. 10).

Only a few constricted-neck jars could be reconstructed to provide information concerning vessel body form. However, the vessel body shapes can best be discussed within the subcategories of constricted-neck jars, which include narrow-collar jars (fig. 10), face-neck jars (fig. 11), and bilobed jars (fig. 12).

Constricted-neck jars are never common at Jargampata and range in frequency between 1.2% and 5.2% with a tendency to become less frequent in the final phases. No constricted-neck jar fragments show evidence of having been exposed to fire, so it seems likely that they were for storage, for transport of liquids, and also for serving liquids.

Narrow-Collar Jars 1.1.1.1

Narrow-collar jars are the most common of the constricted-neck jars (fig. 10). They lack the modeled and/or painted faces of face-neck jars but must be very closely related in conception. These jars frequently receive painted decoration on the collar or elaboration of the rims. The mouth diameters range from 6 cm. to 12 cm. and collar heights from 2.5 cm. to 11 cm. However, it appears that vessel bodies ranged in size from huge jars with small mouths (fig. 10B, C), which must have been for storage, to small serving vessels (fig. 10X).

The only complete vessels of this shape category are two unbroken jars and a fragmentary miniature jar from mixed strata in the House Group (fig. 10A; plate 15I, J). The collars of the miniatures have recurved wall profile forms with a bulge in the neck and constrictions at the body-neck juncture and just below the rim. This seems to imitate the form of some large narrow-collar jars (fig. 10P, Q, R). The miniatures have an elongated body with conical base and two vertically placed handles on the vessel shoulders. Interestingly, the handles are not on opposite sides of the vessel but are set to one side. This feature seems to have no utility on unpainted jars but probably originated in Middle Horizon 1B with face-neck jars, which have elaborate decorative panels on the vessel body below the face. The width of the decorated zone required the handles to be placed slightly toward the rear (Menzel 1968: 72). Another miniature vessel, slightly larger but of this same shape with a bulge in the collar and handles displaced to one side, was found in a Middle Horizon cache elsewhere in the Pampas River valley. A number of other miniatures from the House Group may also imitate the narrow-collar jar (plate 15K-O), suggesting an important ritual function. The large jars were probably for storage or transport of food and beverages, while the miniatures may have had similar functions for ceremonial materials.

The narrow-collar jar never reaches a frequency of more than 4.7% of the vessels in any phase at Jargampata, and its frequency dwindles steadily to a low of 1.2% in the Illaura Phase.

Face-Neck Jars 1.1.1.2

Face-neck jars have shapes similar to narrow-collar jars but also have modeled and painted faces on the jar collars (fig. 11). No specimens from the analyzed samples could be reconstructed, but one example from the House Group was more complete (fig. 11E; plate 11A). This vessel has a flat

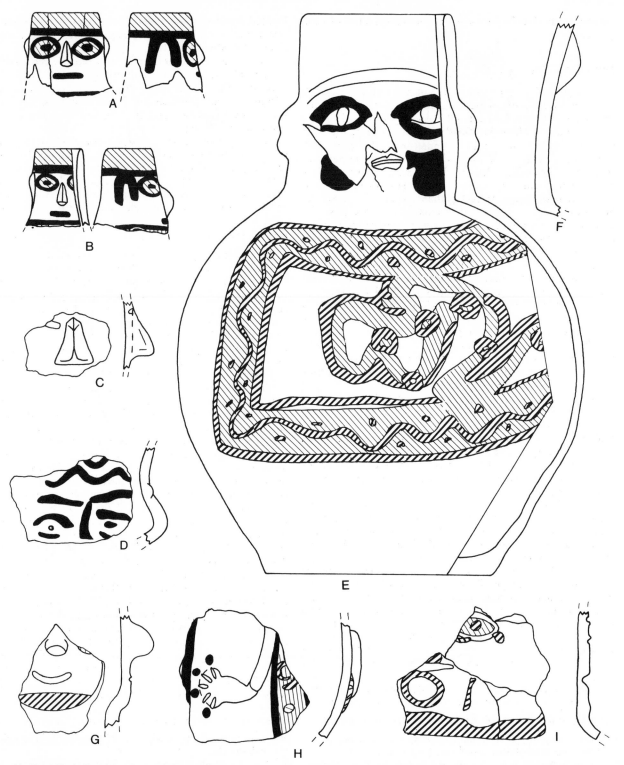

Figure 11. Face-Neck Jars 1.1.1.2   (Scale = ½)

A   Late Patibamba I (?); House Group, S4 stratum 2; D=3 cm.; 2.1.2.5 on red
B   Late Patibamba I (?); House Group, CW stratum 4A; D=2.5 cm.; black, white, gray on red
C   Early Patibamba; E2 x S15 stratum 9
D   Early Patibamba (?); House Group, CX stratum 2; 2.1.1.3
E   Late Patibamba I; House Group, CX strata 4, 5, S4 stratum 2; D=8 cm.; 2.1.3.1

F   Early Patibamba (?); House Group, CX stratum 2
G   Early Patibamba (?); House Group, CX stratum 2; 2.1.2.1 on natural
H   Early Patibamba; E2 x S13 stratum 9; 2.1.4.1 on natural; 4.1
I   Middle Patibamba; North Unit, S11 stratum E; 2.1.2.1 on natural

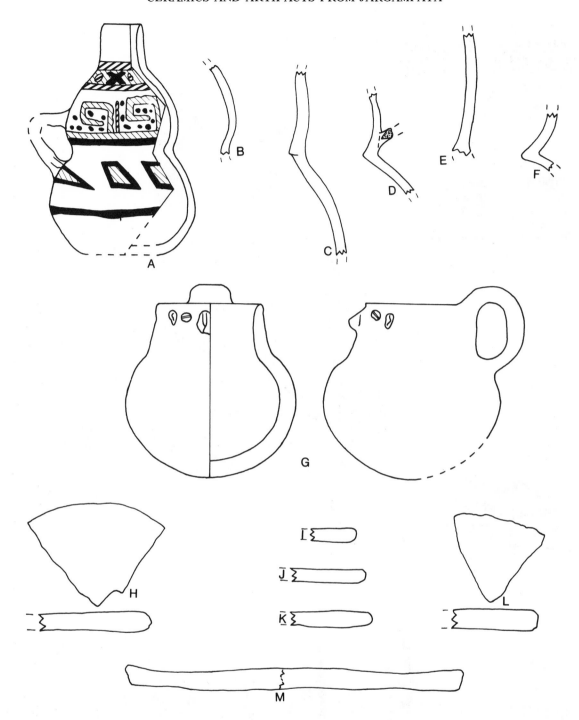

Figure 12. A–G: Bilobed Jars 1.1.1.3; H–M: Ceramic Disks 1.8   (Scale = ½)

A Late Patibamba I (?); House Group, S1 floor, CW stratum 4; D=2 cm., D of constriction=5 cm.; 2.1.3.1 on red; 3.7

B Late Patibamba I; North Unit, S11 stratum D1; D of constriction=9 cm.

C Late Patibamba I; North Unit, S11 stratum D1; D of constriction=7 cm.

D Late Patibamba I; North Unit, S10 stratum D1; D of constriction=11 cm.

E Late Patibamba II; North Unit, S11 stratum D; D of constriction=9 cm.

F Late Patibamba II; North Unit, S11 stratum D; D of constriction=11 cm.

G Late Patibamba I; House Group, S4 stratum 2; D=6 cm.

H Late Patibamba II; North Unit, S11 stratum D; D=12 cm.

I Middle Patibamba; North Unit, S11 stratum E; D=16 cm.

J Early Patibamba; E2 x S14 stratum 9; D=18 cm.

K Early Patibamba; E2 x S15 stratum 9; D=16 cm.

L Late Patibamba II; North Unit, plaza floor; D=16 cm.

M Early Patibamba; E2 x S15 stratum 9; D=18.5 cm.

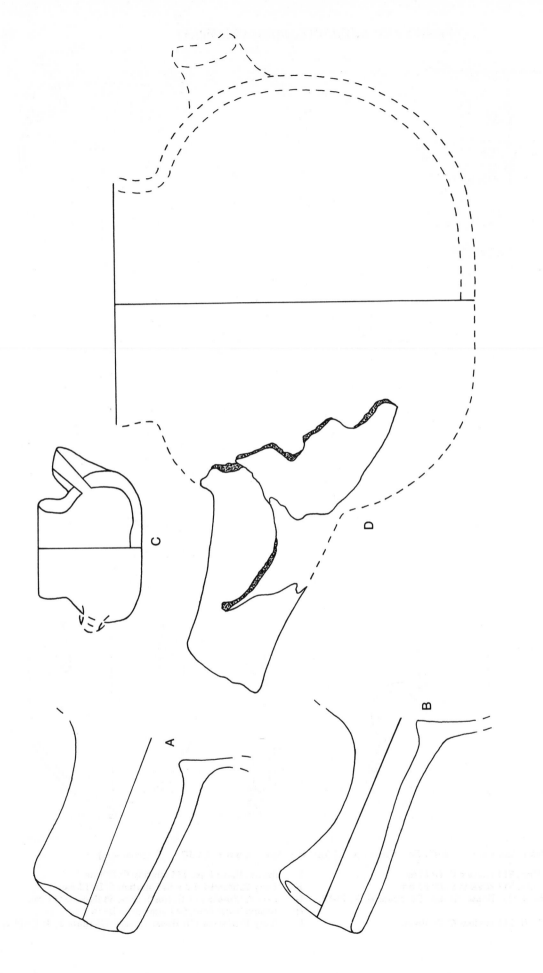

Figure 13. Side-Spout Jars 1.1.2 (Scale = ½)

A   Late Patibamba I or II; House Group, CW stratum 4; D of spout=7 cm.

B   Late Patibamba I (?); House Group, CW strata 1, 2; D of spout=6 cm.

C   Late Patibamba I (?); House Group, CW stratum 5, S4 stratum 3; D=5 cm., D of spout=1.5 cm.

D   Illaura; North Unit, S11 stratum C1; D of spout=5 cm.

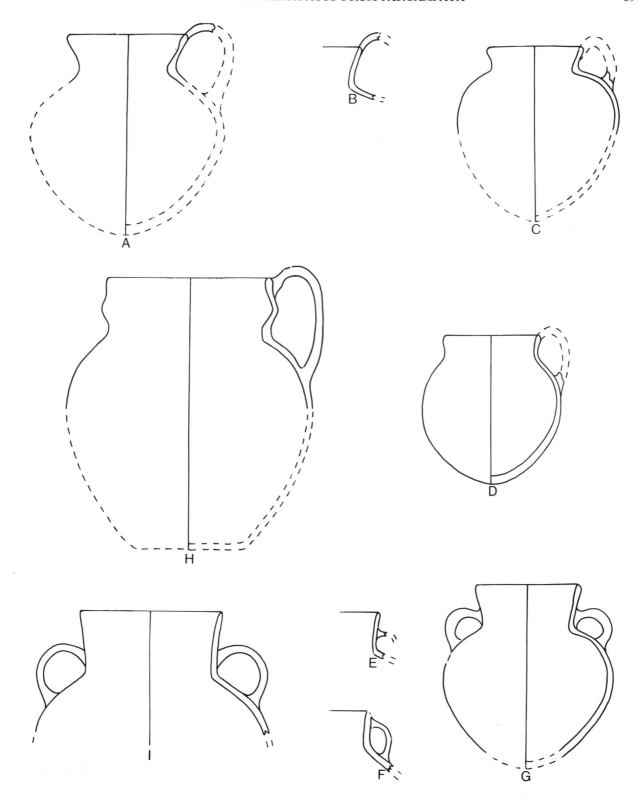

Figure 14. Flaring-Neck Jars 1.1.3   **A–G: Size Variant A 1.1.3A; H–I: Size Variant B 1.1.3B**   (Scale = ¼)

A   Illaura; North Unit, S11 stratum C; D=12cm.

B   Illaura; North Unit, S11 stratum C; D=12 cm.

C   Late Patibamba I (?); House Group, S6 strata 6, 7, EI-17; D=10 cm.

D   Illaura; North Unit, S11 stratum C; D=10cm.

E   Illaura; North Unit, S11 stratum C; D=9cm.

F   Early Patibamba; E2 x S15 stratum 5; D=12 cm.

G   Late Patibamba I or II; North Unit, S8 floor; D=11 cm.

H   Illaura; North Unit, S11 stratum C; D=16 cm.

I   Early Patibamba (?); House Group, CX strata 3, 4; D=14 cm.

base. Unfortunately, it could not be determined whether it had had handles.

Face-neck jars varied considerably in size, with mouth diameters ranging from 4 cm. to 9 cm. or more. Frequently, the facial features were produced with press molds and then painted. Generally there is a broad, decorated area on the body of the jar below the face (fig. 11E), which may include the hands and arms of the person represented (fig. 11H).

Face-neck jars are rare in the Jargampata samples and are present at a frequency of 1% or lower in the first two phases only. The last three phases lack these vessels totally, but the presence of press molds (plate 15B-D) and contemporary specimens from the House Group indicates that they had not disappeared from the ceramic inventory. However, it seems that face-neck jars may have been absent by the Illaura Phase.

Bilobed Jars   1.1.1.3

Bilobed jars are composite forms consisting of a spherical body section with a smaller more or less spherical section above (fig. 12A-G; plate 11B, D). The material recovered indicates only two spheres, but the possibility of three or more cannot be discounted. Both round and flattened bottoms appear, and the mouth may be large and open like a face-neck jar or tapering and spouted like a bottle. Like other narrow-collar jars, they are appropriate recipients of painted or modeled decoration.

Two handle modes are represented, both of rather thick clay straps. One handle type unites the two vessel spheres and is located about halfway between the base and lip (fig. 12A, D; plate 11B). This form of handle may be related to that found on small lyre-shaped cups (fig. 35M-O). The second handle mode is a looping strap rising from the rim and joining the vessel body on the upper part of the shoulder of the lower sphere (fig. 12G; plate 11D). There can be little doubt that this handle form is derived from the small flaring-neck jars (fig. 14A-D, H).

Bilobed jars are infrequent at Jargampata and are limited to the Late Patibamba I and II phases. It is significant that samples from these phases lack face-neck jars. Although all bilobed pots from the North Unit are plain, one from the House Group has a modeled face on the upper section of the body (fig. 12G; plate 11D) and could have been classified as a face-neck jar. The upper spheres of bilobed vessels are also reminiscent of the bulging collars of some narrow-collar jars (fig. 10A, P-R). It seems that the bilobed vessel, although sometimes similar to a bottle, must be closely related to the constricted-neck jars and developed from these forms. Although none are represented in the Illaura Phase pottery sample, the bilobed vessels with tall, loop handles and modeled faces may have been replacing the more traditional face-neck jars. The similarity of these vessels to the handled, bilobed forms, sometimes with faces, of Early Inca or Killke from Cuzco (Lathrap 1970: plate 52; Larco 1963: fig. 129; Rowe 1970: 559) is striking, and there can be little doubt that the Killke vessels develop into the typical *puños* of Imperial Inca pottery (Pardo 1957: 567, lam. 1). Like the Inca *puños,* the Jargampata bilobed jars were probably serving vessels for liquids.

Side-Spout Jars   1.1.2

No complete side-spout jars could be reconstructed, but a miniature from the House Group (fig. 13C; plate 11C) and various fragments provide a fairly accurate picture of their form. The body form is that of a small jar with a flat or slightly rounded base and a low collar with nearly vertical walls. A horizontal strap handle was placed on the shoulder of the vessel opposite a spout which projected slightly upward from the vessel shoulder (fig. 13). The vessel bodies apparently ranged considerably in size, and, although most spouts were probably placed on jars of not more than 18 cm. in diameter, there are some large spouts which may have come from much larger vessels. None of the examples from Jargampata have painted or modeled decoration, although some are slipped red. However, although they are classified separately, the similarity between these jars and constricted-neck jars suggests they should have been appropriate vehicles for decoration.

Figure 15. Flaring-Neck Jars 1.1.3   B–C Size Variant A 1.1.3A;   D–S Size Variant B 1.1.3B;   A, T–AT: Size Variant C 1.1.3C
(A: Scale = ¼; B–AT: Scale = ½)

A	Late Patibamba I (?); House Group, CZ stratum 5; D=22cm.
B	Late Patibamba I; North Unit, S10 stratum D1; D=9 cm.
C	Early Patibamba; North Unit, E2 x S14 stratum 9; D=7 cm.
D	Late Patibamba I; North Unit, S10 stratum D1; D=15 cm.
E	Early Patibamba; E3 x S13-15 stratum 9; D=12 cm.
F	Early Patibamba; E2 x S13 stratum 9; D=16 cm.
G	Early Patibamba; E2 x S15 stratum 9; D=14 cm.
H	Early Patibamba; E2 x S15 stratum 5; D=15 cm.
I	Early Patibamba; E3 x S13-15 stratum 9; D=16 cm.
J	Late Patibamba I; North Unit, S11 stratum D1; D=16 cm.
K	Illaura; North Unit, S10 stratum C; D=15 cm.
L	Late Patibamba II; North Unit, plaza floor; D=15 cm.
M	Early Patibamba; E2 x S14 stratum 9; D=16 cm.
N	Late Patibamba I; North Unit, S11 stratum D1; D=15 cm.
O	Late Patibamba II; North Unit, plaza floor; D=16 cm.
P	Late Patibamba I; South Unit, S7 stratum 4; D=14 cm.
Q	Late Patibamba I; North Unit, E5 x S10 stratum 4; D=16 cm.
R	Early Patibamba; E2 x S14 stratum 9; D=14 cm.
S	Late Patibamba I; North Unit, S11 stratum D1; D=17 cm.
T	Early Patibamba; E2 x S15 stratum 8; D=22 cm.
U	Early Patibamba; E2 x S15 stratum 9; D=20 cm.
V	Early Patibamba; E2 x S13 stratum 9; D=20 cm.
W	Early Patibamba; E2 x S15 stratum 9; D=23 cm.
X	Late Patibamba I; North Unit, E6 x S9 stratum 4b; D=20 cm.
Y	Early Patibamba; E2 x S15 stratum 6; D=22 cm.
Z	Late Patibamba II; North Unit, plaza floor; D=20 cm.
AA	Early Patibamba; E2 x S15 stratum 8; D=19 cm.
AB	Late Patibamba I; North Unit, S10 stratum D1; D=23 cm.
AC	Late Patibamba I; North Unit, S10 stratum D1; D=19 cm.
AD	Late Patibamba II; North Unit, plaza floor; D=22 cm.
AE	Illaura; North Unit, S11 stratum C1; D=20 cm.
AF	Early Patibamba; E2 x S14 stratum 9; D=23 cm.
AG	Middle Patibamba; North Unit, S11 stratum E; D=22 cm.
AH	Middle Patibamba; North Unit, S11 stratum E; D=20 cm.
AI	Early Patibamba; E3 x S13-15 stratum 4; D=20 cm.
AJ	Illaura; North Unit, S10 stratum C; D=23 cm.
AK	Late Patibamba II; North Unit, S11 stratum D; D=22 cm.
AL	Late Patibamba I; South Unit, S7 stratum 4; D=19 cm.
AM	Early Patibamba; E2 x S15 stratum 9; D=22 cm.
AN	Early Patibamba; E3 x S13-15 stratum 9; D=21 cm.
AO	Late Patibamba II; North Unit, S11 stratum D; D=20 cm.
AP	Illaura; North Unit, S10 stratum C; D=22 cm.
AQ	Illaura; North Unit, S10 stratum C; D=22 cm.
AR	Middle Patibamba; North Unit, S11 stratum E; D=20 cm.
AS	Middle Patibamba; North Unit, S10 stratum E; D=20 cm.
AT	Illaura; North Unit, S11 stratum C; D=21 cm.

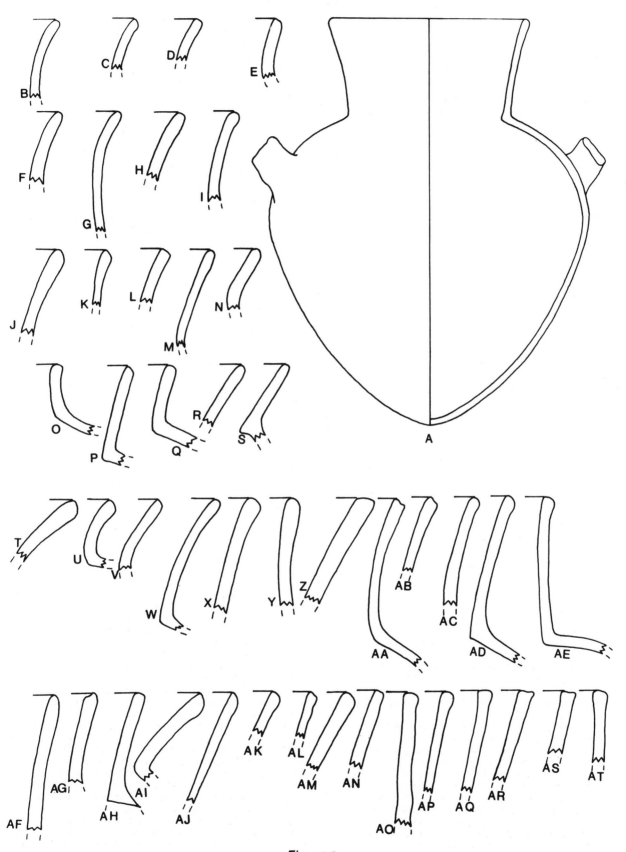

Fig. 15

Bennett (1953: 40, fig. 8G) recognized this form at Wari and called it an olla with shoulder spout. Lumbreras (1959; lam. XIO) has illustrated a decorated specimen, and other decorated examples are known from Conchopata (Chaki-pampa) (Lumbreras, personal communication) and Ayapata (Ravines, personal communication).

Side-spout jars occur in very low frequency throughout the sequence at Jargampata and are still present during the Illaura Phase. There can be little doubt that their primary function was as serving pots to pour liquids such as chicha beer. In rural villages of Ayacucho today, surprisingly similarly shaped aluminum teapots are used to dispense alcohol at village rituals such as cleaning the irrigation canals, branding cattle, and saints' day celebrations.

Flaring-Neck Jars   1.1.3

Another general category of necked jars differentiated from constricted-neck jars and side-spout jars is flaring-neck jars. These vessels contrast with the others discussed in that their necks range from nearly vertical to quite flared, although most have wall angles between 15° and 20°. The collar wall profiles are generally straight or curve outward slightly. Reconstructed specimens indicate that the bodies were elongated and generally had conical bases, although flat or nearly flat bottoms become more common on large specimens from the later phases at Jargampata. Most specimens appear to have had a body height up to twice that of the mouth diameter and a maximum width at the shoulders roughly equal to the height of the vessel body without the collar.

The size range found within this category required its subdivision into size modes. Seven size variants were recognized on the basis of histograms showing the distribution of mouth diameters. Variant A generally ranges between 7 cm. and 12 cm. in mouth diameter, although one specimen with a diameter of 13 cm. was included (figs. 14A-G, 15B, C, E). Variant B ranges between 14 cm. and 18 cm. in mouth diameter (figs. 14H, I, 15D, F-S). These small flaring-neck jars share similar handle modes which distinguish them from constricted-neck or side-spout jars and also from the larger flaring-neck jars. Instead of horizontal or vertical strap handles on the shoulders of the

pot, these jars have strap handles which join the collar to the vessel body. Two alternate modes are represented. One consists of two strap handles on opposite sides of the vessel. One end of the handle is welded to the collar below its rim, while the other is attached to the upper part of the vessel shoulder (fig. 14E-G, I). The second mode consists of a single handle attached to the lip. The strap rises, then loops over and down to join the upper part of the shoulder (fig. 14A-D, H). This handle form is very similar to some Inca vessel handles (Pardo 1957: lam 3) and has sometimes been identified as Late Horizon for this reason (Bonavia 1967-68: 249, lam. 7, 9, fig. 6). However, it shares its general form with handles of vessel form 4 from Ayapata (Ravines 1968: fig. 30) and is clearly a Middle Horizon shape.

Larger flaring-neck jars of size variant C have mouth diameters between 19 cm. and 24 cm. (fig. 15T-AT); those of variant D range from 24 cm. to 29 cm. (fig. 16A-H, M); and those of size variant E range from 30 cm. to 35 cm. (fig. 16J-L, N-W). Very large jars of variant F range in mouth diameter from 36 cm. to 38 cm. (fig. 16Y-AE), and those of variant G range from 41 cm. to 45 cm. or possibly even more (fig. 16AF-AL).

All of the large flaring-neck jars appear to share a single handle mode. Two strap handles are placed on opposite sides of the vessel on the shoulders, although there seems to have been a freedom of choice in placement of the handles in a vertical or horizontal position. Both alternatives appear with about equal frequency.

These jars were not decorated and have rough surface finishes. Some bases have heavy antiplastic inclusions and soot-stained surfaces, indicating that at least some of these jars were used on the fire, probably for food preparation.

The frequency of flaring-neck jars drops from 33.3% in Early Patibamba to 18.6%, 16%, and 12% through Middle Patibamba, Late Patibamba I, and Late Patibamba II respectively. In the final Illaura Phase, the popularity of the category shoots up again to 36.6%. This decline and rise must relate to activities carried on within the North Unit at Jargampata. However, the changes in frequency are not experienced equally by all size variants, as indicated in the detailed ceramic descriptions for each phase which follow in Chapters 9 through 13.

Figure 16. Flaring-Neck Jars 1.1.3   A–H: Size Variant D 1.1.3D;   J–W: Size Variant E 1.1.3E;   Y–AE: Size Variant F 1.1.3F;
AF–AL: Size Variant G 1.1.3G;   I, X: Plastic Decoration on Jars   (Scale = ½)

A	Early Patibamba; E2 x S14 stratum 9; D=26 cm.	U	Early Patibamba; E2 x S15 stratum 9; D=32 cm.
B	Early Patibamba; E2 x S15 stratum 5; D=26 cm.	V	Late Patibamba I; North Unit, E6 x S10 stratum 4b; D=31cm.
C	Early Patibamba; E2 x S14 stratum 7; D=27 cm.		
D	Early Patibamba; E2 x S14 stratum 9; D=26 cm.	W	Early Patibamba; E2 x S15 stratum 6; D=32 cm.
E	Illaura; North Unit, S10 stratum C; D=25 cm.	X	Early Patibamba; E3 x S13-15 stratum 9
F	Early Patibamba; E2 x S14 stratum 9; D=26 cm.	Y	Early Patibamba; E2 x S15 stratum 8; D=38 cm.
G	Late Patibamba I; North Unit, E6 x S9 stratum 4a; D=26 cm.	Z	Early Patibamba; E2 x S14 stratum 9; D=36 cm.
H	Middle Patibamba; North Unit, S11 stratum E; D=26 cm.	AA	Early Patibamba; E2 x S14 stratum 9; D=36 cm.
I	Late Patibamba II; North Unit, S11 stratum D	AB	Late Patibamba I; North Unit, E5 x S10 stratum 4; D=36 cm.
J	Early Patibamba; E2 x S14 stratum 9; D=32 cm.		
K	Late Patibamba I; South Unit, S7 stratum 4; D=34 cm.	AC	Early Patibamba; E2 x S14 stratum 9; D=36 cm.
L	Early Patibamba; E2 x S14 stratum 9; D=31 cm.	AD	Late Patibamba I; North Unit, S10 stratum D1; D=38 cm.
M	Middle Patibamba; North Unit, S11 stratum E; D=29 cm.	AE	Early Patibamba; E2 x S15 stratum 9; D=37 cm.
N	Early Patibamba; E2 x S15 stratum 9; D=33 cm.	AF	Middle Patibamba; North Unit, S11 stratum E; D=45 cm.
O	Illaura; North Unit, S10 and 11 strata C, C1; D=31 cm.	AG	Early Patibamba; E2 x S14 stratum 9; D=41 cm.
P	Early Patibamba; E2 x S15 stratum 7; D=32 cm.	AH	Late Patibamba I; South Unit, S7 stratum 4; D=44 cm.
Q	Illaura; North Unit, S11 stratum D1; D=30 cm.	AI	Late Patibamba I; North Unit, S10 stratum D1; D=43 cm.
R	Middle Patibamba; North Unit, S11 stratum E; D=34 cm.	AJ	Early Patibamba; E2 x S13 stratum 9; D=44 cm.
S	Illaura; North Unit, S11 stratum C; D=33 cm.	AK	Late Patibamba I; South Unit, S7 stratum 3; D=45 cm.
T	Early Patibamba; E2 x S15 stratum 9; D=34 cm.	AL	Early Patibamba; E2 x S14 stratum 7; D=42 cm.

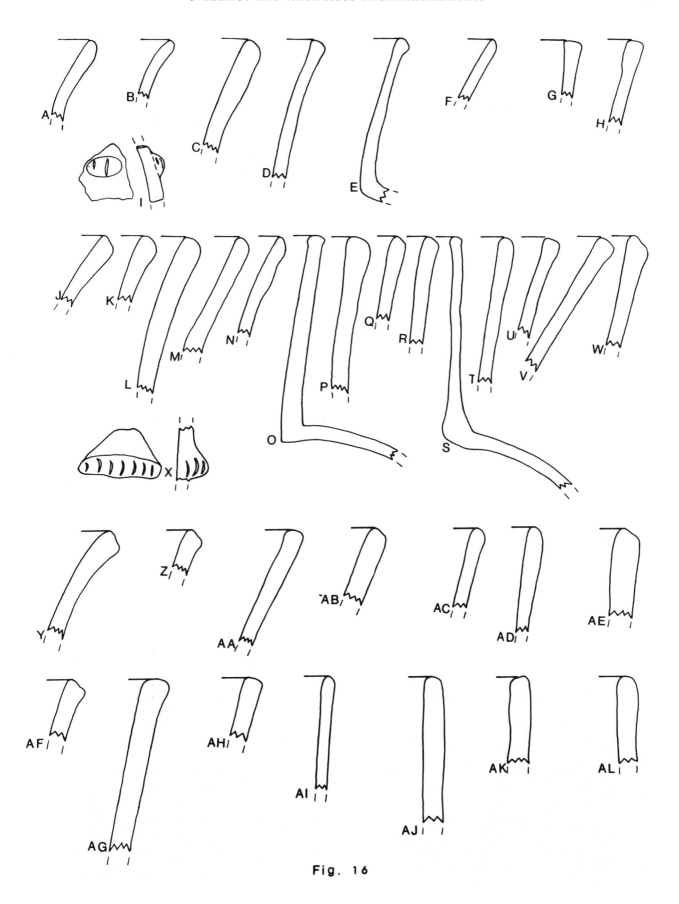

Fig. 16

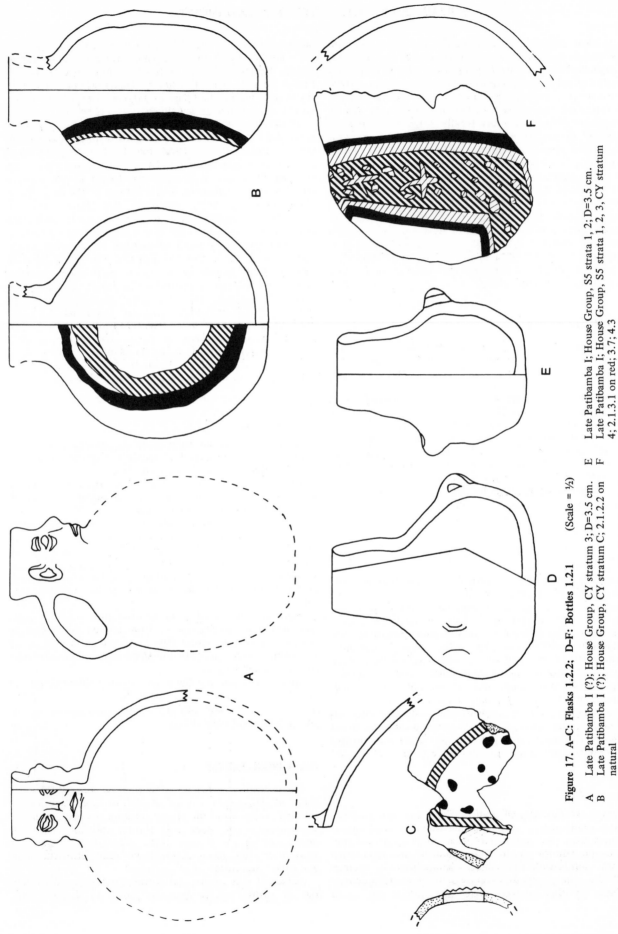

Figure 17. A–C: Flasks 1.2.2; D–F: Bottles 1.2.1 (Scale = ½)

A   Late Patibamba I (?); House Group, CY stratum 3; D=3.5 cm.
B   Late Patibamba I (?); House Group, CY stratum 2; 2.1.2.2 on natural
C   Middle Patibamba; North Unit, S11 stratum E; 2.1.3.1 on red
D   Late Patibamba I (?); House Group, CY stratum 3, CW stratum 4; D=3.5 cm.
E   Late Patibamba I; House Group, S5 strata 1, 2; D=3.5 cm.
F   Late Patibamba I; House Group, S5 strata 1, 2, 3, CY stratum 4; 2.1.3.1 on red; 3.7; 4.3

It is clear that flaring-neck jars are the most common utility vessels at Jargampata. Unfortunately, the information available for utility wares from other sites in Ayacucho is largely limited to descriptions of paste, finish, and surface color, making it useless for comparison. Certainly some of these forms are present at Wari (Bennett 1953: fig. 8H, J), but there are others which are totally outside the range of Jargampata shapes. It is equally clear that the jars with widely flared rims from hilltop sites which I (W. Isbell 1972) have termed the "CB" series are very different from those of Jargampata. The CB pottery is found on high elevation sites in the Pampas valley, and although insecurely dated it may represent a parallel and completely different ceramic tradition. It seems likely that careful investigation of utility pottery from sites around Ayacucho will reveal a number of distinct traditions which maintained their integrity on local sites. If such traditions can be defined, it may become possible to interpret the varied pottery found in Wari and other urban centers.

CLOSED FORMS   1.2

This general category, which includes vessels with constricted mouths or spouts, is less unified than others established for Jargampata pottery. Closed forms are always rare, never more than 3.5% of the vessels from a phase, and may not have been a particularly important component of the potter's ceramic inventory. Early Patibamba has the lowest frequency of closed forms and Illaura has the highest. These vessels may have been increasing in popularity at Jargampata very late in the Middle Patibamba Phase or in Late Patibamba I. If so, they may not have had such clearly defined rules for form and decoration as the jars and open bowls which constitute the largest percentage of the pottery throughout the occupation.

The subcategories of closed forms are bottles, flasks, and incurving bowls.

Bottles   1.2.1

There are no bottles identified in the ceramic samples selected for analysis. This may be a result of the rarity of the form or of the bias of samples taken mostly from the North Unit, since specimens do occur in the House Group (fig. 17D-F). They include coarsely finished examples with surfaces like utility pots (fig. 17E), plain, red-slipped specimens (fig. 17D), and others with painted decoration (fig. 17F). It would appear that bottles had several size modes, but all had subglobular bodies and rather broad-mouthed, slightly tapering spouts. Bases were generally flat, and two handles were set opposite one another or offset to one side in a horizontal or vertical position near the vessel shoulders. Although certainly not identical, the bottles from Ayapata are generally similar (Ravines 1968: figs. 35-40).

Flasks   1.2.2

Flasks have disk-shaped bodies. They have two circular, flattened sides with a seam uniting them. A small spout protrudes from the seam, and there may be a flattened bottom opposite the spout. Two modes of side seams with temporal implications have been distinguished by Menzel (1968: 76), and they have been recognized as subcategories of flasks in this analysis. The first, which has been numbered 1.2.2.1, is a flask with flattened side seam (fig. 17C; Menzel 1968: fig. 29). This form is characteristic of Middle Horizon 1B, but it is also found on conservative Epoch 2A specimens. The single fragmentary example from the Middle Patibamba Phase at Jargampata probably represents a conservative 2A specimen.

Flasks with tightly curved side seams have been numbered 1.2.2.2 and are later than those with flattened seams (Menzel 1968a: fig. 24; 1964: figs. 11, 19). They belong to progressive Middle Horizon 2A specimens and Epoch 2B samples. Only one such flask was found in the selected samples from Jargampata, and it belongs to the final Illaura Phase which probably postdates the Middle Horizon. However, two fragmentary examples from the House Group at Jargampata (fig. 17A, B) have tightly curved side seams. One example has painted decoration on a rather rough surface, while the second was slipped red but has a modeled face and strap handle on the spout. Both these examples came from the same stratum of the House Group, where they were associated with an exotic, imported vessel with skull motif (fig. 40E; plate 16D) and fragments of a large, hollow-tripod-support bowl (fig. 32A). Since these hollow supports do not appear in the Jargampata ceramic samples until Late Patibamba I, it seems likely that all of these vessel fragments belong to Middle Horizon 2B, although the stratigraphic associations from the House Group are subject to question.

Incurving Vessels   1.2.3

Incurving vessels are subglobular bowls with walls which have a convex curve and a constricted mouth (fig. 18). Some of the bowls might be referred to as neckless ollas or tecomates, although the wall angles at the rim are rarely more than -45° and have a mean of about -30°, which seems rather low for a neckless olla.

Few incurving vessels could be reconstructed, but there is a considerable range of variation in size. Bottoms were either curved to form a continuous spherical body or moderately flattened and united to the body by a continuous curve. Both plain and decorated bowls are found, and only one of the larger specimens has a handle (fig. 18L).

Paste and surface finish range from quite coarse to quite fine, and it is not atypical to find painted decoration on coarse examples or rather fine paste and surface finish on the plain bowls, especially the small ones, which probably served as drinking cups.

Incurving vessels are the most common closed forms but are still infrequent at Jargampata. They are least common in the first two phases and undergo a slight increase in the later phases, especially Illaura.

OPEN BOWL FORMS   1.3

Open bowl forms are the most popular generalized vessel shape at Jargampata. A total of 458, or more than half of the 895 vessels from the eleven selected samples, belong to this category. All vessels with flaring walls are defined as open bowl forms if they lack necks or other complex sections of a composite form. Bowls, cups, urns, tumblers, and other such forms are all included.

Generally the open bowl forms from Jargampata have flat or slightly curved bottoms joined to simple profile

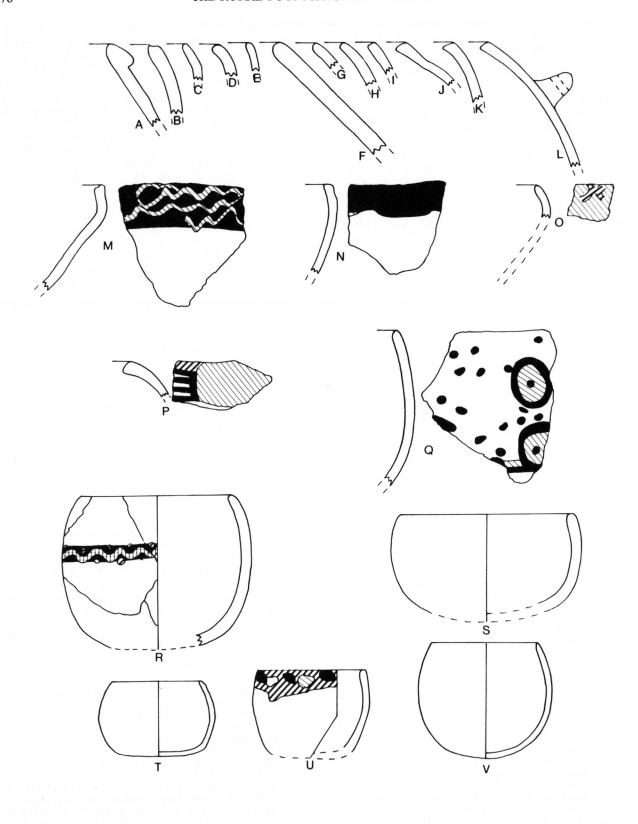

Fig. 18

vessel walls by a continuous curve. However, there are some forms with recurved wall profiles or sharp basal angles. Open bowl forms rarely have handles, but exceptions include oversize bowls and small lyre-shaped cups. Support modes include both hollow and solid tripods, ring bases, and solid pedestals. Subcategories of open bowl forms are plain bowls, decorated bowls, tripod bowls, ring-base bowls, pedestal bowls, lyre-shaped cups, and straight-sided cups.

It seems likely that all of the open bowl forms, except perhaps for oversize bowls, were designed to be serving vessels. The popularity of the category is interesting since it begins low in Early Patibamba, with these shapes accounting for only 45.8% of the vessels. There is a very gradual increase through the next three phases, which contain 54.9%, 55.3%, and 61.9%, respectively; but following the temporal hiatus which ends with the Illaura Phase, the frequency of open bowl forms has dropped to 39% of the vessels in the sample.

Plain Bowls   1.3.1

Bowls may be differentiated from cups in that bowls have mouth diameters about twice their depth while cups have heights roughly equal to their mouth diameters. Jargampata plain bowls generally have straight or incurving, convex wall profiles. An outcurving, concave profile is fairly common in the early phases, but disappears completely by Late Patibamba II except on oversize plain bowls. Bottoms are generally slightly curved to nearly flat and are united to the vessel walls by a continuous curve. By definition, plain bowls lack decoration, and there are no handles on plain bowls except for oversize examples. Bowls with special supports have been classified separately.

Plain bowls generally have a hard, orange paste with well-distributed fine antiplastic inclusions. The surfaces are coarsely polished and may be natural orange to brown or slipped red. Two subcategories of plain bowls have been distinguished on the basis of size—regular-size and oversize plain bowls. A separate category was set up for all miniature vessels, but the frequency of miniature plain bowls indicates that three size modes probably existed.

Plain bowls do not vary greatly in frequency through the sequence at Jargampata. Their highest frequency is 18.2% in Early Patibamba, from which they decline only slightly in subsequent phases.

Regular-Size Plain Bowls   1.3.1.1

Regular-size plain bowls account for most of the plain bowls. They range in mouth diameter from 12 cm. to 23 cm., but most have diameters between 15 cm. and 18 cm., a measurement which changes only slightly throughout the occupation (fig. 19A-BG). It would appear that in Early Patibamba there existed only a single, highly variable shape mode for regular-size plain bowls. However, throughout the sequence at Jargampata there is a progressive development of a bimodality within the range of variation. By the Illaura Phase there were two shapes which could be distinguished, although it is difficult to say whether the separation was accomplished. One plain bowl form generally has straight, flaring walls with a tight basal curve and large mouth diameter (fig. 19F, N, R, U, W), while the second is smaller and has more vertical walls and an open curve uniting the walls and base (fig. 19AT-AZ). It is clear that these shapes reflect a distinction between interior- and exterior-decorated bowls, whose shapes also become more contrastive throughout the sequence. The former shape relates to interior-decorated bowls, while the latter is similar to exterior-decorated bowls. However, these two bowl forms may not be limited to Jargampata and may have a considerable time depth in the Ayacucho area. Menzel (1968a: figs. 1, 2a) has reconstructed two Epoch 1A bowl forms. One, from the site of Acuchimay, clearly relates to Jargampata interior-decorated bowl forms, and the other, from the site of Chakipampa, or Conchopata, is very similar to the exterior-decorated bowls.

The frequency of regular-size plain bowls remains relatively constant throughout the sequence at Jargampata.

Oversize Plain Bowls   1.3.1.2

Oversize plain bowls are similar to regular-size examples in shape, paste, and other attributes, but are larger and range in mouth diameter from 24 cm. to 40 cm. However, most specimens fall between 24 cm. and 26 cm. (figs. 19BH-BR, 20). These large vessels are also frequent recipients of a pair of horizontal strap handles placed a centimeter or two below the rim (figs. 19 BP, 20A, B).

The frequency of oversize bowls is low, making it difficult to distinguish changes in form. However, fairly complete examples from the House Group suggest that two shape modes may have existed and that they were

---

Figure 18. Incurving Vessels 1.2.3   (Scale = ½)

A   Late Patibamba II; North Unit, plaza floor; D=9 cm.
B   Early Patibamba; E2 x S13 stratum 9; D=20 cm.
C   Late Patibamba I; North Unit, E5 x S11-12 stratum 4; D=36 cm.
D   Late Patibamba II; North Unit, S11 stratum D; D=13 cm.
E   Late Patibamba I; North Unit, S11 stratum D1; D=17 cm.
F   Early Patibamba; E3 x S13-15 stratum 4; D=26 cm.
G   Illaura; North Unit, S11 stratum C; D=12 cm.
H   Illaura; North Unit, S11 stratum C1; D=30 cm.
I   Late Patibamba I; North Unit, S10 stratum D1; D=18 cm.
J   Illaura; North Unit, S10 stratum C; D=25 cm.
K   Late Patibamba I; North Unit, S10 stratum D1; D=12 cm.
L   Late Patibamba I; South Unit, S7 strata 2, 3, 4; D=22 cm.
M   Illaura; North Unit, S11 stratum C; D=18 cm.; 2.1.2.5 on natural; 3.5.1.4; 4.5.3.2

N   Late Patibamba II; North Unit, plaza floor; D=12 cm.; 2.1.2.5 on natural; 3.5.1.4
O   Late Patibamba I; North Unit, S11 stratum D1; D=15 cm.; 2.1.2.1 on natural (?); 3.12
P   Middle Patibamba (?); House Group, CY stratum 5; D=18 cm.; 2.1.3.1 on natural
Q   Middle Patibamba (?); House Group, CW stratum 5 ; D=9 cm.; 2.1.2.5 on red; 4.6, 4.13.1
R   Illaura (?); North Unit, S11 strata C1, E; D=9 cm.; 2.1.3.9 on red; 3.5.1.5; 4.5.1.2
S   Late Patibamba I (?); House Group, CW strata 4, 6; D=9.5 cm.
T   Late Patibamba I (?); House Group, CX stratum 4; D=5 cm.
U·   Late Patibamba I or II; House Group, CW strata 2, 4, CX stratum 3, S1 strata 1, 2; D=6 cm.; 2.1.3.1 on natural; 3.5.2
V   Late Patibamba I; House Group, CW stratum 4; D=6 cm.

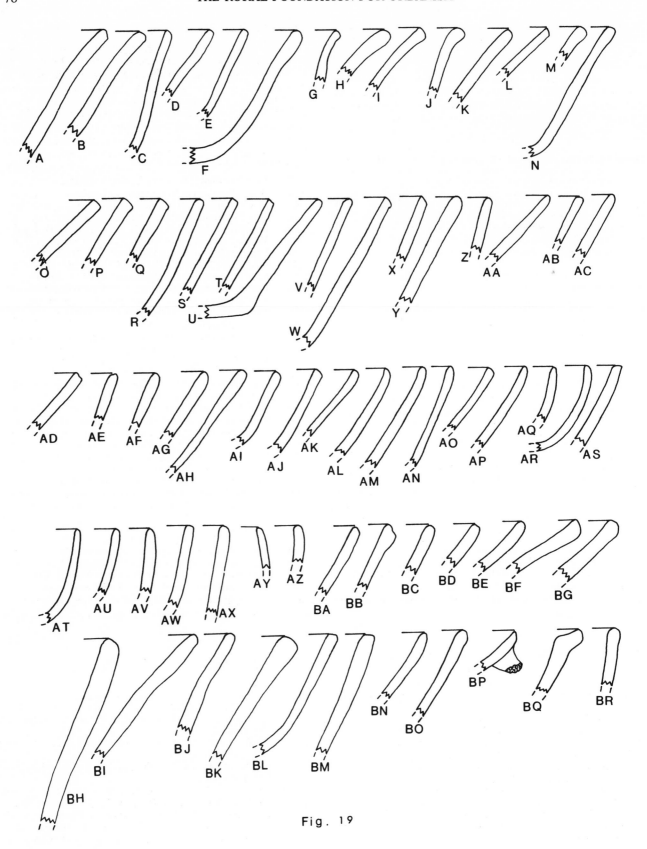

Fig. 19

Figure 19. A–BG: Plain Bowls, Regular Size 1.3.1.1; BH–BR: Plain Bowls, Oversize 1.3.1.2   (Scale = ½)

A	Late Patibamba I; North Unit, S10 stratum D1.
B	Late Patibamba I; North Unit, E5 x S10 stratum 4; D=16 cm.
C	Late Patibamba I; North Unit, E6 x S9 stratum 4b; D=19 cm.
D	Late Patibamba I; North Unit, E6 x S10 stratum 4b; D=18 cm.
E	Middle Patibamba; North Unit, S11 stratum E; D=14 cm.
F	Late Patibamba I; North Unit, E6 x S10 stratum 4b; D=17 cm.
G	Late Patibamba I; North Unit, S10 stratum D1; D=19 cm.
H	Early Patibamba; E2 x S15 stratum 9; D=20 cm.
I	Late Patibamba I; North Unit, S11 stratum D1; D=19 cm.
J	Late Patibamba I; South Unit, S7 stratum 4; D=17 cm.
K	Early Patibamba; E2 x S15 stratum 9; D=18 cm.
L	Early Patibamba; E2 x S15 stratum 7
M	Late Patibamba II; North Unit, plaza floor; D=18 cm.
N	Middle Patibamba; North Unit, S10 stratum E; D=18 cm.
O	Early Patibamba; E2 x S15 stratum 9; D=22 cm.
P	Late Patibamba I; North Unit, S11 stratum D1; D=18 cm.
Q	Late Patibamba II; North Unit, S11 stratum D; D=17 cm.
R	Late Patibamba I; South Unit, S7 stratum 4; D=20 cm.
S	Middle Patibamba; North Unit, S11 stratum E; D=17 cm.
T	Early Patibamba; E2 x S15 stratum 9; D=16 cm.
U	Illaura; North Unit, S11 stratum C; D=19 cm.
V	Early Patibamba; E2 x S14 stratum 9; D=21 cm.
W	Late Patibamba I; South Unit, S7 stratum 4; D=18 cm.
X	Early Patibamba; E2 x S15 stratum 7; D=19 cm.
Y	Middle Patibamba; North Unit, S11 stratum E; D=12 cm.
Z	Early Patibamba; E3 x S13-15 stratum 7; D=18 cm.
AA	Late Patibamba I; North Unit, S11 stratum D1; D=13 cm.
AB	Illaura; North Unit, S11 stratum C; D=18 cm.
AC	Late Patibamba II; North Unit, S11 stratum D; D=20 cm.
AD	Middle Patibamba; North Unit, S11 stratum E; D=16 cm.
AE	Illaura; North Unit, S11 stratum C1; D=11 cm.
AF	Late Patibamba II; North Unit, S10 stratum D; D=18 cm.
AG	Illaura; North Unit, S10 stratum C; D=14 cm.
AH	Late Patibamba II; North Unit, E5 x S10 stratum 3; D=20 cm.

AI	Early Patibamba; E2 x S13 stratum 9; D=16 cm.
AJ	Illaura; North Unit, S11 stratum C; D=13 cm.
AK	Late Patibamba I; North Unit, S11 stratum D1; D=11 cm.
AL	Late Patibamba II; North Unit, plaza floor; D=20 cm.
AM	Late Patibamba II; North Unit, S11 stratum D; D=20 cm.
AN	Middle Patibamba; North Unit, S10 stratum E; D=15 cm.
AO	Early Patibamba; E3 x S13-15 stratum 9; D=18 cm.
AP	Illaura; North Unit, S10 stratum C; D=18 cm.
AQ	Early Patibamba; E2 x S14 stratum 9; D=16 cm.
AR	Late Patibamba I; North Unit, S10 stratum D1; D=15 cm.
AS	Late Patibamba II; North Unit, plaza floor, D=16 cm.
AT	Illaura; North Unit, S11 stratum C1; D=11 cm.
AU	Early Patibamba; E2 x S15 stratum 7; D=12 cm.
AV	Late Patibamba I; North Unit, E5 x S10 stratum 4; D=16 cm.
AW	Late Patibamba I; North Unit, S10 stratum D1; D=13 cm.
AX	Early Patibamba; E2 x S15 stratum 9; D=22 cm.
AY	Late Patibamba II; North Unit, S11 stratum D; D=12 cm.
AZ	Late Patibamba I; South Unit, S7 stratum 4; D=17 cm.
BA	Early Patibamba; E3 x S13 stratum 9; D=18 cm.
BB	Late Patibamba I; North Unit, E5 x S10 stratum 4; D=20 cm.
BC	Late Patibamba II; North Unit, S11 stratum D; D=18 cm.
BD	Illaura; North Unit, S11 stratum C1; D=15 cm.
BE	Late Patibamba I; North Unit, E5 x S9 stratum 4; D=20 cm.
BF	Early Patibamba; E3 x S13-15 stratum 9; D=23 cm.
BG	Early Patibamba; E2 x S14 stratum 5; D=20 cm.
BH	Early Patibamba; E2 x S14 stratum 9; D=40 cm.
BI	Late Patibamba I; North Unit, S11 stratum D1; D=26 cm.
BJ	Early Patibamba; E2 x S15 stratum 5; D=26 cm.
BK	Early Patibamba; E2 x S15 stratum 9; D=29 cm.
BL	Late Patibamba I; North Unit, E6 x S9 stratum 4b; D=24 cm.
BM	Late Patibamba II; North Unit, E5 x S9 stratum 3; D=32 cm.
BN	Late Patibamba II; North Unit, plaza floor; D=24 cm.
BO	Late Patibamba II; North Unit, S11 stratum D; D=24 cm.
BP	Early Patibamba; E3 x S13-15 stratum 9; D=26 cm.
BQ	Late Patibamba I; North Unit, E6 x S9 stratum 4b; D=28 cm.
BR	Early Patibamba; E3 x S13-15 stratum 9; D=24 cm.

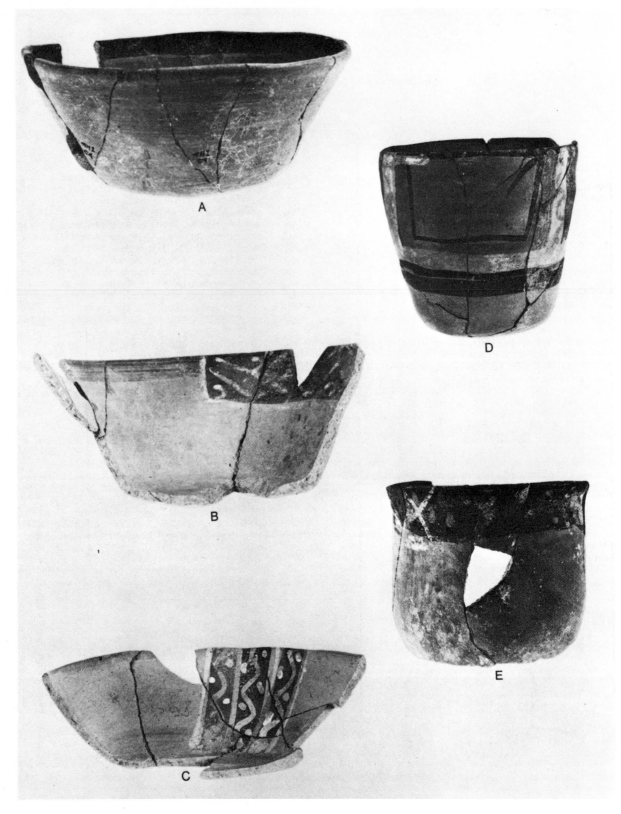

Plate 12. Open Bowl Forms 1.3   (Scale = ½)

A   Interior-Decorated Bowl; 1.3.2.1; Figure 24D
B   Interior-Decorated Bowl; 1.3.2.1; Figure 27A
C   Interior-Decorated Bowl; 1.3.2.1; Figure 22J

D   Straight-Sided Cup; 1.3.7; Figure 35 A1-A2
E   Lyre-Shaped Cup; 1.3.6; Figure 35F

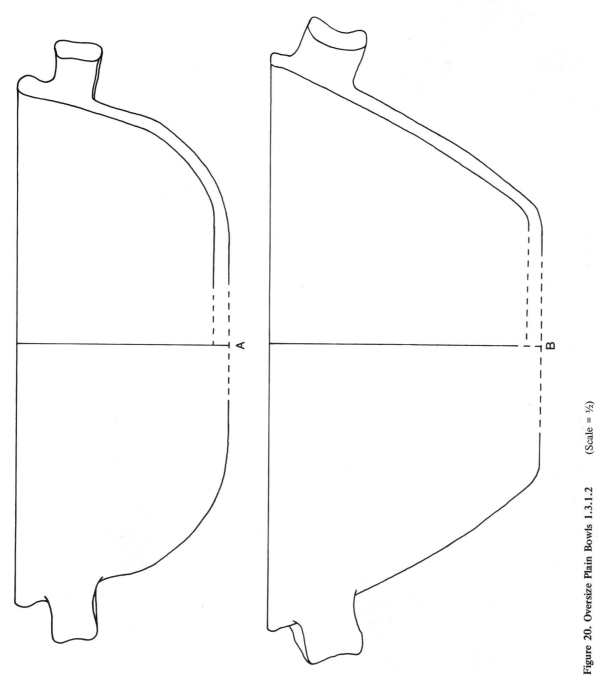

Figure 20. Oversize Plain Bowls 1.3.1.2   (Scale = ½)

A   Middle Patibamba or Late Patibamba I (?); House Group, CW strata 3, 4, 6; D=29 cm.

B   Middle Patibamba or Late Patibamba I (?); House Group, CW strata 3, 4, 6, S6 strata 6, 7; D=31 cm.

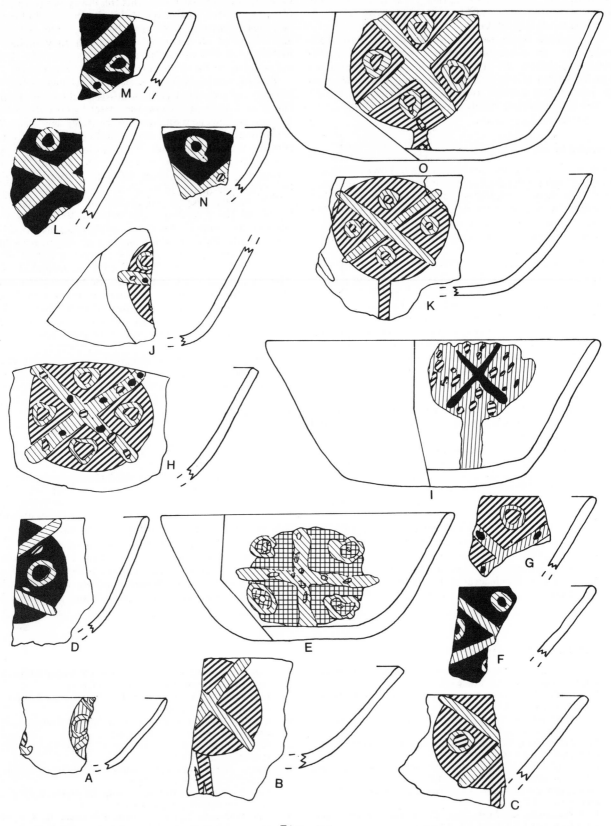

Fig. 21

essentially the same found among plain bowls and the interior-decorated (fig. 20B) contrasted with exterior-decorated bowls (fig. 20A).

The oversize bowls were more common in Early Patibamba than in subsequent phases, and they probably disappeared before the Illaura Phase. A single specimen from the Illaura sample was probably redeposited. It seems that plain bowls reduced to a single size mode with both oversize and miniature bowls eliminated by the time of the reoccupation of Jargampata.

Decorated Bowls   1.3.2

Decorated bowls are similar to plain bowls in shape, paste, and surface finish, but differ from them in that they more frequently receive a red slip and all have painted decoration. As for plain bowls, there is a regular-size mode, an oversize mode, and also a miniature size, although they have been classified with miniature vessels for seriational purposes.

A very sharp distinction exists between bowls with interior painted decoration and those with exterior painted decoration. Of a total of 246 decorated bowls from the five phases at Jargampata, only two have both interior and exterior decoration. All others are painted on one surface only. The distinction between the two vessel classes is made sharper by the presence of design themes and shape features such as tripod tab supports which are exclusively associated with one or the other class. Consequently, three subcategories of decorated bowls have been distinguished: interior-decorated bowls, exterior-decorated bowls, and a residual group of bowls with both interior and exterior painting. In the first two subgroups, there are both regular-size and oversize subdivisions.

The frequency of all decorated bowls is a rather low 21.4% in Early Patibamba but is higher in the following three phases with a peak in Late Patibamba II of 40.1%. However, in the Illaura Phase reoccupation the frequency drops to only 20.3%, and oversize as well as miniature modes are absent.

The frequency of interior- and exterior-decorated bowls shifts considerably during the occupation, and much of the gain in popularity experienced by decorated bowls following Early Patibamba can be attributed to the rise in frequency of exterior-decorated bowls. While bowls with exterior decoration account for only 12.2% of the Early Patibamba decorated bowls, this frequency jumps to 33.3% of the decorated bowls from Middle Patibamba. In the next two phases, exterior-decorated bowls account for 41.4% and 32.8% of all decorated bowls, and they maintain a frequency of 40% of the Illaura Phase in spite of a decline in frequency of the entire category of decorated bowls.

In Early Patibamba it is difficult to distinguish between interior- and exterior-decorated bowls on the basis of shape, but in each successive phase the vessel forms become more distinct. As time goes on, interior-decorated specimens have larger mouths, greater wall angles, and tightly curved unions between the base and walls. Exterior-decorated bowls have smaller diameters, more vertical walls, and open curves uniting base and wall. These differences are obvious from the statistics presented in the phase descriptions.

The sudden rise in popularity of exterior-decorated bowls and the progressive differentiation in form between interior- and exterior-decorated groups suggest that following Early Patibamba the potters at Jargampata came under the strong influence of a ceramic tradition which already had a clearly defined exterior-decorated bowl category. The sudden change in the use of decorative colors and the introduction of new design themes in Middle Patibamba also support the interpretation that a strong external influence began with this phase. It is interesting that the hypothesized external influence made itself felt immediately in color usage and design themes and in the popularity of vessel shape categories but only very gradually modified the shape categories themselves. I suspect this indicates a continuity of local potters and potting tradition in spite of the introduction of new attributes and activities from elsewhere.

Interior-Decorated Bowls   1.3.2.1

Interior-decorated bowls have painted decoration on unpigmented, natural light or light red-slipped surface on the inside of the vessel, and during the first four phases sometimes on the rim as well (figs. 21-27E). These bowls range in size from an 11 cm. to a 36 cm. mouth diameter. This includes both regular-size and oversize groups and miniature bowls with interior decoration as well.

The decorative colors used on these bowls are white, dark red, black, gray, orange, yellow, brown, light red, and a distinct crusty black. However, bowls with more than four colors are extremely rare, and Illaura specimens lack

Figure 21. Interior-Decorated Bowls 1.3.2.1   (Scale = ½)

A   Middle Patibamba; North Unit, S10 stratum E; D=14 cm.; 2.1.3.2 on natural; 3.1.2.1; 4.4.1.1

B   Late Patibamba I; North Unit, E5 x S10 stratum 4; D=20 cm.; 2.1.2.1 on red; 3.1.2, 3.1.4

C   Late Patibamba I; North Unit, S11 stratum D1; D=14 cm.; 2.1.2.1 on red; 3.1.2.1, 3.1.4; 4.4.1.1

D   Late Patibamba I; South Unit, S7 stratum 4; D=23 cm.; 2.1.3.1 on natural; 3.1.2.4; 4.4.1.1

E   Late Patibamba I; South Unit, S7 strata 3, 4; D=16 cm.; 2.1.2.7 on natural; 3.1.3.1, 3.1.4; 4.6

F   Late Patibamba II; North Unit, plaza floor; D=16 cm.; 2.1.3.1 on natural; 3.1.2.4; 4.4.1.1

G   Late Patibamba II; North Unit, S11 stratum D; D=17 cm.; 2.1.3.8 on red; 3.1.2.2; 4.4.1.1, 4.13.4

H   Late Patibamba II; North Unit, E5 x S11-12 stratum 4; D=17 cm.; 2.1.3.1 on natural; 3.1.2.2; 4.13.4

I   Late Patibamba I or II; House Group, CY feature E1-6e; D=18 cm.; 2.1.3.8 on red; 3.1.2.3, 3.1.4; 4.13.1

J   Late Patibamba II; North Unit, E5 x S10 stratum 2; 2.1.3.1 on natural; 3.1.2.2; 4.13.4

K   Late Patibamba I or II; House Group, CY stratum 3; D=17 cm.; 2.1.2.1 on red; 3.1.2.1; 4.4.1.1

L   Illaura; North Unit, S11 stratum C; D=22 cm.; 2.1.2.5 on natural; 3.1.2.1; 4.4.1.1

M   Illaura; North Unit, S11 stratum C1; D=15 cm.; 2.1.2.5 on natural; 3.1.2.2; 4.4.1.1, 4.13.4

N   Late Patibamba I or II; House Group, S6 stratum 6; D=17 cm.; 2.1.3.1 on natural; 3.1.2.2; 4.4.1.1, 4.13.4

O   Late Patibamba II; House Group, CW strata 3a, 4, 5; D=20 cm.; 2.1.3.5 on red; 3.1.2.2, 3.1.4.1; 4.4.1.1, 4.13.4

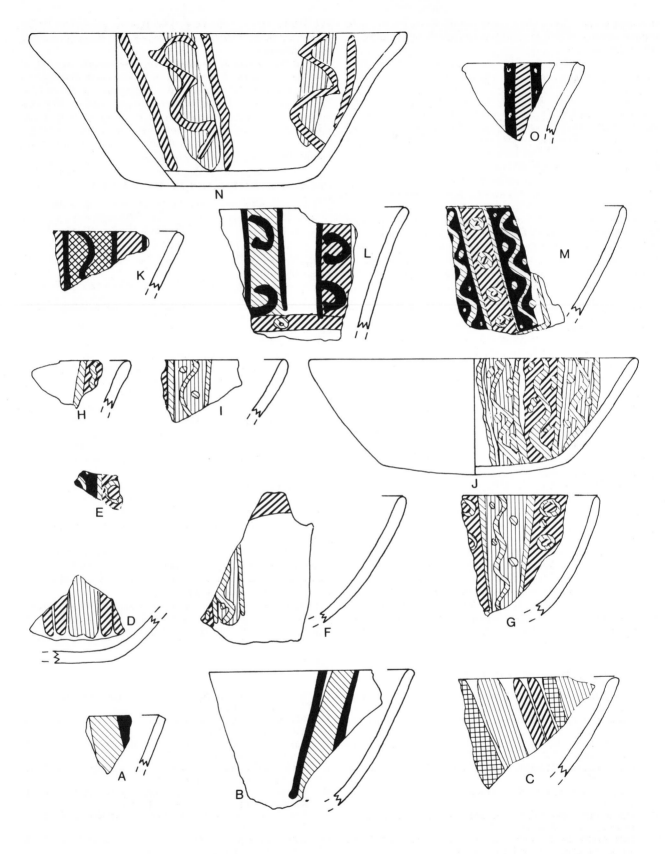

Fig. 22

combinations of more than three colors. Each color has its unique history which is reported in the phase descriptions which follow.

Regular-Size Interior-Decorated Bowls   1.3.2.1.1

Regular-size interior-decorated bowls range in mouth diameter from 11 cm. to 23 cm., but have a mode of 18 cm. through the first three phases and modes of 16 cm. and 17 cm. in the final two phases respectively. The wall angles range from $5°$ to $50°$, but have a mode of $30°$ for all phases except Early Patibamba, where these bowls have wall angles with a mode of $25°$. The vessel walls are generally straight or slightly convex, but outcurving, concave walls occur in low frequencies through the first three phases. Lips are generally rounded, exterior-curved, or flattened, but interior curves become more frequent in the Illaura Phase. Most rims are unmodified, but the thickened variants E1, F, and D are fairly frequent in the first three phases while the thinned form C replaces the thickened variants in Late Patibamba II and Illaura (fig. 9).

The bowls range in height from 6 cm. to 9 cm., but develop from a range of 6 cm. to 7 cm. in Early Patibamba to a range of 6 cm. to 9 cm. in Late Patibamba I. From this peak, they decline in size to 5.5 cm. to 8.5 cm. in Late Patibamba II, and to 5.5 cm. to 7.5 cm. in Illaura.

Design themes in Early Patibamba are generally single, light-colored horizontal bands (fig. 23A, B); vertical bands in isolation or groups (fig. 22A, E); large panels with geometric filler elements (fig. 26A); a wing design (fig. 25G); and, rarely, representational figures (fig. 25B). In Middle Patibamba, the single-horizontal-band theme frequently becomes two parallel bands, black over red (fig. 24C), and this theme is maintained through the remainder of the sequence (fig. 24D-H). Another very important theme which appears in Middle Patibamba for the first time and continues through the remainder of the sequence is a colored disk with Saint Andrew's cross (fig. 21A). These disks were probably arranged so that four disks occupied the interior bowl walls in opposed pairs. The theme is represented by only a single example in Middle Patibamba, but it becomes a varied and popular local theme (fig. 21A-O) and was almost surely introduced on imported ceramics during Middle Patibamba (fig. 39L; plate 17E).

By Late Patibamba I, the wing-design theme and representational figures have disappeared and single-band themes are almost exclusively dark red, with light colors like white very rarely used. Panels with geometric fillers continue, as do vertical-band themes and horizontal-band arrangements.

Late Patibamba II decoration is very similar to that of the previous phase. Innovations include a single-black-band theme and panels divided into horizontal sections (fig. 26F-I; plate 12D). Illaura ceramics do not indicate any new themes, but show a restriction of color usage within old design themes like the colored disk and Saint Andrew's cross, horizontal- and vertical-band themes, and the apparent disappearance of panel themes.

Oversize Interior-Decorated Bowls   1.3.2.1.2

Oversize interior-decorated bowls range in mouth diameter from 24 cm. to 36 cm., and although they are too infrequent in each phase to establish modes, 24 cm. and 26 cm. are the modes for the entire category. The wall angles range between $10°$ and $50°$, but the mode for the entire category is $35°$.

The wall profile form is most varied in Early Patibamba with straight; incurving, convex; and outcurving, concave modes represented. By Late Patibamba I the outcurving, concave mode is no longer found. It might be that the absence is due to the small sample, but the outcurving wall profile also disappears from regular-size bowls by Late Patibamba II and is preserved only on large, plain, tripod-support bowls. The most common lip treatment is rounded, while rims may be unmodified, or thickened in conformity with modes D, E, or E1 (fig. 9), though there is no obvious temporal difference. None of these vessels could be completely reconstructed, but they were 5 cm. or 6 cm. high, or perhaps taller. The bases were probably flat or slightly curved. Unlike the oversize plain bowls, there is no evidence for handles.

Decoration themes, limited to vessel interiors, are generally similar to those of regular-size bowls with banded designs (fig. 23C), panel designs (fig. 26E), and others. One uncommon specimen, however, has a dark red wavy line with dots on an unmodified clay surface (fig. 24A). This paint was quite eroded, and it is likely that more heavily eroded colors, and especially light colors like white or gray, might be overlooked, resulting in the classification of decorated specimens as plain bowls.

Oversize decorated bowls are very uncommon and never account for more than 1.6% of a phase sample. These vessels are absent from the small Middle Patibamba sample,

---

Figure 22. Interior-Decorated Bowls 1.3.2.1   (Scale = ½)

A   Early Patibamba; E2 x S15 stratum 9; D=18 cm.; 2.1.2.5 on red; 3.2.2

B   Middle Patibamba; North Unit, S11 stratum E; D=18 cm.; 2.1.2.5 on red; 3.2.1

C   Late Patibamba II; North Unit, plaza floor; D=19 cm.; 2.1.3.14 on red-orange; 3.2.2

D   Late Patibamba II; North Unit, plaza floor; 2.1.2.3 on natural; 3.2.2

E   Early Patibamba; E2 x S15 stratum 9; 2.1.3.1; 3.2.2; 4.4.1.3, 4.5.4.1

F   Middle Patibamba; North Unit, S10 stratum E, S11 stratum D; D=16 cm.; 2.1.3.2 on red; 3.2.2, 3.5.1.2; 4.5.4.1

G   Late Patibamba I; North Unit, S10 stratum D1; D=17 cm.; 2.1.3.2 on natural; 3.2.2; 4.4.1.3, 4.5.4.1

H   Late Patibamba II; North Unit, S11 stratum D; D=20 cm.; 2.1.2.1 on natural; 3.2 (?); 4.5.4

I   Late Patibamba II; North Unit, S11 stratum D; D=17 cm.; 2.1.3.2; 3.2.2; 4.5.4.1

J   Illaura; North Unit, S11 stratum C; D=17 cm.; 2.1.3.2 on natural; 3.2.2; 4.5.4.1

K   Early Patibamba (?); House Group, S4 stratum 1; D=22 cm.; 2.1.3.7 on natural; 3.2.2; 4.5.4

L   Early Patibamba (?); House Group, CY stratum 5d; D=22 cm.; 2.1.3.1 on natural; 3.2.2; 4.2, 4.4.1

M   Middle Patibamba (?); House Group, S4 stratum 5; D=18 cm.; 2.1.2.3 on natural; 3.2.2; 4.4.1.3, 4.5.4.1

N   Late Patibamba II (?); House Group, CZ stratum 5; D=20 cm.; 2.1.2.3 on natural; 3.2.3; 4.5.4

O   Early Patibamba (?); House Group, CX stratum 1; D=23 cm.; 2.1.3.1 on natural; 3.2.3 (?); 4.13.4

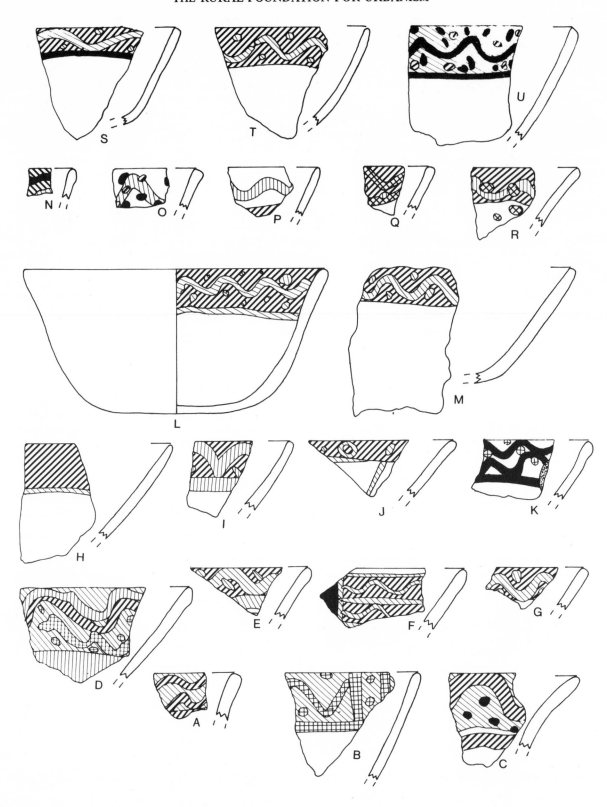

Fig. 23

Figure 23. Interior-Decorated Bowls 1.3.2.1   (Scale = ½)

A   Early Patibamba; E2 x S15 stratum 9; D=18 cm.; 2.1.2.1 on dark red slip; 3.5.1.1; 4.5.2

B   Early Patibamba; E2 x S15 stratum 9; D=16 cm.; 2.1.2.7 on red; 3.5.1.1.1; 4.5.1.1

C   Early Patibamba; E2 x S14 stratum 9; D=32 cm.; 2.1.3.1 on red; 3.5.1.1; 4.5.1.2

D   Middle Patibamba; North Unit, S11 stratum E; D=23 cm.; 2.1.4.5; 3.5.1.1; 4.5.3.1

E   Middle Patibamba; North Unit, S10 stratum E; D=18 cm.; 2.1.2.1 on red; 3.5.1.2; 4.5.2.1

F   Middle Patibamba; North Unit, S11 stratum E; D=17 cm.; 2.1.3.1; 3.5.1.2; 4.5.1

G   Middle Patibamba; North Unit, S11 stratum E; D=18 cm.; 2.1.2.1 on natural; 3.5.1.2; 4.5.1.1

H   Late Patibamba I; North Unit, E6 x S10 stratum 4b; D=22 cm.; 2.1.2.1 on natural; 3.5.1.2

I   Late Patibamba I; South Unit, S7 stratum 4; D=14 cm.; 2.1.2.3; 3.5.1.2; 4.5.1.1

J   Late Patibamba I; North Unit, S10 stratum D1; D=18 cm.; 2.1.2.1 on natural; 3.5.1.2; 4.4.2

K   Late Patibamba I; North Unit, S10 stratum D1; D=17 cm.; 2.1.2.11 on natural; 3.5.1.3; 4.5.2.1

L   Late Patibamba I; South Unit, S7 stratum 4; D=19 cm.; 2.1.2.1 on natural; 3.5.1.2; 4.5.1.1

M   Late Patibamba II; North Unit, S11 stratum D; D=26 cm.; 2.1.2.1 on red; 3.5.1.2; 4.5.1.1

N   Late Patibamba II; North Unit, S11 stratum D; D=?; 2.1.2.1; 4.5.2

O   Late Patibamba II; North Unit, S11 stratum D; D=17 cm.; 2.1.3.1 on red; 4.5.1.2

P   Illaura; North Unit, S10 stratum C; D=18 cm.; 2.1.2.3 on natural; 4.5.1

Q   Illaura; North Unit, S11 stratum C1; D=17 cm.; 2.1.3.13 on red; 3.5.1.2; 4.5.2.1

R   Late Patibamba I (?); House Group, CW stratum 5; D=15 cm.; 2.1.3.13 on natural; 3.5.1.2; 4.5.1.2

S   Middle Patibamba (?); House Group, CX stratum 1; D=14 cm.; 2.1.3.1 on natural; 3.5.1.2; 4.5.1.1

T   Late Patibamba I or II; House Group, CX stratum 4; D=16 cm.; 2.1.2.1 on red; 3.5.1.2; 4.5.1.1

U   Early Patibamba (?); House Group, CX stratum 5; D=16 cm.; 2.1.3.1 on natural; 3.5.1.1; 4.5.1.2

Figure 24. Interior-Decorated Bowls 1.3.2.1   (Scale = ½)

A   Early Patibamba; E2 x S15 stratum 9; D=36 cm.; 2.1.1.1 on natural; 3.8.1

B   Late Patibamba I; North Unit, E6 x S10 stratum 4b; D=20 cm.; 2.1.2.2 on natural; 3.8.1 (?)

C   Middle Patibamba; North Unit, S10 stratum E; D=14 cm.; 2.1.4.1; 3.5.2.3; 4.5.1, 4.5.1.1

D   Late Patibamba I; South Unit, S7 stratum 4; D=19 cm.; 2.1.3.1 on red; 3.5.2.3; 4.5.1.1

E   Late Patibamba II; North Unit, S10 and S11 stratum D; D=16 cm.; 2.1.3.1 on red; 3.5.2.3; 4.5.1.1

F   Late Patibamba II; North Unit, E5 x S10 stratum 2; D=21 cm.; 2.1.3.1; 3.5.2.3; 4.5.1 (?)

G   Late Patibamba I or II (?); House Group, CW strata 3, 4; D=17 cm.; 2.1.3.1 on natural; 3.5.2.3; 4.5.1.1

H   Illaura; North Unit, S10 and 11 strata C, C1; D=16 cm.; 2.1.3.1 on red; 3.5.2.3; 4.5.1, 4.5.1.1

I   Illaura; North Unit, S11 stratum C1; D=14 cm.; 2.1.3.5; 3.5.2.6; 4.5.1, 4.5.1.1

J   Middle Patibamba (?); House Group, CY strata 5, 3c; D=19 cm.; 2.1.3.1 on natural; 3.5.2; 4.5.1.2

K   Late Patibamba I or II; House Group, CY stratum 4; D=16 cm.; 2.1.2.2 on natural; 3.5.2.1

L   Early Patibamba; E3 x S13-15 stratum 9; D=17 cm.; 2.1.3.10 on natural; 3.2.4; 4.9, 4.13.1

M   Early Patibamba (?); House Group, S4 stratum 2; D=20 cm.; 2.1.4.1; 3.2.4 and/or 3.5.1.1.1; 4.9, 4.13.1

N   Early Patibamba (?); House Group, CX stratum 2; D=22 cm.; 2.1.3.8 on red; 3.5.1.1.1 with gray; 4.9, 4.13.1

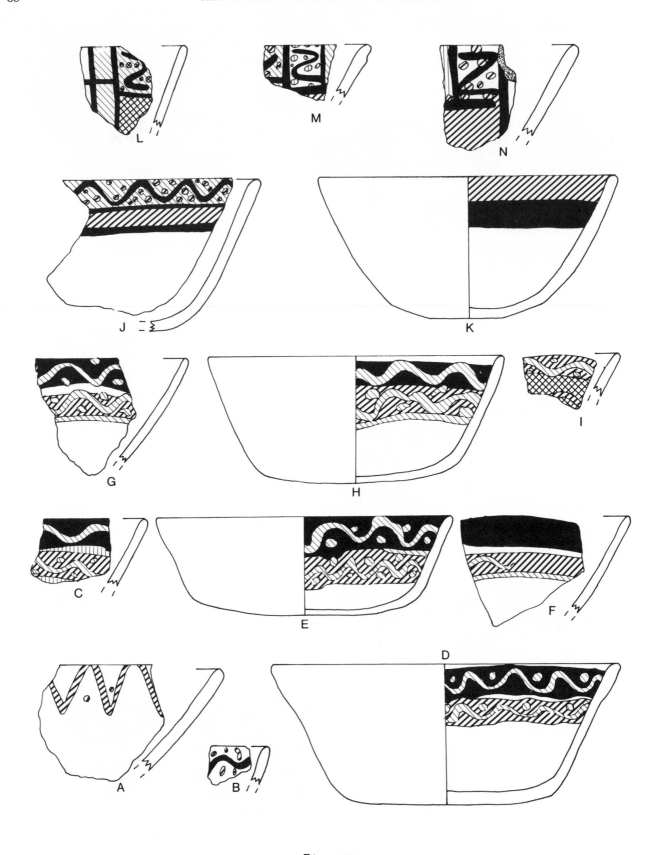

Fig. 24

Plate 13. Interior-Decorated Bowls 1.3.2.1   (Scale = ½)

A1-A2	Figure 21I	C	Figure 24H
B	Figure 21E	D	Figure 26F

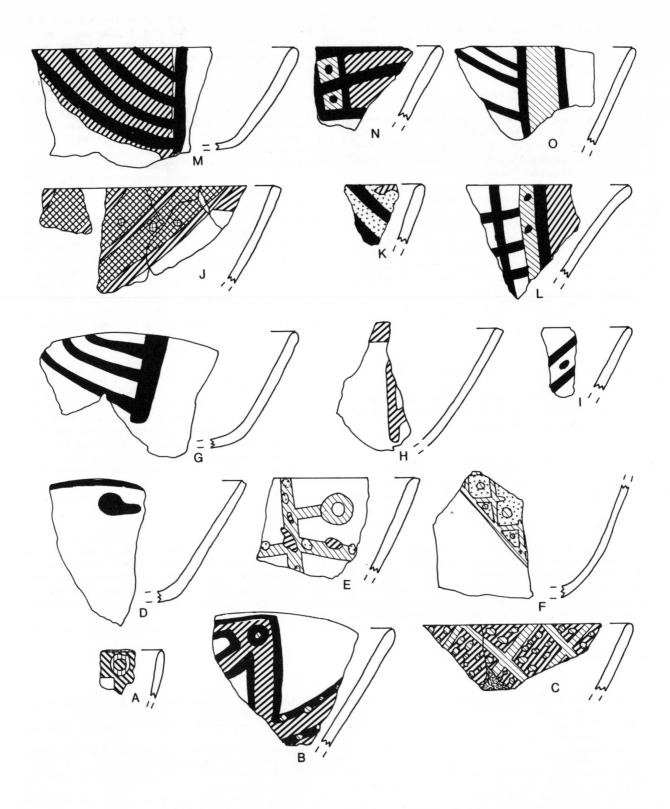

Fig. 25

but this may be due to sample error or the low frequency itself. The Illaura Phase also lacks oversize decorated bowls, and since only a single oversize plain bowl—which appears to be redeposited—was found with the sample, it is likely that the Illaura Phase completely lacks oversize bowls.

Exterior-Decorated Bowls 1.3.2.2

Exterior-decorated bowls have painted decoration on their exterior surface. The paint may be applied to a natural light clay surface or on a thin red slip (figs. 28, 29, 30B-M). In the first four phases, the rim may also be intentionally decorated, but not in the final Illaura Phase.

These bowls range in mouth diameter from 10 cm. to 27 cm. and so include both oversize and regular-size examples. However, the single oversize specimen is unique among the samples, and there are no exterior-decorated miniature bowls represented. The decorative colors employed are the same used on interior-decorated bowls, and, as is the case with the interior designs, combinations of more than four colors are rare in the first four phases while Illaura Phase bowls lack combinations of more than three colors.

As pointed out in the discussion of decorated bowls, exterior-decorated bowls are rare in Early Patibamba. There are only five examples, which account for 2.6% of the phase sample. However, the frequency of this vessel class rises to 10.8% in Middle Patibamba and continues to increase slightly in the following two phases. In Illaura, the frequency drops to 8.1%, but this reflects a decrease in popularity of all bowl forms, and the ratio between interior- and exterior-decorated bowls remains more or less constant following Early Patibamba.

Regular-Size Exterior-Decorated Bowls 1.3.2.2.1

Regular-size exterior-decorated bowls range in mouth diameter from 10 cm. to 22 cm. In Early Patibamba, these bowls are very similar to regular-size interior-decorated examples, but they proceed to differentiate from them in mouth diameter. The sample of exterior-decorated bowls from the Early Patibamba Phase is too small to provide a mode, but the mean mouth diameter of 17.3 cm. compares with a mean of 17.7 cm. for regular-size interior-decorated bowls of the same phase. The Middle Patibamba sample is also too small for a clear mode, but the mean of the more popular exterior-decorated bowls is 14 cm., compared with

17.4 cm. for regular-size interior-decorated bowls. In Late Patibamba I, the mean for the regular-size exterior-decorated bowls is 16.8 cm. and the mode is 17 cm., while interior-decorated bowls have a mean of 18.4 cm. and a mode of 18 cm. In Late Patibamba II, the exterior-decorated class has a mean and mode of 15.3 cm. and 14 cm. compared to 17.1 cm. and 16 cm. for the interior-decorated group. Illaura Phase regular-size exterior-decorated bowls have mean and modal mouth diameters of 12.8 cm. and 12 cm. compared with 17.8 and 17 cm. respectively for regular-size interior-decorated bowls.

A comparable progressive differentiation can be seen in wall angles, although the response is more gradual. Early Patibamba and Middle Patibamba regular-size exterior-decorated bowls have means of 20° and 23° respectively compared with mean wall angles for interior-decorated bowls of 27.8° and 32.5° and modes of 25° and 30° for the same phases. Late Patibamba I exterior-decorated bowls have equally popular modes of 15° and 20° with a mean of 20.3°, while interior-decorated specimens have a mode and mean of 30°. From this phase on, the interior-decorated bowls change little, with wall angle means of 28° and 28.5° and modes of 30° and 30° for Late Patibamba II and Illaura. However, the wall angles of exterior-decorated bowls continue to decline, with means of 15.6° and 11.5° and modes of 15° and 15° for the same phases.

Wall profiles remain quite constant throughout the sequence with straight and incurving convex the most popular forms. Rounded lips are popular throughout the sequence, but interior curves are common in the first two phases; exterior curves common in the first, third, and fourth; and flattened rims more popular in the last four phases. Most rims are unmodified, but thickened forms E, D, and E1 are occasional alternatives in the last four phases.

Vessel height does not seem to vary greatly, with specimens rarely greater than 7.5 cm. or less than 5.5 cm. high until the small Illaura Phase bowls, which may be as short as 4 cm. The bottoms are flat to gently curved and are united to the walls by an open curve.

Decorative themes for Early Patibamba cannot be abstracted because of the small sample, but one specimen has a design similar to a theme which is common on interior-decorated bowls. This theme is based upon a single light-colored band, white or gray, with filler elements (fig. 28B). Wavy lines (fig. 28A) and more amorphous designs are also found.

Figure 25. Interior-Decorated Bowls 1.3.2.1   (Scale = ½)

A Middle Patibamba; North Unit, S11 stratum E; D=17 cm.; 2.1.2.3 on red; 3.3.2; 4.4.1.4

B Early Patibamba; E2 x S16 stratum 9; D=20 cm.; 2.1.3.1 on red; 3.9; 4.4.1, 4.13.4

C Middle Patibamba; North Unit, S11 stratum E; D=19 cm.; 2.1.2.1 on red; 3.7; 4.13.1

D Late Patibamba I; North Unit, E6 x S10 stratum 4b; D=18 cm.; 2.1.1.3 on red

E Late Patibamba II; North Unit, plaza floor; D=13 cm.; 2.1.4.3 (light red, dark red, and white design is on a black slip not shown in illustration); 4.4.2, 4.13.4

F Late Patibamba II; North Unit, E5 x S9 stratum 2; 2.1.2.6 on natural; 3.14; 4.13.1

G Early Patibamba; E2 x S16 stratum 9; D=16 cm.; 2.1.1.3 on red; 3.6.1

H Middle Patibamba; North Unit, S11 stratum E; 2.1.1.1 on natural; 3.6.1, 3.5.1.2

I Illaura; North Unit, S11 stratum C1; D=17 cm.; 2.1.1.3 on red; 3.3.3 (?)

J Middle Patibamba; North Unit, S10 stratum E; 2.1.3.15 on natural; 3.6, 3.5.1.2; 4.13.1

K Late Patibamba I; South Unit, S7 stratum 4; D=18 cm.; 2.1.3.17

L Early or Middle Patibamba; House Group, CX stratum 1; D=22 cm.; 2.1.3.1 on red; 3.6.2; 4.13.1

M Early Patibamba; House Group, CX stratum 2; D=16 cm.; 2.1.2.2 on natural; 3.6.1

N Early or Middle Patibamba; House Group, CX stratum 2; 2.1.3.1 on natural; 3.6.1; 4.13.1

O Early or Middle Patibamba; House Group, CX stratum 2; D=24 cm.; 2.1.3.1 on natural; 3.6.2

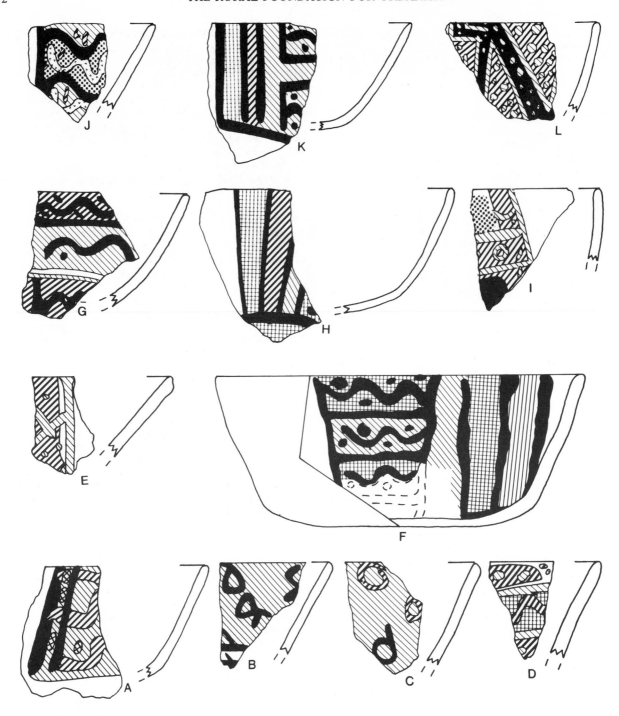

Figure 26. Interior-Decorated Bowls 1.3.2.1   (Scale = ½)

A   Early Patibamba; E2 x S13 stratum 9; D=18 cm.; 2.1.4.2 on red; 3.3.1; 4.5.3

B   Late Patibamba I; North Unit, E5 x S9 stratum 4; D=16 cm.; 2.1.2.1 on red; 3.3 (?); 4.1

C   Late Patibamba I; North Unit, S11 stratum D1; D=19 cm.; 2.1.3.1; 4.1

D   Late Patibamba I; North Unit, S11 stratum D1; D=18 cm.; 2.1.3.4 on red; 3.3.1.1; 4.5.1, 4.13.1

E   Late Patibamba I; North Unit, S10 stratum D1; D=24 cm.; 2.1.2.1 on natural; 3.3.1; 4.13.1

F   Late Patibamba II; North Unit, plaza floor; D=20 cm.; 2.1.4.9 on natural; 3.3.1.1, 3.4.1; 4.5.1.1

G   Late Patibamba II; North Unit, plaza floor; D=22 cm.; 2.1.3.1 on red; 3.3.1.1; 4.5.1, 4.5.1.1

H   Late Patibamba II; North Unit, E9 x S6 stratum 3; D=16 cm.; 2.1.4.6 on natural; 3.4.1

I   Late Patibamba II; North Unit, E6 x S9 stratum 3; D=21 cm.; 2.1.4.7 on natural; 3.3.1.1; 4.4.2

J   Late Patibamba II; North Unit, S11 stratum D; D=18 cm.; 2.1.5.1 on red; 3.3.1; 4.5.3.1

K   Late Patibamba II; North Unit, E5 x S10 stratum 2; D=16 cm.; 2.1.4.6 on red; 3.4.2; 4.5.1.1

L   Illaura; North Unit, S11 stratum C; D=20 cm.; 2.1.3.1; 3.3.3; 4.13.1

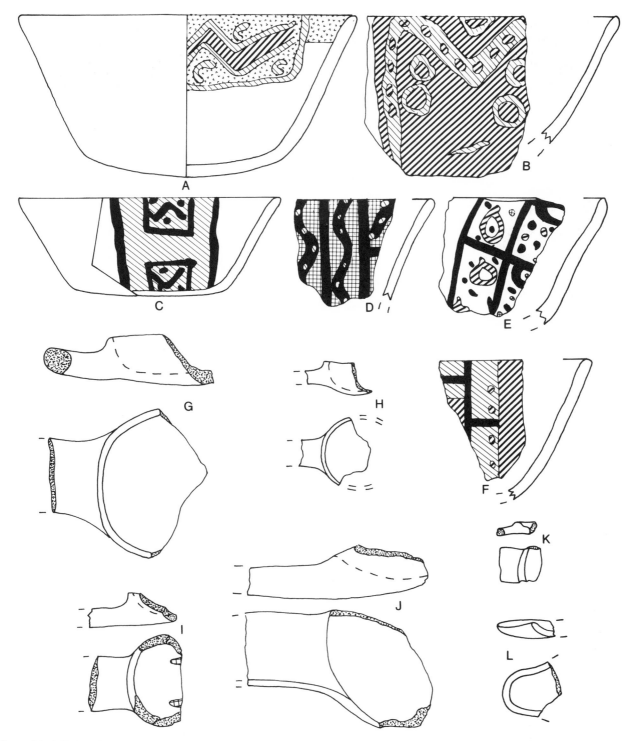

Figure 27. A–F: Interior-Decorated Bowls 1.3.2.1; G–L: Spoons 1.5   (Scale = ½)

A   Late Patibamba I or II; House Group, CY strata 3, 3d, 4, S4 strata 1, 2, S5 stratum 2, CX stratum 1; D=18 cm.; 2.1.3.17 on natural; 3.3.3, 3.5.1.2; 4.2

B   Late Patibamba I or II; House Group, CW stratum 4, S5 stratum 2, CX stratum 2, CY stratum 3; D=14 cm.; 2.1.2.1 on red; 3.3.3 (?); 4.4.2, 4.13.4

C   Late Patibamba I or II; House Group, CW strata 3II, 3III; D=14 cm.; 2.1.2.5 on natural; 3.4.2; 4.5.1.1

D   Early or Middle Patibamba (?); House Group, CY stratum 5; D=22 cm.; black, white, orange; 3.4.2 (?); 4.13.4

E   Late Patibamba I or II (?); House Group, CY strata 4, 5; 2.1.3.9 on red; 3.14; 4.1, 4.13.2

F   Late Patibamba I or II (?); House Group, S4 strata 2, 4; D=16 cm.; 2.1.3.1; 4.13.1

G   Early Patibamba (?); House Group, CX stratum 2

H   Early Patibamba (?); House Group, CX stratum 1

I   Early Patibamba; E2 x S14 stratum 9; 2.1.1.4 on natural

J   Early Patibamba; E2 x S14 stratum 9

K   Illaura; North Unit, S11 stratum C1

L   Early Patibamba; E2 x S15 stratum 9

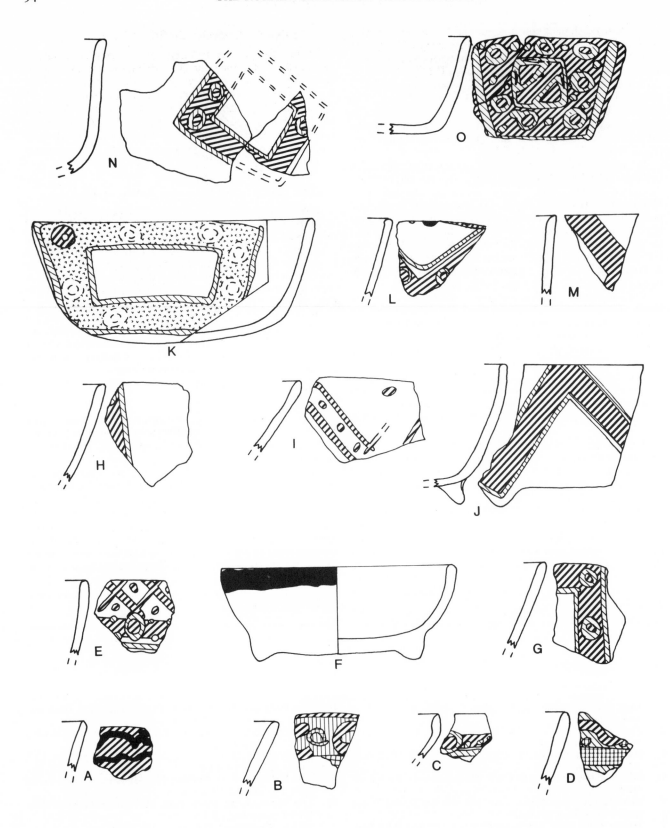

Fig. 28

Single-band themes continue into Middle Patibamba (fig. 28C) and some possibly transitional forms (fig. 28D) may provide an antecedent for double horizontal bands (fig. 30J), which survive until Late Patibamba II (fig. 30K-M).

A very distinctive and diagnostic theme is composed of three parallel bands, black over dark red over black. This theme is limited to exterior-decorated bowls. It makes its appearance in Middle Patibamba and remains popular through Late Patibamba II and, perhaps, the Illaura Phase (fig. 29B-J).

In Late Patibamba I, a new theme consisting of a rectangle formed by a broad band appears on exterior-decorated bowls. This theme continues through Late Patibamba II (fig. 28G, H, K, O), and, placed in diagonal position, is characteristic of Late Patibamba II and Illaura (fig. 28M, N). It is interesting that this theme was first found on an interior-decorated bowl in Middle Patibamba but did not survive as a theme for interior-decorated bowls. A broad band forming a zigzag circling the bowl exterior occurs in Late Patibamba I and II (fig. 28I, J, L, M).

Vertical bands, which are common on interior-decorated bowls from Early Patibamba on, do not appear on exterior-decorated bowls until Late Patibamba I (fig. 30C, D). However, once vertical bands become associated with the exterior-decorated bowl, they continue through the Illaura Phase (fig. 30E-I).

The single light band which characterizes Early Patibamba and Middle Patibamba disappears in Late Patibamba I but reappears as a single black band in the Illaura Phase, where it is probably adopted from interior-decorated bowls (fig. 28F).

Perhaps the most significant modification which offsets regular-size exterior-decorated bowls and distinguishes them from regular-size interior-decorated bowls is the addition of tripod tab supports. These are small, solid supports added to the bottom of a vessel. They first appear in Late Patibamba I (figs. 28G, J, 29D, 32D; plate 14A) and continue through Late Patibamba II (fig. 29G; plate 14F) and into Illaura (figs. 28F, 30I; plate 14C). These bowls have been treated as a subclass of tripod bowls because of their temporal significance, but they could also be considered a subclass of exterior-decorated bowls since all specimens appear to have had some kind of exterior decoration.

Oversize Exterior-Decorated Bowls   1.3.2.2.2

There is only one example of an oversize exterior-decorated bowl among the pottery samples from Jargampata. The specimen comes from the Late Patibamba I Phase from rooms S10 and S11. It has a mouth diameter of 27 cm. and a rather highly flared wall angle of 30°. There are traces of red and black paint on the exterior, but the design theme cannot be recognized. This unique bowl may represent a very infrequent category or may be the product of an innovative potter.

Interior- and Exterior-Decorated Bowls   1.3.2.3

Bowls with interior and exterior decoration are sufficiently scarce to suggest that they either belong to a very rare category or fall outside the rules for pottery at Jargampata. One small sherd from Middle Patibamba comes from a bowl which had an exterior band design and an interior design which cannot be definitely recognized. A second specimen, much more complete, comes from Late Patibamba II (fig. 30A). It has an exterior design composed of three parallel horizontal bands and an interior theme based on groups of vertical bands. In the detailed description of Late Patibamba II ceramics, I have discussed several attributes of this bowl which lead me to believe that it was produced at Jargampata by a foreign potter.

Tripod Bowls   1.3.3

Tripod bowls constitute a subgroup of open bowl forms but have been divided into solid-tripod-support bowls (1.3.3.1), hollow-tripod-support bowls (1.3.3.2), and tripod tab-foot bowls (1.3.3.3).

Solid-tripod-support bowls (fig. 31) are present in low frequency from Early Patibamba through Late Patibamba II and are lacking in the Illaura sample. The first tripod supports at the site are solid, round legs (fig. 31D), but in Late Patibamba II a more rectangular form of support appears (fig. 31C). The solid supports were placed on oversize plain bowls which may have had horizontal handles just below the rims (fig. 31A, H). It is interesting that these bowls retain outcurving, concave wall profiles into Late Patibamba II when that wall profile mode had disappeared from other bowls.

Figure 28. Exterior-Decorated Bowls 1.3.2.2   (Scale = ½)

A   Early Patibamba; E2 x S14 stratum 9; D=20 cm.; 2.1.1.3 on dark red; 3.8.2

B   Early Patibamba; E2 x S14 stratum 9; D=14 cm.; 2.1.4.4 on natural; 3.5.1.6; 4.1, 4.2

C   Middle Patibamba; North Unit, S10 stratum E; D=12 cm.; 2.1.2.1 on cream; 3.5.1.2; 4.4.2, 4.13.1

D   Middle Patibamba; North Unit, S11 stratum E; 2.1.3.4 on red-brown; 3.5.1.1; 4.5.1.2

E   Late Patibamba II; North Unit, S11 stratum D; D=17 cm.; 2.1.2.1 on natural; 3.7; 4.4.2

F   Illaura; North Unit, S11 strata C, C1; D=12 cm.; 2.1.1.3 on natural; 3.5.1.4

G   Late Patibamba I; North Unit, E6 x S10 stratum 4b; D=14 cm.; 2.1.2.1 on natural; 3.3.2; 4.4.1.4

H   Late Patibamba I; North Unit, E6 x S9 stratum 4b; D=18 cm.; 2.1.2.1 on natural; 3.3.2

I   Late Patibamba I; North Unit, E6 x S9 stratum 4; D=18 cm. (?); 2.1.1.1 on natural; 3.3.3; 4.13.1

J   Late Patibamba I; North Unit, E5 x S9 stratum 4; D=15 cm.; 2.1.2.1 on natural; 3.3.3

K   Late Patibamba II; North Unit, plaza floor; D=14 cm.; 2.1.3.17 on natural; 3.3.2; 4.4.1.4

L   Late Patibamba II; North Unit, E2 x S10 stratum 3; D=10 cm.; 2.1.3.1 on natural; 3.3.3; 4.4.1.4

M   Late Patibamba II; North Unit, S11 stratum D; D=14 cm.; 2.1.1.1 on natural; 3.3.2.1

N   Illaura; North Unit, S11 stratum C; D=15 cm.; 2.1.2.1 on natural; 3.3.2.1; 4.4.1.4

O   Late Patibamba I or II; House Group, S5 stratum 2; D=11 cm.; 2.1.2.1; 3.3.2; 4.4.1.4

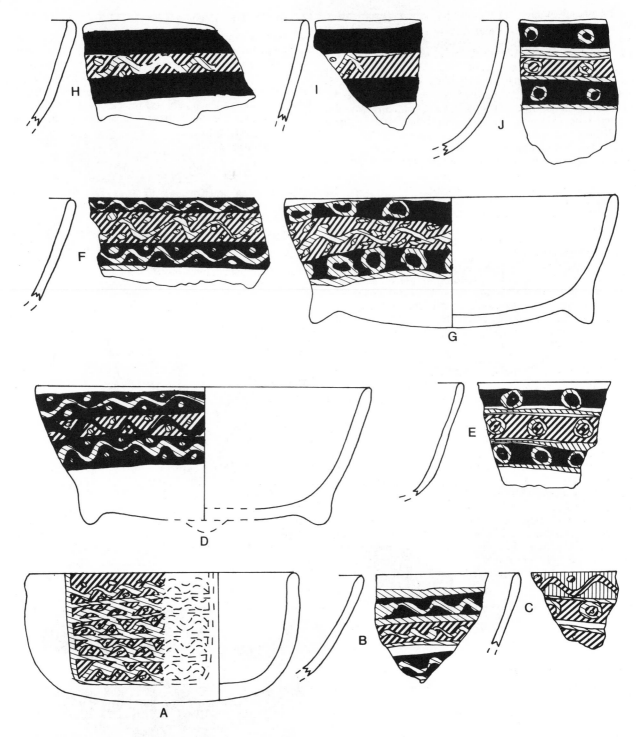

Figure 29. Exterior-Decorated Bowls 1.3.2.2   (Scale = ½)

A   Late Patibamba I or II; House Group, CY strata 3, 3c, 4;
    D=14.5 cm.; 3.3.1.1; 4.5.1.1
B   Middle Patibamba; North Unit, S10 stratum E; D=15 cm.;
    2.1.3.1 on natural; 3.5.3.1; 4.5.1
C   Late Patibamba I; North Unit, S11 stratum D1; D=17 cm.;
    2.1.3.2 on red; 3.5.3.4; 4.5.1.1, 4.6
D   Late Patibamba I; South Unit, S7 strata 3, 4; D=18 cm.;
    2.1.3.1 on red; 3.5.3.1; 4.5.1.1
E   Late Patibamba I; North Unit, S10 stratum D1; D=18 cm.;
    2.1.3.1 on red; 3.5.3.1; 4.6

F   Late Patibamba I; North Unit, S10 stratum D1; D=17 cm.;
    2.1.3.1 on red; 3.5.3.1; 4.5.1.1
G   Late Patibamba II; North Unit, plaza floor; D=18 cm.; 2.1.3.1
    on red; 3.5.3.1; 4.4.1.2, 4.5.1.2.1
H   Late Patibamba II; North Unit, E5 x S10 stratum 2; D=18 cm.;
    2.1.3.1 on natural; 3.5.3.1; 4.5.1.1
I   Illaura; North Unit, S11 strata C, C1; D=15 cm.; 2.1.3.1 on
    natural; 3.5.3.1; 4.5.1.1
J   Late Patibamba I or II; House Group, CW strata 2, 4, CY
    stratum D; D=15 cm.; 2.1.3.1 on natural; 3.5.3.1; 4.4.1.2

Plate 14. Exterior-Decorated Bowls 1.3.2.2   (Scale = ½)

A   Tripod Tab Foot; 1.3.3.3; Late Patibamba I; South Unit, S7 stratum 4; D=17 cm.; 2.1.3.1 on natural; 3.5.3.1; 4.4.1.2, 4.5.1.2.1

B   Hollow Tripod Support; 1.3.3.2; Figure 32C

C   Tripod Tab Foot; 1.3.3.3; Figure 30I

D   Figure 29A

E   Figure 28K

F   Tripod Tab Foot; 1.3.3.3; Figure 29G

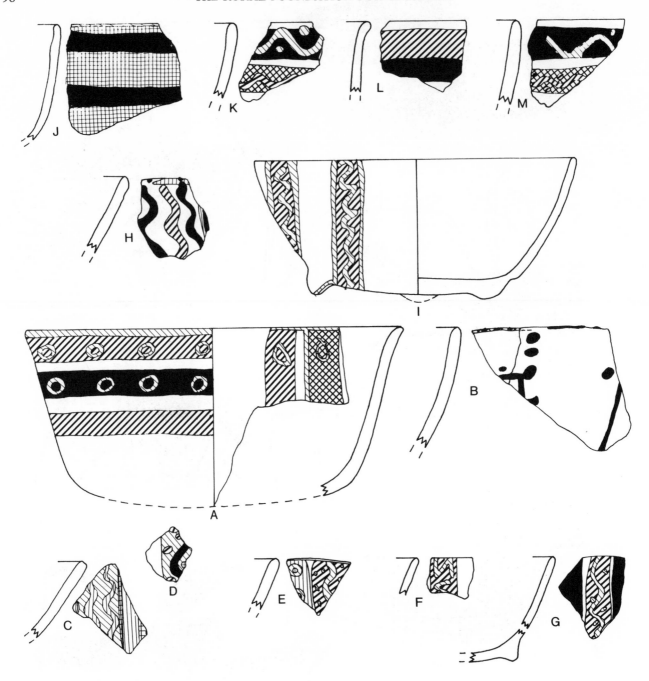

Figure 30. A: Interior- and Exterior-Decorated Bowl 1.3.2.3; B–M: Exterior-Decorated Bowls 1.3.2.2   (Scale = ½)

A   Late Patibamba II; North Unit, plaza floor; D=20 cm.; interior 2.1.3.5 on red, exterior 2.1.3.1 on natural; interior 3.2.2, exterior 3.5.3.2; interior 4.4.1.3, exterior 4.4.1.2

B   Early Patibamba; E2 x S15 stratum 9; D=18 cm.; 2.1.2.10 on red; 3.10.1; 4.7

C   Late Patibamba I; North Unit, E5 x S10 stratum 4; D=17 cm.; 2.1.3.16 on natural; 3.2.2 (?); 4.5.5

D   Late Patibamba I; South Unit, S7 stratum 4; 2.1.4.6 on red-brown; 4.5.4.1

E   Late Patibamba II; North Unit, E6 x S9 stratum 3; D=18 cm.; 2.1.3.2 on natural; 3.2.2; 4.4.1.3, 4.5.4.2

F   Late Patibamba II; North Unit, S10 strata D, D1; D=17 cm.; 2.1.2.1 on natural; 3.2.3 (?); 4.8

G   Illaura; North Unit, S11 stratum C1; 2.1.3.1 on natural; 3.2.2; 4.5.4.1

H   Late Patibamba I (?); House Group, CX stratum 1; D=20 cm.; 2.1.3.8 on natural; 4.5.5

I   Illaura; North Unit, S10 stratum C; D=17 cm.; 2.1.2.1 on natural; 3.2.3; 4.5.4

J   Middle Patibamba; North Unit, S11 stratum E; D=14 cm.; 2.1.2.5 on orange; 3.5.2.5

K   Late Patibamba I; North Unit, S11 stratum D1; D=18 cm.; 2.1.4.2 on natural; 3.5.2.2; 4.5.1, 4.5.1.1

L   Late Patibamba II; North Unit, plaza floor; D=14 cm.; 2.1.2.1 on natural, possible traces of white decoration; 3.5.2.1

M   Late Patibamba II; North Unit, S11 stratum D; D=22 cm.; 2.1.4.2 on natural; 3.5.2.2; 4.5.1.1

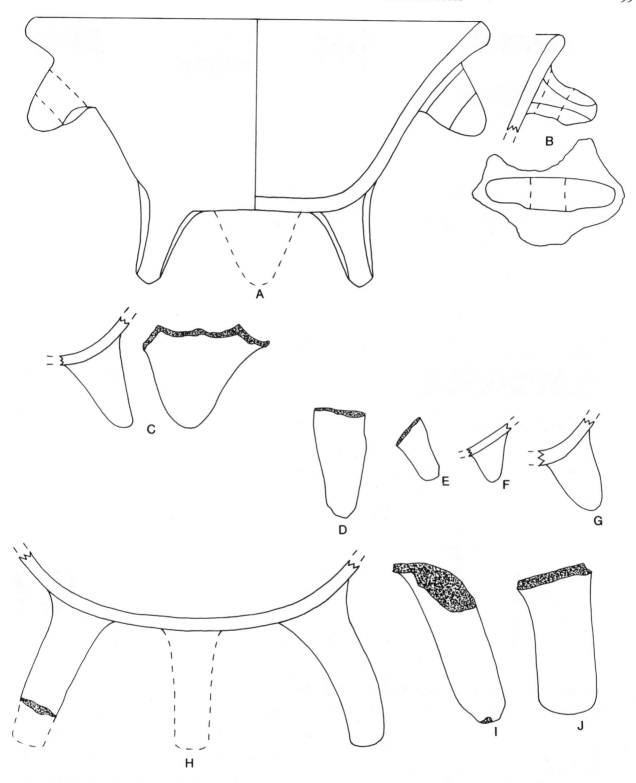

Figure 31. Solid-Tripod Bowls 1.3.3.1   (Scale = ½)

A   Late Patibamba II; North Unit, W8 x N12-13 stratum 3; D=24 cm.

B   Late Patibamba II; North Unit, E5 x S10 stratum 2; D=30 cm.

C   Late Patibamba II; North Unit, plaza floor

D   Early Patibamba; E3 x S13 stratum 9

E   Early Patibamba (?); House Group, CW stratum 2

F   Late Patibamba I (?); House Group, CW stratum 2

G   Late Patibamba I or II; House Group, CY stratum 3

H   Middle Patibamba (?); House Group, CY stratum 4

I   Early Patibamba (?); House Group, CY stratum 5

J   Early Patibamba (?); House Group, CY stratum 5

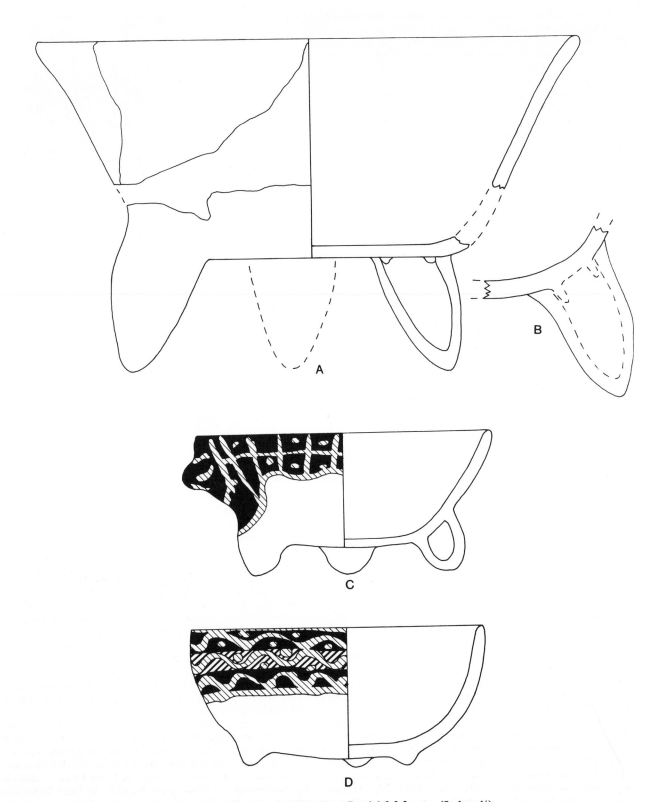

Figure 32. A–C: Hollow-Tripod-Support Bowls 1.3.3.2; D: Solid-Tab-Foot Bowl 1.3.3.3   (Scale = ½)

A   Late Patibamba I or II; House Group, CY strata 3a, 4, CW
     stratum 4; D=30 cm.
B   Late Patibamba I or II; House Group, CX stratum 5

C   Late Patibamba I or II; House Group, S4 strata 1, 5, CW strata
     3II, 3III; D=16.5 cm.; 2.1.2.5 on red, with modeled adornos
     below rim; 3.14 (?) or 3.5.1.4; 4.13.1
D   Late Patibamba I; South Unit, S7 stratum 4; D=16 cm.; 2.1.3.1
     on red; 3.5.3.1; 4.5.1, 4.5.1.1

Hollow tripod supports are represented by only two large fragmentary examples in the Late Patibamba I and II phase samples. It seems likely that this form of support did not appear at Jargampata until Late Patibamba I. More complete specimens from the House Group show that the large hollow tripods were also supports for oversize bowls, apparently with outcurving, convex wall profiles (fig. 32A, B). Unfortunately, there is no evidence for handles.

Small hollow tripod supports also occur on one bowl from the House Group (fig. 32C; plate 14B). The specimen came from mixed strata in room S4 but probably belongs to Late Patibamba I. The modeled adornos below the rim of this vessel make it quite reminiscent of tripod vessels which made their appearance in the North Highlands at the beginning of Cajamarca IV (Reichlen 1970: 492, 497-98), when various Middle Horizon influences are particularly evident. It seems likely that the extensive use of tripod bowls may be a Middle Horizon 2B characteristic.

Tripod tab feet are attached to the base of exterior-decorated bowls. These small, solid supports appear for the first time in Late Patibamba I and continue in use through the Illaura Phase (figs. 28F, J, 29D, G, 30G, I, 32D; plate 14A, C, F). It is important to note that a close association between this bowl form and the three-horizontal-band decorative theme is probably established at Jargampata in spite of the fact that the sudden appearance of the form suggests introduction. However, the three-band design theme appears in Middle Patibamba (fig. 29B), while the tab feet are not represented until Late Patibamba I.

It is likely that this vessel shape, the tripod-support form, was introduced to Jargampata from Wari. Bennett (1953: fig. 13A) illustrates a bowl fragment with similar supports. The single-light-band design theme on the vessel would seriate earlier than Late Patibamba I in terms of the progression of decorative themes at Jargampata.

Although this bowl form has not been given much attention, it may be an important diagnostic feature of Late Middle Horizon. Similar bowls have been reported by David Browman (personal communication) from the Huancayo area; the National Museum in Lima has a particularly nice specimen on display; and Lumbreras (1959: lam. XIS) illustrates another example with a typical Middle Horizon design, except that this bowl, in contrast with the others, has interior decoration.

Ring-Base Bowls 1.3.4

Ring-base bowls, a subcategory of open bowl forms, are very rare at Jargampata. Only one such base was recovered; it belongs to the Middle Patibamba Phase (fig. 33B). The only other specimen came from mixed strata in the House Group. It has interior decoration based on a grid pattern with dots, which is very rare at Jargampata but reminiscent of a fragmentary vessel from the House Group which may have copied Cajamarca-style decoration (fig. 38B). It seems significant that the single ring-base bowl at Jargampata occurs in a phase dated as Middle Horizon 2A, which must be broadly contemporary with the Epoch 2A offerings from Ayapata that include ring-base bowls in imitation of Cajamarca styles (Ravines 1968: 32-33; figs. 31-34). Both of these samples predate the proliferation of tripod supports at Jargampata in Epoch 2B. Similarly, in Cajamarca, Reichlen (1970: 492) recognizes that ring bases of Cajamarca III predate tripod bowls of Cajamarca IV.

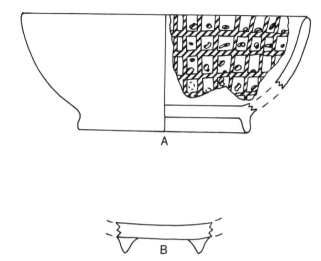

Figure 33. Ring-Base Bowls 1.3.4   (Scale = ½)

A   Late Patibamba I (?); House Group, S4 strata 3, 4; 2.1.1.1 on natural; 3.14; 4.13.1
B   Middle Patibamba; North Unit, S11 stratum E

Pedestal Bowls 1.3.5

Pedestal bowls have solid pedestal supports, straight or slightly outcurving walls, and a coarse paste and surface finish like that characteristic of undecorated jars. None of the specimens recovered show traces of a colored slip or any painted decoration (fig. 34).

This very distinctive vessel shape is a characteristic but low-frequency component of Jargampata pottery from Early Patibamba through the Illaura Phase. It has not previously been recognized as a component of Middle Horizon pottery. However, I have collected fragments of these bases from Conchopata (Chakipampa), and Lumbreras (personal communication) confirms finding similar bases in his excavations at that site. Beyond this, I know of no other sites where these vessels are found, including Wari. Consequently, this form may become an important indicator of subcultural groups in and around Ayacucho during the Middle Horizon.

The origin of these pedestal bowls may be found in the Ayacucho area, but the form seems to be out of place in the Central Highlands. No related vessel shapes are reported from the area, and the most similar form which I have seen is represented by two decorated pedestal bowls illustrated by Nordenskiold (1930: plate XLVIA, B) from Rurenabaque on the Beni River of Bolivia. One of these vessels has decoration which indicates Tiahuanaco influence, and exterior-decorated tripod vessels from the Mojos (Nordenskiold 1930: plate XLIXA-C) suggest that we may need to consider a possible role for this lowland zone during the Middle Horizon.

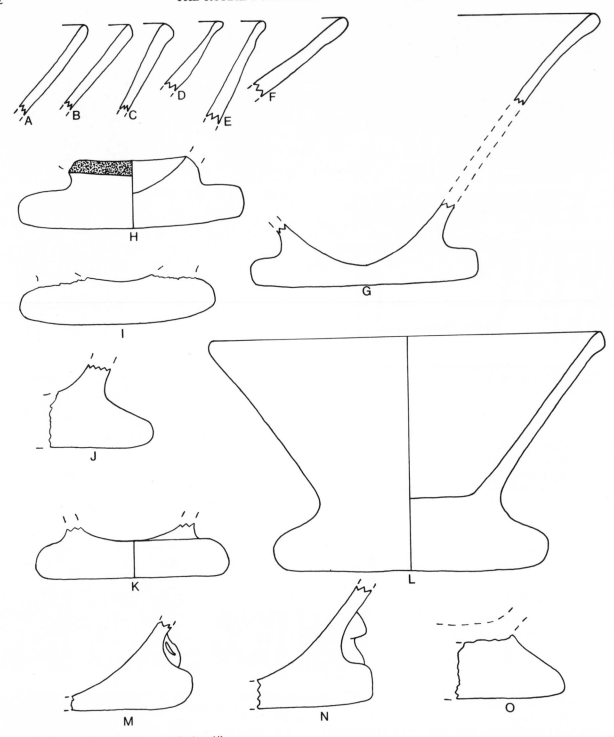

Figure 34. Pedestal Bowls 1.3.5   (Scale = ½)

A   Early Patibamba; E2 x S15 stratum 9; D=18 cm.
B   Early Patibamba; E2 x S15 stratum 9; D=14 cm.
C   Illaura; North Unit, S11 stratum C; D=17 cm.
D   Middle Patibamba; North Unit, S11 stratum E; D=21 cm.
E   Illaura; North Unit, S11 stratum C; D=22 cm.
F   Late Patibamba II; S11 stratum D; D=20 cm.
G   Late Patibamba II; North Unit, plaza floor; D=24 cm.; D of base=12 cm.
H   Late Patibamba I; South Unit, S7 stratum 4; D of base=12 cm.
I   Middle Patibamba; North Unit, S11 strata E, C; D of base=10.5 cm.

J   Early Patibamba; E3 x S13-15 stratum 9; D of base=16 cm.
K   Middle Patibamba; North Unit, S11 stratum E; D of base=10 cm.
L   Illaura; North Unit, S10 stratum C1; D=21cm.; D of base=14.5 cm.
M   Early Patibamba; E2 x S15 stratum 8; D of base=15 cm.
N   Early Patibamba; E2 x S15 stratum 9; D of base=16 cm.
O   Early Patibamba; E2 x S15 stratum 9; D of base=14 cm.

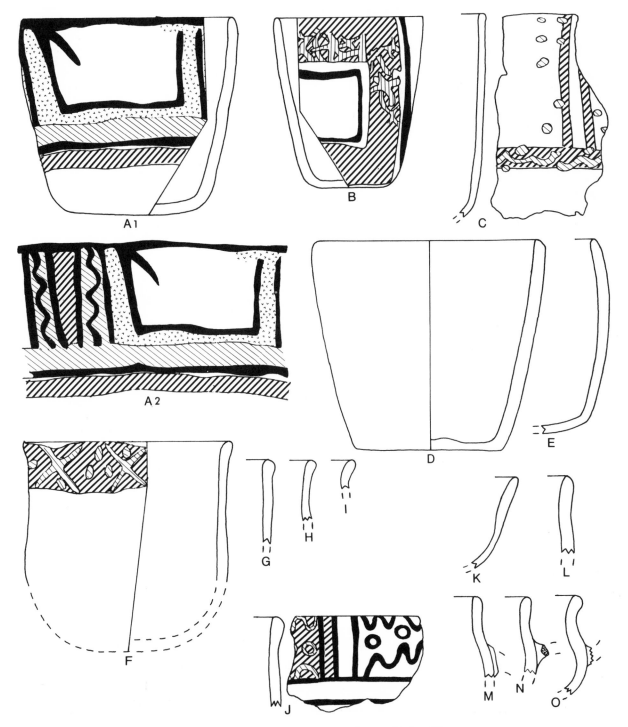

Figure 35. A–E: Straight-Sided Cups 1.3.7; F–O: Lyre-Shaped Cups 1.3.6   (Scale = ½)

A1 and A2   Late Patibamba I; South Unit, S7 strata 3, 4; D=11.5
  cm.; 2.1.4.3 on natural; 3.4.1; 4.5.4
B   Late Patibamba I or II; House Group, CY strata 2, 3, 4; D=8
  cm.; 2.1.3.8 on red; 3.3.2
C   Illaura; North Unit, S11 stratum C; D=9 cm.; 2.1.2.1 on
  natural; 3.5.1.2.1; 4.5.1.1, 4.13.1
D   Late Patibamba I or II; House Group, CY strata 3, 3a; D=13
  cm.
E   Late Patibamba I or II; House Group, CY stratum 4; D=12 cm.
F   Late Patibamba II; North Unit, plaza floor; D=11 cm.; 2.1.2.1
  on natural; 3.7.1; 4.13.1

G   Illaura; North Unit, S10 stratum C; D=8 cm.
H   Illaura; North Unit, S10 stratum C; D=7cm.
I   Late Patibamba II; North Unit, plaza floor; D=12 cm.
J   Late Patibamba I or II; House Group, CX stratum 4; D=9 cm.;
  2.1.3.1 on red; 3.4.1 (?); 4.4.2, 4.5.1
K   Early Patibamba; E2 x S15 stratum 9; D=13 cm.
L   Early Patibamba; E3 x S13-15 stratum 9; D=9 cm.
M   Late Patibamba II; North Unit, S11 stratum D; D=9 cm.
N   Late Patibamba I (?); House Group, CW stratum 4; D=8 cm.
O   Late Patibamba I; South Unit, S7 stratum 4; D=8 cm.

Lyre-Shaped Cups   1.3.6

Lyre-shaped cups compose an infrequent subcategory of open bowl forms. They are distinctive in having a recurved wall profile or inverted bell shape. Their temporal distribution at Jargampata is subject to question. Two rims from the Early Patibamba Phase have the appropriate wall profiles (fig. 35K, L) but have mouth diameters considerably greater than most lyre-shaped cups, which tend to have a diameter about equal to or slightly less than their height. The next example is from Late Patibamba I and also has a fairly large mouth diameter relative to its height (fig. 35O). This specimen has a small handle, which is why it is classified in a subcategory of lyre-shaped cups (1.3.6.1) which appears in Late Patibamba I.

Late Patibamba II witnessed a greater popularity of lyre-shaped cups, both with and without handles (fig. 35F, I, M), although the walls are frequently quite straight and the category may have been merging with straight-sided cups. A decorated specimen from the House Group which may be contemporary with this phase also has rather straight walls. Illaura Phase lyre-shaped cups are also nearly straight in wall profile (fig. 35G, H).

Straight-Sided Tall Cups   1.3.7

Straight-sided cups have mouth diameters about equal to their height and straight or very slightly incurving, convex wall profiles (fig. 35A-E). They may derive from lyre-shaped cups since they first appear in Late Patibamba I and then only in a low frequency. There are no examples from Late Patibamba II, but there is one from the Illaura Phase. This form was frequently decorated and apparently was more common in the House Group than in the North Unit, where the only examples found were from the Illaura Phase.

MINIATURE VESSELS   1.4

Miniature vessels were separated from other vessel shape categories because of their chronological significance. These vessels do not appear in any samples until Late Patibamba I

and are found in Late Patibamba II and possibly in the Illaura Phase. They may be distinguished from regular-size vessels in that they are smaller. Miniature bowls have mouth diameters of less than 10 cm. and usually have wall thicknesses of .4 cm. or less. Only in the Illaura Phase, when some regular-size bowls became very small, is it probable that the miniature bowls were not distinguished from the regular-size category (fig. 36N-U). Other miniature vessel forms are so much smaller than the regular-size specimens that they could hardly have been functional. These include narrow-collar jars (figs. 10A, 36H; plate 15I-L), side-spout jars (fig. 13C), flaring-neck jars (fig. 36I; plate 15M-O), and some vessels which may be cups or bowls (fig. 36G, J-M; plate 15G, H).

It is significant that all miniature forms except for miniature bowls were absent from the North Unit and were found only in the House Group.

SPOONS   1.5

Spoons are rare at Jargampata, and there are only four from all the samples analyzed. They show a curious temporal distribution, with three from the Early Patibamba Phase (fig. 27I, J, L) and one from the Illuara Phase (fig. 27K). The absence of spoons during Middle Patibamba through Late Patibamba II is partially confirmed by the lack of spoons in the House Group, except from fill which probably represents Early Patibamba refuse (fig. 27G, H) and three specimens in Cajamarca style (plate 18B-D).

Most spoons made at Jargampata have solid prismatic handles and circular or ovoid bowls (fig. 27G-J), but one specimen from the Early Patibamba sample was made of a thin piece of clay modeled into an elongated trough with a continuous handle and bowl (fig. 27L).

COLANDERS   1.6

Colanders are very infrequent at Jargampata, and none were found in the ceramic samples selected for analysis. However, two fragmentary examples were recovered from

---

Plate 15.
(Scale = 1/2)

A   Pedestal Bowl; 1.3.5; Figure 34L
B   Press Mold; 1.7; Late Patibamba II; North Unit, S10 stratum D; D=7 cm.
C   Press Mold; 1.7; Late Patibamba II; North Unit, plaza floor; D=8 cm.
D   Press Mold; 1.7; Late Patibamba I; North Unit, S10 stratum D1; D=5 cm.
E   Colander; 1.6; Early Patibamba (?); House Group, CX stratum 4
F   Colander; 1.6; Early Patibamba (?); House Group, CX stratum 2
G   Miniature Vessel; 1.4; Figure 36M
H   Miniature Vessel; 1.4; Figure 36L
I   Miniature Vessel; 1.4; Narrow-Collar Jar; 1.1.1.1; Figure 10A
J   Miniature Vessel; 1.4; Narrow-Collar Jar; 1.1.1.1; Middle Patibamba or Late Patibamba I; House Group, S4 stratum 2; D=.6 cm.
K   Miniature Vessel; 1.4; Necked Jar; 1.1; Late Patibamba I (?); House Group, S4 subfloor offering; D=1.2 cm.

L   Miniature Vessel; 1.4; Necked Jar; 1.1; Late Patibamba I (?); House Group, S4 subfloor offering
M   Miniature Vessel; 1.4; Necked Jar; 1.1; Late Patibamba I (?); House Group, S1 floor; D=2.8 cm.
N   Miniature Vessel; 1.4; Necked Jar; 1.1; Late Patibamba I (?); House Group, S4 stratum 1; D=3 cm.
O   Miniature Vessel; 1.4; Necked Jar; 1.1; Late Patibamba I (?); House Group, CW stratum 4; D=3.3cm.
P   Scraper-Polisher; 1.9; Illaura; North Unit, S10 stratum C
Q   Possible Scraper-Polisher; 1.9; Figure 36F
R   Scraper-Polisher; 1.9; Late Patibamba I; House Group, S4 stratum 3
S   Scraper-Polisher; 1.9; Late Patibamba I or II; North Unit, S9 floor
T   Bilobed Jar (?); 1.1.2 (?); Late Patibamba I or II; House Group, CW stratum 4
U   Bilobed Jar (?); 1.1.2 (?); Late Patibamba I or II; House Group, CW stratum 4
V   Flask (?); 1.2.2 (?); Late Patibamba I or II; House Group, CW stratum 4; D=4 cm.

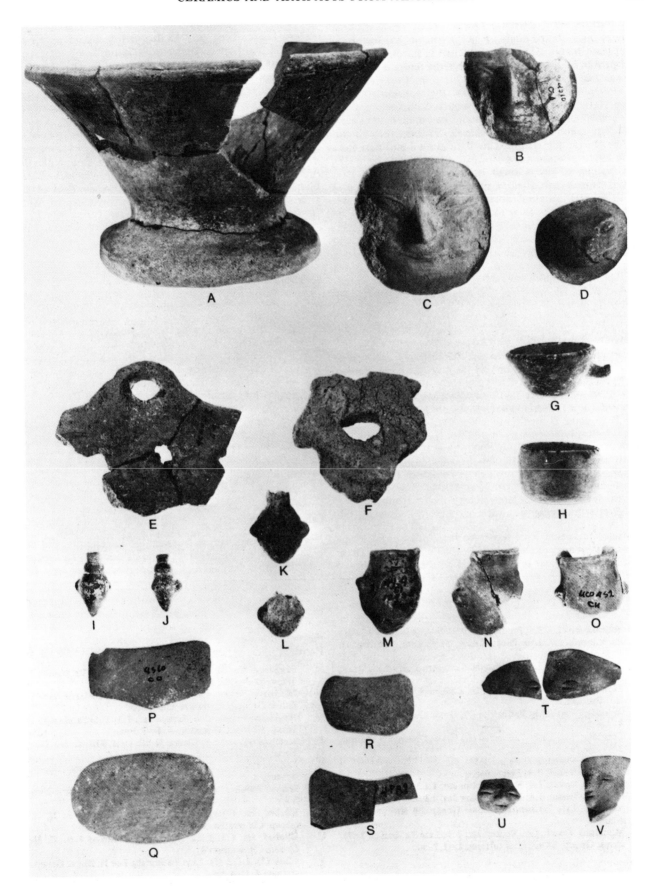

upper strata in the House Group. Their association is unclear, and they might have belonged to the final occupation of the House Group or been included with the late gravel fill, which contains primarily Early Patibamba refuse.

One colander fragment includes a rim with a handle rising vertically from it. The irregular holes were small, probably not more than 1 cm. or 1.5 cm. in diameter (plate 15E). The second colander fragment has holes about 2 cm. in diameter and is a much thicker piece of pottery (plate 15F).

The shape of these vessels remains unclear, and, because of the irregularity of the single rim sherd caused by the handle, mouth diameter cannot be measured. However, the paste and finish are coarse like that of undecorated jars.

PRESS MOLDS 1.7

Press molds from Jargampata are small, very shallow disks which were almost exclusively shaped for the making of human or animal faces. It is likely that they were used in the manufacture of face-neck jars.

There are no press molds from either Early or Middle Patibamba, but this may be a factor of the sample size and the rarity of these artifacts. Late Patibamba I has two molds. One is a face, probably an animal and perhaps a feline (plate 15D). The second mold was for the production of a pair of human hands with the fingertips almost touching. Both could have been used for producing face-neck jars, but the animal face might also have produced adornos such as the one found just below the rim of an exterior-decorated, hollow-tripod-support bowl from the House Group (fig. 32C; plate 14F).

Two press molds from Late Patibamba II are both human faces appropriate for face-neck jars (plate 15B, C). There is no evidence for large molds which might have been used for producing whole vessels or sections of vessels.

CERAMIC DISKS 1.8

Ceramic disks from Jargampata are flat, circular slabs of fired clay which range in diameter from about 12 cm. to 19.5 cm. and are from .7 cm. to 1.2 cm. thick (fig. 12H-M). They are infrequent, but are found from Early Patibamba through Late Patibamba II. Their finish and paste are coarse, like that of undecorated jars, and none have slip or decoration. The function of the disks remains obscure, but they may have served as slab bases upon which potters manufactured vessels.

SCRAPER-POLISHERS 1.9

Scraper-polishers were probably used by potters for finishing ceramic vessels (fig. 36A-D; plate 15P, R, S). Most are sherds from plain vessels which have been worked into their finished form by grinding the edges. Usually several sides became rather deeply concave through wear (plate 15S). Other scraper-polishers are made of stone (plate 19H), while some ceramic specimens must have been manufactured exclusively as potters' tools since the edges show little or no evidence of finishing by grinding.

Scraper-polishers appear in the ceramic samples in Middle Patibamba and are found throughout the rest of the sequences at Jargampata.

Two ceramic plaques, one from Late Patibamba II (fig. 36E) and one from the Illaura Phase (fig. 36F; plate 15Q), do not have the shape which is characteristic of most scraper-polishers. The former was modeled in its completed form, while the latter was worked out of a large sherd. These artifacts have been included with scraper-polishers, but it is possible that they belong to a distinct category. Two stone plaques from the House Group (plate 19F, G) may also belong to this unknown category. Elsewhere in the Central Highlands, Ravines (personal communication) found a rectangular ceramic plaque, which had been intentionally manufactured but showed no signs of edge abrasion, with the Ayapata pottery offerings of Middle Horizon 2A.

EXOTIC VESSELS 1.10

The exotic-vessel category includes all pottery which is foreign to Jargampata and the five stylistic phases established at the site. Most of these vessels were identified by their distinctive paste, although many were equally salient in surface finish, decorative colors, design, and quality of workmanship. The departures from the typical qualities of Jargampata pottery lead to the conclusion that these vessels were imported to the site. However, there are also some vessels which have typical Jargampata paste but are stylistically exceptional.

Almost all the exotic sherds from the ceramic samples selected for analysis have paste and decorative characteristics which associate them with fancy, elite pottery from Wari or other centers of prestige in the Ayacucho area. In consequence, these vessel fragments provide an index of interaction between Jargampata and more important centers. Early Patibamba, which probably predates the occupation of the North Unit, provides a ceramic sample which contains only .5% exotic pottery. Middle Patibamba represents the early occupation of the North Unit, and the local pottery shows considerable stylistic impact from outside sources. In this phase the frequency of exotic pottery jumps to 2%. Late Patibamba I witnessed the structural modification of the North Unit and possibly an intensification of Wari centralization; exotic pottery accounts for 6.4% of the ceramic sample in this phase. Late Patibamba II represents the disruption of the Wari state and the abandonment of many centers, including Jargampata. Exotic imported pottery drops to 1.8% of the sample, which may still include redeposited pieces. The Illaura Phase postdates horizon styles associated with Wari and the cultural interchange which these styles indicate. There is very little change in ceramics between Late Patibamba II and Illaura, but exotic pottery has disappeared completely.

The exotic pottery from the ceramic samples is very fragmentary, but it plays an important role in dating the phases at Jargampata in relation to major Middle Horizon sites and in the seriation of ceramic styles established by Menzel (1964, 1968a). Important pieces which can be dated were discussed in Chapter 5 and are dealth with in each of the phase descriptions.

There was only one exotic sherd in the Early Patibamba sample (fig. 39J), but an elite piece from E1-1 of E2-3 x S13-14 (fig. 43) is probably contemporary. This incurving bowl with profile feline-headed angel (fig. 39K; plate 16C) indicates that some fancy elite materials were moving from

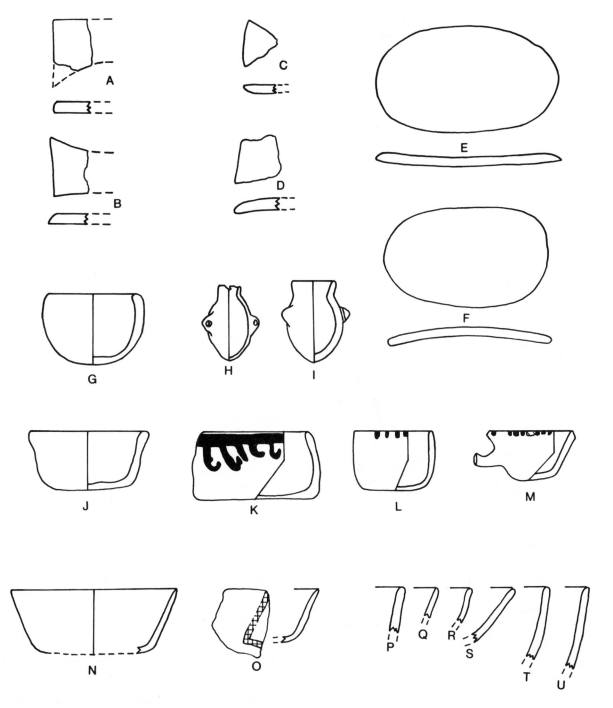

Figure 36. A–D: Sherd Scraper-Polishers 1.9; E–F: Possible Scraper-Polishers; J–U: Miniature Vessels 1.4 (Scale = ½)

A Late Patibamba I; North Unit, S11 stratum D1
B Late Patibamba I (?); House Group, CW stratum 3a
C Middle Patibamba; North Unit, S11 stratum E
E Late Patibamba II; North Unit, S10 stratum D
F Illaura; North Unit, S10 stratum C
G Early or Middle Patibamba (?); House Group, CY stratum 5; D=5 cm.
H Late Patibamba (?); House Group, S4 intrusive subfloor offering; D=1.2 cm.
I Late Patibamba I (?); House Group, S4 stratum 1; D=2.5 cm.
J Late Patibamba I (?); House Group, S5 strata 1, 2; D=6.5 cm.
K Late Patibamba I or II (?); House Group, CY stratum 4, CW stratum 4; D=6 cm.; 2.1.1.3 on red; 3.5.1.5

L Late Patibamba I (?); House Group, CW stratum E; D=4.5 cm.; 2.1.1.3 on red
M Unknown; House Group, S4 stratum 1; D=4.5 cm.; 2.1.2.1 on red
N Late Patibamba I; North Unit, S11 stratum D1; D=9 cm.
O Late Patibamba I; North Unit, E6 x S9 stratum 4a; D=9 cm.; 2.1.1.4
P Late Patibamba II; North Unit, S10 stratum D; D=8 cm.
Q Late Patibamba II; North Unit, S11 stratum D; D=9 cm.
R Late Patibamba II; North Unit, S11 stratum D; D=8.5 cm.
S Illaura; North Unit, S11 stratum C; D=9 cm.
T Illaura; North Unit, S11 stratum C; D=8 cm.
U Illaura; North Unit, S11 stratum C; D=9 cm.

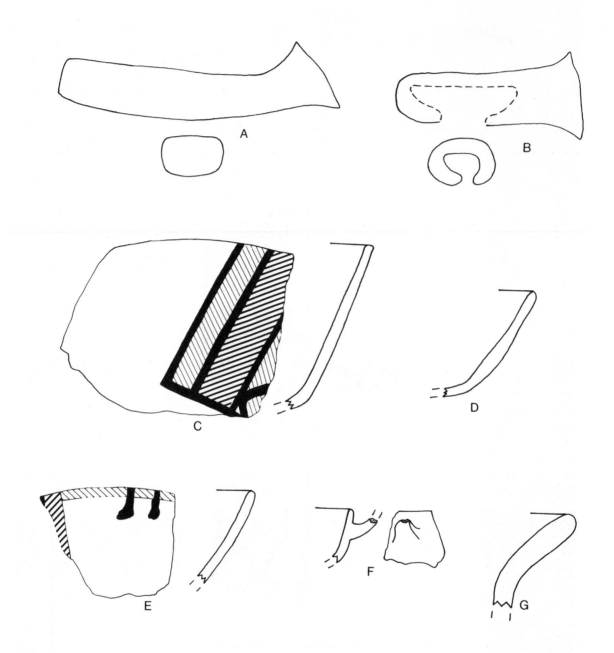

Figure 37. Element 11 Sherds   (Scale = ½)

A   Element 11; solid handle
B   Element 11; hollow handle
C   Element 11; D=22 cm.; 2.1.3.1 on red-brown; 3.2.2; 4.5.4
D   Element 11; D=16 cm.

E   Element 11; D=21 cm.; 2.1.3.1 on red-brown; 3.5.1.1, 3.2.2 (?)
F   Element 11; D=4 cm.
G   Element 11; D=22 cm.

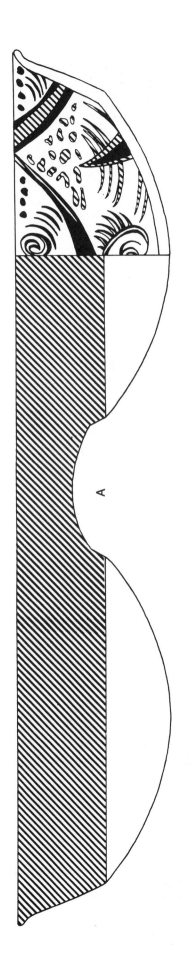

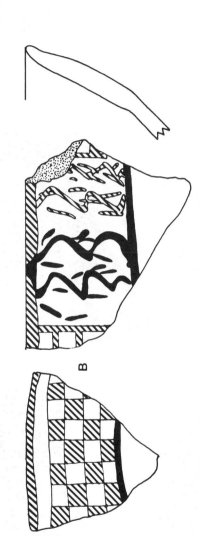

Figure 38. Cajamarca-Style Vessels (Scale = 1:1)

A Late Patibamba I (?); House Group, CX strata 4, 5; D of each bowl = 11 cm.; 2.1.2.1 on natural

B Late Patibamba I (?); House Group, CX stratum 5; D=16 cm.; 2.1.2.1 on natural

Plate 16. Fine Elite Vessels   (Scale = 1/2)

A	Figure 39C	E	Figure 40F
B1-B2	Figure 39D1, D2	F1-F2	Figure 40A1, A2
C	Figure 39K	G1-G2	Figure 40B1, B2
D	Figure 40E		

Plate 17. Fine Elite Vessels   (Scale = 1/2)

A1-A2	Figure 41E	D	Figure 39E
	Figure 39G	E	Figure 39L
C	Figure 39B	F	Figure 39I

Wari or another center of prestige to rural Jargampata prior to the establishment of the North Unit. Middle Patibamba ceramics include two exotic pieces (fig. 39G, L; plate 17B, E).

Both phases probably belong to Middle Horizon Epoch 2A (Menzel 1964, 1968a), although interaction between Jargampata and Wari certainly increased in Middle Patibamba. Several exotic vessels from the House Group probably belong to Middle Horizon 2A and are therefore contemporary with Early or Middle Patibamba. A small, slightly incurving bowl (fig. 40B1, B2; plate 16G1, G2) has two vertical chevron bands dividing the vessel into two parts. Each panel has a variant of the "ray design with approximate symmetry" (Menzel 1968a: 73), and, although this particular specimen is somewhat distinctive in its treatment of recurved rays, it seems to share a general form with such designs from Epoch 1B Chakipampa (Menzel 1968a: fig. 35) and Epoch 2A Atarco A (Menzel 1968a: fig. 19a).

A fragment of an imported bowl with both interior and exterior decoration (fig. 39A1, A2; plate 18E) has an interior design which derives from the terminal Early Intermediate Period fusion of Nazca and Huarpa with the early Middle Horizon Conchopata style. The design depicts a profile of a spotted-and-horned animal which shares a fanged mouth, ring nose, hornlike projections on top of the head, and body spots with Middle Horizon 1A specimens from Acuchimay (Menzel 1968a: 57, figs. 2b-6). However, the Jargampata specimen lacks a zigzag band framing the upper side of the body and shares with Epoch 2A spotted-and-horned animals an orientation upright to the rim (Menzel 1968a: 73, fig. 7). Tentatively, this design theme seems best dated as Middle Horizon 1B, although it may be an archaic Epoch 2A specimen. The bowl fragment was found on the disturbed floor of room S1, where it may have been part of the furnishings which accompanied a human mummy. If this is so, the piece may already have been quite old. In fact, it may have been only a sherd since no more fragments of this bowl, easily identified by its distinctive paste, were found throughout the House Group.

An imported, oversized interior-decorated bowl with outcurving, concave walls and representational designs which probably depict llamas (fig. 41E; plate 17A1, A2) may also belong to Middle Horizon 2A. Representational designs occur only in Early Patibamba and Middle Patibamba, which may provide cross-dating for this specimen.

One face-neck jar (fig. 40C) has a nearly spherical body and cylindrical neck more characteristic of Middle Horizon

2A than 2B on the South Coast (Menzel 1968a: 81). However, the specimen was in association with a face-neck jar which is clearly Epoch 2B (fig. 40A1, A2; plate 16F1, F2), and both were probably redeposited from room S1.

Fragments from four exotic, oversize bowls were found in the House Group. Two are plain (fig. 41B, D) and cannot be dated stylistically, although one accompanied the burned textile offering below the foundation of the north wall of room S4, which was a fairly late addition to the House Group. The other two bowls have interior decoration (fig. 41A, C; plate 18G) and are so similar that they may have formed a pair. Both came from mixed strata but originally were probably grave furniture in room S1. They have interior designs based upon rectilinear, geometric, stylized wings. The stylized wing placed diagonally to a vessel rim occurs at Jargampata only in Early and Middle Patibamba (fig. 25H-M), suggesting that these imported bowls also belong to Middle Horizon 2A. However, Menzel (1964: fig. 28) reports similar wing motifs on interior-decorated bowls of Middle Horizon Epoch 2B from the South Coast. Consequently, the dating of these specimens remains in question.

Late Patibamba I and II belong to Middle Horizon Epoch 2B. This period certainly represents the time of maximum interaction between Jargampata and Wari. Late Patibamba I includes sixteen imported vessel fragments (fig. 39C, E, F, H, I; plates 16A, 17D, F). The most diagnostic of these comes from an exotic lyre-shaped cup with front-face deity head (fig. 39C; plate 16A). This specimen is the same kind of vessel as a more complete example from the House Group which was probably part of the grave furniture on the floor of room S1 (fig. 29D1, D2; plate 16B1, B2). Both of these cups were discussed in Chapter 5, and it is clear that they belong to Middle Horizon Epoch 2B (Menzel 1968a: 76, 89). Unfortunately, the seriation of fancy, lay elite pottery is not yet sufficiently detailed to permit definite stylistic dating to subepochs for the other imported pieces from Late Patibamba I.

Late Patibamba II includes three exotic sherds, only one of which is decorated (fig. 39B; plate 17C). This sherd is sufficiently eroded to suggest it may not have been an original inclusion in Late Patibamba II refuse.

A substantial number of vessels from the House Group probably belong to Middle Horizon 2B and should be contemporary with these two phases. The lyre-shaped cup (fig. 39D1, D2; plate 16B1, B2) has been discussed elsewhere, but it provides an important date for at least some of the human remains placed in room S1. A face-neck

---

Figure 39. Fine Elite Vessels   (Scale = ½)

A   Early Patibamba (?); House Group, S1 floor; D=13 cm.; interior—black, white, gray, yellow, dark red on dark red; exterior—black, white, dark red, gray, yellow on dark red

B   Late Patibamba II; North Unit, S11 stratum D; D=7 cm.; black, white, yellow on light red.

C   Late Patibamba I; North Unit, S10 stratum D1, S11 stratum D; D=10 cm.; black, gray, dark red, white, yellow on light red

D1 and D2   Late Patibamba I (?); House Group, CW strata 3, 4III, CX stratum 3; D=10 cm.; black, gray, dark red, white, yellow on light red

E   Late Patibamba I; North Unit, S11 stratum D1; black, white, dark red, yellow on light red

F   Late Patibamba I; North Unit, S10 stratum D1; black, white, dark red on light red

G   Middle Patibamba; North Unit, S11 stratum E; D=11 cm.; black, white, yellow on dark red

H   Late Patibamba I; North Unit, E6 x S9 stratum 4b; black, white, and possible traces of yellow on light red

I   Late Patibamba I; North Unit, E6 x S10 stratum 4b, S11 stratum D1; D=15 cm.; black, white on light red

J   Early Patibamba; E2 x S14 stratum 9; D=17 cm.; black, dark red on natural

K   Early Patibamba (?); E2 x S14, E3 x S13-15 feature El-1; D=7.5 cm.; black, white, dark red, gray on light red

L   Middle Patibamba; North Unit, S10 stratum E; D=16 cm.; black, white, gray on light red

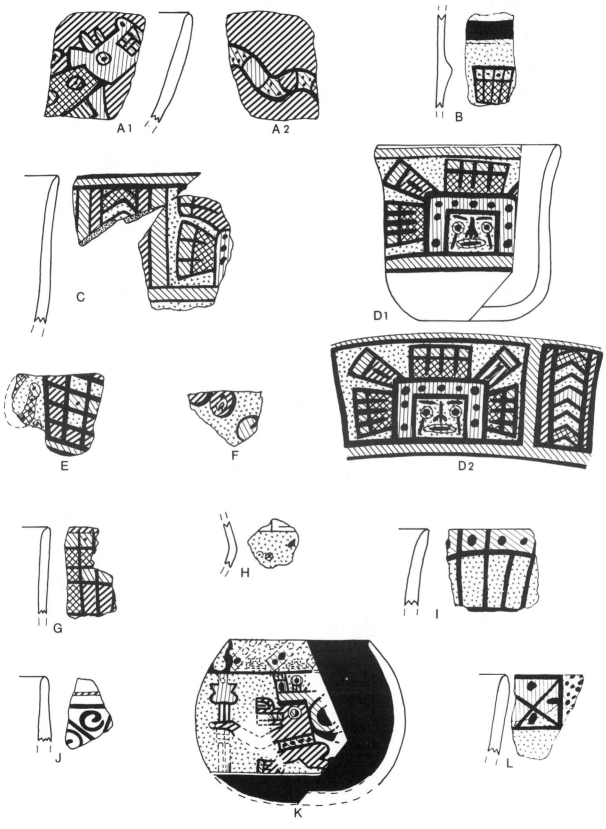

Fig. 39

Figure 40. Fine Elite Vessels   (Scale = ½)

A1 and A2   Late Patibamba I (?); House Group, CX strata 5, 5a; D=4 cm.; black, white, gray on orange

B1 and B2   Early Patibamba or Middle Patibamba (?); House Group, CX strata 3, 4, S5 stratum 2; D=6.5 cm.; black, white, gray on light red

C   Middle Patibamba (?); House Group, CX strata 4, 5, CZ stratum 5; D=4 cm.; black, white, dark red on brown

D   Late Patibamba I (?); House Group, CZ strata 5, 7; D=8 cm.; black, white on red

E   Late Patibamba I or II; House Group, CY stratum 3d, CW stratum 6; D=8.5 cm.; black, white, dark red, light red on dark red

F   Late Patibamba I or II (?); House Group, CY stratum 3d; D=7 cm.; black, white, gray, light red, dark red on light red

G   Late Patibamba I or II(?); House Group, CW stratum 3; black, gray on light red

H   Late Patibamba I (?); House Group, CY stratum 5; black on orange-red

I   Late Patibamba I; House Group, S1 floor, CW stratum 4b; D=5 cm.; black, white on light red

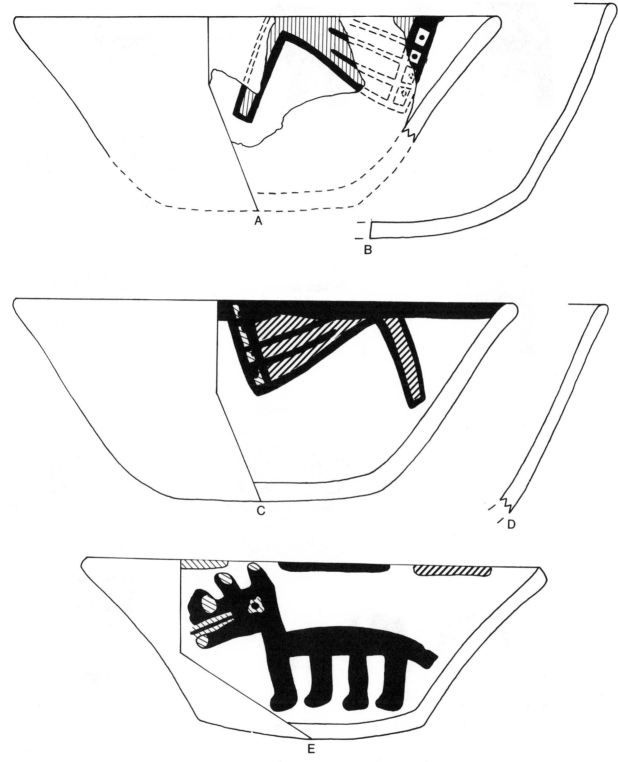

Figure 41. Fine Elite Vessels   (Scale = ½)

A   Late Patibamba I (?); House Group, S1 floor, CW stratum 1, S4 strata 1, 2; D=26 cm.; black, gray on red slip

B   Late Patibamba I (?); House Group, CY strata 3, 3c, 4; D=26 cm.

C   Late Patibamba I (?); House Group, S1 floor and fill, S4 stratum 1, CW strata 1, 3a; D=27 cm.; black, dark red, white on red

D   Late Patibamba (?); House Group, S4 subfoundation offering; D=26 cm.

E   Early Patibamba or Middle Patibamba (?); House Group, CY stratum 6a; D=25 cm.; black, white, dark red on red

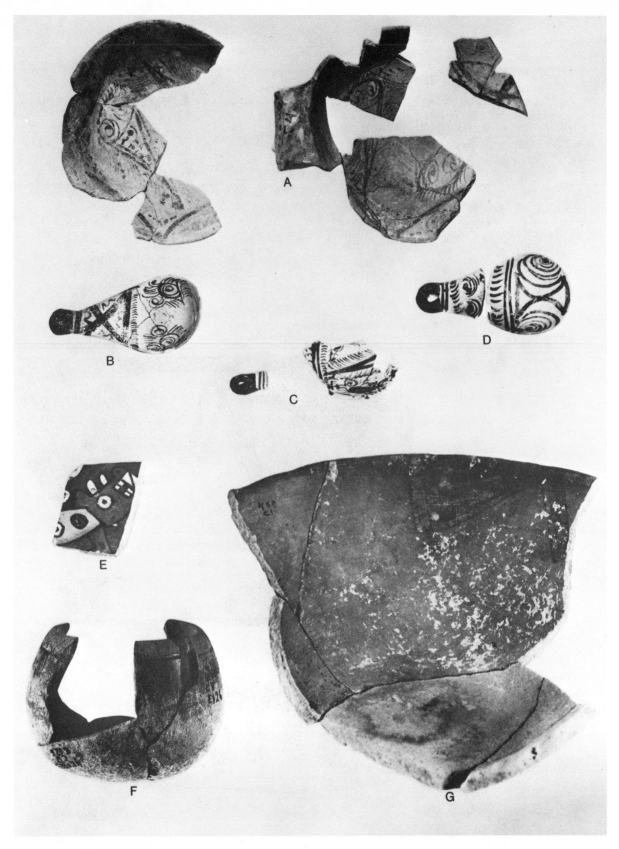

Plate 18. Fine Elite and Imported Vessels   (Scale = 1/2)

A   Figure 38A

B   Cajamarca Spoon; House Group, S6 strata 6, 7

C   Cajamarca Spoon; House Group, S6 stratum 6, S2 stratum 3,
CW stratum 3a

D   Cajamarca Spoon; House Group, CW strata 4, 4II

E   Figure 39A1, A2

F   Figure 40D

G   Figure 41C

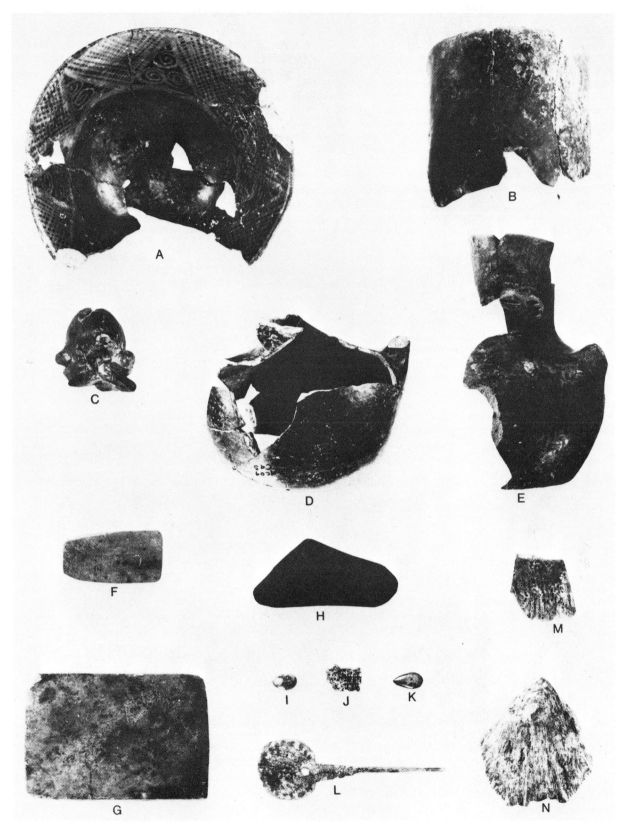

Plate 19. A–E: Black Decorated Vessels; F–N: Nonceramic Artifacts   (Scale = ½)

A	Figure 42E	H	Stone Scraper-Polisher; Illaura; North Unit, S11 stratum C1
B	Figure 42G	I	Stone Bean Effigy; House Group, S6 stratum 6
C	Figure 42C	J	Stone Alpaca Effigy; House Group, S6 stratum 6
D	Figure 42D1, D2	K	Stone Teardrop Form; House Group, S1 floor
E	Figure 42B1, B2	L	Metal *Tupo*; North Unit, S9 fill
F	Stone Plaque; House Group, CW stratum 3	M	Worked *Spondylus* Shell; North Unit, plaza floor.
G	Stone Plaque; House Group, CW stratum 3	N	Unworked Oyster (probably *Ostrea*); House Group, S4 stratum 5

jar (fig. 40A1, A2) and probably the fragment of another (fig. 40H) have tapered spouts tilted slightly to the rear, very prominent shoulders, and bodies which taper toward the base. All these characteristics are diagnostic of Middle Horizon 2B (Menzel 1968a: 81). An incurving bowl with skull theme (fig. 40E; plate 16D) was associated with hollow tripod supports which appear first in Late Patibamba I. This suggests an Epoch 2B date for the bowl.

Several other pieces of imported pottery were found in the House Group but cannot be dated because of a lack of diagnostic features. One fragment (fig. 40G) may come from a bilobed bottle, a form which does not appear in the Jargampata ceramic samples until Late Patibamba or Middle Horizon 2B. It is worth noting that an Epoch 2B burial from the South Coast also has a bilobed bottle (Menzel 1964: fig. 24).

The small cup with straight sides (fig. 40F; plate 16E) is another shape which does not appear in local pottery at Jargampata until Late Patibamba I. The exotic incurving bowl (fig. 40D; plate 18F) and small jar collar (fig. 40I) cannot be dated but are likely to be late.

A number of black decorated (Bennett 1953: fig. 16; Menzel 1964: 18-19) vessel fragments were found in the House Group (fig. 42; plate 19B-E), but none were found in the ceramic sample selected for analysis. However, Late Patibamba I includes three exotic sherds which have glossy black surfaces and gray paste. These black undecorated vessel fragments probably establish the phase association for the black decorated ware from the House Group. Furthermore, one regular-size interior-decorated, black decorated bowl (fig. 42E; plate 19A) came from the floor of room S8 of the North Unit. Since a number of pieces were scattered about the floor, the bowl must have been dropped there just before the abandonment of the site, late in Late Patibamba I or in Late Patibamba II. It seems likely, then, that the plain black lyre-shaped cup (fig. 42G; plate 19B); the two curious face-neck vessels with laterally elongated bodies (fig. 42B1, B2, D1, D2; plate 19D, E); the animal effigy head (fig. 40C; plate 19C) and the collar fragment (fig. 42F), which may have come from other face-neck vessels; and the incurving bowl (fig. 40F) all belong to the Late Patibamba I Phase.

Since Late Patibamba I or Middle Horizon 2B represents the period of maximum exchange between Jargampata and centers of greater prestige, it is most likely that other exotic ceramics which cannot be dated belong to this phase. Most interesting are three spoons (plate 18B-D) in typical Cajamarca III Cursive Floral style (Reichlen 1970: 492). They have hard, white paste characteristic of the North Highlands and were produced by artisans very competent in executing the distinctive cursive design elements and themes. It is probable that the spoons were manufactured at Cajamarca and imported to the Central Highlands.

Another specimen with obvious Cajamarca affiliation is a vessel which consists of two small bowls with diameters of about 11 cm. each, which were joined by a solid bridge between the bowl rims and walls (fig. 38A; plate 18A). The bowls have slight basal angles, turned-out lips, and round bottoms, which are very unusual at Jargampata. The interiors of both bowls were painted in a pure cursive floral design which can be duplicated on materials from Wari (Bennett 1953: plate 11C; Lumbreras 1960: lam XVA-D) and on the exotic spoons from Jargampata (plate 18B-D). However, the hard, light paste characteristic of Cajamarca pottery is distinct from the dark, sand-tempered paste of this double vessel. Its paste is not identical to that of Jargampata since it is a bit darker and somewhat softer, but the texture and antiplastic inclusions are typical of the local paste. Consequently, it seems likely that the double vessel was made at Jargampata or in the Ayacucho area but was fired in a distinctive fashion. In any case, the vessel was manufactured and decorated by an artist highly skilled in the Cajamarca style of a paste very similar to that found at Jargampata.

A second vessel with slight base angle, turned-out lip, and rounded bottom also appears to copy Cajamarca styles (fig. 38B). In this case, there is no doubt that the paste is local and that the artist who decorated the vessel did not have a good understanding of Cajamarca designs. The inept cursive painting does not duplicate any design themes found at Jargampata, but employs design elements from Jargampata decoration in a combination not quite right for Cajamarca. The grid, or checkerboard, pattern is perhaps more successful in the hands of the Jargampata potter, who was strongly oriented to rectilinear geometric designs. Similar checkerboards are found on vessels which imitate Cajamarca bowls from Ayapata (Ravines 1968: fig. 31).

A third bowl with ring base from the House Group may also have meant to copy Cajamarca styles (fig. 33A). The rectangular grid with dots does not occur elsewhere at Jargampata and may copy the Cajamarca checkerboard. However, the paste is local, and the shape attributes are characteristic of Jargampata, except for the ring base, which is uncommon.

These last ceramic pieces suggest at least three kinds of interaction between the Wari region and the Cajamarca area of the North Highlands. The three spoons (plate 18B-D) indicate direct trade between centers in the Ayacucho area and the North Highlands. Small portable items were apparently carried between the regions, perhaps by trade specialists. It seems significant that fragments of Cajamarca bowls are found at Wari, while rural Jargampata has only the smallest and most easily transported ceramics—spoons. A carefully controlled redistribution must have taken place in the great urban centers.

Second, the double vessel (fig. 38A; plate 18A) suggests the presence in the Ayacucho area and perhaps even at Jargampata of artisans who were very well trained in

---

Figure 42. Black Decorated Vessels   (Scale = ½)

A   Late Patibamba I or II; House Group, CW stratum 5; D=5 cm.; red on black

B1 and B2   Late Patibamba I or II; House Group, CY strata 4, 5, CW stratum 5; D=6 cm.; red on black.

C   Late Patibamba I or II; House Group, CW stratum 4III; red on black

D1 and D2   Late Patibamba I or II; House Group, CW stratum 4; red on black

E   Late Patibamba I or II; North Unit, S8 floor; D=15 cm.; red on black

F   Late Patibamba I or II; House Group, CY stratum 5; D=5 cm.; red on black

G   Late Patibamba I or II; House Group, S5 strata 1, 2; D=10 cm.; plain black

Fig. 42

Cajamarca styles and worked in local clay but produced vessels of North Highland design. These artisans may have come from the North Highlands or been trained by North Highlanders. In any case, this indicates movement of craft specialists rather than their products alone. The presence of a locally made Cajamarca-style bowl at Jargampata but only spoons of imported Cajamarca ware may indicate a prestige interval between the two wares.

Third, the bowls with derived Cajamarca attributes (figs. 33A, 38B) indicate that local rural potters attempted to imitate a foreign product which must have had considerable prestige and value but with which they were only poorly acquainted.

A final sample of exotic vessels at Jargampata consists of locally manufactured pots which fall outside the stylistic variation defined for the five phases represented in the ceramic samples selected for analysis. A group of seven diagnostic vessel fragments came from a feature in the House Group which was labeled both Element 11 and Element 1 until it was recognized to be continuous (fig. 37). The feature is composed of gravel and underlies the floor of corridor CX, its west wall, and parts of room S1 and S3 (fig. 4). It is this gravel fill into which burial 3 intruded. There can be no doubt that feature Element 1 or 11 predates the construction of the House Group, and the pottery contained in the gravel must be early also. Three open bowls, which include two regular-size interior-decorated specimens (fig. 37C, E) and one regular-size plain bowl (fig. 37D) might belong to Early Patibamba. The black-outlined, vertical-band theme and the narrow, horizontal, white band have clear parallels in Early Patibamba. However, there are two horizontal "frying pan handles" (fig. 37A, B), a small cup or miniature bowl with an odd handle (fig. 37F), and a jar neck with vertical collar and flaring rim (fig. 37G). None of these features are found in Early Patibamba or the later phases. Several Huarpa sherds were collected from the surface of the Jargampata ridge area, and it is likely that the site had a sparse and sporadic occupation for much longer than the five phases represented in the North Unit and South Unit samples. These sherds from Element 11 include forms unknown in the five phases described and provide some indication of what pre–Early Patibamba ceramics may have looked like. However, it is likely that the vessels from the samples do not predate Early Patibamba by much since the bowls share so many characteristics with Early Patibamba bowls. The surprising part of the sample is the presence of shape features which are absent in Early Patibamba.

NONCERAMIC ARTIFACTS

Nonceramic artifacts from Jargampata were not subjected to analysis and remain in storage for future examination. However, preliminary impressions will be outlined here to provide a more accurate picture of the materials recovered from Jargampata.

Perhaps the most salient feature of the artifact inventory is the scarcity of chipped stone tools. A single fragment of an obsidian projectile point was recovered in the House Group, and a few unmodified flakes of obsidian and chert were found elsewhere in the North and South Units. In corridor CX of the House Group, some of the mixed strata from the south end of the corridor contained a large number of crudely flaked pieces of low-quality slate. These artifacts range in size from 10 cm. to about 80 cm. and look like very coarse blades or unfinished artifacts. The size and crudity of most specimens might suggest that they were intended for digging tools, although the stone does not seem hard enough to withstand heavy use. Similar but slightly better finished pieces of the low-quality slate were collected from the surface of the site of Ayaurqo opposite the town of San Miguel (fig. 2).

Ground stone objects were mostly limited to grinding stones for the preparation of foods. One *batan* and a rocker grinder were found in the North Unit, on the low bench in front of the wall of the South Gallery at E4 x S9. Other grinding stones were found near their original positions in corridors CX and CW of the House Group and in the northwest corner of room S7. Very few of these showed deliberate shaping through pecking or grinding. Most *batans* are simply large, flat stones of appropriate size and shape, which could not be distinguished from those in use in modern rural homes today. In fact, several disappeared from the excavations and were recovered in the houses of local residents where they had been taken to be used. The grinding stones or *manos* are elongated and convex on the abraded surface. They could have been used by sliding or rocking. One fragment of a stone bowl was recovered from corridor CW of the House Group.

Other ground stone objects include a scraper-polisher of stone (plate 19H), the two stone plaques (plate 19F, G) which were discussed with pottery scraper-polishers, and several small cylinders from the North Unit which may have been pestles.

Tiny stone objects manufactured from a hard green stone were found in the House Group. Most common were small, irregular green beads from about .4 cm. to .8 cm. in diameter with biconically drilled holes. One bead of a lighter green is ground into a disk .6 cm. in diameter. These beads were found only in the House Group, and mostly in the disturbed soil from room S1, where they may have comprised grave offerings.

Among other tiny objects made from the same green stone is an animal effigy from the floor of room S6. The animal appears to be a camelid with very long wool, perhaps an alpaca (plate 19J). It is exactly 2 cm. long and 1.5 cm. tall at the top of the ears. Three flattened teardrop forms were found, two on the floor of room S1 and one in corridor CY (plate 19K). A green stone effigy of a *Phaseolus vulgaris* bean was found on the floor of room S6 (plate 19I) along with a small green stone sphere .75 cm. in diameter. A green stone cube 2.3 cm. long, 1.5 cm. wide, and .9 cm. thick with two biconical holes through the short axis was found in corridor CY. Finally, a fragment of a blue turquoise bead was found on the floor of room S6.

The only objects in clear association with a burial were found with burial 5 in the east end of corridor CZ. Two light-colored, soft, spherical stone beads with diameters of 1.9 cm. and 2.2 cm. and biconical holes were found, along with thirteen tubular bone beads ranging from .8 cm. to 3 cm. long and .5 cm. to .8 cm. thick and one tubular shell bead 2.5 cm. long and .4 cm. thick which may be *Spondylus* shell.

Shell is not uncommon at Jargampata and all is of marine origin. Genera represented include *Ostrea*, *Pecten*, and, most commonly, *Spondylus* (plate 19M, N). There are thirteen fragments of *Spondylus* from the House Group and three from the North Unit. These last three come from the west end of the plaza floor and the floor of room S9, which

indicates that they are late, belonging to Late Patibamba I or II. All show evidence of having been worked. The shells were cut into long trapezoids and sometimes ground smooth on the exterior surface. The final form resembles a small adze blade 4 cm. to 8 cm. long and about 2.5 cm. to 4 cm. wide. However, the edges were never sharpened. None of the specimens have holes drilled in them.

Oyster shell was apparently handled quite differently. One complete shell came from room S4, but all other pieces are finished ornaments. One oyster shell ornament from room S4 is circular, 2.5 cm. in diameter and .2 cm. thick, with two biconical holes .5 cm. apart near the edge. A second oyster shell, also from room S4, is rectangular, 2.5 cm. wide by 3.4 cm. long, and has biconical holes in two corners. The third ornament came from corridor CW and is not complete. It is 1.7 cm. wide and 2.7 cm. long but was longer. It also has biconical holes in two corners.

One *Pecten* shell which is now broken was probably used as an ornament in complete form. It has two biconical holes just below the hinge.

A number of thin tubular and small disk-shaped shell beads were found in various parts of the House Group. At present they have not been identified by genus or species, but some pinkish beads may be made from *Spondylus* while white specimens may come from some kind of *Venus* clam.

Metal objects are very rare at Jargampata, and only three fragmentary objects—all shawl pins or *tupos*—were found. However, in contrast with the fancy pottery, shell objects, and Cajamarca imports, which were more common in the House Group, two fairly large copper *tupos* come from the North Unit while only one very small specimen was found in the House Group. The best-preserved specimen is 10 cm. long and came from room S9 (plate 19L). The other specimen, from the plaza floor, consists of part of the flattened head of a pin, but was probably larger than the complete example. The *tupo* from the House Group came from mixed strata of room S2 and is only 5.3 cm. long and very modest in appearance.

Table 1. Distribution of Vessel Shape Categories Listed by Percentage within Samples and Phases

	Early Patibamba Sample A	Early Patibamba Sample B	Early Patibamba Entire Phase	Middle Patibamba Entire Phase	Late Patibamba I Sample A	Late Patibamba I Sample B	Late Patibamba I Sample C	Late Patibamba I Entire Phase	Late Patibamba II Sample A	Late Patibamba II Sample B	Late Patibamba II Sample C	Late Patibamba II Sample D	Late Patibamba II Entire Phase	Illaura Entire Phase
1.1	47.8	41.4	45.8	33.3	23.1	33.3	34.0	30.9	21.8	10.0	29.2	46.2	26.9	49.4
1.1.1	5.2	5.2	5.2	2.9	3.1	4.1	6.0	4.2	3.6		3.4	7.7	3.6	1.2
1.1.1.1	4.5	5.2	4.7	2.0	3.1	1.4	6.0	2.7	3.6		1.1	7.7	2.4	1.2
1.1.2	1.5		1.0	1.0	1.5	2.0	2.0	1.9			3.4		1.8	.6
1.1.3	32.8	34.5	33.3	18.6	10.8	19.0	14.0	16.0	9.1	10.0	13.5	15.4	12.0	36.6
1.1.3A	1.5	1.7	1.6	1.0		1.4		.8			1.1	7.7	1.2	5.8
1.1.3B	6.7	5.2	6.3	2.0	3.1	6.8	6.0	5.7	3.6		1.1		1.8	4.7
1.1.3C	8.2	13.8	9.9	6.9	3.1	5.4	2.0	4.2	3.6		5.6	7.7	4.8	12.8
1.1.3D	3.0	6.9	4.2	2.9	1.5	.7		.8			1.1		.6	1.7
1.1.3E	6.7	3.4	5.7	2.9	1.5		2.0	.8	1.8	10.0			1.2	8.1
1.1.3F	4.5	1.7	3.6	1.0	1.5	1.4		1.1						.6
1.1.3G	2.2	1.7	2.1	2.0		3.4	4.0	2.7			1.1		.6	2.9
1.2	.7	1.7	1.0	1.0	1.5	2.7	2.0	2.3	3.6		1.1		1.8	3.5
1.2.3	.7	1.7	1.0		1.5	2.7	2.0	2.3	3.6		1.1		1.8	2.9
1.3	42.5	53.4	45.8	54.9	58.5	53.1	58.0	55.3	69.1	90.0	53.9	53.8	61.9	39.0
1.3.1	15.0	25.9	18.2	13.7	29.2	13.6	14.0	17.6	10.9	10.0	12.4	7.7	11.4	13.4
1.3.1.1	10.4	20.7	13.5	12.7	21.5	12.9	14.0	15.3	7.3	10.0	11.2		9.0	12.8
1.3.1.2	4.5	5.2	4.7	1.0	7.7	.7		2.3	3.6		1.1	7.7	2.4	.6
1.3.2	21.6	20.7	21.4	32.4	26.2	25.2	32.0	26.7	50.9	80.0	29.2	38.5	40.1	20.3
1.3.2.1	17.9	20.7	18.8	20.6	16.9	15.6	14.0	15.6	30.9	50.0	20.2	30.8	26.3	12.2
1.3.2.1.1	13.4	8.6	12.0	12.7	10.8	5.4	12.0	8.0	14.5	30.0	11.2	15.4	13.8	8.1
1.3.2.2	3.7		2.6	10.8	9.2	9.5	18.0	11.1	18.2	30.0	9.0	7.7	13.2	8.1
1.3.2.2.1	2.2		1.6	4.9	6.2	6.1	16.0	8.0	16.3	20.0	5.6	7.7	10.2	5.8
1.3.3	.7	1.7	1.0		3.7	4.1	8.0	4.6	3.6		1.1	15.4	3.0	4.1
1.3.5	3.0	5.2	3.6	2.9			2.0	.4	1.8		2.2		1.8	2.3
1.3.6	1.5		1.0				2.0	.4	3.6				1.2	1.2
1.5	2.2		1.6											.6
1.1.1.2	.7	0.0	.5	1.0										
1.3.2.1.2	1.5	1.7	1.6		1.5	.7		.8	1.8		1.1		1.2	
1.3.3.1	.7	1.7	1.0			1.4		.8	1.8			7.7	1.2	
1.8	2.2		1.6	1.0		.7		.4	1.8		1.1		1.2	
1.10	.7		.5	2.0	6.2	6.8	4.0	6.4			3.4		1.8	
1.2.2.1				1.0										
1.3.4				1.0										
1.2.2				1.0										
1.3.2.3				1.0					1.8				.6	
1.9				2.0		.7		.4			1.1		.6	1.7
1.3.2.2.2						.7		.4						
1.1.1.3						2.7		1.5			2.2		1.2	
1.3.3.2						.7		.4			1.1		.6	
1.3.3.3					3.1	2.1	8.0	3.4	1.8			7.7	1.2	4.1
1.3.6.1							2.0	.4			1.1		.6	
1.3.7							2.0	.4						.6
1.4					1.5	.7	2.0	1.1			3.4		1.8	1.7
1.7					1.5	.7		.8	1.8		1.1		1.2	
1.2.2.2														.6

Table 2. Distribution of Decorative Attributes Listed by Percentage within Samples and Phases

	Early Patibamba Sample A	Early Patibamba Sample B	Early Patibamba Entire Phase	Middle Patibamba Entire Phase	Late Patibamba I Sample A	Late Patibamba I Sample B	Late Patibamba I Sample C	Late Patibamba I Entire Phase	Late Patibamba II Sample A	Late Patibamba II Sample B	Late Patibamba II Sample C	Late Patibamba II Sample D	Late Patibamba II Entire Phase	Illaura Entire Phase
2.1.1.1	.7	1.7	1.0	3.9	4.6	4.1		3.4	5.5		1.1		2.4	2.9
2.1.1.3	6.0	10.3	7.3	2.0	3.1	3.4		2.7	9.1	10.0	6.7		7.2	2.3
2.1.2.1	1.5	1.7	1.6	5.9	9.2	4.8	2.0	5.3	7.2	10.0	10.1		8.4	2.3
2.1.2.2		1.7	.5	1.0	4.6	1.4		1.9	3.6				1.2	3.5
2.1.2.5	2.2		1.6	6.9	3.1	1.4		1.5	1.8		2.2		1.8	3.5
2.1.2.9	.7		.5	1.0										1.2
2.1.3.1	5.2		3.6	4.9	1.5	1.4	2.0	5.0	12.7	10.0	3.4	30.8	9.0	2.9
2.1.3.5		1.7	.5		1.5	1.4		1.1	1.8		1.1		1.2	1.2
3.2.2	2.2		1.6	2.0	3.1	2.7		2.3	5.5	20.0	1.1		3.6	2.9
3.5.1.6	.7		.5											.6
3.10.1	.7		.5			.7		.4			1.1		.6	.6
4.5.1.1	.7		.5	2.0		2.0	18.0	4.6	9.1	10.0	3.4	7.7	6.0	4.6
4.5.2	.7		.5								1.1	7.7	1.2	.6
4.5.1.2	.7		.5	1.0			4.0	.8			1.1		.6	.6
4.13.4	.7	1.7	1.0			.7		.4	1.8		2.2		1.8	.6
4.13.1	1.5		1.0	4.9	3.1	2.7		2.3	3.6		3.4	7.7	3.6	1.2
4.5.4	.7		.5	1.0			2.0	.4			1.1		.6	1.7
4.5.4.1	.7		.5	1.0	1.5	.7		.8			1.1		.6	1.7
2.1.4.4	.7		.5											
2.1.4.8		1.7	.5											
2.3.3	1.5		1.0											
2.3.5	.7		.5											
3.2.4	.7		.5											
3.6.2	.7		.5											
3.8.2	.7		.5											
3.15	3.0		2.1											
3.13	.7		.5											
4.5.3	.7		.5											
4.7	.7		.5											
4.9	.7		.5											
4.10	1.5		1.0											
2.1.1.2	2.2		1.6	3.9										
2.1.4.1	.7		.5	1.0		.7		.4						
2.1.3.10	1.5		1.0		3.1			.8						
2.1.2.7	1.5		1.6	1.0			2.0	.4						
2.1.2.10	2.2		1.6			.7		.4						
2.1.4.2	.7		.5		1.5	.7		.8		10.0	1.1		1.2	
2.1.4.6	.7		.5				.2	.4		10.0		7.7	1.2	
2.3.4	.7		.5								1.1		.6	
3.2.1	.7		.5	1.0										
3.5.1.1	2.2		1.6	2.0										
3.5.1.1.1	1.5		1.0	1.0										
3.9	1.5		1.0	1.0										
3.6	.7	1.7	1.0	2.9										
3.6.1	.7	1.7	1.0	1.0										
3.3.1	1.5	1.7	1.6			.7		.4			1.1		.6	
3.5.1.1.2	.7		.5			.7		.4						

	Early Patibamba Sample A	Early Patibamba Sample B	Early Patibamba Entire Phase	Middle Patibamba Entire Phase	Late Patibamba I Sample A	Late Patibamba I Sample B	Late Patibamba I Sample C	Late Patibamba I Entire Phase	Late Patibamba II Sample A	Late Patibamba II Sample B	Late Patibamba II Sample C	Late Patibamba II Sample D	Late Patibamba II Entire Phase	Illaura Entire Phase
3.10		1.7	.5	1.0	4.6			1.1						
3.8.1	1.5		1.0		1.5			.4						
3.4.2	.7		.5									7.7	.6	
4.4.1	.7		.5	1.0										
4.13.5		3.4	1.0	1.0										
4.1	1.5		1.0		1.5	.7		.8						
4.13.3		1.7	.5		1.5	.7		.8						
4.2	.7		.5		1.5			.4						
4.4.1.3	.7		.5			1.4		.8	1.8	10.0			1.2	
4.3	1.5	1.7	1.6			.7		.4			1.1		.6	
4.13.2	1.5	1.7	1.6		1.5			.4		10.0	2.2	7.7	2.4	
5.1	1.5		1.0		1.5			.4						
5.2	.7		.5	1.0			.4	.8			1.1		.6	
5.3	.7		.5			.7		.4		10.0			.6	
2.1.4.5				1.0										
2.3.2				1.0										
2.1.3.15				1.0										
3.2				2.9										
3.5.2.5				1.0										
3.5.2.7				1.0										
3.5.2.8				1.0										
2.1.3.4				1.0		.7		.4						
2.1.3.16				1.0	1.5			.4						
2.1.3.8				2.0							1.1		.6	
2.1.2.3				2.0			2.0	.4	1.8		1.1	1.0	.6	
2.1.3.2				2.0		2.7		1.5	1.8	10.0	1.1		1.8	1.7
3.7				1.0							1.1		.6	
3.1.2.1				1.0		.7		.4	3.6				1.2	.6
3.3.2				1.0	4.6	2.0		2.3	1.8		1.1		1.2	.6
3.3.2.1				1.0							1.1		.6	1.2
3.5.1.2				6.9	1.5	1.4	4.0	1.9		10.0			.6	1.2
3.5.2.3				1.0		2.0		.4	1.8		1.1	15.4	2.4	.6
3.5.3.1				1.0		1.4	14.0	3.4	7.2		1.1	7.7	3.6	1.2
4.5.3.1				1.0	1.5			.4			1.1		.6	
4.4.2				1.0		.7		.4	1.8	10.0	2.2		2.4	
4.4.1.1				1.0		.7	2.0	.8	5.5		1.1		2.4	1.2
4.4.1.4				1.0	3.1			.8	1.8	10.0			1.2	.6
4.5.1				2.9		1.4	2.0	1.1	1.8			7.7	1.2	1.7
4.5.2.1				1.0		.7		.4						.6
5.4				1.0	1.5	.7		.8			1.1		.6	.6
5.5				1.0		1.4	12.0	3.1	7.2		1.1	7.7	3.6	.6
5.6				1.0			2.0	.4			2.2	7.7	1.8	.6
2.1.1.4					1.5	.7		.8						
2.1.2.11					1.5	.7		.8						
2.1.3.12					1.5	.7		.8						
2.1.5.2							2.0	.4						
3.1.2					1.5			.4						
3.1.1.1						1.4		.8						
3.1.3.2						.7		.4						
3.5.3.4							2.0	.4						

	Early Patibamba Sample A	Early Patibamba Sample B	Early Patibamba Entire Phase	Middle Patibamba Entire Phase	Late Patibamba I Sample A	Late Patibamba I Sample B	Late Patibamba I Sample C	Late Patibamba I Entire Phase	Late Patibamba II Sample A	Late Patibamba II Sample B	Late Patibamba II Sample C	Late Patibamba II Sample D	Late Patibamba II Entire Phase	Illaura Entire Phase
3.12						.7		.4						
3.1.3.1							2.0	.4						
4.5.5					1.5			.4						
2.1.2.14						.7		.4		10.0			.6	
2.1.3.11						.7		.4			1.1		.6	
2.1.3.17						.7		.4	1.8				.6	
2.1.3.7						.7		.4						.6
2.1.4.3							4.0	.8	1.8				.6	
3.1.4					1.5	1.4		1.1			1.1		.6	
3.3.3					3.1			.8		10.0			.6	1.2
3.1.1						.7		.4			1.1		.6	.6
3.1.2.4							2.0	.4	1.8				.6	
3.3.1.1						.7		.4	5.5	10.0			2.4	
3.3.2.2						.7		.4	1.8				.6	
3.5.1.3						.7		.4	1.8				.6	
3.5.2.1						.7		.4	1.8				.6	
3.5.2.2						1.4		.8			1.1		.6	
3.5.2.4						.7		.4	1.8				.6	
3.4.1							2.0	.4	3.6	10.0			2.4	
4.4.1.2						.7	2.0	.8	5.5		2.2		3.0	
4.6					1.5	1.4	2.0	1.9						.6
5.7						.7		.4	7.2	10.0			3.0	
2.1.2.8									1.8				.6	
2.1.3.14									1.8				.6	
2.1.4.9									1.8				.6	
2.3.1									1.8				.6	
2.1.4.7										10.0			.6	
2.1.2.4											1.1		.6	
2.1.5.1											1.1		.6	
3.5.3.2									1.8				.6	
3.5.3.3									1.8				.6	
3.7.1									1.8				.6	
3.1.4.1											1.1		.6	
3.5.1											1.1		.6	
3.8											1.1		.6	
3.14												7.7	.6	
4.5.1.2.1									3.6				1.2	
4.5.4.2										10.0			.6	
4.8											1.1		.6	
2.1.3.9									1.8				.6	.6
2.1.2.6											1.1	7.7	1.2	.6
3.1.2.3									1.8				.6	1.2
3.2.3									1.8		1.1		1.2	1.2
3.5.1.4									1.8		1.1		1.2	1.7
3.1.2.2											2.2	7.7	1.8	.6
2.1.3.3														.6
2.1.3.13														.6
3.5.1.2.1														.6
3.5.1.5														.6
3.5.2.6														.6
4.5.3.2														.6

9

Ceramics of the Early Patibamba Phase

STRATIGRAPHIC ASSOCIATION

Early Patibamba pottery is isolated in six strata lying outside the enclosure wall of the North Unit (fig. 43). Four excavation trenches, labeled E2-5, contained ceramics of this style. The samples of pottery selected for analysis came from six square meters labeled E2-3 x S13-15. Stratum 9 is the oldest deposition containing Early Patibamba ceramics and probably corresponds to the period immediately before the construction of the North Unit enclosure and to the first building period. However, the relationship between the stratum and the perimeter wall is not totally clear since the base of the wall penetrates well below stratum 9, although it was impossible to distinguish an excavation cutting through the stratum for the construction of the wall. It is likely that such an excavation was no wider than the wall foundation it accommodated.

Strata 4 through 8 also contain Early Patibamba ceramics. However, I suspect that these alluvial deposits with only sparse refuse are not primary cultural deposits but represent materials eroded and washed from higher up on the slope. Materials on or near the surface which were redeposited in these five strata are sherds and refuse from stratum 9, and therefore the absolute vertical position of a sherd is not useful for relative dating. In spite of the fact that the upper strata were probably formed after the abandonment of Jargampata, the materials they contain are the same found in stratum 9.

Early Patibamba ceramics probably belong to Middle Horizon Epoch 2A.

VESSEL SAMPLE

A total of 192 vessel fragments represents the Early Patibamba Phase. This sample has been treated as a single unit, but statistics are also presented on Early Patibamba Subphase A and Subphase B in case some significant differences occur between the samples. These represent stratum 9 and strata 4 through 8 respectively. The sample for Subphase A includes 134 pieces and that for Subphase B consists of fifty-eight fragments.

Only diagnostic sherds were included in the analysis. Plain body sherds were not examined. Of the 192 separate pieces studied, all but nine fragments were sorted into shape categories. These nine decorated body sherds included in the sample but not assigned to shapes prevent the sum of the frequency of all vessel shape categories from totaling 100%. Furthermore, because sherds assigned to a general category may not include features of shape or size upon which more refined subcategories are based, the frequencies of these subgroups may not total 100% of the more inclusive category. For example, a heavy conical base can be included as representative of necked jars, but it is impossible to assign it to the category of narrow-collar jar, or side-spout jar, or flaring-neck jar. Consequently, such a vessel fragment cannot be included in the more specific categories.

The vessel shapes which are most frequent in the Early Patibamba sample are necked jars and open bowl forms. These groups are equally frequent, accounting for 45.8% each of all the vessels present. Together, therefore, they account for 91.7% of the sample from the phase.

NECKED JARS   1.1

Eighty-eight necked jars represent 45.8% of the ceramics from the Early Patibamba Phase. These include sixty-four jars, or 47.8%, from Subphase A, and twenty-four jars, or 41.4%, from Subphase B. None of these jars could be completely reconstructed, so certain aspects of shape remain uncertain. However, all the jars have circular horizontal profiles and probably all had strap handles made of clay bands with slightly kidney bean–shaped sections. There is a considerable range in size of handles, suggesting that they were attached to vessels of varying sizes.

Strap handles were placed on the shoulders of large vessels in either a horizontal or a vertical position, apparently in approximately equal frequencies. Smaller jars generally had handles linking the middle of the neck to the upper part of the shoulder or, as indicated in one case,

---

Figure 43. West Face of E3 x S13-15

Pre-1 Rock and gray soil accumulation at base of wall.
1 Dark brown, hard-packed soil with numerous eroded sherds and stones.
2 Black clayish soil with few stones.
3 Red-brown sandy soil with fine gravel.
E1.1 Loose gravel, rocks, and sherds
4 Fine yellow-brown sand with few rocks.
5 Fine yellow-brown sand separated from stratum 4 by a thin line with fine gravel.
6 Fine yellow-brown sand separated from stratum 5 by a thin line with fine gravel.

7 Friable red-brown sand with large rocks probably fallen from wall.
8 Thin band of red clayish soil.
9 Gray-black ashy soil with charcoal, large quantities of sherds, gravel, and rocks. This is the major occupation stratum and probably represents the construction period for the North Unit enclosure wall.
10 Red-brown sand and gravel. Sterile.
11 Yellow-brown sand and gravel. Sterile.

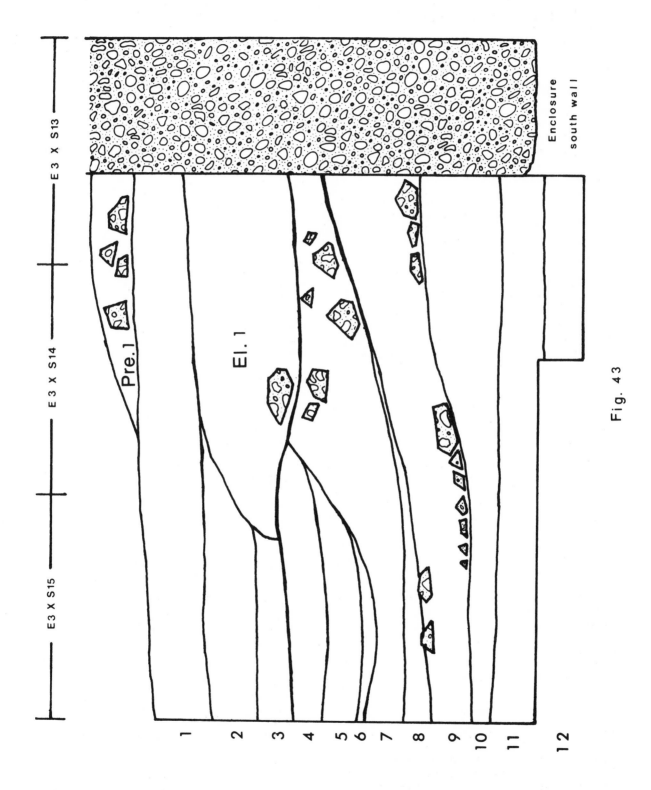

Fig. 43

looping from the rim to the shoulder (fig. 14).

Only two bases were recovered, but both are conical, one from a large and one from a small jar. If this is the only base form, it suggests that body forms were generally elongated. However, it is possible that rounded bases were not recognized during the analysis.

A single example of an appliqué adorno was found. It is a fillet of clay about 4 cm. long welded to the body of the jar parallel to the juncture of the neck and shoulder. The long fillet was incised with vertical lines (fig. 16X). Spouts occur only on side-spout jars.

Decoration is rare on necked jars, and painted design was probably limited to jars of the constricted-neck group, including both narrow-collar jars and face-neck jars. Side-spout jars may also have been decorated, but none were reconstructed.

Constricted-Neck Jars   1.1.1

Constricted-neck jars include ten examples, which represent 5.2% of the Early Patibamba Phase. The sample from Subphase A includes seven examples, or 5.2%, while Subphase B has three examples which also total 5.2%. This general group was often decorated by rim elaborations or painted designs.

Narrow-Collar Jars   1.1.1.1

Nine rims from narrow-collar jars represent 4.7% of the Early Patibamba Phase pottery (fig. 10D-F, H-J, P, U, Y). These include six examples, or 4.5%, of the Subphase A sample, and three specimens, or 5.2%, from Subphase B. These vessel fragments may be described as follows:

	Sample A	Sample B	Entire Phase
Mouth Diameter			
range	8-12cm.	7-12cm.	7-12cm.
mode	10-12cm.	–	9-12cm.
mean	10.2cm.	9.3cm.	9.9cm.
Wall Angle			
range	0-10°	0-10°	0-10°
mode	0	10°	0
mean	2.5°	6.7°	3.9°
Wall Profile Mode			
primary	A	A	A
secondary	E	B	E, B
Lip Treatment Mode			
primary	A	A	A
secondary	B	D	B, D
Rim Modification Mode			
primary	E3	A	E3
secondary	A	E3	A
Neck Thickness			
range	.5-.7cm.	.5-.6cm.	.5-.7cm.
mode	.5cm.	.5cm.	.5cm.
mean	.58cm.	.53cm.	.57cm.

The height of the collars of these jars varied from about 7 cm. to 10 cm. Two collars have painted decorations composed of black, cross-shaped elements repeated in horizontal strings below the rim (fig. 10U). Neither of these has rim elaboration, suggesting that painting and rim thickening may be alternate forms of decoration.

Face-Neck Jars   1.1.1.2

A single fragment of a face-neck jar represents .5% of the phase and .7% of Subphase A. The sherd is small and has an appliqué nose and a deep oblique incision for the eye. No paint was preserved on the surface. The face was modeled on a part of the collar, which bulged outward in an E wall profile form (fig. 11C). This same wall profile occurs on narrow-collar jars of the Early Patibamba Phase.

Several additional sherds from unidentified closed vessel forms have painted or painted and appliqué decoration. These sherds probably come from face-neck jars. One example has an appliqué arm and hand lying on a panel defined by a gray band (fig. 11H). This suggests that Early Patibamba face-neck jars were finished with appliqué and incised features representing limbs. Modeling of body and face features is a characteristic of Middle Horizon Epoch 1B in the Robles Moqo style (Menzel 1964: 21-31) and survives in more rudimentary form into early Epoch 2.

Side-Spout Jars   1.1.2

Two small fragments of laterally placed spouts represent 1% of the Early Patibamba Phase ceramics, or 1.5% of the Subphase A sample (see fig. 13). The entire vessel shape cannot be reconstructed, but it seems likely that it belonged within the category of necked jars.

One spout was covered with a fairly thick matte red slip, while the other was plain or slipped with a thin light-red coating applied very sparsely. The spout diameters are 7 cm. and 3.5 cm. indicating a considerable size variation in this vessel category.

Flaring-Neck Jars   1.1.3

Flaring-neck jars account for sixty-four vessels, or 33.3% of the Early Patibamba ceramics (figs. 14, 15). The sample from Subphase A contains forty-four specimens, or 32.8%, while Subphase B includes twenty examples of flaring-neck jars, a total of 34.5%. These vessels range considerably in size, and mouth diameters show a clearly multimodal distribution. The general category may be described as follows:

	Sample A	Sample B	Entire Phase
Mouth Diameter			
range	7-45cm.	12-42cm.	7-45cm.
mean	26.1cm.	23.2cm.	25.2cm.
Wall Angle			
range	0-40°	(-5)-50°	(-5)-50°
mode	15-30°	10-25°	15-25°
mean	21.5°	20°	21°
Wall Profile Mode			
primary	B	B	B
secondary	A	A	A
Lip Treatment Mode			
primary	C	C	C
secondary	A, D	A	A
Rim Modification Mode			
primary	A	A	A
secondary	E	E	E
Neck Thickness			
range	.5-1.4cm.	.4-1.1cm.	.4-1.4cm.
mode	.7cm., 1.2cm.	.6cm., 1.1cm.	.7cm.
mean	.74cm.	.67cm.	.72cm.

Collar heights of flaring-neck jars vary considerably. Generally, large-mouth jars tend to have tall collars, while small jar collars are shorter, although there are enough exceptions to prevent the formulation of a rule. Collars range from about 3 cm. to over 10 cm. in height.

Flaring-Neck Jars: Size Variant A   1.1.3A

Three small flaring necks represent 1.6% of the Early Patibamba Phase pottery (figs. 14E, 15C, E). Two examples from Subphase A represent 1.5%, while one specimen from Subphase B accounts for 1.7% of the pottery. These necks may be characterized as follows:

	Sample A	Sample B	Entire Phase
Mouth Diameter			
range	7-12cm.	12cm.	7-12cm.
mode	–	12cm.	12cm.
mean	9.5cm.	12cm.	10.3cm.
Wall Angle			
range	15-30°	10°	10-30°
mode	–	10°	–
mean	22.5°	10°	18.3°
Wall Profile Mode			
primary	B	A	B
secondary	–	–	A
Lip Treatment Mode			
primary	C, C1	A	–
secondary	–	–	–
Rim Modification Mode			
primary	A, E1	A	A
secondary	–	–	E1
Neck Thickness			
range	.5-.6cm.	.6cm.	.5-.6cm.
mode	–	.6cm.	.6cm.
mean	.55cm.	.6cm.	.56cm.

The collars of this small-jar category appear to have been short, varying between 2.5 and 3.5 cm. in height.

A single handle indicates that at least some flaring-neck jars of this size had strap handles which joined the middle of the collar to the upper part of the vessel shoulder (fig. 14F). A second small fragment suggests a tall, looping handle from the rim to the shoulder (fig. 14A-D, H).

Flaring-Neck Jars: Size Variant B   1.1.3B

Twelve jar fragments of this group represent 6.3% of the Early Patibamba ceramics (fig. 15F-I, M, R). Nine from Subphase A account for 6.7% and three from Subphase B represent 5.2% of each sample. These vessels may be described as follows:

	Sample A	Sample B	Entire Phase
Mouth Diameter			
range	14-18cm.	14-16cm.	14-18cm.
mode	16cm.	–	16cm.
mean	15.4cm.	15cm.	15.3cm.
Wall Angle			
range	20-40°	(-5)-25°	(-5)-40°
mode	25°	–	25°
mean	28.1°	13.3°	24.1°
Wall Profile Mode			
primary	B	B	B
secondary	A	A	A
Lip Treatment Mode			
primary	A	A	A
secondary	C	D	C, D
Rim Modification Mode			
primary	A	A	A
secondary	C	E2	C, E2
Neck Thickness			
range	.5-.7cm.	.4-.7cm.	.4-.7cm.
mode	.5cm., .7cm.	–	.5cm., .7cm.
mean	.6cm.	.57cm.	.59cm.

Neck height ranged to over 5 cm.

Flaring-Neck Jars: Size Variant C   1.1.3C

Flaring-neck jars of this size group include nineteen examples, or 9.9% of the ceramics for the phase (fig. 15U, V, W, Y, AA, AF, AI, AM, AN). Subphase A contains eleven, or 8.2%, while Subphase B has eight specimens accounting for 13.8% of the ceramics. These jars may be described as follows:

	Sample A	Sample B	Entire Phase
Mouth Diameter			
range	20-23cm.	19-22cm.	19-23cm.
mode	22cm.	–	22cm.
mean	21.5cm.	20.1cm.	20.9cm.
Wall Angle			
range	5-35°	10-50°	5-50°
mode	15°	20°	20°
mean	21.4°	28.8°	24.5°
Wall Profile Mode			
primary	B	B	B
secondary	A	A	A
Lip Treatment Mode			
primary	C	C	C
secondary	D	D	D
Rim Modification Mode			
primary	A	E	A
secondary	E	D	E
Neck Thickness			
range	.5-.7cm.	.4-.8cm.	.4-.8cm.
mode	.7cm.	.6cm.	.6-.7cm.
mean	.63cm.	.63cm.	.63cm.

The height of collars in this group of flaring-neck jars appears to distribute bimodally. One group has a height of about 3.5 to 4 cm. while another set ranges between 6.5 and 8 cm.

Flaring-Neck Jars: Size Variant D   1.1.3D

Eight necked jars of this size group represent 4.2% of the Early Patibamba Phase pottery (fig. 16A-D, F). There are four specimens, or 3%, and four specimens, or 6.9%, from Subphases A and B respectively. These vessels may be characterized as follows:

	Sample A	Sample B	Entire Phase
Mouth Diameter			
range	26-28cm.	24-27cm.	24-28cm.
mode	26cm.	–	26cm.
mean	26.5cm.	25.5cm.	26cm.
Wall Angle			
range	20-35°	5-25°	5-35°
mode	30°	25°	25-30°
mean	28.3°	17.5°	22.9°

Wall Profile Mode			
primary	B	B	B
secondary	A	A	A
Lip Treatment Mode			
primary	C	C	C
secondary	A, C1	A, D	A
Rim Modification Mode			
primary	–	A	A
secondary	A,C,E,H	D	–
Neck Thickness			
range	.5-.7cm.	.5-1.1cm.	.5-1.1cm.
mode	.6cm.	.5cm.	.5-.6cm.
mean	.6cm.	.68cm.	.64cm.

The jar necks indicate that the collars ranged to 6 or 7 cm. or perhaps even higher.

Flaring-Neck Jars: Size Variant E   1.1.3E

Eleven flaring-neck jars of this size variant represent 5.7% of the Early Patibamba ceramics (fig. 16L, N, P, T, U, W). Subphases A and B include nine specimens, or 6.7%, and two examples, or 3.4%, respectively. The group may be characterized as follows:

	Sample A	Sample B	Entire Phase
Mouth Diameter			
range	30-34cm.	32cm.	30-34cm.
mode	–	32cm.	32cm.
mean	32.1cm.	32cm.	32.9cm.
Wall Angle			
range	10-35°	5-15°	5-35°
mode	–	–	15°
mean	20°	10°	18.2°
Wall Profile Mode			
primary	B	A	A
secondary	A	–	B
Lip Treatment Mode			
primary	C	C	C
secondary	D	C1A	D
Rim Modification Mode			
primary	E	E, F	E
secondary	A, D	–	A
Neck Thickness			
range	.7-1.2cm.	1-1.1cm.	.7-1.2cm.
mode	.9cm.	–	.5 cm.
mean	.94cm.	1.05cm.	.96cm.

The height of necks seems to be greater than 6 or 8 cm.

Flaring-Neck Jars: Size Variant F   1.1.3F

Early Patibamba includes seven jars of this category, which represent 3.6% of the ceramic sample from the phase (fig. 16Z, AA, AC, AE). Subphases A and B include six examples, or 4.5%, and one example, or 1.7%, respectively. The category may be described as follows:

	Sample A	Sample B	Entire Phase
Mouth Diameter			
range	36-37cm.	38cm.	36-38cm.
mode	36cm.	38cm.	36cm.
mean	36.2cm.	38cm.	36.4cm.

Wall Angle			
range	5-25°	30°	5-30°
mode	20-25°	30°	20-25°
mean	18.3°	30°	20°
Wall Profile Mode			
primary	A	B	A
secondary	B	–	B
Lip Treatment Mode			
primary	C,C1,C1A	C1A	C,C1,C1A
secondary	D	–	D
Rim Modification Mode			
primary	A	F	A
secondary	D,E,F,G	–	F
Neck Thickness			
range	.6-1.4cm.	1cm.	6-1.4cm.
mode	.9cm.	1cm.	.9cm.
mean	.98cm.	1cm.	.98cm.

The height of these necks was more than 6 or 7 cm. in most cases.

Flaring-Neck Jars: Size Variant G   1.1.3G

This large-jar category includes four examples, or 2.1% of the Early Patibamba ceramics (fig. 16AG, AJ, AL). There are three examples, or 2.2%, from Subphase A and one specimen, or 1.7%, from Subphase B. The category may be described as follows:

	Sample A	Sample B	Entire Phase
Mouth Diameter			
range	41-45cm.	42cm.	41-45cm.
mode	–	42cm.	–
mean	43.3cm.	42cm.	43cm.
Wall Angle			
range	0-15°	0	0-15°
mode	0	0	0
mean	5°	0	3.8°
Wall Profile Mode			
primary	A	A	A
secondary	–	–	–
Lip Treatment Mode			
primary	D	A	D
secondary	C	–	A,C
Rim Modification Mode			
primary	A,C,E	E	E
secondary	–	–	A,C
Neck Thickness			
range	1.1-1.3cm.	1.1cm.	1.1-1.3cm.
mode	–	1.1cm.	1.1cm.
mean	1.2cm.	1.1cm.	1.18cm.

The height of the necks of these vessels was more than 6 cm. and probably ranged between 8 and 10 cm.

CLOSED FORMS   1.2

Closed-form vessels are rare in Early Patibamba ceramics, and two identifiable vessel fragments represent only 1% of the sample. However, there are decorated body sherds which come from unidentified closed forms, indicating that the frequency of this general category may have been greater. Although the decorated sherds might have come from constricted-neck jars, it is possible that they represent

vessels such as bottles or flasks which cannot be recognized until later phases.

Incurving Vessels   1.2.3

Two rims from incurving vessels represent 1% of the Early Patibamba ceramics (fig. 18B, F). One sherd from Subphase A represents .7%, while one fragment from Subphase B is 1.7% of the subphase sample. These incurving vessels would be best considered as bowls and may be described as follows:

	Sample A	Sample B	Entire Phase
Mouth Diameter			
range	20cm.	26cm.	20-26cm.
mode	20cm.	26cm.	–
mean	20cm.	26cm.	23cm.
Wall Angle			
range	(-20°)	(-45°)	(-20)-(-45)°
mode	(-20°)	(-45°)	–
mean	(-20°)	(-45°)	(-32.5°)
Wall Profile Mode			
primary	D	A	–
Lip Treatment Mode			
primary	C1A	A	–
Rim Modification Mode			
primary	D	A	–
Neck Thickness			
range	.7cm.	.9cm.	.7-.9cm.
mode	.7cm.	.9cm.	–
mean	.7cm.	.9cm.	.8cm.

There is no evidence for handles, base form, decoration, or other attributes associated with incurving vessels.

OPEN BOWL FORMS   1.3

Vessels of open bowl form are very common in Early Patibamba and include eighty-eight examples, or 45.8% of the sample. There are fifty-seven examples, or 42.5%, and thirty-one specimens, or 53.4%, in Subphases A and B respectively. The frequency of open bowls is equal to that of necked jars, and together they make up over 90% of the Early Patibamba pottery. Bowls become increasingly more popular until the end of the sequence at Jargampata in the Illaura Phase.

Plain Bowls   1.3.1

A total of thirty-five plain bowls represents 18.2% of the phase sample. Twenty vessels, or 15% of Subphase A, and fifteen vessels, or 25.9% of Subphase B belong to this category. The vessels may be described as follows:

	Sample A	Sample B	Entire Phase
Mouth Diameter			
range	12-40cm.	12-29cm.	12-40cm.
mode	18cm.	18cm., 20cm.	18cm.
mean	21cm.	19.7cm.	20.4cm.
Wall Angle			
range	10-60°	10-65°	10-65°
mode	30°	55°	30°
mean	29.8°	34.7°	31.9°
Wall Profile Mode			
primary	A	A,B,D	A
secondary	D	–	D
Lip Treatment Mode			
primary	A	A	A
secondary	C,D	C	C
Rim Modification Mode			
primary	A	A	A
secondary	D	E,E2	D,E,E2
Wall Thickness			
range	.4-1.0cm.	.4-.9cm.	.4-1.0cm.
mode	.5cm.	.5cm.	.5cm.
mean	.57cm.	.57cm.	.57cm.

All open bowls have circular horizontal profiles and flat to slightly curved bases. Bowls with tripod or pedestal bases or other elaborations are excluded from the category, although since most of the vessels are represented by rim sherds it is possible that fragments from these other categories may be included in the general category of plain bowls.

Regular-Size Plain Bowls   1.3.1.1

Regular-size plain bowls are the largest component of the plain bowl group, and twenty-six examples represent 13.5% of the phase sample (fig. 19H, K, L, O, T, V, X, Z, AI, AO, AQ, AU, AX, BA, BF, BG). Subphase A includes fourteen specimens, or 10.4%, while Subphase B contains twelve examples, or 20.7% of the subphase sample. This group may be described as follows:

	Sample A	Sample B	Entire Phase
Mouth Diameter			
range	12-22cm.	12-22cm.	12-22cm.
mode	18cm.	18cm., 20cm.	18cm.
mean	18cm.	17.8cm.	17.9cm.
Wall Angle			
range	10-45°	10-50°	10-50°
mode	30°	55°	30°
mean	28.6°	32.5°	30.4°
Wall Profile Mode			
primary	A	A,B,D	A
secondary	D	–	D
Lip Treatment Mode			
primary	A	A,C	A
secondary	D	–	C,D
Rim Modification Mode			
primary	A	A	A
secondary	D	E,E2	D,E,E2
Wall Thickness			
range	.4-.7cm.	.4-.7cm.	.4-.7cm.
mode	.5cm.	.5cm.	.5cm.
mean	.54cm.	.51cm.	.52cm.

Few of the regular-size plain bowls could be completely reconstructed, but they appear to have varied between 4 and 6 cm. in height, although some examples were perhaps a bit taller. No handles were attached to these bowls, nor is there evidence for any plastic decoration. The bases were slightly curved to almost flat, with a continuous tight curve forming the angle between the base and the vessel wall.

Oversize Plain Bowls   1.3.1.2

There are nine examples of oversize plain bowls which account for 4.7% of the Early Patibamba ceramic sample (fig. 19BH, BJ, BK, BP, BR). Six bowls, or 4.5% of the sample, are found in Subphase A, while three specimens, or 5.2%, are present in Subphase B. The oversize plain bowls may be described as follows:

	Sample A	Sample B	Entire Phase
Mouth Diameter			
range	24-40cm.	25-29cm.	24-40cm.
mode	24cm.	–	24cm.
mean	28cm.	27cm.	27.7cm.
Wall Angle			
range	10-60°	30-65°	10-65°
mode	20°	–	20°
mean	32.5°	43.3°	36.1°
Wall Profile Mode			
primary	A	A,B,D	A
secondary	D	–	D
Lip Treatment Mode			
primary	A	A	A
secondary	C	D1	C,D1
Rim Modification Mode			
primary	A	A	A
secondary	D,E	E,E2	E
Wall Thickness			
range	.5-1.0cm.	.6-.9cm.	.5-1.0cm.
mode	.5cm.	.9cm.	.5cm.
mean	.63cm.	.8cm.	.69cm.

No oversize plain bowls could be reconstructed, but these vessels were not only larger in mouth diameter but also taller than regular-size plain bowls. One specimen was more than 10 cm. tall, while a second was about 8 cm. tall.

One rim sherd has a horizontal strap handle 5 cm. below the rim and parallel to it. It is likely that two such handles were placed on opposite sides of the vessel. No other evidence for appliqué or plastic elaboration was found, and unfortunately there is no indication of base form.

Decorated Bowls   1.3.2

The Early Patibamba sample includes forty-one decorated bowls which represent 21.4% of the pottery vessels. Subphase A includes twenty-nine examples, or 21.6%, while Subphase B has twelve specimens accounting for 20.7% of that sample. These vessels can often be recognized from sherds which lack rims, and only twenty-nine of the examples have rims sufficiently complete for measurement. The group may be characterized as follows:

	Sample A	Sample B	Entire Phase
Mouth Diameter			
range	11-37cm.	17-26cm.	11-37cm.
mode	18cm.	18cm., 19cm.	18cm.
mean	19cm.	19.5cm.	19.1cm.

Wall Angle			
range	15-50°	10-40°	10-50°
mode	25°	–	25°
mean	28.5°	22.5°	27.6°
Wall Profile Mode			
primary	A	A	A
secondary	D	B	D
Lip Treatment Mode			
primary	A	A	A
secondary	C	D	C,D
Rim Modification Mode			
primary	A	A	A
secondary	E1	D,F	E1
Wall Thickness			
range	.4-.7cm.	.5-.6cm.	.4-.7cm.
mode	.5cm.	.5cm.	.5cm.
mean	.55cm.	.52cm.	.54cm.

Decoration of these bowls is limited to painting, and no examples of plastic decoration were found. Seven colors could be distinguished, but each color varies considerably. The variation seems to be a result of the thickness of pigments applied, the firing temperatures, and other conditions which may not have been rigorously controlled by cultural rules. The designs are painted on a light-colored surface, which ranges from buff-orange to red-brown. Generally, the surface is unslipped or slipped with a clay comparable to the paste. However, many bowls have splotchy areas of light red which probably represent a thin slip irregularly applied. Occasionally the slip is thicker and covers all or most of the bowl. In these cases, the slipped surface ranges from light red to light brown, but it never reaches the bright red characteristic of most of the pottery from Wari. Frequently the undecorated surface of the bowl was more carefully slipped than the decorated surface. All surfaces and colors are matte and lack luster or polish.

Black is the most frequently used color for painted decoration. Not only are there more sherds with black paint, but black is also the most common color on sherds which have been painted with only a single color. Black is most frequently used for painting lines of designs, and its second most common use is as an outline for decoration zones. The third most common use of black is for dots, and the next is for wavy lines and other design elements. Only rarely does black appear as a horizontal band in the Early Patibamba Phase.

Next to black, the most frequently used color is white. Usually this pigment is thin, fails to totally cover the base color, and has a slightly chalky appearance. In other cases there is a thickly applied white paint which has a more creamy color but may be the same preparation.

White does occur without other colors, but usually it is part of a polychrome scheme. Most often it is used for the background of large zones or fields, which are outlined with a color such as black and decorated with small geometric elements. In the Early Patibamba Phase white is frequently used for broad bands—more frequently horizontal than vertical—and occasionally for design elements such as dots or wavy lines. Only a single decorated bowl from the phase has white used as an outline. This is significant because in later phases white is frequently an outline color.

The third most common color is dark red. It ranges from red-purple to brown-red but has a full complement of intermediate colors. However, this red paint contrasts with

the light red slip. Usually dark red is combined with other colors and it only rarely appears as an isolated decorative color. In Early Patibamba it is generally used for design elements such as wavy lines, dots, and small geometric forms. The next most common uses are for lines forming designs and as a background color for zones or fields which were decorated with small elements in other colors. There are a few cases of dark red being used as an outline and for a vertical band. However, in the Early Patibamba sample dark red is never used as a horizontal band. One example has a broad, dark red horizontal line which may provide some antecedent for the dark red horizontal bands of later phases. This banded design theme first appears during the Middle Patibamba Phase. It is based upon two dark red horizontal bands and a black horizontal one and is totally absent in Early Patibamba.

The remaining four colors occur rarely, and only in combination with polychrome schemes. Yellow is restricted to space-filling dots and a single example of a vertical band. Orange is used only for dots and other geometric elements. Brown also occurs as geometric elements except in one case where it is used as an outline color. Gray is rare and appears only as a horizontal band and zone or field color, suggesting that it may be structurally equivalent to white.

The most common single-color designs are painted in black, and white or dark red schemes are infrequent. Two-color arrangements are most common and include, in descending popularity, black and white, white and brown, dark red and black, and black and yellow. Three-color designs combine dark red, white, and black; black, white, and yellow; and, in one case, dark red, white, and yellow. Polychrome painting is only slightly less common than three-color painting and includes examples of black, white, dark red, and gray; dark red, brown, orange, and gray; white, dark red, orange, and gray; black, white, dark red, and orange; and black, dark red, brown, and orange. No bowls are decorated with more than four colors.

Throughout the sequence at Jargampata the selection of design theme and design layout was dependent upon whether a bowl was to be decorated on the interior or the exterior. The difference between the interior- and the exterior-decorated bowls becomes increasingly obvious in the progressive differentiation of these two shapes. However, in the Early Patibamba Phase the two bowl forms are not well differentiated and the exterior-decorated bowls are quite uncommon.

Interior-Decorated Bowls 1.3.2.1

Thirty-six bowls with interior decoration represent 18.8% of the vessels from this phase. There are twenty-four specimens, or 17.9%, and twelve specimens, or 20.7%, from samples A and B respectively. Only twenty-six examples have rims sufficiently complete to provide mouth diameter and wall angle measurements.

Regular-Size Interior-Decorated Bowls 1.3.2.1.1

There are twenty-three bowls of this category which account for 12% of the Early Patibamba ceramics. However, if all identifiable decorated bowls could be measured, the frequency of this category would probably increase. Eighteen examples are from Subphase A and represent

13.4%, while five pieces from Subphase B total 8.6% of that sample. The vessels may be described as follows:

	Sample A	Sample B	Entire Phase
Mouth Diameter			
range	11-22cm.	17-19cm.	11-22cm.
mode	18cm.	18cm., 19cm.	18cm.
mean	17.6cm.	18.2cm.	17.7cm.
Wall Angle			
range	15-45°	15-40°	15-45°
mode	25°	–	25°
mean	28.1°	27°	27.8°
Wall Profile Mode			
primary	A	A	A
secondary	D	B	D,B
Lip Treatment Mode			
primary	A	A	A
secondary	C,D	C,D	C,D
Rim Modification Mode			
primary	A	A	A
secondary	E1	F	E1,F
Wall Thickness			
range	.4-.7cm.	.5-.6cm.	.4-.7cm.
mode	.5cm.	.5cm.	.5cm.
mean	.54cm.	.52cm.	.53cm.

Regular-size interior-decorated bowls range between 6 and 7 cm. in height. They have no handles or other plastic modification. The bases are gently curved to nearly flat, with the base and the wall joined by a tight curve.

Decoration is limited to painting on the interior, or on the rim and interior, over a natural orange surface or a thin red slip. The seven colors described above for all decorated bowls are found on bowl interiors.

The most frequent design theme is based upon a horizontal band 1.5 to 3 cm. wide located just below the bowl rim (fig. 23A, B). These bands are painted in light colors, such as white or gray, and may carry geometric design elements such as wavy lines and dots in dark colors, such as dark red, black, or brown. There are no examples of multiple horizontal bands or of dark red bands, which are so common in later phases.

Vertical bands also occur on Early Patibamba regular-size interior-decorated bowls. These bands are between 1 and 2 cm. wide and occur in isolation or in themes which combine several parallel bands in alternating colors (fig. 22A, E). Light colors are more common, but when an alternating pattern is selected, one dark and one light color appear and the bands are generally outlined in black. The vertical bands are often decorated with geometric elements including wavy lines, circles, dots, Z shapes, hooks, and combinations of these.

Large fields or panels are frequent design themes. These panels were probably arranged symmetrically on the inside of the vessel in sets of two or four. They are usually outlined by a dark line such as black, and, although sometimes unoutlined, are usually a light color such as white or gray. Dark geometric elements such as wavy lines, dots, or irregular markings adorn the light background. Frequently the decorative elements are arranged in unoutlined horizontal bands (fig. 26A).

A wing theme is another common design on bowl interiors. The wing is placed so it hangs at an angle of 30° to 40° from the rim of the bowl (fig. 25G, L). Groups of diagonal lines may represent segments of the wing.

Representational themes are extremely rare in all the decorated pottery from Jargampata, but the few cases which probably represent real or mythical forms are from the Early Patibamba Phase (fig. 25B).

Other infrequent themes on interior-decorated bowls include painted bands, which are outlined with contrastive colors and have a single row of dots through the center of the band, and wavy lines with dots between the crests. Some bowls have rim decoration consisting of a wide line of .5 to .8 cm. or of short, dark-colored bars painted on the rim.

Oversize Interior-Decorated Bowls   1.3.2.1.2

Three oversize interior-decorated bowls account for 1.6% of the Early Patibamba refuse. There are two specimens from Subphase A representing 1.5% and one example from Subphase B which accounts for 1.7% of the sample. This group of vessels may be described as follows:

	Sample A	Sample B	Entire Phase
Mouth Diameter			
range	32-36cm.	26cm.	26-36cm.
mode	–	26cm.	–
mean	34cm.	26cm.	31.3cm.
Wall Angle			
range	40-50°	10°	10-50°
mode	–	10°	–
mean	45°	10°	33.3°
Wall Profile Mode			
primary	B1,D	A	A,B1,D
secondary	–	–	–
Lip Treatment Mode			
primary	A	D	A
secondary	–	–	D
Rim Modification Mode			
primary	A	D	A
secondary	–	–	D
Neck Thickness			
range	.6-.7cm.	.5cm.	.5-.7cm.
mode	.6cm., .7cm.	.5cm.	–
mean	.65cm.	.5cm.	.6cm.

The overall height of these bowls remains unknown since none could be completely reconstructed. However, they were more than 6 cm. tall and probably considerably taller. There is no evidence for handles or other plastic modification on these vessels.

Decoration themes and elements appear to be essentially the same as on regular-size interior-decorated bowls. One vessel has a wide white band below the rim. The band is decorated with a wavy line in dark red, and a thick dark red line nearly 1 cm. wide is painted below the white band (fig. 23C). This may be a progressive feature in anticipation of horizontal red bands. Another sherd with a distinct theme has a dark red wavy line and dots painted on the natural surface below the rim (fig. 24A).

Exterior-Decorated Bowls   1.3.2.2

Exterior-decorated bowls are rare in the Early Patibamba Phase, and five sherds represent 2.6% of the vessel sample. All five examples come from Subphase A, where they account for 3.7% of the sample. Only three of the five fragments are sufficiently complete to permit measurements.

Regular-Size Exterior-Decorated Bowls   1.3.2.2.1

Early Patibamba contains three regular-size bowls, 1.6% of the sample. All these come from Subphase A, where they constitute 2.2% of the sample. However, there are two body fragments from bowls of this shape which could not be measured for mouth diameter. If these were included, they would raise the frequency of the group to 2.6% of the phase. They may be described as follows:

Mouth Diameter	
range	14-20cm.
mode	–
mean	17.3cm.
Wall Angle	
range	15-25°
mode	–
mean	20°
Wall Profile Mode	
primary	A
secondary	D
Lip Treatment Mode	
primary	A,B,C
secondary	–
Rim Modification Mode	
primary	A
secondary	–
Wall Thickness	
range	.5-.6cm.
mode	.5cm.
mean	.53cm.

The regular-size exterior-decorated bowls are distinguished from regular-size interior-decorated bowls in that the former have smaller mouth diameters and lower wall angles. The difference between the categories is very slight in the Early Patibamba material but becomes more obvious in later phases.

None of the bowls could be reconstructed, so the overall height—which was more than 7 cm. in one case—and the base form remain unknown. There are no indications of plastic modification on these vessels.

Decoration is limited to painting on the plain or red-slipped vessel exterior. Design themes are similar to those of interior-decorated bowls. White or gray bands occur just under the rim and also well below the rim. These light bands are between 1.5 and 2 cm. wide and are decorated with geometric elements including wavy lines, hooks, and loops in darker colors (fig. 28B). Dark wavy lines, sometimes in groups, are painted on a thick red slip (fig. 28A), and amorphous dots and dashes are frequently scattered about a vessel surface. Rim decoration includes cross-bars or bars and dots in combination with exterior decoration.

Tripod Bowls   1.3.3.1

Two solid supports in the Early Patibamba ceramic sample represent 1% of that sample. One example, or .74%, is from Subphase A, and one specimen, or 1.7%, is from Subphase B. The former is a solid irregular cylinder 5.5 cm. long and 2.7 cm. thick at the top, which is broken (fig. 31D). The tip shows wear, supporting the assumption that the cylinder served as a leg on a vessel. The Subphase B specimen is 8.5 cm. long from the broken upper end, which is 3.8 cm. thick, to the worn tip, which is about 2.8 cm. thick.

The wear on both of these cylinders suggests that they were legs. Because the only vessels with support legs in later phases are tripod vessels, it seems likely that these legs were also tripods attached to oversize bowls, which may have had horizontal handles below their rims.

Pedestal Bowls   1.3.5

There are seven fragments of pedestal-base bowls, which represent 3.6% of the pottery from the Early Patibamba sample. Four of these come from Subphase A, where they account for 3% of the ceramics, while three specimens account for 5.2% of the Subphase B ceramics. Only two rims (fig. 34A, B), both from Subphase A, supply the description which follows:

Mouth Diameter	
range	14-18cm.
mode	–
mean	16cm.
Wall Angle	
range	40°
mode	40°
mean	40°
Wall Profile Mode	
primary	A,D
secondary	–
Lip Treatment Mode	
primary	D
secondary	–
Rim Modification Mode	
primary	A
secondary	–
Wall Thickness	
range	.5-.6cm.
mode	–
mean	.55cm.

The pedestal bowls are distinctive because their surface finish is rough and striated and provides an appearance more appropriate for necked jars than for bowls.

The height of Early Patibamba pedestal bowls is not well indicated. The bases of the vessels average between 2 and 3 cm. high, and the bowls were certainly more than 5 or 6 cm. tall. Two solid bases from Subphase A have large base diameters of 14 and 16 cm. They show different techniques of manufacture, one in which the bottom of the bowl was welded to the solid base (fig. 34O) and the other in which the bowl and the solid base were manufactured in a single unit (fig. 34J). Three base fragments from Subphase B

include one of the former type and two of the latter. This second pair also has a characteristic unique to the Subphase B sample, the addition of clay fillet lugs to the constricted portion of the pedestal (fig. 34M, N).

Lyre-Shaped Cups   1.3.6

There are two rim sherds from the Early Patibamba Phase which may represent lyre-shaped cups (fig. 35K, L). If so, this shape accounts for about 1% of the phase sample, although both pieces come from Subphase A, where they represent 1.5% of the ceramics. These vessels may be described as follows:

Mouth Diameter	
range	9-13cm.
mode	–
mean	11cm.
Wall Angle	
range	5-20°
mode	–
mean	12.5°
Wall Profile Mode	
primary	E
secondary	–
Lip Treatment Mode	
primary	A
secondary	–
Rim Modification Mode	
primary	A
secondary	A
Wall Thickness	
range	.5-.6cm.
mode	–
mean	.55cm.

There is reason to question the assignment of these sherds to this vessel shape category. They are either divergent prototypes or are erroneously included. It may be that the larger (fig. 35K) is actually an atypical regular-size plain bowl, while the smaller (fig. 35L) is a particularly well-finished collar from a narrow-collar jar. This shape is absent from the Middle Patibamba sample, and if the identification of this shape in Early Patibamba is incorrect, the lyre-shaped cup appears at Jargampata only in Late Patibamba I with the onset of Middle Horizon 2B.

The diagnostic features which suggest that these specimens are fragments of lyre-shaped cups are the nearly vertical walls and the recurving wall profile. One specimen appears to have had a height of about 5 cm., while the other was taller. The base of one vessel was joined to the wall by a continuous, rather gentle curve and was probably slightly rounded. There is no indication of painted decoration or plastic modification.

SPOONS   1.5

Early Patibamba ceramics include three fragments of spoons, which represent 1.6% of the sample. All of these come from Subphase A, where they account for 2.2% of

the subphase sample. Two of these spoons have nearly circular bowls attached to solid prismatic handles (fig. 27I, J). These examples are large enough to be considered dippers. A third small spoon is distinct in manufacture. It is made of a single sheet of clay modeled to form a bowl and a trough-shaped handle rather like a small scoop (fig. 27L).

CERAMIC DISKS   1.8

Three sherds from this phase, or 1.6%, come from flat ceramic disks (fig. 12J, K, M). All are from Subphase A, where they represent 2.2% of that sample. These disks have the rough, striated, and unslipped surfaces and coarse temper characteristic of necked jars. The disks are about 1 cm. thick and have diameters of 16 cm., 18 cm., and 18.5 cm.

EXOTIC VESSELS   1.10

One sherd, or .5% of the ceramic sample from the Early Patibamba Phase, has a fine, spongy-textured, cream-colored paste with very fine temper (fig. 39J). This sherd from Subphase A is outside the range of variation of Jargampata paste and probably represents an import. The fragment is from an open bowl, which may be described as follows:

Mouth Diameter	17cm.
Wall Angle	5°
Wall Profile	A
Lip Treatment	A
Rim Modification	C
Wall Thickness	6cm.

The sherd is heavily eroded, but the interior was covered with a dark red slip. The exterior may have been natural or perhaps slipped with a cream or buff color similar to the paste. The vessel exterior was decorated with two parallel lines in dark red and black just below the rim and a design composed of crossed black lines and loops. The width of the lines and the design are atypical for Jargampata ceramics and most resemble the ring-base bowls reminiscent of Cajamarca IV which were found by Ravines (1968: 31-33, lam. XX31) in the Middle Horizon 2A offerings at Ayapata.

A fragmentary incurving bowl with profile feline-headed angel (fig. 39K; plate 16C) came from several sections of El-1 of E2-3 x S13-14. This piece shows extreme erosion, indicating that it lay on the surface for a long time before its inclusion in El-1. As discussed in Chapter 5, the vessel is probably contemporary with the Early Patibamba Phase and represents another imported ceramic piece. The angel theme can be best dated as Middle Horizon Epoch 2A by comparison with data published by Menzel (1964, 1968a).

The single imported vessel from the Early Patibamba ceramic sample and the piece from El-1 both appear to date to Middle Horizon 2A and probably predate the construction of the North Unit. The very low frequency of .5% imported pottery in this phase may be a product of the kind of refuse sampled, but it may also indicate a rather low level of direct interaction with the large center of Wari, where such elite pottery was probably manufactured. It is significant that very little of the imported pottery from the House Group can be definitely dated as earlier than Middle Horizon 2B. A bowl with a spotted-animal theme (fig. 39A; plate 18E) from the floor of room S1 depicts the mythical animal in so conservative a fashion that an Epoch 1 date seems likely. However, the orientation of the animal to the rim of the bowl and the absence of the zigzag band framing the upper part of the body (Menzel 1968a: 57, figs. 2-7) may indicate a conservative or even archaic Epoch 2 product. A small bowl (fig. 40B; plate 16G) may also be early, but other pieces appear to belong to Epoch 2 and to Epoch 2B, where stylistic dating is sufficiently refined. These imported pieces tend to support the idea that during the Early Patibamba Phase there was considerably less interaction with Wari than in the succeeding three phases.

Figure 44. West Face of 1-Meter Cut across East End of Room S10

A   Rock and dark soil.
B   Clayish soil, dark gray at the top but becoming more red-brown at the bottom. Contains rocks and some sherds in greater concentrations toward the bottom.
C   Friable gray silty soil with some gravel and rocks, numerous sherds, and some charcoal.
C1   Hard surface at the base of stratum C with numerous sherds and charcoal flakes lying on it.
D   Hard brown clayish soil with fewer sherds and little charcoal.

D1   Soil softer and more gray than D but not sharply distinguished from D. Contains far more sherds and charcoal.
E   Red-brown sandy soil with fine gravel, charcoal, and sherds.
F   Yellow-brown sand and gravel. Sterile.
Terrace Fill   Hard brown clay and gravel.
Fill   More sandy red-brown clay and gravel.

10
Ceramics of the Middle Patibamba Phase

STRATIGRAPHIC ASSOCIATION

Two rooms in the northwest sector of the North Unit were labeled S10 and S11. Following the original construction of the enclosure in the Early Patibamba Phase, this section was part of the plaza. A low terrace outlined the later form of the room, and it was against this that refuse of the Middle Patibamba Phase was allowed to accumulate. The construction of a single room, which consisted of both S10 and S11, assured that this refuse would not be removed in the periodic cleanings to which the plaza must have been subjected (figs. 5, 6).

The excavation of S10 and S11 produced a sequence from the first refuse which accumulated in the North Unit through the second and final abandonment. The lowest cultural stratum, labeled stratum E, was found in both rooms and represents the first postconstruction occupation which can be identified within the North Unit (fig. 44).

The remains include a pottery flask which can be stylistically placed in Middle Horizon 2A and carbon fragments dated at A.D. 700±110.

VESSEL SAMPLE

The sample of Middle Patibamba Phase ceramics is composed of 102 vessel fragments, all from stratum E of S10 and S11. All but five decorated body sherds were assigned to vessel shape categories. Frequencies of vessel shapes were calculated on the basis of 102 vessels, which prevents the frequencies of identified vessel shapes from reaching 100%.

Like the pottery from the Early Patibamba Phase, the Middle Patibamba ceramics consist primarily of various necked jars and open bowl forms. Together, these two general categories account for 88.2% of the sample from the phase. This represents a slight but insignificant reduction in the frequency of these shapes, but while in Early

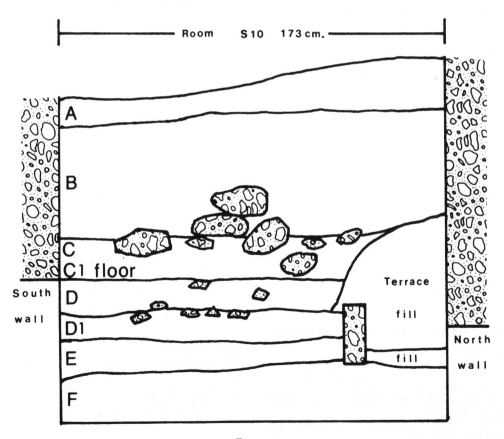

Fig. 44

Patibamba each general category accounted for about 45% of the sample, in Middle Patibamba the necked jars decrease to only 33.3% while open bowl forms increase to 54.9% of the sample.

NECKED JARS   1.1

Necked jars of this phase have circular horizontal profiles. Strap handles were placed on the shoulders of larger vessels in either horizontal or vertical positions, while smaller vessels of the flaring-neck jar group had handles from the collar to the upper part of the shoulder.

Six rough and coarsely tempered jar bases were found. Five of these are conical and come from vessels of varying sizes; one base is flat and is joined to the vessel wall with a tight curve. At the edge of the flat base, there is a slight recurve which creates a somewhat salient base like that on the face-neck jars from the House Group (fig. 11E). It seems likely that there may have been round bases which were not identified.

There is no evidence for plastic decoration on any necked jars except for face-neck jars. Painted decoration is also restricted to face-neck jars.

Constricted-Neck Jars   1.1.1

Three constricted-neck jars represent 2.9% of the Middle Patibamba ceramic sample. This represents a decrease from the Early Patibamba Phase, which may be simply a function of the small sample. Although several Early Patibamba vessels in this general category were decorated, only one Middle Patibamba face-neck jar bears evidence of decoration.

Narrow-Collar Jars   1.1.1.1

There are two rims from this category, which represent 2% of the pottery sample for the phase (fig. 10O, R). These vessels may be described as follows:

Mouth Diameter
range	9-10cm.
mode	—
mean	9.5cm.

Wall Angle
range	0-5°
mode	—
mean	2.5°

Wall Profile Mode
primary	B,E
secondary	—

Lip Treatment Mode
primary	C,C1A
secondary	—

Rim Modification Mode
primary	E1,E3
secondary	—

Neck Thickness
range	.6-.8cm.
mode	—
mean	.7cm.

There are no marked changes in narrow-collar jars from Early to Middle Patibamba. The increased neck thickness and the absence of straight wall profiles are not features continued into later phases. However, the curved E wall profile, which produces a collar with constrictions below the rim and at the body-neck juncture (fig. 10R), is a feature present primarily in Early and Middle Patibamba. This shape characteristic is apparently represented in miniature vessels found in the House Group in disturbed strata (fig. 10A).

No vessels could be reconstructed, but the collars of these jars were frequently more than 8 cm. high. Decoration is absent.

Face-Neck Jars   1.1.2

Only one fragment of a face-neck jar was present in the Middle Patibamba refuse, and the shape accounts for only 1% of the sample (fig. 11I). The fragment is small and reveals little about shape, though it is likely that the shape is similar to that of narrow-collar jars. The wall profile of the neck is straight or slightly concave. This suggests that necks with constrictions and central bulges, which were common in narrow-collar and face-neck jars of Early Patibamba and still present in the Middle Patibamba narrow-collar jars, are decreasing in popularity in the face-neck jar category as well.

The mouth diameter of the Middle Patibamba face-neck jar was about 10 cm., and the paste is coarse like that of other necked jars. Although there is no evidence for base form, it is likely that the bottoms were flat.

The eye on the collar appears to have been produced in a mold. This is the first evidence for press molding at Jargampata. The eye was painted white with a dark red, almost brown, pupil. A dark red ring below the mouth may represent face paint, tattooing, or perhaps piercing of the lower lip and the use of a labret.

Side-Spout Jars   1.1.2

One side-spout jar, or 1% of the ceramic sample, is represented by the base of a spout. The inside diameter at the base of the spout is 3.4 cm. A large sherd, from a jar with a horizontal strap handle placed low on the shoulder at the widest point of the body, may have belonged to the spouted vessel. If so, the mouth diameter was about 11 cm. and the maximum diameter of the vessel was about 14 cm.

Flaring-Neck Jars   1.1.3

There are nineteen fragments of flaring-neck jars, which represent 18.6% of the Middle Patibamba sample. This is a rather dramatic drop from the frequency of 33.3% for this general category in Early Patibamba. In later phases the frequency of these vessels continues to decline until the post–Middle Horizon Illaura Phase when it returns to about the same as in Early Patibamba. This suggests that the discrepancies in frequency between the phases are a factor of function and are related to activities in the North Unit.

In spite of the general decrease in frequency of flaring-neck jars, the distribution of the vessels within size categories does not change significantly. Thirteen of the jars had rims complete enough to provide the following description:

Mouth Diameter
range	10-45cm.
mean	26.2cm.

Wall Angle
range	5-25°

mode	15°
mean	15.8°
Wall Profile Mode	
primary	A
secondary	B
Lip Treatment Mode	
primary	D
secondary	A,B,C,C1
Rim Modification Mode	
primary	A
secondary	D,E,E1,G
Neck Thickness	
range	.5-1.4cm.
mode	.6cm.
mean	.72cm.

The most salient change in flaring-neck jars in Middle Patibamba is the reduction in wall angle. Not only are these collars more nearly vertical, but the range of wall angles is reduced. These trends continue into later phases, although they are not as marked as in the small Middle Patibamba sample.

The height of collars is not well indicated among the pieces recovered, but most range between 5 and 7 cm.

Flaring-Neck Jars: Size Variant A   1.1.3A

One rim sherd from this vessel category represents 1% of the Middle Patibamba ceramic sample. The jar may be described as follows:

Mouth Diameter	10cm.
Wall Angle	10°
Wall Profile	A
Lip Treatment	A
Rim Modification	A
Neck Thickness	.5cm.

The height of the neck of this vessel was about 4 or 5 cm.

Flaring-Neck Jars: Size Variant B   1.1.3B

Two vessel fragments of this size group represent 2% of Middle Patibamba ceramics. However, only one rim can be measured to provide a description:

Mouth Diameter	15cm.
Wall Angle	20°
Wall Profile	A
Lip Treatment	C
Rim Modification	A
Neck Thickness	.5cm.

Neck height was about 4 cm.

Flaring-Neck Jars: Size Variant C   1.1.3C

This vessel shape category is represented by seven vessel fragments, or 6.9% of the phase sample (fig. 15AG, AH, AR, AS). As in Early Patibamba, this is the most popular size variant among the flaring-neck jars. Five fragments provided measurements which could be abstracted for the description which follows:

Mouth Diameter	
range	20-24cm.

mode	20cm.
mean	21.2cm.
Wall Angle	
range	15-25°
mode	15°
mean	17°
Wall Profile Mode	
primary	A
secondary	B
Lip Treatment Mode	
primary	D
secondary	B,B1A
Rim Modification Mode	
primary	A
secondary	D,H
Neck Thickness	
range	.6-.7cm.
mode	.6cm.
mean	.64cm.

In contrast with Early Patibamba flaring-neck jars of this size, the height of the collars appears to have a single broad mode with a range between 4 and 7 cm.

Flaring-Neck Jars: Size Variant D   1.1.3D

This size group includes three examples, or 2.9% of the Middle Patibamba sample (fig. 16H, M). Along with size variant E, it is the second most popular variant for flaring-neck jars. Two rims could be measured and can be described as follows:

Mouth Diameter	
range	26-29cm.
mode	–
mean	27.5cm.
Wall Angle	
range	15-25°
mode	–
mean	20°
Wall Profile Mode	
primary	A
secondary	–
Lip Treatment Mode	
primary	C,D
secondary	–
Rim Modification Mode	
primary	A,G
secondary	–
Neck Thickness	
range	.7-.8 cm.
mode	–
mean	.75cm.

The neck height of these jars was generally about 7 cm.

Flaring-Neck Jars: Size Variant E   1.3.3E

Three sherds from jar necks of this size variant represent 2.9% of the Middle Patibamba vessels (fig. 16R). This is the second most popular size variant. Two rim sherds provide the description which follows:

Mouth Diameter	
range	34cm.
mode	34cm.
mean	34cm.

Wall Angle
range	10-20°
mode	–
mean	15°

Wall Profile Mode
primary	A,B
secondary	–

Lip Treatment Mode
primary	A,C
secondary	–

Rim Modification Mode
primary	E
secondary	–

Neck Thickness
range	.6-.8cm.
mode	–
mean	.7cm.

These large collars had heights in excess of 6 cm.

Flaring-Neck Jars: Size Variant F   1.1.3F

This category is represented by a single sherd, which accounts for 1% of the phase sample. The relative frequency of the category has dropped considerably from Early to Middle Patibamba. The single example lacks a rim, but must have had a mouth diameter of about 38 cm.

Flaring-Neck Jars: Size Variant G   1.1.3G

Two sherds from this size group represent 2% of the Middle Patibamba assemblage (fig. 16AF). They may be described as follows:

Mouth Diameter
range	42-45cm.
mode	–
mean	43.5cm.

Wall Angle
range	5-15°
mode	–
mean	10°

Wall Profile Mode
primary	A
secondary	–

Lip Treatment Mode
primary	B,C1
secondary	–

Rim Modification Mode
primary	A,E1
secondary	–

Neck Thickness
range	.9-1.4cm.
mode	–
mean	1.15cm.

Unfortunately, both of these rim sherds were broken well above the body-neck juncture so they provide no indication of the height of the necks.

CLOSED FORMS   1.2

Closed vessels are infrequent in the Middle Patibamba assemblage. Only one vessel fragment could be identified by shape category, but five decorated body sherds probably came from other closed vessels, and it seems likely that there was a substantial increase within this general category between Early and Middle Patibamba.

Flat Side Seam Flask   1.2.2.1

Several sherds from a large flask represent 1% of the sample of Middle Patibamba vessels (fig. 17C). The body of the flask had a flattened shape resembling a tambourine with a diameter of about 22 cm. and a thickness of 6 or 7 cm. from one side to the other. The seam which joins the two sides of the vessel is gently curved to nearly flat with an easily visible angle at the point of the juncture of the sides with the seam. This is a vessel shape diagnostic of Middle Horizon Epoch 1B and 2A (Menzel 1968: 76).

Little of the Middle Patibamba flask is preserved, and both the spout and the rim are missing. The side seam was decorated with white, black, and dark red to purple paint on a rather dark red-brown slip. The interior surface is rough natural orange, and the paste is typical of other Jargampata pottery.

OPEN BOWL FORMS   1.3

The Middle Patibamba assemblage contains fifty-six vessels which belong to open bowl forms. This represents a total of 54.9% of the sample—a slight gain over the frequency of the same general category in the Early Patibamba Phase. The greatest gain, however, was in decorated—and particularly exterior-decorated—bowls.

Plain Bowls   1.3.1

There are fourteen plain bowls, which represent 13.7% of the Middle Patibamba ceramic sample. In terms of frequency within the open bowl form category, plain bowls decline in popularity between Early and Middle Patibamba. The group may be described as follows:

Mouth Diameter
range	12-26cm.
mode	15-17cm.
mean	17.2cm.

Wall Angle
range	25-45°
mode	30-35°
mean	34°

Wall Profile Mode
primary	A
secondary	B

Lip Treatment Mode
primary	A
secondary	B,D,D1

Rim Modification Mode
primary	A
secondary	D,E

Wall Thickness
range	.4-1.1cm.
mode	.5cm.
mean	.55cm.

Vessel shape remains relatively unchanged from the Early Patibamba Phase. A slight reduction in vessel mouth diameter is made more obvious by the reduced frequency of oversize plain bowls, but the regular-size plain bowls show some reduction as well.

Regular-Size Plain Bowls 1.3.1.1

Thirteen regular-size plain bowl sherds represent 12.7% of the Middle Patibamba ceramic assemblage (fig. 19E, N, S, Y, AD, AN). The group may be characterized as follows:

Mouth Diameter
range	12-21cm.
mode	15-17cm.
mean	16.4cm.

Wall Angle
range	25-45°
mode	30-35°
mean	34.1°

Wall Profile Mode
primary	A
secondary	B

Lip Treatment Mode
primary	A
secondary	B,D,D1

Rim Modification Mode
primary	A
secondary	E1

Wall Thickness
range	.4-1.1cm.
mode	.5cm.
mean	.55cm.

Few of these bowls could be reconstructed, but they apparently ranged between 5 and 7 cm. in height. This represents a small gain in height over plain bowls of the Early Patibamba Phase. Bases were slightly curved to almost flat with a gentle, continuous curve uniting the bottom to the wall. However, there is a secondary mode represented by two sherds which have flat bases with sharp angles.

Oversize Plain Bowls 1.3.1.2

Oversize plain bowls drop in popularity between Early and Middle Patibamba, and a single example represents 1% of the vessels from the phase. This specimen may be described as follows:

Mouth Diameter	26cm.
Wall Angle	30°
Wall Profile	A
Lip Treatment	A
Rim Modification	E1
Wall Thickness	.6cm.

The vessel could not be reconstructed to its base, but the wall height was greater than 5 cm.

Decorated Bowls 1.3.2

Middle Patibamba includes thirty-three decorated bowls, which represent 32.4% of the total vessel sample. This demonstrates that there is a considerable increase in the popularity of decorated bowls in this phase. Eighteen vessel fragments have rims, which permit the description which follows:

Mouth Diameter
range	12-23cm.
mode	18cm.
mean	16.4cm.

Wall Angle
range	10-50°
mode	30°
mean	30.6°

Wall Profile Mode
primary	A
secondary	D

Lip Treatment Mode
primary	A
secondary	C,D

Rim Modificaton Mode
primary	A
secondary	E1

Wall Thickness
range	.3-.6cm.
mode	.5cm.
mean	.51cm.

Decoration is restricted to painting on a natural or red-slipped surface. As on Early Patibamba decorated bowls, the red slip is frequently very thin and it is often difficult to determine its presence or absence from a single sherd. In spite of this continuity in treatment of the design background, the Middle Patibamba use of colors represents a considerable change from Early Patibamba practices.

On the Middle Patibamba decorated bowls, white has replaced black as the most frequently used color. As before, this pigment continues to appear alone, but it is usually used in combinatination with other colors. The most common uses for white include wavy lines and dots in more complex polychrome designs. Next in frequency is the outlining of design zones with white. This practice, which occurred on only one Early Patibamba sherd, established a new mode which continued through succeeding phases. White fields and bands are present in the Middle Patibamba Phase but have become the exception rather than the rule. These large background areas are now generally painted another color, and white appears to be used to paint around other color blocks or to add small design elements. Occasionally white lines are used to construct decorative themes.

Dark red is the second most frequently used color, and like white it is only rarely found alone. Its most common use, as a broad horizontal band, is a characteristic of Middle Patibamba which originates in the phase and continues into succeeding phases. Some vertical bands are also found, but the second most frequent use of dark red is for plain and wavy lines painted upon zones of another color. Dark red outlines are absent and do not reappear in the remainder of the Jargampata sequence.

Black, which was the most popular color in Early Patibamba, has dropped to third position in this phase. The frequency of vessels which have only black decorations has also declined, and on most vessels where the pigment appears it is used for the major design lines within polychrome schemes. Black bands, mostly horizontal, have become quite common, and there is only a single example of black being used as an outline color.

As in the Early Patibamba Phase, the remaining colors appear infrequently and only in combination with other pigments. Orange and gray are more common than yellow and brown. Gray continues to serve a function like that of white and is used for wavy lines and, less frequently, for

bands and design fields. Orange continues to appear primarily as dots and is occasionally used for wavy lines. One orange band may have been intended to be dark red. Yellow and brown appear exclusively as background colors for design fields.

The only pigments which occur alone on bowls are white, black, and dark red. Black in all combinations, has decreased in frequency and this is reflected in a decrease in the frequency of bowls which are decorated with one color only. This decrease is in spite of an increase in the popularity of single-color decoration in white or dark red.

Two-color painting is more common than single-color decoration. Popular combinations are dark red and white, black and white, and dark red and gray. Three-color painting is only slightly less common than bichrome and includes especially dark red, white, and black; and dark red, black, and gray. Polychrome combinations are rare and are limited to black, white, dark red, and gray; and white, dark red, orange, and gray.

The separation of interior- and exterior-decorated bowls becomes more explicit in the Middle Patibamba Phase. There are several new design themes which are associated with one category or the other.

Interior-Decorated Bowls   1.3.2.1

There are twenty-one decorated bowls which have interior painting only. This represents 20.6% of the phase sample. All of these vessels which can be measured are of regular size, and the oversize interior-decorated bowl is not represented in the sample.

Regular-Size Interior-Decorated Bowls   1.3.2.1.1

Regular-size interior-decorated bowls include thirteen specimens, which represent 12.7% of the vessel sample for the phase. They may be described as follows:

Mouth Diameter	
range	14-23cm.
mode	, 18cm.
mean	17.4cm.
Wall Angle	
range	15-50°
mode	30°
mean	33.5°
Wall Profile Mode	
primary	A
secondary	D
Lip Treatment Mode	
primary	A
secondary	C,D
Rim Modification Mode	
primary	A
secondary	E1
Wall Thickness	
range	.4-.6cm.
mode	.5-.6cm.
mean	.54cm.

These data show that although there are some modifications in decorative motifs these interior-decorated bowls belong to the same tradition as those of the Early Patibamba Phase. The slight increase in flair of the wall angle in Middle Patibamba probably is not significant and it does not continue into later phases.

Generally the interior-decorated bowls ranged between 6 and 7.5 cm. in height, although some small examples with mouth diameters around 14 cm. are as short as 4 cm. The bases are slightly curved, with tight curves uniting the bottoms to the vessel walls.

Paint was applied on a red slip or natural light surface on the interior or rim. The most common decorative theme is a broad horizontal band just below the rim. This theme derives from the white bands of the Early Patibamba Phase. However, although white bands still occur (fig. 23D), dark red bands are the most popular (fig. 23E-G). These bands are decorated with combinations of lines and dots.

There is a new design theme which appears in Middle Patibamba. It consists of two parallel bands placed horizontally one below the other. This new theme continues as part of the Jargampata ceramic tradition throughout the remainder of the sequence. The only combination of colors is a black band over a dark red band. These in turn may be decorated with wavy lines and dots (fig. 24C). It is interesting that exterior-decorated bowls are becoming much more popular in this phase, and on these there is also a two-horizontal-band decoration theme. Several color combinations occur, but never the black over red band combination, which is typical of interior decoration only. However, it may be that this new theme is introduced from more progressive exterior-decorated bowls. On the other hand, the theme might have developed locally with the use of painted lines to separate horizontally placed design elements on broad bands (fig. 23F). If this is the case, there must be a temporal hiatus between Early and Middle Patibamba.

Diagonal lines, which probably constitute a wing design or degenerate wing design, are common in Middle Patibamba (fig. 25H, J). This is a conservative theme which continues from Early Patibamba but becomes so transformed that the theme can hardly be considered to have survived in the local style beyond the Middle Patibamba Phase.

Vertical bands, both in isolation (fig. 22B) and in multiple series (fig. 23F), also continue from Early to Middle Patibamba. However, a progressive elaboration of the multiple-vertical-band theme is the decoration of all the bands with wavy lines with dots instead of alternating between circles and wavy lines with dots.

A particularly important design theme appears in this phase and continues through the remainder of the sequence at Jargampata. This theme is a colored disk and Saint Andrew's cross (fig. 21A), which is strictly limited to vessel interiors on the local ceramics. Based on evidence from later, more complete vessels, it seems likely that four colored disks were arranged symmetrically in quadrants of the vessel. The theme was probably introduced from centers of greater prestige since the basic design occurs on an imported vessel exterior (fig. 39L; plate 17E) and is found in similar form at Wari (Bennett 1953: figs. 11J, 13B, 20A). At Jargampata, the colored disk is generally decorated with a Saint Andrew's cross in contrasting color and circles or dots in the four quadrants of the disk. Only one example of this theme was found in the small Middle Patibamba sample, but it becomes a popular and diagnostic aspect of the Jargampata style.

Another theme which occurs with low frequency on vessel interiors is a rectangle formed by a broad painted band (fig. 25A). This is a theme which is found more frequently on exterior-decorated bowls, and on interiors it

is limited to Middle Patibamba and Late 'Patibamba I. Decorating fields or bands with crossing diagonal lines and dots (fig. 25C), which give the impression of cross-hatching, also appears in low frequency in Middle Patibamba.

Exterior-Decorated Bowls   1.3.2.2

The Middle Patibamba vessel sample includes eleven fragments of exterior-decorated bowls. They account for 10.8% of the sample, which is a dramatic increase over the 2.6% which this group constitutes in Early Patibamba. It seems that the Middle Patibamba ceramic sample represents a stylistic divergence from Early Patibamba, which reflects functional changes or foreign influence, or perhaps both. Unfortunately, only five of the eleven bowls have rims sufficiently preserved for measurement.

Regular-Size Exterior-Decorated Bowls   1.3.2.2.1

All of the five exterior-decorated bowls which could be measured are of regular size. These vessels represent 4.9% of the sample, but it seems likely that the remaining exterior-decorated bowls are also in the regular-size range and would more than double this frequency. The group may be described as follows:

Mouth Diameter
range	12-16cm.
mode	−
mean	14cm.

Wall Angle
range	10-35°
mode	−
mean	23°

Wall Profile Mode
primary	D
secondary	A

Lip Treatment Mode
primary	A
secondary	B,D

Rim Modification Mode
primary	A
secondary	E2,G

Neck Thickness
range	.3-.5cm.
mode	.5cm.
mean	.44cm.

Comparison of these bowls with regular-size interior-decorated bowls and the examination of both groups from Early Patibamba shows that the exterior-decorated bowls are becoming smaller in mouth diameter and their walls are becoming more vertical relative to interior-decorated bowls.

Vessel heights range between 6 and 7 cm., and bases are gently curving with an open curve uniting the bottom with the vessel walls.

Painted decoration is restricted to the vessel exterior or rim and exterior, and it emphasizes themes based on horizontal bands. There are conservative themes similar to those of Early Patibamba which consist of a single band, often white or gray, below the rim, which may be decorated with geometric elements such as wavy lines with dots or circles (fig. 28C). However, some have broad outlines or decoration lines which may copy multiple-band designs or perhaps provide a stylistic bridge between single- and multiple-band themes (fig. 28D).

A progressive theme which appears in Middle Patibamba is composed of two horizontal bands (fig. 30J). These occur in several color combinations and may carry geometric decorations.

A single bowl fragment is decorated with a three-band theme which becomes much more popular in succeeding phases. This theme consists of a black band above a red band above another black band. On the Middle Patibamba example, the bands are separated by thin white lines and are decorated with wavy white lines (fig. 29B). This theme is particularly diagnostic of Late Patibamba I and II, where it is almost always associated with tripod tab supports. However, although the black, red, black banding appears in Middle Patibamba, there is no evidence for the tab supports.

One exterior-decorated bowl is decorated with a vertical-band theme which consists of a dark red band outlined in white.

Interior- and Exterior-Decorated Bowls   1.3.2.3

A single small sherd, which represents only 1% of the Middle Patibamba vessels, comes from a decorated open bowl which had painted decoration on both the interior and exterior surfaces. The fragment is part of the base and wall of the bowl and cannot be accurately measured. The exterior had a horizontal band design, of which only the lowest black band outlined in white is preserved. The interior had a broad black line running across the bottom and up the wall, possibly associated with the colored disk and Saint Andrew's cross theme. Of nearly 1,200 vessel segments examined from the excavations at Jargampata, only this and one bowl from Late Patibamba II have both interior and exterior decoration.

Tripod Bowls   1.3.3

There is no evidence for tripods of any sort in the Middle Patibamba vessel sample. However, their presence in the preceding Early Patibamba Phase and the succeeding Late Patibamba I Phase suggests that the seeming absence of tripods in Middle Patibamba is a result of sample error.

Ring-Base Bowls   1.3.4

One ring-base bowl accounts for 1% of the Middle Patibamba vessel sample (fig. 33B). Only the base of this vessel was recovered, making it impossible to reconstruct the vessel shape or even to be sure that the vessel was a bowl. The paste is typical of Jargampata, but both the interior and exterior of the vessel were blackened as though they had been burned. There are slight traces of red paint on the vessel interior.

The ring base is only .7 cm. high and has a diameter of 4.3 cm. The narrow and rounded lower surface of the base shows considerable abrasion from use.

Pedestal Bowls   1.3.5

Three vessel fragments from pedestal bowls account for 2.9% of the Middle Patibamba sample (fig. 34D, I, K). Two of these are represented by solid bases, while the third—which is probably a separate vessel—is a rim sherd. This single rim may be described as follows:

Mouth Diameter	21cm
Wall Angle	40°
Wall Profile	D
Lip Treatment	B
Rim Modification	G
Wall Thickness	.5cm.

The vessel walls from these bowls were over 5 cm. tall, probably closer to 10 cm. The two bases are 10 and 10.5 cm. in diameter. The Middle Patibamba pedestal bowls appear to be taller and have larger mouth diameters and smaller base diameters than their counterparts in the Early Patibamba Phase.

Both of the bases from this phase were modeled separately and the walls of the bowl were welded to their upper surfaces (fig. 34I, K). There are no appliqué lugs or other decoration on these bowl bases.

CERAMIC DISKS   1.8

A coarsely finished sherd from a flat disk accounts for 1% of the Middle Patibamba vessel sample. This pottery slab is .7 cm. thick and has a diameter of 16 cm.

SCRAPER-POLISHERS   1.9

The Middle Patibamba ceramic sample includes two sherds, or 2% of the vessel sample, which have one edge ground smooth (fig. 36C, D). Both are plain sherds which have probably been ground smooth through use, possibly scraping the surfaces of unfired pottery vessels.

EXOTIC VESSELS   1.10

Two sherds represent vessels which are atypical of Jargampata pottery. These vessels are probably imported pieces and account for about 2% of the Middle Patibamba Phase ceramics. Although still small, this frequency represents a substantial increase over the .5% imported ceramics in Early Patibamba.

One sherd comes from an exterior-decorated bowl form (fig. 39L; plate 17E), which can be described as follows:

Mouth Diameter	16cm.
Wall Angle	10°
Wall Profile	A
Lip Treatment	A1
Rim Modification	A
Wall Thickness	.7cm.

The vessel's height was greater than 4 cm., but its size and form cannot be reconstructed. The paste is light red and fine textured and has a finely crushed grit temper with a few larger particles of sand. The interior and exterior of the bowl were slipped with a relatively even, thick red slip which has a low gloss on the exterior. There is a black line on the interior just below the rim, and the upper surface of the rim has dark red sections and white sections which are crossed by black bars.

The exterior of the vessel has a white band about 2 cm. wide below the rim. Black dots were painted on the band. Enclosed in a black rectangle is a gray disk with a black

Saint Andrew's cross and dots in the quadrants. This imported sherd probably reveals the origin of the disk and Saint Andrew's cross which appears on local, regular-size interior-decorated bowls in this phase and becomes so popular in succeeding phases (fig. 21). This design occurs at Wari, where it seems to have had an evolutionary progression from simple crosses (Bennett 1953: fig. 11H, K) and crosses with dots in their quadrants (Bennett 1953: fig. 20A; Lumbreras 1960: lam. XVJ) on one hand and larger filler dots (Lumbreras 1960: lam. XIIF) on the other, to dots with crosses (Bennett 1953: fig. 11F, G), disks with crosses and dots in quadrants (Bennett 1953: fig. 13B; Lumbreras 1960: lam. XIIIF), and outlined rectangles with Saint Andrew's crosses and dots in the quadrants (Bennett 1953: fig. 11J).

The second imported vessel is represented by a very small rim fragment which cannot be measured (fig. 39G; plate 17B). However, the mouth diameter was less than that of most bowls, and the shape was probably a cup or perhaps the neck of a narrow-collar jar. The paste is similar to that of the other imported sherd, and the exterior and rim of the interior were slipped with a smooth, low-gloss red. The exterior is decorated with black lines which form a grid of white, yellow, and red sections.

The increase in the volume of elite vessels imported in Middle Patibamba certainly affected the appearance of new decorative themes and perhaps also the changes in vessel shape frequencies. These changes follow the construction of the North Unit at Jargampata and probably all indicate a substantial strengthening of direct Wari influence and control in the San Miguel valley during this phase.

The stratigraphy within the House Group was badly disturbed, but there is one large bowl which, on stylistic grounds, may belong to Middle Patibamba or possibly even the Early Patibamba Phase (fig. 41E; plate 17A). The bowl was probably not moved after its original deposition, and I suspect the stratum may predate Late Patibamba I. The vessel has an interior decoration of two figures of animals, which are probably llamas, and rectangular designs with vertical bars. Representational figures are absent from Jargampata pottery following the Early Patibamba Phase, and the outward curve of the vessel wall is more common in the first two phases at the site than in later phases. The bowl has a faint impression on its exterior of a llama and rectangular design, suggesting that it was fired while stacked in an identical bowl. However, no fragments of other examples were found in the House Group, and the piece comes from the workshop of a specialist.

Another vessel from the House Group which may belong to this phase is a face-neck jar (fig. 40C) with shape characteristics intermediate between those of Middle Horizon 2A and 2B for the South Coast (Menzel 1968a: 81). However, fragments of this vessel were clearly associated with pieces of another face-neck jar (fig. 40A; plate 16F), which is clearly Epoch 2B in shape.

There are a number of fragments of exotic vessels from the House Group which cannot be dated, but it is significant that none are clearly as early as Early Patibamba, while only very few might be considered to be from the Middle Patibamba Phase. However, in the following phase the importation of pottery must have increased greatly.

11
Ceramics of the Late Patibamba I Phase

STRATIGRAPHIC ASSOCIATION

The large quantity of Late Patibamba I pottery from excavation units indicates that this phase represents the most intensive occupation at Jargampata, or at least the most intensive for those parts of the site which were investigated. The frequency of foreign vessels demonstrates a maximum of interaction with outside sites. However, the phase is very close in time to the dramatic abandonment of Jargampata.

Two samples of Late Patibamba I ceramics were collected within the North Unit, while a third sample came from room S7 in the South Unit. Most of the pottery from the House Group also belongs to this or the succeeding phase, but because of the extensive mixing within the House Group no single sample could be satisfactorily isolated for analysis.

The relative dating of the Late Patibamba I Phase is clear from the stratigraphy of rooms S10 and S11 (fig. 44). Late Patibamba I ceramics were found in stratum D1 overlying stratum E, which contained materials of the Middle Patibamba Phase. Stratum D1 was capped in turn by stratum D which contained pottery of the Late Patibamba II Phase.

From the southeastern part of the plaza of the North Unit a second sample of Late Patibamba I materials was selected for analysis. Stratum 4 of units E5-6 x S9-10 contained abundant sherds which had collected near the walls enclosing the plaza. Stratum 4 lay upon nearly sterile stratum 5 which contained a few body sherds and one rim from the collar of a narrow-collar jar (fig. 10T). This sherd has its closest parallels in the Early Patibamba Phase (fig. 10U). Along the east enclosure wall, it was possible to observe a slight difference between the upper and lower part of stratum 4, which might provide a basis for sub-dividing the sample; however, since very few sherds were collected with this provenience distinction, it was not considered in the analysis. It may be that a very sparse Middle Patibamba component was represented in the bottom of the stratum.

Overlying stratum 4 in E5-6 x S9-10 is stratum 3 which contains pottery of the Late Patibamba II Phase (fig. 45).

All the pottery from room S7 in the South Unit appears to belong to the Late Patibamba I Phase, except possibly the redeposited materials of strata 1 and 2 which were excluded from the sample. Stratum 4 consisted of a floor with a substantial number of sherds lying on or slightly above it. Many sherds from stratum 3 belonged to the same vessels found in stratum 4, so the materials from both strata were treated as a single sample (fig. 46).

A radiocarbon age determination on small fragments of charcoal from stratum D1 of room S10 provided a date of A.D. 765±90 (GX-1933). This indicates that Late Patibamba I ceramics may date to as much as 100 years later than Middle Patibamba Phase pottery.

VESSEL SAMPLE

The Late Patibamba I ceramic sample consists of 262 fragmentary vessels. All but seven decorated body sherds were assigned to vessel shape categories.

Descriptive statistics listed below have been compiled for each of the three samples as well as for the entire phase. The Late Patibamba IA sample comes from E5-6 x S9-10, stratum 4, and consists of sixty-five vessels. Sample IB is from rooms S10 and S11, stratum D1, and includes 147 vessels, while sample IC from room S7 contains fifty vessels.

Two general shape categories predominate in this phase. Necked jars and open bowl forms together account for 86.3% of the pots. The slight reduction in the frequency of these two groups is due to an increase in the popularity of infrequent, minor forms. In Late Patibamba I, a trend continues which was observed from Early to Middle Patibamba. This is the increase in frequency of open bowl forms at the expense of necked jars. In this phase, open bowl forms account for 55.3% of the vessels, while necked jars have dropped to a frequency of 30.9%. The three samples are remarkably consistent, with IA showing 58.5% and 23.1%, IB 53.1% and 33.3%, and IC having 58% and 34%, respectively, for open bowl forms and necked jars. This is surprising considering the probability that room S7 in the South Unit had a function very different from that of the North Unit where the remaining two samples were collected.

NECKED JARS   1.1

The necked jars of Late Patibamba I retain the same shape characteristics found in the previous two phases. The two groups with the smallest mouth diameters have strap handles from the collar to the upper shoulder, while larger jars have horizontal or vertical handles placed on the shoulders. Conical bases account for about half of the jar bottoms, but large, flat bases with moderately sharp basal angles indicate that a flat-bottomed jar was becoming more popular.

There is no indication of body-neck juncture ornaments or any plastic decoration of the Late Patibamba I jars. In fact, there are no face-neck jars from this or later phases. However, it seems unlikely that the category of face-neck jars had disappeared since fragments of press molds for faces (plate 15D) are present in Late Patibamba I as well as the following phase. However, it seems likely that the narrow-collar jar and the face-neck jar may have been merging to form a new category which makes its appearance in this phase. This is the bilobed jar (fig. 12B, C, D), which is a variant of constricted-neck jars. Some examples from the House Group have painted decorations or a modeled face on the upper lobe or neck (fig. 12A, G).

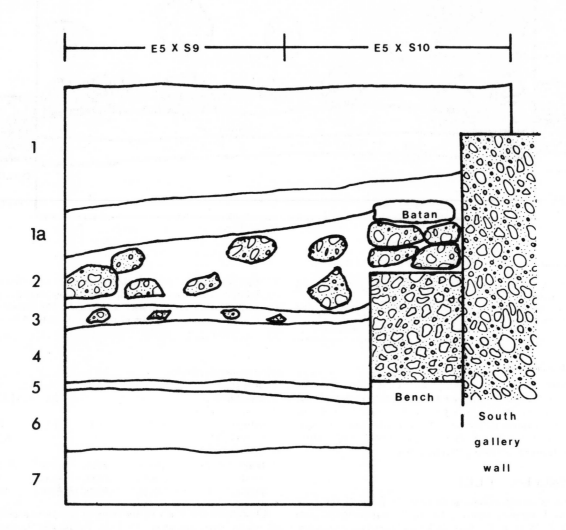

Figure 45. East Face of E5 x S9-10

1   Dark brown clayish soil with few rocks, little gravel.
1a   Lighter red-brown clayish soil.
2   Light brown, ashy soil with numerous rocks and fine gravel. Sherds are more numerous.
3   Finer light brown soil, more ashy in texture with fewer rocks, finer gravel, and more numerous sherds.
4   Gray-brown soil with ash and charcoal, fine gravel, and numerous sherds. Becomes more dense at the bottom. To the east this stratum becomes rapidly thinner until the bottom forms the plaza floor.

5   Darker brown sandy soil with fine gravel and few sherds.
6   Yellow-brown sandy soil with gravel. Sterile.
7   Yellow-brown sandy soil with gravel. Separated from stratum 6 by thin line of gravel.

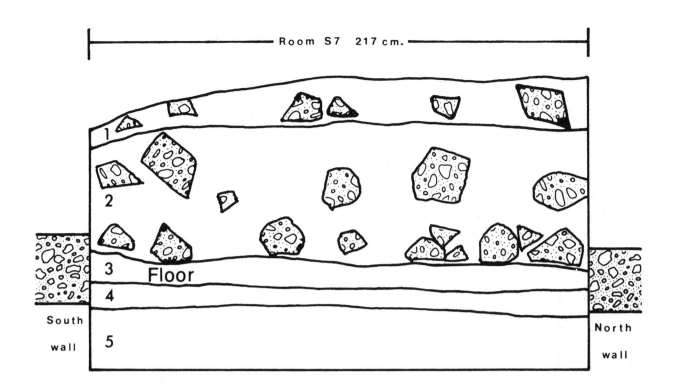

Figure 46. East Face of 1-Meter Cut across West End of Room S7

1 Yellow-brown to gray sandy clay with numerous rocks and some sherds.
2 Dark brown clayish soil with many rocks and some gravel and eroded sherds.

3 Fine gray-brown silty soil becoming more ashy toward the bottom. Little gravel and no large rocks; some sherds.
4 Coarser yellow-gray silt with many sherds. The surface of this stratum is hard packed with many sherds lying upon it.

Constricted-Neck Jars   1.1.1

Jars with constricted necks include eleven examples, or 4.2% of the Early Patibamba I ceramic sample. Sample IA contains two specimens, or 3.1%; sample IB has six pieces, or 4.1%; and sample IC includes three constricted-neck jars, which account for 6% of that sample. There is very little change in frequency from previous phases.

Narrow-Collar Jars   1.1.1.1

A total of seven collars with rims, or 2.7% of the Late Patibamba I ceramic sample, belong to narrow-collar jars (fig. 10G, L, N, Q, S, V). Sample IA includes two examples, or 3.1% of the sample; IB has two rims, or 1.4%; while IC contains three pieces, or 6% narrow-collar jars. These vessels may be described as follows:

	Sample IA	Sample IB	Sample IC	Entire Phase
Mouth Diameter				
range	7-9cm.	10cm.	9-11cm.	7-11cm.
mode	–	10cm.	11cm.	10-11cm.
mean	8cm.	10cm.	10.3cm.	9.6cm.
Wall Angle				
range	0°	0-10°	(-10)-(-15)°	(-15)-10°
mode	0°	–	(-10°)	0°
mean	0°	(-5°)	(-12°)	(-3.6°)
Wall Profile Mode				
primary	A	A	A	A
secondary	B	B	E	B,E
Lip Treatment Mode				
primary	A,C	A1,D	A	A
secondary	–	–	C1	A1,C,C1,D
Rim Modification Mode				
primary	C,E1	A,E	E1	E1
secondary	–	–	–	A,C,E
Neck Thickness				
range	.4cm.	.6cm.	.6cm.	.4-.6cm.
mode	.4cm.	.6cm.	.6cm.	.6cm.
mean	.4cm.	.6cm.	.6cm.	.54cm.

Changes in the form of the neck of the narrow-collar jar are slight, but apparent. In Late Patibamba I, the wall angles become progressively inclined inward and the wall profile becomes generally straight. Only a single recurved collar wall is present (fig. 10Q), and it is somewhat atypical. The most popular rim modification form is an exterior thickening with exterior bevel. In features such as neck thickness, lip treatment, and wall profile, the Late Patibamba I narrow-collar jars are more similar to those of Early Patibamba than those of Middle Patibamba.

The overall height of the collars is rarely preserved but was probably about 10 cm. to 12 cm. Vessel body shape is indefinite since no examples could be completely reconstructed.

Two necks from sample IA have painted decoration on a thin red slip over the exterior surface. The colors employed are black and white and black, white, and yellow. The design themes are not evident, but appear to be distinct from the patterns associated with bowls. However, some design elements, such as circles, are similar to those

employed on bowls during the phase, while crosses establish continuity with Early Patibamba I (fig. 10V). One collar with exterior thickened rim and exterior painted decoration is a combination unique to the phase.

Face-Neck Jars   1.1.1.2

No examples of face-neck jars were identified among the pottery sample from Late Patibamba I. However, a clay mold for producing a face (fig. 23D) was probably intended for the manufacture of face-neck vessels, although this example from sample IB probably represents an animal rather than a human. Another piece of a mold from sample IA represents a pair of hands with the fingertips pointing toward one another but not quite touching. It is common for the hands of individuals represented on face-neck jars to rest upon the chest or stomach with the fingers not quite touching. Consequently, it seems likely that this second mold fragment may also have been used for the production of face-neck jars. The mixed strata of the House Group include two small face-neck jars (fig. 11A, B) and a large example (fig. 11E) which probably date to Late Patibamba I.

Bilobed Jars   1.1.1.3

The near disappearance of the face-neck jar in this phase is accompanied by the appearance of a new vessel shape which is closely related to narrow-collar and face-neck jars and may be an analogue for the face-neck jar. The new vessel form has two, or perhaps more, spherical body sections stacked vertically to produce a composite vessel shape with a form like a figure 8. Four fragments, or 1.5% of the Late Patibamba I ceramics, are from vessels of this shape, but all four specimens come from sample IB, where they represent 2.7% of the sample (fig. 12B-D).

None of the bilobed vessels from these examples could be reconstructed, and no rims were reconstructed. The diameter of the upper sphere appears to have varied between 7 cm. and 12 cm., while the lower sphere was probably 50% to 100% larger than the upper section. Vertical strap handles were attached to the vessel exteriors, and overall body height probably ranged between 12 cm. and 20 cm. Reconstructed specimens from mixed strata within the House Group probably belong to this or the succeeding phase. One example shows that the bilobed jar could have a narrow spout and suggests its classification as a bottle (fig. 12A; plate 11B). A second vessel plus fragments of several others show that crude appliqué features could convert the upper lobe into a face reminiscent of the face-neck jar (fig. 12G; plates 11D, 15T, U, V).

A tall, looping pitcher handle attached to the bilobed vessel was probably transposed to this new vessel from the smallest sizes of flaring-neck jars. However, these vessels are very reminiscent of Killke or Inca vessels.

Side-Spout Jars   1.1.2

Five fragmentary spouts from side-spout jars account for 1.9% of the sample of vessels from the Early Patibamba I Phase. A single specimen from sample IA represents 1.5%, while three pieces from sample IB total 2%, and one from IC represents 2% of the subphase sample. None of these vessels could be reconstructed, but they probably had a substantial size range, as the spouts vary between 3 cm. and

5 cm. in diameter. Four spouts have a matte red slip and the remaining piece is unslipped.

Flaring-Neck Jars   1.1.3

There are forty-two fragmentary flaring-neck jars, which represent 16% of the vessels from this phase. This frequency indicates a decline in popularity, although the drop is less dramatic than that between Early and Middle Patibamba. The sherds include seven, or 10.8%, from sample IA; twenty-eight, or 19%, from sample IB; and seven, or 14%, from sample IC. Only twenty-seven of the jar fragments have rims complete enough for measurement.

The group of flaring-neck jars may be described as follows:

	Sample IA	Sample IB	Sample IC	Entire Phase
Mouth Diameter				
range	15-36cm.	8-43cm.	14-45cm.	8-45cm.
mean	24cm.	21cm.	24.1cm.	23.1cm.
Wall Angle				
range	5-35°	0-35°	0-15°	0-35°
mode	20°	20°	15°	20°
mean	20.7°	18.8°	14.3°	17.8°
Wall Profile Mode				
primary	A	A	A	A
secondary	B	B	B	B
Lip Treatment Mode				
primary	C1A	A	C	C
secondary	D	C,D	A	A
Rim Modification Mode				
primary	A	A	A	A
secondary	E1,H	D	E,E1	E1,D
Neck Thickness				
range	.5-1.1cm.	.5-.8cm.	4-1.2cm.	.4-1.2cm.
mode	.6cm.	.5cm.	–	.6cm.
mean	.7cm.	.61cm.	.73cm.	.65cm.

The decrease in mean mouth diameter within this shape category reflects a shift in the popularity of size categories between Middle Patibamba and Late Patibamba I. The frequency of the largest size jars actually increases between the phases, but this is more than compensated for by the increasing popularity of small- and medium-mouth jars and the decrease in frequency of most larger size groups. The wall angle shift suggests a return in Late Patibamba I to a neck or collar more similar to those of Early Patibamba. Lip treatment also resembles Early Patibamba samples more than the Middle Patibamba collection.

No flaring-neck jars from these samples could be completely reconstructed, but a specimen from the House Group which probably belongs to the Late Patibamba I Phase (fig. 15A) provides good evidence for body form. Bases were generally conical, but flat or gently curved bottoms also occur. A small jar from room S9 in the North Unit (fig. 14G) possesses the same general form. The collars varied in height from 4 cm. to slightly over 10 cm. Generally, short collars are found on vessels of the smallest size groups while large vessels have necks 6 cm. or more tall. However, even the vessels with mouth diameters greater than 40 cm. have collars which probably did not exceed 11 cm. or perhaps 12 cm.

Flaring-Neck Jars: Size Variant A 1.1.3A

Two fragmentary vessels from this category represent .8% of the total ceramic refuse for the phase, although both come from sample IB where they represent a substantially higher frequency (fig. 15B, D). Considering the overall frequency, however, this category varies little from Early Patibamba.

The two vessels of this category may be described as follows:

	Sample IB and Entire Phase
Mouth Diameter	
range	8-12cm.
mode	—
mean	10cm.
Wall Angle	
range	10-20°
mode	
mean	15°
Wall Profile Mode	
primary	A,B
secondary	—
Lip Treatment Mode	
primary	A,D
secondary	—
Rim Modification Mode	
primary	A
secondary	—
Neck Thickness	
range	.5cm.
mode	.5cm.
mean	.5cm.

The collars of these small jars were probably not very high. One preserved example was about 3.5 cm. tall. There is no information on aspects of form or handles.

Flaring-Neck Jars: Size Variant B 1.1.3B

This size variant is the most popular among the flaring-neck jars of Late Patibamba I. There are fifteen specimens, which account for 5.7% of the ceramic sample (fig. 15J, N, P, Q, S). Two, ten, and three sherds represent 3.1%, 6.8%, and 6%, respectively, for samples IA, IB, and IC. This high frequency is similar to that found in Early Patibamba and contrasts with that of Middle Patibamba. In terms of the frequency of size variant B within the flaring-neck jars, this phase represents a popularity peak and a gain over both earlier phases.

Ten sherds, two from IA, five from IB, and three from IC, provide all essential measurements and may be described as follows:

	Sample IA	Sample IB	Sample IC	Entire Phase
Mouth Diameter				
range	15-16cm.	14-17cm.	14-16cm.	14-17cm.
mode	—	16cm.	—	16cm.
mean	15.5cm.	15.6cm.	15cm.	15.4cm.
Wall Angle				
range	20-35°	15-35°	15-20°	15-35°
mode	—	15°,20°	15°	—
mean	27.5°	23°	17°	27°
Wall Profile Mode				
primary	A,B	A	B	A
secondary	—	B	A	B
Lip Treatment Mode				
primary	C,C1A	C	C	C
secondary	—	A	C1	A,D
Rim Modification Mode				
primary	A	A	—	A
secondary	—	E,E1	—	E,E1
Neck Thickness				
range	.5-.7cm.	.5-.7cm.	.6cm.	.5-.7cm.
mode	—	.6cm.	.6cm.	.5-.7cm.
mean	.6cm.	.6cm.	.6cm.	.6cm.

Neck height generally ranged between 3 cm. and 5 cm., although one jar may have had a collar which was slightly taller.

Flaring-Neck Jars: Size Variant C 1.1.3C

Eleven sherds of this size group represent 4.2% of the Late Patibamba I ceramics (fig. 15X, AB, AC, AL). Sample IA includes two, or 3.1%; sample IB contains eight, or 5.4%; and sample IC has one flaring-neck jar of this size variant, or 2% of the vessels within the sample. In both previous phases, this size group was the most popular within the flaring-neck jars. Its drop to the secondary position is only temporary, and the group recovers its primary position in Late Patibamba II.

Only five sherds, two from IA, two from IB, and one from IC, were complete enough to provide the measurements upon which the following description is based:

	Sample IA	Sample IB	Sample IC	Entire Phase
Mouth Diameter				
range	20cm.	19-23cm.	19cm.	19-23cm.
mode	20cm.	—	19cm.	19-20cm.
mean	20cm.	21cm.	19cm.	20.2cm.
Wall Angle				
range	15-20°	20°	20°	15-20°
mode	—	20°	20°	20°
mean	17.5°	20°	20°	19°
Wall Profile Mode				
primary	A,B	B	A	B
secondary	—	—	—	A
Lip Treatment Mode				
primary	A,C1	A,C1A	C1	A,C1
secondary	—	—	—	C1A
Rim Modification Mode				
primary	A,E1	D,E	E1	E1
secondary	—	—	—	A,D,E
Neck Thickness				
range	.5-.7cm.	.6cm.	.4cm.	.4-.7cm.
mode	—	.6cm.	.4cm.	.6cm.
mean	.6cm.	.6cm.	.4cm.	.56cm.

None of the collars are preserved to their entire height, but two fragments indicate necks over 6 cm. tall and there are no suggestions of short collars associated with this size variant of flaring-neck jar.

Flaring-Neck Jars: Size Variant D   1.1.3D

In Late Patibamba I, this size variant declined drastically in popularity. The low frequency established in this phase continues through the remainder of the occupation at Jargampata. Two sherds represent .8% of the total Late Patibamba I sample, or 1.5% of sample IA and .7% of IB, each of which include a single example (fig. 16G).

Only the single sherd from sample IA was complete enough to provide a description:

Mouth Diameter	26cm.
Wall Angle	5°
Wall Profile	A
Lip Treatment	D
Rim Modification	H
Neck Thickness	.6cm.

The height of the collars cannot be determined, although it was more than 3 cm.

Flaring-Neck Jars: Size Variant E   1.1.3E

Vessels of this size category decline in this phase as do those of size variant D. Two sherds represent .8% of the entire sample, or 1.5% of sample IA and 2% of sample IC, each of which have a single example (fig. 16K, V). The two sherds provide the following description:

	Sample IA	Sample IC	Entire Phase
Mouth Diameter			
range	31cm.	34cm.	31-34cm.
mode	31cm.	34cm.	—
mean	31cm.	34cm.	32.5cm.
Wall Angle			
range	30°	15°	15-30°
mode	30°	15°	—
mean	30°	15°	22.5°
Wall Profile Mode			
primary	A	B	A,B
secondary	—	—	—
Lip Treatment Mode			
primary	D	C	C,D
secondary	—	—	—
Rim Modification Mode			
primary	H	E	E,H
secondary	—	—	—
Neck Thickness			
range	.8cm.	.8cm.	.8cm.
mode	.8cm.	.8cm.	.8cm.
mean	.8cm.	.8cm.	.8cm.

The neck height of one jar was more than 7 cm.; neither was complete.

Flaring-Neck Jars: Size Variant F   1.1.3F

Three fragments of collars from vessels of this size variant represent 1.1% of the ceramic sample for the phase (fig. 16AB, AD). One sherd, or 1.5% of the IA sample, and two sherds, or 1.4% of the IB sample, demonstrate that this size variant is also declining in popularity.

Two relatively complete collar fragments provide the following description:

	Sample IA	Sample IB	Entire Phase
Mouth Diameter			
range	36cm.	38cm.	36-38cm.
mode	36cm.	38cm.	—
mean	36cm.	38cm.	37cm.
Wall Angle			
range	20°	10°	10-20°
mode	20°	10°	—
mean	20°	10°	15°
Wall Profile Mode			
primary	A	A	A
secondary	—	—	—
Lip Treatment Mode			
primary	C1A	C	C,C1A
secondary	—	—	—
Rim Modification Mode			
primary	A	D	A,D
secondary	—	—	—
Neck Thickness			
range	1.1cm.	.8cm.	.8-1.1cm.
mode	1.1cm.	.8cm.	—
mean	1.1cm.	.8cm.	.95cm.

Neither sherd is preserved above a collar height of 4 cm., although it appears that the neck was probably considerably taller.

Flaring-Neck Jars: Size Variant G   1.1.3G

A total of seven collar fragments of this size group represents 2.7% of the vessel sample from Late Patibamba I (fig. 16AH, AI, AK). Five sherds from sample IB represent 3.4%, while two from sample IC total 4%. This is the only large-size variant of flaring-neck jars which shows a substantial gain in popularity during this phase.

Four collar rims, two from each subphase, provide the following description:

	Sample IB	Sample IC	Entire Phase
Mouth Diameter			
range	43cm.	44-45cm.	43-45cm.
mode	43cm.	—	43cm.
mean	43cm.	44.5cm.	43.8cm.
Wall Angle			
range	0-5°	0-15°	0-15°
mode	—	—	0°
mean	2.5°	7.5°	5°
Wall Profile Mode			
primary	A	A	A
secondary	—	—	—
Lip Treatment Mode			
primary	C,D	B1A,D	D
secondary	—	—	B1A,C
Rim Modificaton Mode			
primary	A,D	A	A
secondary	—	—	D
Neck Thickness			
range	.6-.8cm.	.9-1.2cm.	.6-1.2cm.
mode	—	—	—
mean	.7cm.	1.1cm.	8.8cm.

The maximum preserved height of any of these large collars is 6 cm., although the original height was probably somewhat more.

CLOSED FORMS 1.2

As in the earlier phases, closed vessel forms continue to be rare in Late Patibamba I, though their relative increase in this phase is obvious. There are six vessel fragments, representing 2.3% of the phase sample, which come from incurving bowls (fig. 18C, E, I, K, L, O). However, seven decorated body sherds which could not be assigned to shape categories probably come from closed forms such as bottles or flasks. If these are added, the frequency of closed forms would double, indicating a dramatic increase. This higher frequency is, however, similar to that found in the Middle Patibamba Phase after unassigned decorated body sherds are added to the sum of closed vessels.

Incurving Vessels 1.2.3

Six vessel fragments from incurving vessels account for 2.3% of the ceramic sample for the phase (fig. 18C, E, I, K, L, O). One from sample IA represents 1.5%, four from sample IB total 2.7%, and one fragment from IC accounts for 2% of that sample. In Late Patibamba I, the incurving vessel is quite rare, but it achieves a popularity increase over earlier phases which continues through the remainder of the occupation at Jargampata.

The sample of six incurving bowls may be described as follows:

	Sample IA	Sample IB	Sample IC	Entire Phase
Mouth Diameter				
range	36cm.	12-18cm.	22cm.	12-36cm.
mode	–	–	–	–
mean	36cm.	15.5cm.	22cm.	20cm.
Wall Angle				
range	(-25°)	(-15)-(-35)°	(-45°)	(-15)-(-45)°
mode	(-25°)	–	(-45°)	(-25°)
mean	(-25°)	(-26.3°)	(-45°)	(-29.1°)
Wall Profile Mode				
primary	D	D	D	D
secondary	–	–	–	–
Lip Treatment Mode				
primary	A	A,D	D	A,D
secondary	–	–	–	–
Rim Modification Mode				
primary	A	A	A	A
secondary	–	G	–	G
Neck Thickness				
range	.5cm.	.4-.6cm.	.5cm.	.4-.6cm.
mode	.5cm.	.4cm.	.5cm.	.4cm., .5cm.
mean	.5cm.	.48cm.	.5cm.	.48cm.

One incurving vessel with a mouth diameter of 22 cm. has a handle made from a horizontal tab of clay about 3.5 cm. long with a hole punched vertically through it. The tab handle is placed 3.5 cm. below the rim and parallel to it (fig. 18L). There is very little information concerning vessel body form, but it appears that two modes may have been used. One form appears to have had a continuous curve to the body wall, creating a vessel of globular or subglobular shape, while the second form probably had more nearly straight walls flaring from the base to a shoulder from which they curved inward to the neckless mouth. The one with straight wall profile was decorated with a dark red link design on a white zone—probably a banded design theme—just below the rim (fig. 18O).

OPEN BOWL FORMS 1.3

Open bowl forms, which include vessels generally classed as bowls and cups, are the most popular shapes in Late Patibamba I. There are 145 examples, which account for 55.3% of the total vessel sample from the phase. Thirty-eight examples from sample IA represent 58.5%, while seventy-eight pieces from sample IB account for 53.1%. Twenty-nine specimens from sample IC total 58% of that subphase sample. The high frequency of these vessels is substantially similar to that found in the Middle Patibamba Phase as well as in Late Patibamba II but represents a gain over the frequency found in Early Patibamba.

Plain Bowls 1.3.1

Plain bowls constitute 17.6% of the pottery from this phase, forty-six fragmentary specimens. Sample IA contains nineteen pieces, or 29.2%; IB has twenty, or 13.6%; while sample IC has seven bowls, or 14% of the subphase sample. The frequency of plain bowls has increased in this phase from a lower popularity in Middle Patibamba and they now have a popularity almost equal to that found in Early Patibamba. However, it is interesting to note that the frequencies of samples IB and IC, which come from the North Unit and the South Unit respectively, are low and are comparable to Middle Patibamba, while sample IA, also from the North Unit, has an unusually high frequency of plain bowls.

A total of forty vessel fragments provide the following description:

	Sample IA	Sample IB	Sample IC	Entire Phase
Mouth Diameter				
range	12-33cm.	10-26cm.	15-20cm.	10-33cm.
mode	–	17cm.	17cm.	17cm.
mean	19.8cm.	16.5cm.	17.4cm.	17.4cm.
Wall Angle				
range	5-50°	10-50°	5-30°	5-50°
mode	25°,40°	–	30°	30°
mean	28.4°	30.3°	22°	28.3°
Wall Profile Mode				
primary	D	A	A	D
secondary	B,C	D,B	D	A
Lip Treatment Mode				
primary	A	A	A,C	A
secondary	C	D	D	C
Rim Modification Mode				
primary	A	A	D	A
secondary	E,C,D	C	A	E
Wall Thickness				
range	.4-.8cm.	.4-.7cm.	.4-.6cm.	.4-.8cm.
mode	.5cm.,.6cm.	.5cm.	.6cm.	.5cm.,.6cm.
mean	.6cm.	.53cm.	.54cm.	.57cm.

Progressive trends include a very slightly noticeable tendency for the wall angles of plain bowls to decrease. In addition to this, outcurving wall profiles are becoming less common and are entirely absent from sample IC. In other aspects, including mouth diameter, the plain bowls of this phase are like those of the earlier phases. Base form was generally slightly curved to nearly flat, with a continuous curve joining the bottom to the walls. However, there are fragments of two flat bases, one with a sharp basal angle.

Regular-Size Plain Bowls   1.3.1.1

There are forty fragmentary regular-size plain bowls, which account for 15.3% of all the Late Patibamba I ceramic sample (fig. 19A-D, F, G, I, J, R, W, AA, AK, AR, AV, AW, AZ, BE). Sample IA includes fourteen pieces, or 21.5%; sample IB has nineteen, or 12.9%; and IC has seven regular-size plain bowls, 14% of the ceramic sample. These vessels may be described as follows:

	Sample IA	Sample IB	Sample IC	Entire Phase
Mouth Diameter				
range	12-21cm.	10-20cm.	15-20cm.	10-21cm.
mode	18cm.,20cm.	17cm.	17cm.	17cm.
mean	17.4cm.	15.9cm.	17.4cm.	17.4cm.
Wall Angle				
range	5-50°	10-50°	5-30°	5-50°
mode	40°	30°	30°	30°
mean	30.7°	29°	22°	28.7°
Wall Profile Form				
primary	D	A	A	D
secondary	B	D	D	A
Lip Treatment Form				
primary	A	A	A,C	A
secondary	C	D	D	C,D
Wall Thickness				
range	.4-.7cm.	.4-.6cm.	.4-.6cm.	.4-.7cm.
mode	.5cm.,.6cm.	.5cm.	.6cm.	.5cm.,.6cm.
mean	.55cm.	.52cm.	.54cm.	.54cm.

The regular-size plain bowls demonstrate the trend observed in the general category of plain bowls—the reduction in flare or wall angle. This reverses the move toward greater wall angles observable from Early Patibamba to Middle Patibamba. The wall angles of these Late Patibamba I vessels are more similar to those of Early Patibamba than to those of the Middle Patibamba Phase, as are various aspects of vessel shape.

The height of these bowls ranges between 4.5 cm. and 9 cm., with some positive correlation between mouth diameter and height. This sample demonstrates the continuation of a trend toward deeper bowls. All of the bases recovered are nearly flat with a continuous curve—tighter in the case of more flaring bowls and more gentle on specimens with nearly vertical walls—which unites the wall with the base.

Oversize Plain Bowls   1.3.1.2

Six fragmentary oversize plain bowls represent 2.3% of the vessels from Late Patibamba I (fig. 19BI, BL, BQ). Five sherds, or 7.7% of the sample, come from subphase IA, while one sherd, or .7%, comes from sample IB, and the subphase IC sample lacks these vessels entirely. The high frequency of these vessels in Early Patibamba compared with the low frequency in Middle Patibamba and both Late Patibamba IB and IC strongly suggests that the form is associated with special activities and is not represented in certain samples for that reason.

Oversize plain bowls may be described as follows:

	Sample IA	Sample IB	Entire Phase
Mouth Diameter			
range	24-33cm.	26cm.	24-33cm.
mode	24cm.	26cm.	24cm.
mean	26.6cm.	26cm.	26.5cm.
Wall Angle			
range	10-25°	50°	10-50°
mode	25°	50°	25°
mean	22°	50°	26.7°
Wall Profile Mode			
primary	D	B	D
secondary	C	–	B,C
Lip Treatment Mode			
primary	A,C	A	A
secondary	C1	–	C
Rim Modification Mode			
primary	D,E	A	A
secondary	A	–	E
Wall Thickness			
range	.6-.8cm.	.7cm.	.6-.8cm.
mode	.8cm.	.7cm.	.8cm.
mean	.74cm.	.7cm.	.73cm.

Few of these bowls could be reconstructed to provide overall shape, but the wall angles have decreased in this phase as they have for regular-size plain bowls. The overall vessel height appears to have ranged from about 7.5 cm. to perhaps 10 or 12 cm. The bases were gently curved, although there are some flat bottoms from plain bowls which may have been from oversize bowls.

Decorated Bowls   1.3.2

The Late Patibamba I vessel sample includes seventy fragmentary decorated bowls, which account for 26.7% of the collection. This frequency represents a popularity intermediate between that in the Early Patibamba and the Middle Patibamba phases. Seventeen sherds, or 26.2% of sample IA; thirty-seven sherds, or 25.2% of sample IB; and sixteen sherds, or 32% of sample IC, are from these decorated vessels.

A total of forty-five sherds with measurable rims provide the following description:

	Sample IA	Sample IB	Sample IC	Entire Phase
Mouth Diameter				
range	14-29cm.	13-27cm.	14-23cm.	13-29cm.
mode	20cm.,22cm.	17cm.,18cm.	19cm.	17cm.,18cm.
mean	19.3cm.	17.7cm.	17.7cm.	18.2cm.
Wall Angle				
range	10-45°	15-45°	5-35°	5-45°
mode	35°	35°	–	30°
mean	29.2°	29.2°	18.6°	25.9°
Wall Profile Mode				
primary	A	A	A	A
secondary	D	D	D	D

Lip Treatment Mode				
primary	D	A	C,D	D
secondary	C	B,C	A	A,C
Rim Modification Mode				
primary	A	A	A	A
secondary	D,E	B,E1	B,D	B,D,E1
Wall Thickness				
range	.4-.6cm.	.4-1.1cm.	.5-.6cm.	.4-1.1cm.
mode	.5cm.	.5cm.	.6cm.	.5cm.
mean	.53cm.	.57cm.	.58cm.	.55cm.

The painted decoration of Late Patibamba I is derived from Middle Patibamba. Although many aspects of shape are more indicative of Early Patibamba, it is clear that the use of color, design elements, and design themes is descended from Middle Patibamba. Paint was applied on a natural orange to light brown surface or on a red slip. Frequently, the red slip is thin and splotchy and fails to completely cover the surface of the bowl.

As in Middle Patibamba, white continues to appear more often than any other color, but it never occurs as a monochrome. It is used only in combination with other pigments in complex designs. Most frequently, white is used for space-filling elements such as dots, wavy lines, or other elements on bands or panels. White outlines around colored zones and fine white lines in linear designs are also common. The white bands and fields which were so common in Early Patibamba are very rare. It appears that white has progressed to being a color for lines or dots on or around another color from its former position as a color spread over large backgrounds or zones.

Dark red is the second most popular color and appears occasionally as the only color although generally it is combined with one or more other colors. In contrast with white, dark red is most often used to fill zones or paint bands rather than for linear elements. Its most common uses are for horizontal bands and, second, for colored disks decorated with Saint Andrew's crosses. Uncommon are dark red dots and other elements such as wavy lines. Vertical bands are very rare.

Black rates third in popularity during Early Patibamba I. It was frequently used as the only decorative color on bowls or was combined into bichrome or polychrome schemes. Its most common use is for horizontal bands, which are usually combined with dark red bands. Black lines in linear designs continue to be common, and black dots, wavy lines, and other elements used as space fillers are frequent. However, the use of black as an outline color continues to be rare, although it is slightly more common than in Middle Patibamba. The use of black for a colored disk decorated with Saint Andrew's cross is a progressive feature. This occurs on a single specimen which comes from sample IC and would be at home in the Late Patibamba II sample.

The remaining colors used in this phase appear infrequently and are used primarily in combination with other colors. Gray and yellow are next in popularity after black. Gray is used for bands, both horizontal and vertical, and for rim decorations. There is only a single case of gray being used for a wavy line space-filler element. Most of the gray paints are darker than those of the previous phase, but the use of the color is unchanged. However, gray has become more distinct from white because the structural position of white has shifted, leaving the use of gray more parallel to that of black.

Yellow appears as horizontal bands and as space-filler elements such as dots and wavy lines. The next most frequently used color, brown, is used for both design elements and colored fields or disks which are further decorated with contrasting colors. However, Late Patibamba I is the only phase in which brown was used as a monochrome decoration. Orange is the rarest color and appears only as space-filling dots.

An additional color appearing in low frequency in Late Patibamba I is light red. Although light reds had been present at Jargampata since Early Patibamba, their use seems to have been limited to slips. Some of the dark red paints of the first phases also vary in color so that they are as light as the light red of Late Patibamba I. However, I have distinguished light red in this phase as a separate color because it appears on the same vessel with—and in contrast to—the dark red paint. Light red dots appear occasionally in polychrome designs which include dark red.

Late Patibamba I is a period of experimentation with color, and there is a considerable amount of variation. The first five-color design—black, white, dark red, brown, and yellow—is found in the progressive IC sample. Monochromes continue at about the same level of popularity as in Middle Patibamba, with dark red or black the most frequent color. Bichrome schemes are slightly more common than monochromes, with dark red and white the favorite combination. Slightly less common are dark red with black and black with white. Trichromes are about as popular as bichromes, with the most common combination being dark red, white, and black. Other popular combinations include dark red, white, and gray and dark red, white, and yellow. Polychromes are infrequent, with dark red, white, black, and yellow and dark red, white, black, and light red being the only examples which occur more than once.

The decorated bowls clearly separate into two classes, interior-decorated bowls and exterior-decorated bowls. By Late Patibamba I, these groups have become distinct in terms of mouth diameter and wall angle as well as many design themes which are associated with one or the other group. Perhaps one of the most diagnostic new features which also continues into later phases at Jargampata is the short, solid-tripod tab support. These supports are used exclusively on exterior-decorated bowls.

Interior-Decorated Bowls   1.3.2.1

Forty-one of the seventy decorated bowls of Late Patibamba I have interior decoration. They account for 15.6% of the ceramic sample for the whole phase. Eleven pieces, 16.9%, are from sample IA; twenty-three, 15.6%, from IB; and seven, 14%, come from sample IC. It would appear that the interior-decorated bowls suffer a slight decline in popularity in Late Patibamba I, perhaps due to gains in the frequency of exterior-decorated bowls.

Only twenty-three of the interior-decorated bowl fragments were sufficiently complete for measurement of the mouth diameter to be made.

Regular-Size Interior-Decorated Bowls   1.3.2.1.1

A total of twenty-one of the twenty-three interior-decorated bowls are regular-size specimens. This represents only 8% of the phase sample, but this frequency would be higher if more fragments could be measured. Perhaps more

significant is that regular-size pieces account for 91.3% of the interior-decorated bowls which could be measured. Seven pieces, or 10.8%, come from sample IA; eight examples, or 5.4%, from IB; and six examples, or 12%, come from sample IC.

The regular-size interior-decorated bowls may be described as follows:

	Sample IA	Sample IB	Sample IC	Entire Phase
Mouth Diameter				
range	16-22cm.	14-19cm.	14-23cm.	14-23cm.
mode	20cm.,22cm.	17cm.,18cm.	19cm.	18cm.
mean	19.9cm.	17.3cm.	18.2cm.	18.4cm.
Wall Angle				
range	15-45°	20-40°	20-35°	15-45°
mode	35°	–	25°,30°	30°
mean	32.1°	30°	27.5°	30°
Wall Profile Mode				
primary	A	A	A	A
secondary	D	D	C,D	D
Lip Treatment Mode				
primary	C,D	A	D	D
secondary	–	B	–	A,C
Rim Modification Mode				
primary	A	A	A	A
secondary	–	E1	D	D,E1
Wall Thickness				
range	.4-.6cm.	.5-1.1cm.	.5-.6cm.	.4-1.1cm.
mode	.5cm.	.5cm.	.5cm.,.6cm.	.5cm.
mean	.5cm.	.63cm.	.55cm.	.56cm.

The shapes of these bowls deviate little from those of the Middle Patibamba Phase. Vessel height increases slightly, ranging between 6 cm. and 9 cm., with the greater heights generally associated with bowls of larger mouth diameter. All of the bases recovered are nearly flat, with continuous curves uniting the vessel bottoms and walls.

Painted decoration is limited to the interior of the bowls, or occasionally the rim and the interior. Generally the decoration is on a red-slipped or natural light orange to brown surface.

A common design theme in Late Patibamba I, which develops from Middle Patibamba pottery, is the colored disk with Saint Andrew's cross (fig. 21B-D; plate 13A). In this phase, the theme is both more common and more varied. The colored disk is generally dark red, but one example is brown and another is black. Typically, the disk is decorated with a cross placed diagonally, but in some examples the cross is omitted and in one unique case the cross is placed vertically (fig. 21E; plate 13B). In almost all cases, the cross is white. Generally a single circle was added in each quadrant formed by the cross on the circular disk, but variants include circles with a central dot, dots alone, or nothing at all. In one progressive example from sample IC, the cross has dots on it (fig. 21E; plate 13B).

The disks with Saint Andrew's cross were apparently arranged so that one of the four disks was placed in each quadrant of the vessel. A Late Patibamba I innovation was the connection of disks by a broad line running down the vessel wall and across the bottom (fig. 20A2).

Another common design theme is a broad horizontal band immediately below the bowl rim (fig. 23H-L). This is a theme which has a continuous development from Early Patibamba. However, the white band characteristic of the first phase was supplemented by a dark red band in Middle Patibamba, while by Late Patibamba I the white band had disappeared and was replaced by a dark red band or by a band of another color such as brown, an innovation in this phase.

The horizontal band is usually decorated with a wavy line and dots, multiple wavy lines and dots, circles, or some other space-filler elements. Some examples have plain bands, but it may be that the decorative elements which are usually white have worn off.

A two-band theme which originated in Middle Patibamba continues into Late Patibamba I (fig. 24D). The only combination which is represented is a black band over a dark red one. Like the single bands, the parallel bands have space-filler elements such as wavy lines and dots which are generally painted in white.

The design theme of diagonal lines composing a wing motif has disappeared in Early Patibamba I and does not reappear in the samples of vessels from later phases.

Groups of vertical bands constitute a popular design theme (fig. 22G). As in the earlier examples of this theme, the bands are often decorated with elements such as wavy lines, dots, or circles. There is no evidence for the presence of single-vertical-band themes in this phase.

A Middle Patibamba theme which continues into Late Patibamba I is the broad band forming a rectangle. However, in this phase the theme becomes associated with exterior-decorated bowls and it occurs only once on a bowl interior.

Another design theme is a field painted white and decorated with space-filler elements in contrasting colors (fig. 26B, C). Outlined panels are also found (fig. 26D), and a progressive innovation in this phase is the division of the panel into horizontal rows which are decorated with wavy lines and dots. However, this new design becomes more common in Late Patibamba II.

Oversize Interior-Decorated Bowls   1.3.2.1.2

Only two vessel fragments, or 8.7% of the vessel sample, are from oversize interior-decorated bowls. However, this low frequency might have been higher if a larger portion of the bowls had been sufficiently complete to measure. One vessel, or 1.5% of the subphase sample, comes from sample IA, and the one vessel, or .7%, comes from sample IB.

The oversize interior-decorated bowls may be described as follows:

	Sample IA	Sample IB	Entire Phase
Mouth Diameter			
range	29cm.	24cm.	24-29cm.
mode	29cm.	24cm.	–
mean	29cm.	24cm.	26.5cm.
Wall Angle			
range	35°	45°	35-45°
mode	35°	45°	–
mean	35°	45°	40°
Wall Profile Mode			
primary	D	A	A,D
secondary	–	–	–
Lip Treatment Mode			
primary	A	C	A,C
secondary	–	–	–

Rim Modification Mode			
primary	E	E1	E,E1
secondary	–	–	–
Wall Thickness			
range	.4cm.	.7cm.	.4-.7cm.
mode	.4cm.	.7cm.	–
mean	.4cm.	.7cm.	.55cm.

The height of these oversize bowls is not preserved in the fragmentary materials, nor is there any evidence of base form.

Painted decoration is limited to the vessel interior. One example is an innovative theme composed of a broad line or band which is outlined by a contrasting color. The band forms a zigzag around the vessel wall. This new theme also appears on bowl exteriors in this and the succeeding phase. The second bowl has an outlined and decorated panel theme like that found on many regular-size interior-decorated bowls (fig. 26E).

Exterior-Decorated Bowls   1.3.2.2

There are twenty-nine examples of bowls decorated on the exterior surface, which represent 11.1% of the Late Patibamba ceramic sample. This vessel category is slowly gaining popularity, both in absolute frequency and in frequency relative to interior-decorated bowls. Six vessels, or 9.2% of the subphase samples, are from sample IA; fourteen, or 9.5%, from sample IB; and nine pieces, or 18%, from subphase IC. A total of twenty-two vessels could be measured for mouth diameter.

Regular-Size Exterior-Decorated Bowls   1.3.2.2.1

Twenty-one exterior-decorated bowls, or 8% of the phase sample, are of regular size. Four, or 6.2% of the subphase, are from sample IA; nine, or 6.1%, are from IB; and eight, or 16%, come from subphase IC. It is worth noting that 95.5% of the exterior-decorated bowls which were measured have regular-size mouth diameters. They may be described as follows:

	Sample IA	Sample IB	Sample IC	Entire Phase
Mouth Diameter				
range	14-18cm.	13-18cm.	16-19cm.	13-19cm.
mode	–	17cm.	–	17cm.
mean	16cm.	16.4cm.	17.5cm.	16.8cm.
Wall Angle				
range	10-35°	15-35°	5-20°	5-35°
mode	–	35°	15°	15°,20°
mean	22.5°	26.7°	11.9°	20.3°
Wall Profile Mode				
primary	A,D	A	A,D	A
secondary	–	D	–	D
Lip Treatment Mode				
primary	D	A,B	C	C,D
secondary	–	C	A	A
Rim Modification Mode				
primary	A	A	A	A
secondary	D	E2	C,D	D
Wall Thickness				
range	.5cm.	.4-.6cm.	.6cm.	.4-.6cm.
mode	.5cm.	.5cm.	.6cm.	.5cm.
mean	.5cm.	.52cm.	.6cm.	.55cm.

These figures reveal that the shape features which differentiate exterior-decorated bowls from interior-decorated bowls—including smaller mouth diameter and lower wall angles—become more obvious from Middle Patibamba to Late Patibamba I. The height of the bowls, which ranges between about 5.5 cm. and 7.5 cm., remains unchanged.

The most outstanding innovation associated with exterior-decorated bowls in Late Patibamba I is the appearance of solid tab supports added in sets of three to the bases of some of these vessels (figs. 29D, 32D). The innovation seems sufficiently important to include this type as a new vessel category (1.3.3.3) within a group of tripod-support bowls. However, since all of the tab-support vessels which are reasonably complete have exterior decoration and the tab supports occur only on exterior-decorated bowls, the establishment of a new category may be artificial. These tab-support bowls are treated along with other exterior-decorated vessels in this description.

The tripod-tab-support vessels are particularly interesting because they appear suddenly without antecedent and are rather popular. However, many have bottoms sufficiently curved that when they are set on a flat surface the tab supports do not touch the surface. Other bowls from the same sample rest firmly on their supports, so it seems that there is no chronological significance in the apparent functional or nonfunctional nature of the supports.

Decoration on the regular-size exterior-decorated bowls is limited to painting on the exterior, or the rim and exterior, except for a few examples from sample IC, which qualify as exterior-decorated bowls on the basis of their shapes but have painting on the rim only. There are three main design themes employed. First is a theme composed of two horizontal bands, second a three-horizontal-band arrangement, and third the painting of broad bands forming rectangles.

Decoration composed of two broad bands in contrasting colors parallel to the bowl rim is common in Late Patibamba I. This theme, which first appeared in Middle Patibamba, now consists of bands of equal width, and there are several color combinations, including a dark red band over a black band, a black over a yellow band, and a gray over a dark red band, in that order of popularity. The colored bands are sometimes outlined with white lines and decorated with space-filler elements painted in white or dark red. The elements are typically wavy lines and dots, circles, or circles and dots (fig. 30K).

The single-horizontal-band exterior decoration which was so popular in Early Patibamba is absent in the sample from Late Patibamba I, although it reappears in a modified form in the later phases at Jargampata.

More popular than the two-band decorative theme is a theme composed of three horizontal bands on the vessel exterior. There is a single combination of colors, a black band over a dark red band over another black band. Occasionally, the colored bands are outlined with white lines, but it is more common to find a single white line below the three bands or no white outlines at all. Generally the bands are decorated with wavy lines and dots, circles, or circles and dots, or, very rarely, wavy lines alone (figs. 29D-F, 32D; plate 14A).

It is particularly common to find tripod tab supports on exterior-decorated bowls with the three-band design theme (figs. 29D, 32D; plate 14A). Although the design theme originates in Middle Patibamba (fig. 29D), it is interesting

to note that there is no evidence for tripod tab supports in that phase, so apparently the decorative theme and the supports appear separately in the Jargampata sequence.

The third most popular design theme for exterior-decorated bowls in Late Patibamba I is a rectangle formed by a broad band about 1.5 cm. wide. The band is generally dark red, outlined in white, and is often decorated with white circles (fig. 28G, H). Some variants have concentric, nested rectangles, and there is a theme which consists of a broad zigzag band which circles the bowl (fig. 28I, J).

An infrequent design theme on exterior-decorated bowls is a group of vertical bands decorated with multiple wavy lines or a wavy line with dots (fig. 30C, D).

Oversize Exterior-Decorated Bowls   1.3.2.2.2

Only one example, or .4% of the entire sample of vessels for the phase, is an oversize bowl with exterior decoration. This represents only 4.5% of the exterior-decorated bowls which could be measured. The specimen, from sample IB, may be described as follows:

Mouth Diameter	27cm.
Wall Angle	30°
Wall Profile	D
Lip Treatment	A
Rim Modification	A
Wall Thickness	.5cm.

This bowl fragment has red and black paint on an unslipped background. The design theme cannot be identified, and there is no information for overall height or base form.

Tripod Bowls   1.3.3

Tripod bowls represent only about 1% of the Early Patibamba ceramic sample and are absent from the Middle Patibamba remains. However, in Late Patibamba I there is an increase in both frequency and variety. Twelve tripod-vessel fragments account for 4.6% of the ceramic sample.

Subphase IA includes two fragmentary exterior-decorated bowls with tripod tab-shaped feet (fig. 28J), while the IB sample has one exterior-decorated bowl with tab supports (fig. 29D) and two more tab feet from other bowls. This sample also includes two large solid supports with circular cross sections. One which is reasonably complete measures 7 cm. long and 3 cm. thick (fig. 31). Finally, the sample from this subphase included a fragment of a large hollow support which was over 7 cm. tall and about 5 cm. in diameter at the top. It closely resembles more complete examples from the House Group (fig. 32A, B).

Subphase IC includes four exterior-decorated bowls with tripod tab supports (fig. 32D; plate 14A).

Late Patibamba I witnesses the appearance of both tripod tab supports and hollow tripod supports, all apparently attached to bowls which frequently had exterior decoration. There is a vessel reminiscent of the tripod-tab-support bowls with small hollow supports which comes from the House Group (fig. 32C; plate 14B). This vessel, although of a local paste, has features suggestive of the tripod vessels of Cajamarca IV and the "semi-cursive tripod" of terminal Cajamarca III (Reichlen 1970: 492). In

fact, it seems most likely that this expansion of tripods at Jargampata must be contemporary with other colonial Wari styles of Epoch 2B, such as Huacho and Viracochapampa, which contain a substantial number of tripod vessels. Conversely, the pure Epoch 2A styles, such as that which Ravines (1968: 19-46) recovered at Ayapata, appear to lack tripods.

Pedestal Bowls   1.3.5

One fragment of a pedestal bowl represents .4% of the Late Patibamba I Phase sample. Although this is a decline from the frequency of the preceding phases, the following phases have frequencies similar to those found in Early and Middle Patibamba. The single specimen from sample IC is represented by a solid base about 12 cm. in diameter which is modeled together with the walls of the vessel in a single piece (fig. 34H).

Lyre-Shaped Cups   1.3.6

One fragment of a lyre-shaped cup from subphase sample IC represents .4% of the pottery vessels for the entire phase. The wall profile has an S recurve, but the wall was oriented so that the mouth and base diameters are about equal (fig. 35O). This vessel may be described as follows:

Mouth Diameter	8cm.
Wall Angle	0°
Wall Profile	E
Lip Treatment	C
Rim Modification	E2
Wall Thickness	.7cm.

The height of this cup is about 5.5 cm., and the remains of a small handle are attached to the wall at the vessel's widest point. The base is missing, but it appears to have formed a continuous curve with the vessel wall.

Two lyre-shaped cups are reported in the Early Patibamba Phase (fig. 35K, L), but both are very wide-mouthed and perhaps quite short. The form is absent from the Middle Patibamba sample, and it seems likely that Late Patibamba I may actually be the phase during which this vessel shape makes its first appearance at Jargampata. Exotic lyre-shaped cups are present in this phase and may provide the stimulus for local copies.

Straight-Sided Tall Cups   1.3.7

A new shape which does appear in Late Patibamba I is a tall cup with straight or nearly straight walls and a flat bottom. This form is represented by a single example from the progressive IC sample and accounts for .4% of the pottery vessels for the phase (fig. 35A). The specimen may be described as follows:

Mouth Diameter	11cm.
Wall Angle	5°
Wall Profile	A
Lip Treatment	A
Rim Modification	A
Wall Thickness	.5cm.

The height of this cup is 10.5 cm. The base is nearly flat, with a tight curve uniting it to the walls. Decoration

consists of exterior painting in black, white, dark red, and light red. The design theme appears to be a variation on a vertical band and panel arrangement which is repeated three times around the cup. The panel consists of a rectangle made by a light red band outlined with black which is pendent from a black line on the rim. A vertical white band with wavy black line borders the panel on both sides, and a dark red band outlined in black separates each register from its counterparts. Below the panels are two horizontal bands, white and dark red, separated by a black line.

MINIATURE VESSELS   1.4

Another vessel shape category which appears to originate in Late Patibamba I is that of miniature vessels. These miniatures duplicate several vessel shapes but are distinctive because they are much smaller and generally have walls considerably thinner than those of regular-size vessels, in spite of the coarse paste and finish which often characterize the miniatures.

Three fragments from miniatures represent 1.1% of the ceramic sample for the phase. Each of the three subphase samples contains one specimen, representing 1.5%, .7%, and 2% of these samples respectively. It appears that all three specimens are from bowls. Only one shows any trace of decoration, and that consists of a brown line painted on the interior (fig. 36N, O).

Two specimens from sample IA and IB provide the following description:

	Sample IA	Sample IB	Entire Phase
Mouth Diameter			
range	9cm.	9cm.	9cm.
mode	9cm.	9cm.	9cm.
mean	9cm.	9cm.	9cm.
Wall Angle			
range	30°	20°	20-30°
mode	30°	20°	—
mean	30°	20°	25°
Wall Profile Mode			
primary	A	B	A,B
secondary	—	—	—
Lip Treatment Mode			
primary	A1	B	A1,B
secondary	—	—	—
Rim Modification Mode			
primary	E1	A	E1,A
secondary	—	—	—
Wall Thickness			
range	.3cm.	.4cm.	.3-.4cm
mode	.3cm.	.4cm.	—
mean	.3cm.	.4cm.	.35cm.

The height of one of these bowls was 3 cm., and their bases were gently curved like those of larger bowls. Two of the three miniatures are fire blackened, an unusual characteristic for bowls at Jargampata.

There are no other shapes of miniature vessels in the Late Patibamba I ceramic sample, but miniatures from the House Group which probably belong to this or the succeeding phase copy a number of forms, including the side-spout jar and the flaring-neck jar (figs. 10A, 13C).

PRESS MOLDS   1.7

Two pottery molds for the manufacture of relief details represent .8% of the pottery from this phase. One fragmentary specimen comes from subphase IA, where it represents 1.5% of the sample, while a complete mold comes from sample IB and accounts for .7% of the pottery (plate 15D). The mold fragment from sample IA has the impression of two hands with the fingertips almost touching one another. It is likely that it was used for producing face-neck jars with relief hands, although no such vessels were found in the excavations. The second mold is a face, but apparently that of an animal—perhaps a feline. The mold is about 4.5 cm. in diameter and quite deep, so it would have produced a face in high relief. However, the features of the face are in very low relief and are difficult to identify. Although this mold may also have been used in the production of face-neck jars, a tripod bowl from the House Group (fig. 32C; plate 14B) has salient adornos in high relief which might be animal faces and it seems likely that the mold was used to make such a vessel.

CERAMIC DISKS   1.8

A single sherd, .4% of the phase sample, is from a flat pottery disk. This specimen from sample IB had a diameter of about 17 cm. and a thickness of .7 cm. (fig. 12).

SCRAPER-POLISHERS   1.9

A plain sherd from subphase sample IB accounts for .4% of the pottery objects from Early Patibamba I. The distinctive feature of the sherd is that the three edges which have not been recently broken are smoothed to a curve (fig. 36A). It seems likely that the sherd was used as a scraping tool, perhaps in the manufacture of pottery. One of the edges must have had a deep curve appropriate for scraping the exterior of vessel walls.

Close examination of the sherd under a binocular microscope revealed that some of the smooth edges of the sherd showed very little evidence of abrasion, suggesting that the scraper-polisher was manufactured as a tool rather than having been worked out of a broken sherd from a pot. Similar tools, some deliberately prepared and others manufactured by use from large pot sherds, were found in the House Group (fig. 36B).

EXOTIC VESSELS   1.10

The high frequency of sherds which have paste and surface finish distinctive from the typical pottery of Jargampata suggests that Late Patibamba I was a period in which Jargampata experienced a maximum of extrasite contact and interaction. There are sixteen such pieces, which probably represent imports and account for 6.4% of the total ceramic sample for the phase. This is a 300% increase in frequency over Middle Patibamba. Four pieces, or 6.2% of the sample, come from subphase IA; ten pieces, or 6.8%, are from IB; and sample IC has two pieces, or 4% imported ware.

Generally the exotic sherds have glossy surface finishes which contrast with the local matte pottery. The paste, the

vessel shapes, and in some cases the decorative colors are equally outstanding.

Two sherds from sample IA and a third from IB have shiny black surfaces and gray paste, indicating that the pottery was unoxidized and perhaps smudged (Shepard 1965: 106, 221). There is no decoration on these sherds, but it seems likely that they belong to the type that Bennett (1953: fig. 16) and Menzel (1964: 18-19) have termed black decorated pottery, which comes from the Ayacucho valley in Middle Horizon IB and later. One of the sherds came from a vessel of composite form; perhaps it was a neck on a larger body. The black decorated pottery establishes a link to Wari and the Ayacucho valley, strengthening the impression of exterior interaction. A substantial amount of this pottery was found in the House Group.

Another exotic vessel, probably of the lyre-shaped cup form, is represented by four sherds from sample IA which, however, do not fit together. One sherd from sample IB fit onto one of the IA rim sherds (fig. 39I; plate 17F), and judging by its less eroded condition it seems likely that the original context of this vessel was with sample IB. The cup has a mouth diameter of about 14 cm. and a wall angle of about 15°. The upper part of the vessel wall has a slight outward curve, and the lip treatment is rounded, although the rim has been thinned somewhat. The vessel wall is .5 cm. thick. The interior and exterior have a low-gloss red slip, and the exterior is decorated with a pattern of black lines and dots and a white band below the rim. Nearly identical sherds can be found at Wari as well as at other Middle Horizon sites, and the appearance of this ceramic type at Jargampata in Late Patibamba I strengthens the assumption that extrasite ties were intensified at this time.

Another sherd with parallels at Wari is from a vessel with a body diameter of about 14 or 15 cm. The background is red, and painted decoration includes black, white, dark red-purple, and yellow which form a feather motif and reverse S shapes with dots (fig. 39E; plate 17D). This sherd can be compared with Viñaque-style pottery from Wari (Bennett 1953: plate 4A) and provincial centers (Flores Espinoza 1959: foto 4) of Late Middle Horizon 2 (Menzel 1964: 42-43).

Three sherds from a fancy lyre-shaped cup were found in the subphase IB sample. A fourth, a more eroded sherd of the same vessel, came from the stratum overlying sample IB where it was probably redeposited (fig. 39C; plate 16A). The lyre-shaped cup had a mouth diameter of 10 cm. and a wall angle of 10°. The wall profile is slightly recurving, and the lip treatment is rounded in spite of the thinned rim. The wall is .6 cm. thick and has a glossy red slip on the interior and exterior. The exterior decoration consists of a vertical chevron band, two feather motifs attached to a gray band, and other elements which are part of the front-face deity with headdress which has been described by Menzel (1964: 41-42; 1968: 76, 89). This lay elite theme is so highly standardized (Bennett 1953: plate 3F) that even without the whole theme it is quite clear that the vessel belongs to Middle Horizon 2B and was probably imported from Wari itself. A nearly identical lyre-shaped cup was found in the House Group (fig. 39D; plate 16B), where it was probably grave furniture in room S1. This establishes a firm crossdating with Late Patibamba I.

Two additional fancy decorated sherds—one from sample IA and the other from IB—are also probably Wari imports, but the small size and eroded condition prevent the identification of design themes and the dating of these pieces. The sherd from sample IA was part of a closed vessel which may have been modeled into a complex form (fig. 39H). The only identifiable theme is the interlocking meander which often outlines the head of Middle Horizon figures (Lumbreras 1960b: lam. VJ). The sherd from sample IB is from the wall and base of a bowl or cup with exterior design (fig. 39F).

Three undecorated body sherds from sample IB have glossy red finishes, while one from sample IA has a shiny orange surface distinct from the Jargampata ceramics. One rim sherd from sample IB comes from a plain bowl with a low-gloss red finish and a mouth diameter of 17 cm.

Sample IC includes two exotic body sherds with decoration. One is a thick sherd with red slip and is decorated with broad black horizontal bands, while the second has a glossy red slip and is decorated with black, white, and yellow paint.

Although the deposits within the House Group were badly mixed, it is likely that most of the fancy pottery from those rooms belongs to the Early Patibamba I Phase. The lyre-shaped cup (fig. 39D; plate 16B), which is contemporary with the example from sample IB (fig. 39C; plate 16A), probably constituted part of a grave offering originally placed in room S1. Among other vessels from similar contexts is a bowl with a stylistically conservative, but right-side-up, spotted animal derived from fancy Chakipampa A antecedents (Menzel 1968a: 57; figs. 2b, 3-6), which was found on the floor of room S1 (fig. 39A; plate 18E). The bilobed jar or bottle (fig. 12A; plate 11B) may also have come from this room, and three large bowls—two of which have wing motifs (fig. 41A-C; plate 18G)—are probably part of grave offerings. These imported bowls have wing motifs which were apparently common elsewhere during Middle Horizon 2B in spite of the lack of evidence for this theme in the Jargampata pottery of Early Patibamba I.

A cache of vessel fragments found in association in one of the corridors of the House Group includes a fancy bowl with skulls (plate 16D) and two fragmentary flasks with tightly curved side seams (fig. 17A, B), which might also be of Middle Horizon 2B. There is little doubt that the skull vessel is an imported piece, but the flasks were probably manufactured locally. Also found in close association with the skull vessel and flasks were hollow-tripod supports, which appear in Late Patibamba II.

Face-neck jars are not represented in the sample of Late Patibamba I pottery, although there are molds that probably were for their manufacture as well as local examples from the House Group. Five face-neck jars also from the House Group were apparently manufactured elsewhere and imported, as there is an example with very fine red-orange paste and extremely well-finished natural surface which has shape characteristics diagnostic of Middle Horizon 2B (fig. 40A; plate 16F). The nearly tubular or cylindrical neck has become tapered and inclined slightly toward the rear, while the body has the more prominent shoulder and less rounded profile described by Menzel (1968a; figs. 40-41) for Atarco B. A second fragmentary example (fig. 40H) with similar paste may have come from the same source and, although it is incomplete, the backward inclination of the base of the neck suggests the piece is of Epoch 2B as well.

Another face-neck jar which was probably produced locally (fig. 40C) was associated with fragments of the

nearly complete imported jar. It is interesting that the shape features are more conservative, suggesting that the association may be fortuitous, the local piece may have been quite old when included in the deposit, or perhaps that the locally manufactured pottery was more conservative and continued to manifest attributes of Middle Horizon 1 and 2A even when more prestigious centers were producing ceramics with features typical of Epoch 2B. However, these ceramics do provide evidence for an intensified interaction between Jargampata and centers of greater prestige such as Wari. The increase in imported elite pottery suggests that either the quantities of products exported from Jargampata were going up or that they were increasing in value relative to manufactured goods and the services of elite specialists.

Black decorated pottery appears in Late Patibamba I in the North Unit, and it seems reasonable to associate most of the black decorated pottery from the House Group with this phase. There is no black decorated pottery in the subsequent Late Patibamba II sample, although one reasonably complete and rather elaborately decorated bowl (fig. 42E; plate 19A), which came from the surface of the floor in room S8 of the North Unit, must date to the abandonment of the site and must therefore belong to the end of Late Patibamba I or Late Patibamba II. However, the low frequency of imported materials in Late Patibamba II suggests a sharp drop in extrasite exchange, and even if the bowl was scattered on the floor in this phase it was probably imported in Late Patibamba I.

Vessels of black decorated pottery from the House Group include two fragmentary face-neck vessels of unusual form (fig. 42B. D; plate 19D, E). The bodies of these vessels are laterally elongated, and they have high peaks at both ends and decorated center panels which suggest a man wearing a poncho. An almost identical vessel, which must be contemporary with Late Patibamba I and Middle Horizon 2B, has been illustrated by Lumbreras (1959: lam. IXC) from the Galvez Durand collection in Huancayo. Although this vessel shape has not been generally recognized as belonging to the late Wari culture, it must be considered in relationship to the flattened, flask-like vessels with face necks in black ware which are typical of the Late Middle Horizon or the Late Intermediate Period of the North Coast.

A number of sherds from other black ware or black decorated vessels include a lyre-shaped cup form, a small sub-hemispherical bowl, and a modeled head which appears to represent a monkey (fig. 42G, F, C; plate 19B, C).

The ceramics discussed above indicate some form of exchange between Jargampata and sites in the Ayacucho valley. However, that the sphere of interaction was much greater is indicated by three spoons which are typical Cajamarca III Cursive Floral style and are made from a white paste otherwise unrepresented at Jargampata (plate 18B-D). Similar ceramics are found at Wari (Bennett 1953: plate 11), where they may have been manufactured. However, my impression is that the hard white paste of these vessels from Wari and of the spoons from Jargampata is not typical of the Central Highlands, and these ceramics may have been manufactured for export as far away as the North Highlands. The exclusive presence of small, portable items such as spoons supports the idea that long-distance transport may have been involved. Conversely, there are other fragmentary vessels from the House Group which must be local versions of Cajamarca pottery.

A double bowl—a form unknown to me in Cajamarca ceramics—from stratum 4 of corridor CX is painted in typical Cajamarca Cursive Floral style by an artist who executed the designs with great skill. Furthermore, the bowl has a slight basal angle and an out-turned lip, which are North Highlands features not typical at Jargampata (fig. 38A; plate 18A). The skill with which this vessel was painted convinces me that it was manufactured by a potter trained in the North Highland style, but the paste of the vessel is unlike that of the Cajamarca spoons. The paste of this vessel is unlike that of many Wari vessels, and yet it is not exactly like that of Jargampata. Perhaps this vessel represents the product of a Cajamarca-trained artisan resident in the Ayacucho area.

Two vessels show the impact of the Cajamarca style upon the local potters at Jargampata. Two fragments of one bowl from the House Group demonstrate that the slight basal angle and out-turned lip of the northern style were copied (fig. 38B). However, the quickly executed style of painting was apparently beyond the abilities of local potters at Jargampata. Part of the bowl was decorated with cursive squiggles which look as much like the wavy-line–and–dot designs of Jargampata as like the elegant Cajamarca styles they are meant to imitate. The remainder of the vessel was decorated with a gridiron or checkerboard pattern which at least gives the same impression of filled space typical of the Cajamarca style. The second vessel which may imitate Cajamarca is from room S4, strata 3 and 4, of the House Group (fig. 33A). The bowl has one of the only two ring bases found, and although the remainder of the shape is not particularly like that of Cajamarca bowls, the gridiron-and-dots decoration is unlike Jargampata themes and recalls the attempt to copy Cajamarca discussed above. If this vessel were dated by the only other ring base in the site, it would be placed in Middle Patibamba and somewhat closer in time to the ring-base, Cajamarca-style bowls found at Ayapata by Ravines (1968: fig. 31) and attributed to Middle Horizon 2A.

These last Cajamarca copies are probably locally produced by Jargampata potters, as indicated by the paste and the lack of skill in executing the foreign designs.

The Cajamarca-style pottery at Jargampata indicates three kinds of relations with the North Highlands. First, the people of Jargampata, and probably other sites, copied Cajamarca materials and styles in what appears to have been stimulus diffusion. Second, Cajamarca-trained potters and probably other specialists from the North Highlands worked at their own professions in the Ayacucho-Wari area. Third, overland transport moved goods—including some pottery—between the Central Highlands and the North Highlands. Long-range trade, especially with the north, is also indicated by sea shells, including *Spondylus* (plate 19M, N), which must ultimately have come from Ecuador (Paulsen 1974). Metals, of which three examples were found at Jargampata (plate 19L), may also have been important items in long-range trade.

If all of these exotic materials are correctly identified as belonging to the Late Patibamba I Phase at Jargampata, it is particularly interesting to note that as the last days of the Wari polity drew to a close in Middle Horizon 2B the degree of interaction among sites was intensified and trade spheres may have been extended. This contrasts sharply with the period following the Wari collapse during which regional isolation appears to have been the rule. It would seem that either the eclipse of the Wari economic system took place

very suddenly or that the administration recognized the impending collapse and strove to prevent it by a final but unsuccessful intensification of interchange. The increase in elite goods at a site such as Jargampata may indicate that the level of economic specialization and craft production was on the increase—perhaps at the same time that agricultural products were becoming more scarce. This might have increased the cost of urban living until it became prohibitive and resulted in a peaceful but rapid abandonment of the cities.

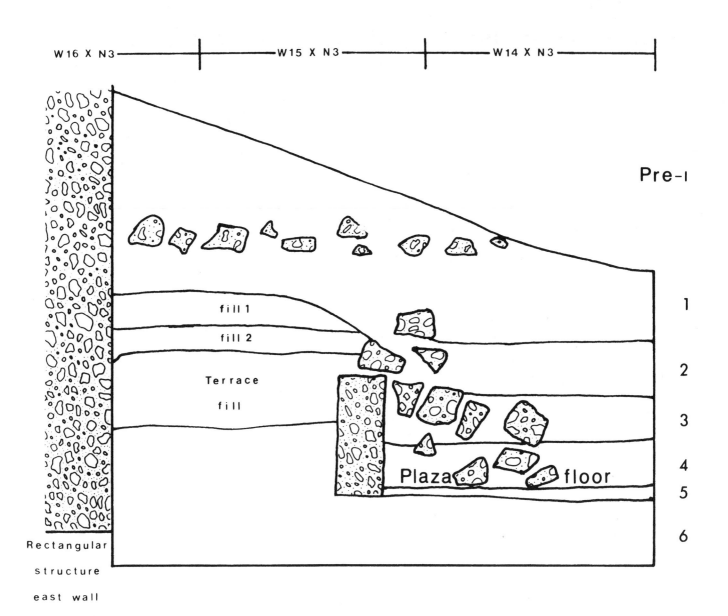

Figure 47. North Face of Cut N3 x W14-16

Pre-1   Dark brown clayish soil with relatively few rocks.
  1   Dark brown soil with some but not many rocks. Separated from Pre-1 by a concentration of rocks fallen from the walls.
  2   Lighter brown sandy clay with rocks and gravel.
  3   Series of fine strata of sand and fine gravel with rocks fallen from walls.
  4   Sandy gravel with rocks and some sherds. Separated from stratum 3 by a thin line of fine gravel. Sherds are most frequent in the bottom of this stratum.

  5   Hard earth floor with ashy texture and many sherds. Sherd concentrations are found under the rocks fallen from the low terrace retaining wall.
Fill 1   Thin stratum of hard, dark clay.
Fill 2   Thin stratum of hard, dark clay. Little difference exists between Fill 1 and this fill, but they separate easily with a trowel.
Terrace Fill   Red-brown sandy clay with fine gravel. Sterile.
  6   Yellow-brown sand and gravel. Sterile.

12
Ceramics of the Late Patibamba II Phase

STRATIGRAPHIC ASSOCIATION

Ceramics of Late Patibamba I and II share so many stylistic attributes that single vessels often cannot be assigned with confidence to one or the other phase. The difference is most accurately described as quantitative rather than qualitative, although there is stratigraphic justification for the separation of phases I and II from two excavations in the North Unit. The pottery of Late Patibamba II appears to represent a final scattering of refuse on the living surfaces at Jargampata as the site was abandoned. If this interpretation is correct, the separate treatment of Late Patibamba II is particularly important for what this material and time period may tell us about the collapse of the Wari polity even though the entire ceramic sample may represent only a fraction of a generation of time.

The relative dating of Late Patibamba II pottery is evident in rooms S10 and S11 (fig. 44), where ceramics of this phase were found in stratum D overlying pottery of Late Patibamba I in stratum D1. Both these strata were covered by materials assigned to the Illaura Phase from strata C and C1. In excavation E5-6 x S9-10 (fig. 45), strata 2 and 3 contained Late Patibamba II ceramics and rested upon stratum 4 which contained Late Patibamba I materials. Although strata 2 and 3 could be visually distinguished from one another, it is improbable that they indicate a long temporal duration for the phase. It is more likely that the small quantity of sherds from stratum 2 represents redeposited material carried by slope wash from above within the North Unit after the west wall collapsed. However, pottery from these two strata has been handled separately since there are some differences between the two samples which cannot be assumed to have resulted from the small sample size.

The final sample of Late Patibamba II pottery is perhaps the most interesting and least contaminated. These sherds come from the surface of the plaza floor of the North Unit from an area approximately 1 meter by 6 meters at the west end of the floor. A low terrace across the west end of the North Unit surrounded the Rectangular Structure and was supported by a stone retaining wall. Much of this wall collapsed onto the plaza floor, sealing the materials which were lying on the floor at the moment of abandonment (fig. 47). It is interesting that a considerable sample of pottery was found beneath the fallen stones while the central area of the plaza was virtually free of refuse. This could indicate that refuse only accumulated along the walls of the North Unit plaza or that the central part of the plaza floor was scoured by erosion prior to the deposition of a meter of alluvium which was a result of the collapse of the west wall of the North Unit enclosure. If the plaza floor was kept reasonably clean while in use, there can be little doubt that the collection of refuse which accumulated against the terrace retaining wall represents a final moment in the occupation of the North Unit and apparently of the urban site of Wari as well.

VESSEL SAMPLE

The sample of Late Patibamba II vessels is composed of 167 fragmentary pots. All but five decorated body sherds from unknown closed forms were assigned to vessel shape categories.

Two general shape categories account for 88% of the total pottery collection. Necked jars account for only 26.9% of the sample, while open bowl forms constitute 61.1% of the collection. This frequency maintains the trend observed through the first three phases at Jargampata of open bowl forms increasing in frequency at the expense of necked jars. However, the frequencies from the various subphase samples may be slightly less consistent than those found in the Late Patibamba I material.

The pottery from the plaza floor beneath the collapsed retaining wall will be referred to as sample IIA. It includes fifty-five vessel fragments, 21.8% necked jars and 69.1% open bowl forms.

Sample IIB comes from stratum 3 of E5-6 x S9-10 and contains only ten vessel fragments. Necked jars account for only 10% of the sample, and open bowl forms constitute the remaining 90%.

Stratum D of rooms S10 and S11 contained the eighty-nine vessel fragments which compose sample IIC. This sample includes 29.2% necked jars, and 53.9% of the sherds are from open bowl forms.

The fourth sample, IID, comes from stratum 2 of E5-6 x S9-10 and includes only thirteen vessels. These consist of 46.2% necked jars and 53.8% open bowls. It is worth observing that if samples IIB and IID were added together, the frequency would be 30.4% necked jars and 69.6% open bowl forms—a frequency very close to that found in the two larger samples.

NECKED JARS 1.1

Necked jars of this phase retain the same basic shape characteristic of earlier jars except for an increase in the popularity of flat or nearly flat bottoms. Two jar bases from sample IIA have a flat and a slightly curved bottom, while four bases from sample IIC include one flat bottom with sharp base angle, two nearly flat bottoms, and a

rounded bottom. There are no conical bases in the sample for the phase, but it seems unlikely that this form, so popular in the early part of the sequence, could have disappeared completely. Furthermore, conical bottoms constitute about 25% of the jar bases from the final Illaura Phase.

The form and placement of handles remain unchanged, as do the constraints upon decoration of jars. One exception, however, is a body sherd from a jar in sample IIA. This sherd has shallow incisions arranged in a vertical band pattern. A possible second exception comes from sample IIC and is probably a body sherd from a jar with a small appliqué pellet with two vertical incisions (fig. 16I). Other examples of plastic decoration are absent, and the face-neck jar is totally lacking in this sample, although there are press molds which were probably used for the manufacture of such jars (plate 15B, C). Some body sherds and bases were slipped red, but it is likely that these belonged to decorated jars of the constricted-neck group.

Constricted-Neck Jars   1.1.1

There are six examples of constricted-neck jars, 3.6% of the pottery from the phase. Sample IIA includes two examples, or 3.6%; sample IIC has three specimens, or 3.4%; while IID has a single example accounting for 7.7% of the vessels.

Narrow-Collar Jars   1.1.1.1

Four narrow-collar jars represent 2.4% of the pottery vessels from the Late Patibamba II sample (fig. 10W, X, Z). Two examples from sample IIA represent 3.6%; one piece from sample IIC is 1.1%; and one specimen from IID accounts for 7.7%. Only three of these necks could be measured to provide the description which follows:

	Sample IIA	Sample IID	Entire Phase
Mouth Diameter			
range	6-8cm.	6cm.	6-8cm.
mode	–	6cm.	6cm.
mean	7cm.	6cm.	6.7cm.
Wall Angle			
range	(-5)-0°	5°	(-5)-5°
mode	–	5°	–
mean	(-2.5°)	5°	0°
Wall Profile Mode			
primary	A	A	A
secondary	–	–	–
Lip Treatment Mode			
primary	A,B	B	B
secondary	–	–	A
Rim Modification Mode			
primary	B,F	A	A,B,F
secondary	–	–	–
Neck Thickness			
range	.4-.5cm.	.4cm.	.4-.5cm.
mode	–	.4cm.	.4cm.
mean	.45cm.	.4cm.	.43cm.

The most outstanding differences between these narrow-collar jars and those of earlier phases are reductions in mouth diameter and in neck thickness. One sherd from sample IID (fig. 10X) has enough of the body to indicate that the entire vessel was quite small, and it seems the reductions in diameter and thickness reflect reductions in vessel size in Late Patibamba II. Also, wall profiles are all straight and none have thickened rims.

Painted decoration is found on three of the four examples. Two have black bands just below the rim (fig. 10X, Z), while the third has a black band about 2 cm. below the rim (fig. 10W). One specimen is more elaborate and has a dark red band below the black band and vertical white lines (fig. 10X). This single black band below the vessel rim is a theme frequently found on jars and bowls of Late Patibamba II and Illaura.

Face-Neck Jars   1.1.1.2

There are no examples of face-neck jars from this phase, but two press molds with human faces (plate 15B, C) were probably used for the production of these vessels. It seems likely that either the frequency of this shape category was on the decline or perhaps that the functional specialization of the shape was changing so that it was no longer represented in refuse of the North Unit.

Bilobed Jars   1.1.1.3

Bilobed jars or bottles made their appearance in Late Patibamba I, and two fragmentary examples from Late Patibamba II represent 1.2% of that vessel sample (fig. 12E, F). Both specimens come from sample IIC, where they account for 22.5% of that sample. However, it should be recognized that, except for bilobed jars from the House Group, all of these vessels belonging to Late Patibamba I came from S10 and S11, stratum D1, which underlies the Late Patibamba IIC sample. The presence of two bilobed jars in the IIC sample might have been a result of redeposition of the earlier materials.

The two fragmentary vessels from this phase are too small to supply complete measurements, but the form and size of the jars is similar to those of Late Patibamba I.

Side-Spout Jars   1.1.2

Three fragments of side-spout jars account for 1.8% of the pottery vessels from this phase (fig. 13). All specimens are from sample IIC, where they represent a total of 3.4% of the refuse. None of the jars could be reconstructed, but the spouts range from 3 cm. to 4.5 cm. in diameter and from 5.7 cm. to 9 cm. in length. Two of the spouts have a thin brown slip on their exterior surfaces.

Flaring-Neck Jars   1.1.3

Flaring-neck jars continue to decline in popularity in Late Patibamba II. Twenty vessel fragments represent 12% of the total sample. Sample IIA contains five, or 9.1%, flaring-neck jars; sample IIB has a single jar, accounting for 10% of the vessels; sample IIC includes twelve jars, or 13.5%; and in sample IID there are two flaring-neck jars which represent 15.4% of the pots. Of the twenty jars, only ten are complete enough to supply the following description:

	Sample IIA	Sample IIB
Mouth Diameter		
range	15-22cm.	32cm.
mean	18.3cm.	32cm.
Wall Angle		
range	(-5)-30°	20°
mode	—	20°
mean	17.5°	20°
Wall Profile Mode		
primary	A,B	A
secondary	—	—
Lip Treatment Mode		
primary	D	B
secondary	C	—
Rim Modification Mode		
primary	E	D
secondary	A,D	—
Neck Thickness		
range	.6-1cm.	.7cm.
mode	.6cm.	.7cm.
mean	.7cm.	.7cm.

	Sample IIC	Sample IID	Entire Phase
Mouth Diameter			
range			
mode	17-42cm.	13cm.	13-42cm.
mean	25cm.	13cm.	21.9cm.
Wall Angle			
range	5-30°	25°	(-5)-30°
mode	5°	25°	20°,25°
mean	16.3°	25°	18°
Wall Profile Mode			
primary	A	B	A
secondary	B	—	B
Lip Treatment Mode			
primary	C,D	A	D
secondary	—	—	C
Rim Modification Mode			
primary	E	D	E
secondary	A	—	A,D
Wall Thickness			
range	.5-1.1cm.	.5cm.	.5-1.1cm.
mode	—	.5cm.	.6cm.
mean	.73cm.	.5cm.	.69cm.

This is a small sample, but it indicates a continuation of the decrease in mouth diameter for this category of vessels. This apparent decrease is produced by a reduction in the frequency of jars with very large mouth diameters. Lip treatment most resembles Middle Patibamba, and there is a high frequency of rims modified by thickening consistent with form E. None of the vessels could be completely reconstructed, but it seems very unlikely that the body form differed significantly from earlier phases, except perhaps for base shape. The neck height ranges from 2.5 cm. to 7.5 cm. There is one example of plastic decoration from sample IIC (fig. 16I). An appliqué pellet about 1.8 cm. by 1 cm. was welded on the body of what was probably a flaring-neck jar. It was placed almost on the shoulder and has two small vertical incisions which were made in wet clay.

Flaring-Neck Jars: Size Variant A   1.1.3A

Two sherds from this size group represent 1.2% of the Late Patibamba II pottery, 1.1% of sample 11C, and 7.7% of sample IID. The single sherd from sample IID which has its rim may be described as follows:

Mouth Diameter	13cm.
Wall Angle	25°
Wall Profile	B
Lip Treatment	A
Rim Modification	D
Neck Thickness	.5cm.

The neck of this jar was not over 4 cm. tall.

Flaring-Neck Jars: Size Variant B   1.1.3B

Three fragments from jars of this size group represent 1.8% of all vessels from Late Patibamba II (fig. 15L, O). Two rim sherds from sample IIA represent 3.6%, and one from sample IIC represents 1.1% of the sample. Although the total frequency is very low, the popularity of vessels of this size has not shifted appreciably compared with other sizes of flaring-neck jars. The group may be described as follows:

	Sample IIA	Sample IIC	Entire Phase
Mouth Diameter			
range	15-16cm.	17cm.	15-17cm.
mode	—	—	—
mean	15.5cm.	17cm.	16cm.
Wall Angle			
range	(-5)-25°	30°	(-5)-30°
mode	—	—	—
mean	10°	30°	20°
Wall Profile Mode			
primary	B	A	B
secondary	—	—	A
Lip Treatment Mode			
primary	D	D	D
secondary	—	—	—
Rim Modification Mode			
primary	A,E	E	E
secondary	—	—	A
Neck Thickness			
range	.6cm.	.6cm.	.6cm.
mode	.6cm.	.6cm.	.6cm.
mean	.6cm.	.6cm.	.6cm.

Neck height was 3.5 cm. and more.

Flaring-Neck Jars: Size Variant C   1.1.3C

This is the most popular size of flaring-neck jar during Late Patibamba II, with eight sherds accounting for 4.8% of the total vessel sample (fig. 15Z, AD, AK, AO). Relative to other sizes of flaring-neck jars, this group gains in popularity from Late Patibamba I and approximates the frequency which characterized Middle Patibamba. Two sherds from sample IIA, or 3.6%, five from sample IIC, or 5.6%,

and one from sample IID, or 7.7%, comprise the total, of which four rim sherds provide the description which follows:

	Sample IIA	Sample IIC	Entire Phase
Mouth Diameter			
range	20-22cm.	20-22cm.	20-22cm.
mode	–	–	20-22cm.
mean	21cm.	21cm.	21cm.
Wall Angle			
range	20-30°	5-25°	5-30°
mode	–	–	–
mean	25°	15°	20°
Wall Profile Mode			
primary	A	A,B	A
secondary	–	–	B
Lip Treatment Mode			
primary	C,D	C,D	C,D
secondary	–	–	–
Rim Modification Mode			
primary	D,E	E	E
secondary	–	–	D
Neck Thickness			
range	.6-1cm.	.5-.7cm.	.5-1cm.
mode	–	–	–
mean	.8cm.	.6cm.	.7cm.

Two rim sherds have neck heights of 7 cm. and 7.5 cm., indicating that the necks of these jars were fairly tall.

Flaring-Neck Jars: Size Variant D   1.1.3D

Jars of this size group declined dramatically in frequency in Late Patibamba I. In this phase, there are no rim sherds which indicate mouth diameter of this size. However, one sherd from a body-neck juncture in sample IIC provides an estimated mouth diameter of 26 cm. indicating that, although infrequent, the size variant had not disappeared.

Flaring-Neck Jars: Size Variant E   1.1.3E

This size variant accounts for 1.2% of the phase. One rim from sample IIB represents 10% and a collar fragment from IIA accounts for 1.8% of the sample. The rim may be described as follows:

Mouth Diameter	32cm.
Wall Angle	20°
Wall Profile	A
Lip Treatment	B
Rim Modification	D
Neck Thickness	.7cm.

The neck of this jar was more than 4 cm. tall.

Flaring-Neck Jars: Size Variant G   1.1.3G

As mentioned above, large jars are quite rare in Late Patibamba II. Size variant F is absent, and a single rim sherd from a vessel of size variant G represents .6% of the vessel sample. This specimen, from sample IIC where it represents 1.1% of the vessels, may be described as follows:

Mouth Diameter	42cm.

Wall Angle	5°
Wall Profile	A
Lip Treatment	C
Rim Modification	A
Neck Thickness	1.1cm.

The neck of this jar was over 6 cm. tall.

CLOSED FORMS   1.2

Closed vessels are infrequent throughout the sequence at Jargampata. In Late Patibamba II, three specimens account for 1.8% of the vessel sample, and all are from incurving bowls. However, there are also five decorated body sherds which probably represent such closed forms as bottles or flasks. It may be that if these small-mouthed pots were properly represented in the vessel sample they would be somewhat more common and might show a slow gain in frequency from Middle Patibamba through Late Patibamba II and into the final Illaura Phase.

Incurving Vessels   1.2.3

Three rim sherds from incurving vessels represent 1.8% of the ceramic sample for the phase and account for all identifiable closed vessels (fig. 18A, D, N). Two rims from sample IIA represent 3.6%, and one from sample IIC accounts for 1.1% of the subphase sample. These incurving pots may be described as follows:

	Sample IIA	Sample IIC	Entire Phase
Mouth Diameter			
range	9-12cm.	13cm.	9-13cm.
mode	–	13cm.	–
mean	10.5cm.	13cm.	11.3cm.
Wall Angle			
range	(-10)-(-30)°	(-25°)	(-10)-(-30)°
mode	–	(-25°)	–
mean	(-20°)	(-25°)	(-21.7°)
Wall Profile Mode			
primary	D	D	D
secondary	–	–	–
Lip Treatment Mode			
primary	A,D	A	A
secondary	–	–	D
Rim Modification Mode			
primary	A,E1	C	A,C,E1
secondary	–	–	–
Wall Thickness			
range	.5-.7cm.	.6cm.	.5-.7cm.
mode	–	.6cm.	–
mean	.6cm.	.6cm.	.6cm.

The features which tend to differentiate these incurving bowls from earlier examples include a decrease in mouth diameter and a reduction in wall angle. None of the vessels could be reconstructed to provide more information on shape.

Only one vessel was decorated, but it carries a theme typical of Late Patibamba I and II. This piece, from sample IIA (fig. 18N), has a single broad black band on the exterior just below the rim.

OPEN BOWL FORMS   1.3

This general category, which includes both bowls and cups, is the most common group of vessels in Late Patibamba II. There are 102 examples, which account for 61.1% of the sample. This demonstrates a continuation of the trend of increasing popularity of open bowl forms seen throughout the first four phases. There are thirty-eight of these vessels from sample IIA, representing 69.1%; sample IIB includes nine, or 90%; sample IIC has forty-eight, or 53.9%; while sample IID includes seven, or 53.8%, open bowl forms.

Plain Bowls   1.3.1

There are nineteen plain bowls, 11.4% of the vessels, from Late Patibamba II (fig. 19M, Q, AC, AF, AH, AL, AM, AS, AY, BB, BC, BM-BO). In spite of the increasing popularity of open bowl forms, plain bowls decrease in frequency, showing that the increment in the general class is due to the rise in popularity of decorated rather than plain bowls. Six plain bowls represent 10.9% of sample IIA; one from sample IIB represents 10%; eleven plain bowls account for 12.4% of sample IIC; while one from sample IID represents 7.7% of that subphase sample. This collection may be described as follows:

	Sample IIA	Sample IIB
Mouth Diameter		
range	16-24cm.	20cm.
mode	16cm.,24cm.	20cm.
mean	19.7cm.	20cm.
Wall Angle		
range	15-35°	35°
mode	–	35°
mean	28.3°	35°
Wall Profile Mode		
primary	D	A
secondafy	A	–
Lip Treatment Mode		
primary	A	A
secondary	B	–
Rim Modification Mode		
primary	A	D
secondary	C,D,H	–
Wall Thickness		
range	.5-.6cm.	.5cm.
mode	.5cm.	.5cm.
mean	.53cm.	.5cm.

	Sample IIC	Sample IID	Entire Phase
Mouth Diameter			
range	12-24cm.	30cm.	12-30cm.
mode	18cm.	30cm.	18cm.
mean	17.5cm.	30cm.	19cm.
Wall Angle			
range	(-10)-35°	30°	(-10)-35°
mode	25°,25°	30°	25°
mean	24.5°	30°	26.6°
Wall Profile Mode			
primary	A	A	A
secondary	D	–	D
Lip Treatment Mode			
primary	B,D	A	A,B
secondary	A	–	D
Rim Modification Mode			
primary	A	D	A
secondary	–	–	D
Neck Thickness			
range	.4-.7cm.	.7cm.	.4-.7cm.
mode	.6cm.	.7cm.	.5cm.
mean	.55cm.	.7cm.	.55cm.

The mean diameter of plain bowls increases slightly in this phase, but more significant is the decrease in wall angle. Outcurving wall profiles are absent in this phase as well as in the following Illaura Phase. The bases of the plain bowls are usually slightly curved or almost flat, with a continuous curve joining the bottom to the wall.

Regular-Size Plain Bowls   1.3.1.1

Fifteen regular-size plain bowls represent 9% of the vessels for the phase (fig. 19M, Q, AC, AF, AH, AL, AM, AS, AY, BB, BC). The frequency of regular-size bowls relative to oversize examples has not changed significantly. Four regular-size bowl fragments from sample IIA account for 7.3%; one from sample IIB represents 10%; and ten from sample IIC total 11.2% of the sample. These bowls may be described as follows:

	Sample IIA	Sample IIB	Sample IIC	Entire Phase
Mouth Diameter				
range	16-20cm.	20cm.	12-20cm.	12-20cm.
mode	16cm.	20cm.	18cm.	18cm.
mean	17.5cm.	20cm.	16.9cm.	17.3cm.
Wall Angle				
range	15-35°	35°	(-10)-35°	(-10)-35°
mode	–	35°	25°,35°	25°
mean	26.3°	35°	25°	26°
Wall Profile Mode				
primary	A,D	A	A	A
secondary	–	–	D	D
Lip Treatment Mc				
primary	A	A	B	A,B
secondary	B,C	–	D	D
Rim Modification Mode				
primary	A	D	A	A
secondary	C,H	–	B,D,E2,H	D
Wall Thickness				
range	.5-.6cm.	.5cm.	.4-.7cm.	.4-.7cm.
mode	.5cm.	.5cm.	.5cm.,.6cm.	.5cm.
mean	.53cm.	.5cm.	.55cm.	.55cm.

These bowls demonstrate the long-range trend of reduction in wall angles from Middle Patibamba to the final Illaura Phase. The heights of the vessels generally range between 5 cm. and 7 cm., although there may be a few which are shorter. The tall bowls 8 cm. or 9 cm. high which were common in Late Patibamba I are absent in this phase. This seems to reverse the trend running from Early Patibamba to Late Patibamba I of bowls becoming slightly deeper. However, decorated bowls are more conservative, with some examples still as deep as 8 cm. All of the bases are very slightly curved with continuous curves joining the walls and bottoms. However, as in Late Patibamba I, the

bowls with more nearly vertical walls have more open curves, while those with highly flared walls have tighter curves uniting the walls to the bases. This bimodality is probably produced by a carryover of the progressive differentiation in shape between interior-decorated and exterior-decorated bowls.

Oversize Plain Bowls 1.3.1.2

There are four oversize plain bowls which account for 2.4% of the Late Patibamba II pottery (fig. 16BM-BO). Two vessel fragments from sample IIA represent 3.6%; one from IIB totals 1.1%; and one from IIC is 7.7% of the sample. These vessels may be described as follows:

	Sample IIA	Sample IIB	Sample IIC	Entire Phase
Mouth Diameter				
range	24cm.	32cm.	24cm.	24-32cm.
mode	24cm.	32cm.	24cm.	24cm.
mean	24cm.	32cm.	24cm.	26cm.
Wall Angle				
range	30-35°	20°	30°	20-35°
mode	–	20°	30°	30°
mean	32.5°	20°	30°	28.8°
Wall Profile Mode				
primary	D	A	A	A,D
secondary	–	–	–	–
Lip Treatment Mode				
primary	A,B	B	D	B
secondary	–	–	–	A,D
Rim Modification Mode				
primary	A,D	D	A	A,D
secondary	–	–	–	–
Wall Thickness				
range	.5-.6cm.	.7cm.	.6cm.	.5-.7cm.
mode	–	.7cm.	.6cm.	.6cm.
mean	.55cm.	.7cm.	.6cm.	.6cm.

The height and base form are not indicated on any fragments from these oversize bowls, although at least one was taller than 7 cm. One specimen not described here has a thick horizontal handle just below the rim (fig. 31B). Its diameter of 32 cm. qualifies it as an oversize plain bowl, but this distinctive handle form, which makes its first appearance in this phase, leaves little doubt that the sherd is from a large, solid-tripod-support vessel. However, it is not clear how many oversize plain bowls may have had tripod supports.

Decorated Bowls 1.3.2

The Late Patibamba II vessel sample includes sixty-seven decorated bowls which account for 40.1% of the sample. This represents a peak popularity for decorated bowls at Jargampata. There are twenty-eight bowls, or 50.9%; eight bowls, or 80%; twenty-six bowls, or 29.2%; and five bowls, or 38.5%, of samples IIA, IIB, IIC, and IID respectively. Forty-three rim sherds provide the following description:

	Sample IIA	Sample IIB
Mouth Diameter		
range	10-24cm.	10-21cm.
mode	14cm.	–
mean	16.8cm.	15.8cm.

Wall Angle		
range	10-40°	5-40°
mode	15°	–
mean	23.7°	22°
Wall Profile Mode		
primary	A	D
secondary	D	A
Lip Treatment Mode		
primary	A	A,B
secondary	B,D	D
Rim Modification Mode		
primary	A	A
secondary	C,D	C
Wall Thickness		
range	.5-.7cm.	.4-.6cm.
mode	.5cm.	.5cm.
mean	.58cm.	.52cm.

	Sample IIC	Sample IID	Entire Phase
Mouth Diameter			
range	12-26cm.	16-21cm.	10-26cm.
mode	17cm.	–	14cm.
mean	16.9cm.	18.3cm.	16.8cm.
Wall Angle			
range	5-35°	15-30°	5-40°
mode	25°,30°	–	30°
mean	22.8°	25°	23.1°
Wall Profile Mode			
primary	A	D	A
secondary	D	A	D
Lip Treatment Mode			
primary	A	A	A
secondary	B,C	C	B
Rim Modification Mode			
primary	A	A	A
secondary	C	D	C,D
Wall Thickness			
range	.4-.7cm.	.4-.5cm.	.4-.7cm.
mode	.4cm.,.5cm.	.5cm.	.5cm.
mean	.51cm.	.47cm.	.52cm.

The trend toward less flaring wall angles which is evident in plain bowls is equally obvious among decorated bowls—primarily among exterior-decorated bowls.

Painted decoration may be placed on either the exterior surface or the interior surface on a thin red slip or the natural light clay. The most frequently used color continues to be white, but as in Late Patibamba I it never occurs alone. White is most frequently used for outlines around colored design areas and for decorative elements or space fillers such as wavy lines, dots, and circles. White is also the most common color for the Saint Andrew's cross, which was placed upon a colored disk, and also occurs occasionally in the lines of a design theme. It is used only very rarely for large zones such as bands or fields, which may be elaborated by adding space-filler elements.

Dark red is the second most frequent color on bowls. It is very rarely used as a monochrome. Generally, dark red is used for large zones of color which are further elaborated with small space-filler elements. These include horizontal bands, disks of color, vertical bands, and large fields. However, dark red also occurs occasionally as dots and wavy lines, but never as an outline color.

Black continues to be the third most frequently used

color, as it has been from Middle Patibamba on. However, in Late Patibamba II it regains some popularity and it is only slightly less common than dark red. Black is the only color which appears frequently as a monochrome. Its most common uses are as a horizontal band, for wavy lines, and for dots. Black outlines are becoming popular once more and, very importantly, black is often used for the colored disk associated with the Saint Andrew's cross.

Other colors used, in order of their popularity, are gray, orange, light red, yellow, and brown. A new color which makes a low-frequency appearance in Late Patibamba II is a distinct black which differs from the black pigment generally used because it is very thick and has a matte, crusty appearance.

Gray is generally used for vertical bands; it is also used for horizontal bands and design fields. This is the old structural position of white, now partially taken over by black. However, white appears to be influencing the use of gray since in this phase gray design elements like dots and the Saint Andrew's cross make their debut.

Orange is more common than in Late Patibamba I, but rather than being used as a space filler, which was typical of earlier phases, it assumes a role like that of dark red. Its most common use is for vertical bands; it is also used for horizontal bands and design fields.

Light red occupies a structural position comparable to that of dark red but complementary to that of orange. It appears only occasionally as bands forming rectangles, dots, wavy lines, and design lines. Yellow has a similar function and appears as horizontal bands and as space-filler dots. Brown does not seem to follow a clear pattern. It appears once as an outline, once as dots, and once for a design field. The infrequent crusty black is used like the regular black—for horizontal bands.

Color combinations have undergone some shifts between Late Patibamba I and Late Patibamba II. Monochrome black designs are more frequent, while dark red monochromes are less popular. Brown or white monochrome designs do not occur. Bichromes increase slightly in frequency with the most popular combinations being dark red and white, dark red and gray, and black and white. Trichromes also gain somewhat in popularity, with the dominant combinations being dark red, black, and white, and dark red, gray, and white. Four-color schemes continue to appear about as frequently as in Late Patibamba I. The most popular combinations are dark red, black, white, and yellow and dark red, black, white, and orange. If we count the crusty black as distinct from the regular black, an example of the use of five colors occurs on a single bowl.

Perhaps the most interesting trend in Late Patibamba II color use is the tendency for minor colors—orange, yellow, light red, and to some degree gray—to take on the structural position and perhaps the identity of the more important dark red, black and white. This reorganization of color combinations may foreshadow the simplification of color schemes in the following Illaura Phase.

Interior-Decorated Bowls   1.3.2.1

Following the relatively low point in popularity reached in Late Patibamba I, interior-decorated bowls more or less stabilize in frequency through Late Patibamba II and the Illaura Phase. There are forty-four examples of interior-decorated bowls which account for 26.3% of the Late Patibamba II vessel sample. Seventeen specimens represent

30.9% of sample IIA; five bowls are 50% of sample IIB; eighteen pieces account for 20.2% of sample IIC; and four interior-decorated bowls from sample IID total 30.8% of that sample. There are twenty-five fragmentary vessels complete enough to provide essential measurements.

Regular-Size Interior-Decorated Bowls   1.3.2.1.1

There are twenty-three interior-decorated bowls with mouth diameters of regular size. This represents only 13.8% of the vessel sample for the phase, although the regular-size bowls account for 92% of those which could be measured, suggesting that the actual frequency of this group should be closer to 25% of the total. Eight of these bowls from sample IIA represent 14.5%; three from sample IIB account for 30%; ten from sample IIC represent 11.2%; and two from sample IID are 15.4%. They may be described as follows:

	Sample IIA	Sample IIB
Mouth Diameter		
range	13-22cm.	14-21cm.
mode	16cm.,19cm.	–
mean	17.9cm.	17cm.
Wall Angle		
range	20-40°	5-40°
mode	30°	–
mean	30.6°	23.3°
Wall Profile Mode		
primary	A,D	D
secondary	–	A
Lip Treatment Mode		
primary	B	A
secondary	A	B
Rim Modification Mode		
primary	A	A
secondary	B	C
Wall Thickness		
range	.5-.7cm.	.5-.6cm.
mode	.6cm.	.5cm.
mean	.58cm.	.53cm.

	Sample IIC	Sample IID	Entire Phase
Mouth Diameter			
range	13-20cm.	16-21cm.	13-22cm.
mode	17cm.	–	16cm.
mean	16.3cm.	18.5cm.	17.1cm.
Wall Angle			
range	15-35°	30°	5-40°
mode	25°,30°	30°	30°
mean	27°	30°	28°
Wall Profile Mode			
primary	A	D	A
secondary	D	–	D
Lip Treatment Mode			
primary	A,B	A	A
secondary	C,D	–	B
Rim Modification Mode			
primary	A	A	A
secondary	C	–	C
Wall Thickness			
range	.4-.6cm.	.4-.5cm.	.4-.7cm.
mode	.5cm.	–	.5cm.
mean	.5cm.	.45cm.	.53cm.

The statistics show that these bowls are very slightly smaller in mouth diameter than those of previous phases. Wall angle, however, remains relatively constant. The height of regular-size interior-decorated bowls ranges between 5.5 cm. and 8.5 cm. This demonstrates that these bowls are the most conservative in their resistance to the reversal of the trend toward deeper bowls. In this phase, regular-size bowls more than 7 cm. tall are rare, and even the conservative interior-decorated specimens are never more than 8.5 cm. deep.

Bases of bowls are slightly curved or almost flat with a continuous, tight curve uniting the bottom to the vessel wall.

Decoration is limited to painting on the vessel interior and, rarely, on the rim as well. As in earlier phases, the paint is applied on a thin red slip or a natural light surface.

A common design theme which links Late Patibamba II to Middle Patibamba and Late Patibamba I is the colored disk and Saint Andrew's cross (fig. 21F-H, J). This theme is still limited exclusively to interior-decorated bowls, but occurs in a number of variants. Most of the colored disks from Late Patibamba I were dark red, while those from Late Patibamba II are nearly as often black as dark red. The black disk which first appears in the Late Patibamba I sample becomes quite popular in Late Patibamba II, and by the final Illaura Phase it virtually replaces the dark red disk.

Crosses placed on the disk are oriented diagonally and are generally white. One Saint Andrew's cross is exceptional because it is gray (fig. 21G). Further decoration of the disk is accomplished by adding circles to the quadrants formed by the cross. Another decorative feature is the addition of dots in contrastive colors on the Saint Andrew's cross (fig. 21G, H, J). This is a Late Patibamba I innovation (fig. 21E) which appears to gain popularity in Late Patibamba II. One fragment of this design theme from the surface of the floor of the South Gallery of the North Unit (fig. 21H) tends to confirm that the galleries were also abandoned in Late Patibamba II.

Another Late Patibamba I innovation which gains popularity in this phase is a broad line which connects colored disks on opposite sides of the bowl. One Late Patibamba II example has contrastive dots on the line.

Decoration composed of a single broad horizontal band placed below the rim continues from earlier phases into Late Patibamba II (fig. 23M, N). Both dark red and brown bands continue from Late Patibamba I, but black bands which are also found are innovations. The single black band is more common on exterior-decorated bowls, but it is diagnostic of Late Patibamba II and the following Illaura Phase. It also shows that black was becoming a more important color, replacing dark red in both the colored-disk and single-band themes.

Single bands are often decorated with wavy lines and may have dots in the same or contrasting colors (fig. 23M, O). However, some bands are plain.

The two-horizontal-band theme continues from Middle Patibamba (fig. 24E, F). As in earlier phases, the only color combination appropriate for interior-decorated bowls is a black band over a dark red band. These may be separated by a white line or may have a white line below them. Generally the bands are decorated with wavy lines or a wavy-line—and—dot motif in white.

Vertical band decoration, which runs through the entire Jargampata sequence, continues to be common (fig. 22H, I)

and typically consists of a group of parallel bands running from the rim to the bottom of the bowl. The bands alternate in color and may be outlined in white and decorated with design fillers like wavy lines and dots. However, unoutlined bands generally lack further decorative elaboration.

The theme of a broad band forming a rectangle does not appear on interior-decorated bowls of this phase, although a possible variant looks like nested rectangles.

A design theme which achieves considerable popularity on interior-decorated bowls in Late Patibamba II is a panel divided into horizontal sections, each of which is decorated with elements such as wavy lines and dots (fig. 26F-I; plate 13D). One example of a panel lacking horizontal divisions is a conservative variant (fig. 26J) which appears as early as Early Patibamba, but the horizontally divided panel seems to be limited to Late Patibamba I and II. Generally the panel design was combined with vertical bands of alternating colors. Closely related and possibly derived from this theme is a panel divided into two small horizontal rectangular zones which were decorated with space-filler elements such as wavy lines and dots (fig. 26K).

Oversize Interior-Decorated Bowls 1.3.2.1.2

Oversize interior-decorated bowls number only two, or 1.2% of the total vessel sample. They account for only 8% of the interior-decorated bowls which could be measured. A single example from sample IIA represents 1.8% of the vessels, while one piece from sample IIC accounts for 1.1% of that sample. These bowls may be described as follows:

	Sample IIA	Sample IIC	Entire Phase
Mouth Diameter			
range	24cm.	26cm.	24-26cm.
mode	24cm.	26cm.	—
mean	24cm.	26cm.	25cm.
Wall Angle			
range	35°	35°	35°
mode	35°	35°	35°
mean	35°	35°	35°
Wall Profile Mode			
primary	A	A	A
secondary	—	—	—
Lip Treatment Mode			
primary	B	A	A,B
secondary	—	—	—
Rim Modification Mode			
primary	D	A	A,D
secondary	—	—	—
Wall Thickness			
range	.5cm.	.7cm.	.5-.7cm.
mode	.5cm.	.7cm.	—
mean	.5cm.	.7cm.	.6cm.

These oversize bowls range only between 5 cm. and 6 cm. in height and have gently curving to nearly flat bases joined to the walls by a tight curve. Decoration is like that for regular-size interior-decorated bowls. The small height and identical handling of decoration suggest that the oversize bowls may have begun to merge with the regular-size category. In this respect, it is significant that the final Illaura Phase lacks oversize bowls all together.

One of the oversize vessels has a design which is a variant

of the colored disk with Saint Andrew's cross theme, while the second has a single-band theme with wavy line and dots (fig. 23M).

Exterior-Decorated Bowls   1.3.2.2

There are twenty-two exterior-decorated bowls accounting for 13.2% of the Late Patibamba II vessel sample, or 32.8% of the decorated bowls. This shows that exterior-decorated bowls continue to increase in absolute frequency as in all previous phases, but for the first time they show a slight decrease in popularity relative to interior-decorated bowls. However, the meaning of this is unclear since the relative proportion between interior-decorated and exterior-decorated bowls in the Illaura Phase is similar to that of Late Patibamba I.

Ten of these bowls from sample IIA represent 18.2%; three from sample IIB represent 30%; eight from sample IIC account for 9%; and one from sample IID represents 7.7% of the vessel sample.

Regular-Size Exterior-Decorated Bowls   1.3.2.2.1

Seventeen of the twenty-two exterior-decorated bowls from Late Patibamba II could be measured, and all are of regular size. Nine, or 16.3%; two, or 20%; five, or 5.6%; and one, or 7.7%, come from samples IIA, IIB, IIC, and IID respectively. They may be described as follows:

	Sample IIA	Sample IIB
Mouth Diameter		
range	10-20cm.	10-18cm.
mode	14cm.	−
mean	14.7cm.	14cm.
Wall Angle		
range	10-30°	15-25°
mode	15°	−
mean	16.7°	20°
Wall Profile Mode		
primary	A	A,D
secondary	D	−
Lip Treatment Mode		
primary	A	B,D
secondary	B,C,D	−
Rim Modification Mode		
primary	A	A
secondary	B,E2	−
Wall Thickness		
range	.5-.6cm.	.4-.6cm.
mode	.5cm.	.4cm.,.6cm.
mean	.51cm.	.5cm.

	Sample IIC	Sample IID	Entire Phase
Mouth Diameter			
range	12-22cm.	18cm.	0-22cm.
mode	17cm.	18cm.	14cm.
mean	16.4cm.	18cm.	15.3cm.
Wall Angle			
range	5-20°	15°	10-35°
mode	10°	15°	15°
mean	12°	15°	15.6°
Wall Profile Mode			
primary	A	A	A
secondary	D	−	D
Lip Treatment Mode			
primary	A,C	C	A
secondary	B	−	C,D
Rim Modification Mode			
primary	A	D	A
secondary	−	−	D
Wall Thickness			
range	.4-.6cm.	.5cm.	.4-.6cm.
mode	.4cm.,.5cm.	.5cm.	.5cm.
mean	.48cm.	.5cm.	.5cm.

The progressive differentiation in form between interior- and exterior-decorated bowls continues in Late Patibamba II. The exterior-decorated bowls are now obviously smaller in mouth diameter and have lower wall angles than the interior-decorated examples. The height of the bowls ranges between 5.5 cm. and 7 cm.—unchanged from the previous phase. Bases are gently curved with a continuous curving union between the vessel bottom and walls. One bowl has small tripod tab supports (fig. 29G; plate 14F).

Decoration is limited to painting on the vessel exterior and, occasionally, on the rim. The design themes are those of Late Patibamba I. The most popular themes are horizontal-band designs and rectangles formed by bands. However, vertical-band themes are also frequent and distinctive.

Double-horizontal-band combinations occur in dark red over black, black over yellow, and gray over dark red. As in previous phases, the colored bands are usually decorated with space-filler elements, most commonly a wavy line or a wavy line with dots painted in white. Occasionally, a white line was painted below the lower band (fig. 30L, M).

The three-parallel-horizontal-band theme is by far the most popular mode of decoration for exterior-decorated bowls. Almost all examples have a black band over a red band over another black band. A white line is sometimes painted below the lowest band, and white design elements such as wavy lines, a wavy line with dots, or a row of circles are added on the bands. It is common in this and the previous phase for the upper and lower black bands to receive circular elements, while the central band is decorated with a wavy line with dots (fig. 29G, H; plate 14F). One infrequent variant is a gray band above two dark red bands, and there is a unique piece with a dark red band over a black band over a dark red band.

One bowl has a light red rectangle formed by a broad band outlined by a white line. Circular space-filler elements are painted on the band (fig. 28K; plate 14E). Another bowl has a similar band theme forming a diamond (fig. 28M), while a second has a zigzag band which may be decorated with space-filler elements (fig. 28L).

An interesting theme which may be diagnostic of Late Patibamba II is the decoration of a horizontal band area with a row of X's. Only one example of this arrangement of space fillers is found on an exterior-decorated bowl (fig. 28E), but it is also found on a Late Patibamba lyre-shaped cup (fig. 35F; plate 12E). Although there are possible antecedents for this arrangement in Middle Patibamba (fig. 25C), it could be that it can be considered a theme diagnostic of Late Patibamba II.

Vertical-band design themes are found on a number of exterior-decorated bowls. Groups of bands alternate color and are decorated with circular elements or wavy-line—and—dot fillers (fig. 30E). However, there is a progressive variant of the vertical-band pattern consisting of an isolated band

decorated with space fillers (fig. 30F). It is likely that these single vertical bands were arranged symmetrically around the exterior of a bowl.

Interior- and Exterior-Decorated Bowls   1.3.2.3

One example of a bowl with both interior and exterior painted decoration is unique in the Late Patibamba II sample and accounts for only .6% of the vessels (fig. 30A). The piece comes from sample IIA, where it represents 1.8% of the vessels. There is only one other pottery vessel of local paste from the Jargampata site which also has interior and exterior decoration. This piece is from the Middle Patibamba Phase and, although it is only a small fragment, it may have had some aspects of design similar to the single piece from Late Patibamba II. Together, these two vessels constitute .17% of the 1,195 fragmentary vessels from the Jargampata excavations which were studied. This low frequency might suggest that these bowls violated local rules of decoration and were produced by either an eccentric local potter or an outsider not familiar with the local tradition. However, it should not be assumed that rules apply only to common products and that infrequent objects are outside the rule system.

This atypical bowl may be described as follows:

Mouth Diameter	20cm.
Wall Angle	15°
Wall Profile	A
Lip Treatment	A
Rim Modification	E2
Wall Thickness	.6cm.

As a hypothesis, I suggest that this bowl with both interior and exterior decoration was produced locally by a person not conversant with the rules for producing Patibamba-style pottery. It is unlikely that the piece is imported, since its paste is not distinguishable from that of other pots on the site. If the bowl were a low-frequency, special product or the output of an eccentric potter, many of the standard attributes of Jargampata pottery should be evident. The bowl, however, has an atypical rim profile which does occur on one other bowl from the same sample (fig. 30L) but seems to be associated with Cajamarca styles (fig. 38A, B). Furthermore, there is a suggestion of a basal angle which is rare in Jargampata pottery, and the bowl's height of 9.5 cm. is outside the range of variation found among other bowls of this phase. Finally, the exterior design of three horizontal bands is interesting. Almost all Jargampata bowls with this design theme have a black band over a dark red band over another black band. This bowl has the reverse combination of a dark red band over a black band over another dark red band, which is known on only one other piece, also from the Late Patibamba II Phase. These various deviations from the local pottery style tend to support the notion that this bowl was produced at Jargampata by a potter trained in the skills of the craft in another community with different rules.

Tripod Bowls   1.3.3

The ceramic sample for Late Patibamba II includes only five vessel fragments from bowls which probably had tripod supports (figs. 29G, 31B, C; plate 14F). This represents 3% of the total sample and is a decline from the frequency in Late Patibamba I. However, it is likely that other sherds from tripod vessels may not have been identifiable, so the frequency may have been higher. Two fragments from sample IIA represent 3.6%, one from sample IIC accounts for 1.1%, and two fragments from sample IID represent 15.4% of the samples.

One nearly complete tripod-tab-foot bowl from sample IIA (fig. 29G; plate 14F) provides evidence for the continuity of this form through Late Patibamba I and II and on into the Illaura Phase. The decoration of this bowl is like that found in Late Patibamba I.

A new form of tripod support makes its appearance in this phase. It is a solid support with nearly rectangular cross section rather like the little tab foot but much larger (fig. 31C). The vessel body to which such supports were added can be reconstructed on the basis of a nearly complete bowl from the floor of the North Gallery of the North Unit (fig. 31A). Stratigraphically, this piece should also belong to Late Patibamba II.

These bowls were large tripod vessels with mouth diameters in the oversize range. Bottoms were flat or nearly flat but were joined to the vessel walls by a tight curve. Wall profile form was slightly outcurving, although this form had disappeared from other bowls by Late Patibamba II. The rims were probably slightly thickened, but the most important diagnostic feature is the pair of thick, horizontal handles placed a couple of centimeters below the rim. These are virtually the only handles from Jargampata which are not formed from clay straps. The bowls were about 10 cm. deep, and the supports added as much as 4 cm. more to their total height. The rim sherd with horizontal handle from IID (fig. 31B) must have belonged to a larger vessel of this shape.

Hollow tripods do not appear in the ceramic sample selected for study until Late Patibamba I. Sample IIC includes a fragment of what appears to be a hollow tripod support. The sherd is small, but was probably like large hollow supports from the House Group (fig. 32A, B). This more nearly complete material from the House Group indicates that the hollow supports were placed on oversize bowls very much like those which had the rectangular solid supports. The bottoms were flat, but united to the walls by a continuous curve, and the wall profiles curved outward slightly. The reconstructed bowl had a depth of about 12 cm., with the supports adding another 6 cm. to the overall height.

A regular-size exterior-decorated bowl with hollow tripod supports from the House Group (fig. 32C; plate 14B) is also very reminiscent of the regular-size exterior-decorated tripod bowls with solid tab-foot supports. This suggests that both regular-size and oversize tripod bowls had hollow and solid support alternatives by Late Patibamba II.

Pedestal Bowls   1.3.5

Three fragments of pedestal bowls represent 1.8% of the Late Patibamba II ceramic sample (fig. 34F, G). This frequency is greater than that of Late Patibamba I but less than that of either Early Patibamba or Middle Patibamba. One vessel from sample IIA represents 1.8% and two pieces from sample IIC represent 2.2% of their respective samples. Two of the vessels with rims provide the following description:

	Sample IIA	Sample IID	Entire Phase
Mouth Diameter			
range	24cm.	20cm.	20-24cm.
mode	24cm.	20cm.	—
mean	24cm.	20cm.	22cm.
Wall Angle			
range	35°	40°	35-40°
mode	35°	40°	—
mean	35°	40°	37.5°
Wall Profile Mode			
primary	B	D	B,D
Secondary	—	—	—
Lip Treatment Mode			
primary	A	A	A
secondary	—	—	—
Rim Modification Mode			
primary	E	E	E
secondary	—	—	—
Wall Thickness			
range	.5cm.	.7cm.	.5-.7cm.
mode	.5cm.	.7cm.	—
mean	.5cm.	.7cm.	.6cm.

From sample IIA, there are a base and a rim sherd which are probably from the same bowl (fig. 34G). The base and vessel walls were modeled together in a single piece. A fragment of a base from sample IIC shows that an alternative mode of manufacture was the welding of the bottom and sides of the bowl to the solid base. The diameter of the solid bases was probably about 12 cm., while the bowl depth was about 12 cm. and the overall height of the vessel about 14 cm.

Lyre-Shaped Cups   1.3.6

The lyre-shaped cup may have made its appearance in Late Patibamba I or perhaps (very infrequently) at an earlier date. In Late Patibamba II, the popularity of these vessels has increased, and three specimens represent 1.8% of the ceramic sample (fig. 35F, I, M). Two vessels come from sample IIA where they represent 3.6% of the pots, and one example is from sample IIC where it accounts for only 1.1% of the pottery. The cup from sample IIC is interesting because it had a handle and is considerably smaller than the other examples. Consequently, it will be treated separately.

Two lyre-shaped cups from sample IIA (fig. 35F, I) may be described as follows:

Mouth Diameter	
range	11-12cm.
mode	—
mean	11.5cm.
Wall Angle	
range	0°
mode	0°
mean	0°
Wall Profile Mode	
primary	A,E
secondary	—
Lip Treatment Mode	
primary	A,E
secondary	—
Rim Modification Mode	
primary	B1,E
secondary	—

Wall Thickness	
range	.5cm.
mode	.5cm.
mean	.5cm.

One of these cups is complete enough to estimate its height at about 11 cm. On the exterior immediately below the rim is a single dark red band with a row of white *X*'s and dots.

The single lyre-shaped cup with handle from sample IIC (fig. 35M) may be described as follows:

Mouth Diameter	4.5cm.
Wall Angle	0°
Wall Profile	E
Lip Treatment	C
Rim Modification	A
Wall Thickness	.5cm.

The small, handled lyre-shaped cup may be diagnostic of Late Patibamba I and II, and it seems reasonable to place a specimen from the House Group (fig. 35N) in that time period.

MINIATURE VESSELS   1.4

Miniature vessels, which appeared first in Late Patibamba I, continue into Late Patibamba II. Three miniature bowls represent 1.8% of the total collection, but all come from sample IIC, where they account for 3.4% of the subphase sample (fig. 36P-R). These specimens may be described as follows:

Mouth Diameter	
range	8-9cm.
mode	8cm.
mean	8.3cm.
Wall Angle	
range	10-20°
mode	—
mean	15°
Wall Profile Mode	
primary	A
secondary	D
Lip Treatment Mode	
primary	A
secondary	B
Rim Modification Mode	
primary	A,C,E2
secondary	—
Wall Thickness	
range	.3-.5cm.
mode	—
mean	.4cm.

These vessels are not preserved to their bottoms, but it appears that at least one bowl was about 2.5 cm. high while one other was probably slightly deeper. None of these miniatures were decorated.

PRESS MOLDS   1.7

Two press molds represent 1.2% of the Late Patibamba II ceramics. One from sample IIA represents 1.8%, and one

from sample IIC accounts for 1.1% of the subphase sample (plate 15C, B). Both are very shallow molds for human faces in very low relief. One mold is about 6 cm., and the other about 8 cm., across and it seems most likely that they were used in the production of rather sizeable face-neck jars. It is significant, however, that face-neck jars are not found in any of the ceramic samples analyzed for either Late Patibamba I or II. However, there are examples from the House Group which must date at least to Late Patibamba I.

CERAMIC DISKS 1.8

Two sherds from flat ceramic disks or plates account for 1.2% of the ceramic sample. One specimen from sample IIA represents 1.8% of the sample. It is coarsely finished and has a diameter of 16 cm. and a thickness of 1.1 cm. (fig. 12L). The second piece, from sample IIC, represents 1.1% of that sample, is 12 cm. across and about 1.2 cm. thick, and has a rough surface finish (fig. 12H).

SCRAPER-POLISHERS 1.9

A single object which may be a scraper-polisher comes from sample IIC (fig. 36E). This elliptical plaque is 10 cm. long, 5.5 cm. wide, and .5 cm. thick. It represents .6% of the total vessel sample, or 1.1% of its subphase sample. Unlike many other scraper-polishers recovered at Jargampata which were manufactured—probably through use—from available sherds, this specimen was obviously manufactured and fired in its present form. Furthermore, the edges do not show the heavy abrasion which should be found on a scraping tool. It seems likely that this piece belongs to an unrecognized class of ceramic objects. Rogger Ravines (personal communication) found a more rectangular ceramic plaque (6.7 cm. long, 3.1 cm. wide, and .7 cm. thick) which had been deliberately manufactured, polished, and fired before being placed with the Middle Horizon 2A ceramic offerings found at Ayapata (Ravines 1968: 19-46).

The form of the sample IIC elliptical disk is distinct from other scraper-polishers which have some concave sides and points at the intersection of the sides. A very similarly shaped stone scraper-polisher from the Illaura Phase (fig. 27H) supports the identification of this shape as a scraper-polisher. However, two rectangular stone plaques from the House Group show neither the abraded edges nor the concave sides which characterize the scraper-polishers (fig. 27F, G). These stone plaques may belong to a category of objects which also includes the elliptical ceramic plaque from Late Patibamba II.

EXOTIC VESSELS 1.10

Only a small number of ceramic features, themes, and vessel shapes differentiate Late Patibamba II from Late Patibamba I. These phases share many similarities which make it difficult to distinguish between them. However, a very significant difference does exist between Late Patibamba I and II. During Late Patibamba I, a substantial quantity of elite pottery was brought into the site. These foreign wares represent 6.4% of the three samples selected for analysis, and it is likely that most of the elite and exotic pottery found scattered through the strata of the House Group belongs to Late Patibamba I as well. In Late Patibamba II, there are only three exotic pieces, which account for 1.8% of the total vessel sample, and this percentage may be inflated. All three pieces come from sample IIC, where they represent 3.4% of the subphase. However, the largest sherd, which probably comes from the partially modeled neck of a polychrome jar (fig. 39B; plate 17C), shows sufficient erosion to suggest that it was redeposited, probably from statum D1 of rooms S10 and S11. The remaining two sherds are undecorated body sherds distinguished on the basis of their distinctive surface finish and paste. These are more likely to represent original inclusions and to belong with Late Patibamba II refuse. However, the remaining samples, which include seventy-eight fragmentary vessels, have no exotic pieces.

This very low frequency of exotic pottery—the lowest since Early Patibamba and the construction of the North Unit—must indicate a disruption of relations with Middle Horizon sites of greater prestige and a reversal of the situations which existed in Late Patibamba I. Goods may have continued to flow from Jargampata to Wari while the reverse flow of elite and high-status items declined. This could imply a new kind of relationship between the two sites or a massive devaluation in the cost of the Jargampata products. On the other hand, the drop in elite pottery could indicate nearly total termination of interaction with the Wari polity. This alternative seems most likely since it is obvious that Late Patibamba II pottery belongs to the late part of Middle Horizon 2B or even to Epoch 3 and represents the final refuse dropped on the floors at Jargampata as the site was abandoned. Menzel (1964: 72) has pointed out that no new stylistic influences from Wari can be detected in its provinces after Middle Horizon 2B and that the scarcity of Epoch 3 pottery at Wari indicates that the site was rapidly abandoned after Epoch 2B and perhaps totally depopulated by the end of Epoch 3.

It is clear that the abandonment of Wari and Jargampata are contemporary. The final ceramic refuse at Jargampata demonstrates a disruption of interaction with Wari as depopulation of both sites began. It is not yet clear whether the depopulation began in the rural sector at sites like Jargampata, at urban centers like Wari, or at both simultaneously. However, one fact is that if Jargampata and other such rural centers supplied essential food commodities to the urban population, their abandonment would soon have starved the cities into abandonment as well. Conversely, the disintegration of the urban or state facilities would not necessarily have required the kind of depopulation of rural sites which is indicated at Jargampata.

13
Ceramics of the Illaura Phase

STRATIGRAPHIC ASSOCIATION

Illaura Phase ceramics were isolated in stratum C and on a living floor labeled stratum C1 in rooms S10 and S11 (fig. 44). The stratigraphy indicates that at the beginning of the Illaura Phase the large room S10 and S11 between the Rectangular Structure and the North Gallery of the North Unit was modified by constructing a partition which divided its area into two connecting rooms (fig. 6). The base of this dividing partition rests at the same level as the stratum C1 living floor, demonstrating the contemporaneity of the features.

No other Illaura materials were found at Jargampata, and the other areas excavated on the site were abandoned in that period. The strata from the North Unit which contain Late Patibamba II pottery show this clearly. Stratum D of rooms S10 and S11 contains a large quantity of rock, probably fallen from the disintegrating walls (fig. 44), while sample IIA was covered by a retaining wall which collapsed into the main plaza of the large enclosure (fig. 47). Sample IIB and D overlie the plaza floor and represent the last materials deposited by human activity in that area. Even sample IID appears to have been redeposited by wash made possible by the collapse of the west wall of the North Unit enclosure (fig. 45).

The South Unit did not produce any Illaura ceramics. The House Group was abandoned and had fallen into decay. However, there are clear signs of later activity. At some time parts of the House Group were excavated and both burials and offerings in room S1 were disturbed (plate 8). An extended burial with deformed skull was placed in the upper strata of corridor CX, and this corridor as well as other parts of the House Group were filled with coarse gravel and potsherds apparently raked together from the surface of the site. Similar activity must be responsible for feature 1 in units E2-3 x S13-15, which is another concentration of gravel and sherds heaped against the exterior of the enclosure wall of the North Unit (fig. 43). Although ceramic associations which would date these features are lacking, all of the activities responsible for them may have been carried out by those who reoccupied Jargampata during the Illaura Phase.

A radiocarbon age determination on small fragments of charcoal collected from stratum C1 of room S10 provided a date of A.D. 1220 ± 120 (GX-1934) for the Illaura Phase. Stratum D lacked sufficient charcoal for dating, but stratum D1 from room 10 provided a date of A.D. 765 ± 90 (GX-1933). It is likely that the fill of stratum D was deposited very slowly as the North Unit deteriorated, but the similarity of Illaura pottery to that of Late Patibamba I and II makes me reluctant to believe that some 450 years separate the two occupations. However, it is obvious that Jargampata was abandoned for some time before the Illaura reoccupation, and the Illaura Phase may tentatively be placed in the Late Intermediate Period. It is equally obvious that the people responsible for the Illaura pottery were little more than campers in the Middle Horizon ruins.

VESSEL SAMPLE

One hundred and seventy-two fragmentary vessels were recovered from strata C and C1 of rooms S10 and S11. Many vessels could be partially reconstructed, and since pieces of the same pots frequently came from each of the subsamples, all of the materials were handled together for the descriptive analysis.

The vessel shape categories established for ceramics of the Patibamba style are equally satisfactory for Illaura pots, and all vessel fragments except four decorated body sherds from unknown closed forms were assigned to shape classes. As in previous phases, necked jars and open bowl forms are the predominant shapes, accounting for 88.4% of the total sample. However, in contrast to the long trend toward a decrease in the frequency of necked jars from a high in Early Patibamba, the Illaura Phase sample has the highest frequency of necked jars and the lowest frequency of open bowl forms of any phase at Jargampata. The Illaura sample includes 49.4% necked jars and 39% open bowl forms. This is not radically different from the 45.8% frequency for each general category in Early Patibamba. It seems likely that these frequencies approximate some standard ratio of vessel shapes produced and broken in generalized activity and that the declining frequency of necked jars and the rise in open bowl forms reflects some specialized activities associated with the North Unit during Middle Patibamba and Late Patibamba I and II.

There can be little doubt that the pottery of the Illaura Phase belongs to the same tradition as that of the four earlier phases at Jargampata. The differences do not warrant its separation from the Patibamba style by use of the name Illaura. However, the name Illaura has been adopted—from the neighboring community from which most of the laborers came—to prevent confusion in the future when ceramic complexes are discovered which fill the temporal hiatus between Late Patibamba II and Illaura.

NECKED JARS   1.1

Illaura Phase jars are nearly identical to those of earlier phases. The horizontal profiles are circular, and handles are apparently unchanged. Small jars frequently have strap handles which link the jar collar to the upper part of the vessel shoulder (fig. 14), while large jars have horizontal or vertical strap handles placed on the vessel shoulders (fig. 15A).

Bases are most frequently very slightly curved with a continuous but tight curve uniting the bottom to the vessel walls. About 75% of the bases recovered are of this nearly flat shape. However, nearly 25% of the bases are still conical, and it seems very likely that most—if not all—of the smaller jars had conical bases.

No Illaura jars were decorated, and forms appropriate for decoration are rare or absent.

Constricted-Neck Jars   1.1.1

This entire category of jars is very infrequent during the Illaura Phase. It appears that the popularity of decorated jars was declining. Two specimens represent only 1.2% of the total sample, and the face-neck jar is absent.

Narrow-Collar Jars   1.1.1.1

Both constricted-neck jars, representing 1.2% of the sample, are narrow-collar jars (fig. 10K, M) lacking decoration. The pair may be described as follows:

Mouth Diameter	
range	11-12cm.
mode	−
mean	11.5cm.
Wall Angle	
range	(-10)-0°
mode	−
mean	(-5°)
Wall Profile Mode	
primary	A,B
secondary	−
Lip Treatment Mode	
primary	A,C
secondary	−
Rim Modification Mode	
primary	C,E
secondary	−
Neck Thickness	
range	.6-.7cm
mode	−
mean	.65cm.

These narrow-collar jars are not particularly distinctive, but they fall on the upper end of the range of variation for earlier specimens in mouth diameter and thickness.

Side-Spout Jars   1.1.2

A single fragment from a side-spout vessel represents .6% of the vessel sample (fig. 13D). This jar could not be completely reconstructed, but the spout is about 9 cm. long and 4.5 cm. in diameter and it seems that the vessel probably had a maximum diameter of about 23 cm.

Flaring-Neck Jars   1.1.3

Flaring-neck jars are the most frequent vessel form in the Illaura Phase ceramic sample. This phase represents their peak of popularity at Jargampata. There are sixty-three fragmentary vessels which represent 36.6% of the total collection. The twenty-three examples which could be measured provide the following description:

Mouth Diameter	
range	9-35cm.
mean	21.39cm.

Wall Angle	
range	0-35°
mode	10°
mean	12.8°
Wall Profile Mode	
primary	A
secondary	B
Lip Treatment Mode	
primary	A,D
secondary	C,C1
Rim Modification Mode	
primary	E
secondary	A,E2,H
Neck Thickness	
range	.4-.9cm.
mode	.6cm.
mean	.58cm.

The reduction in mouth diameter of flaring-neck jar collars which occurred through the first phases of the Jargampata sequence does not continue into the Illaura Phase, but necks do become obviously more vertical and have straighter wall angles. Other significant features of these Illaura jars are the reduction in neck thickness and the rise in popularity of thickened rims—especially the rare form H.

Neck heights range from about 3 cm. on small jars to 10 cm. on the largest specimens.

Flaring-Neck Jars: Size Variant A   1.1.3A

There are ten fragmentary jars with rim diameters or estimated rim diameters within this size group (fig. 14A, B, D, E). They represent 5.8% of the ceramics for the phase and 15.9% of the flaring-neck jars. This demonstrates a substantial increase in their popularity during this final phase, although size variant A has increased in popularity relative to other necked jars throughout the sequence at Jargampata.

Only six rims are complete enough to provide all the measurements for the description which follows:

Mouth Diameter	
range	9-12cm.
mode	9cm.
mean	10cm.
Wall Angle	
range	10-20
mode	−
mean	15°
Wall Profile Mode	
primary	A
secondary	B
Lip Treatment Mode	
primary	C
secondary	B
Rim Modification Mode	
primary	A
secondary	E
Neck Thickness	
range	.4-.6cm.
mode	.6cm.
mean	.53cm.

The height of these jar necks ranges between 2.5 cm. and 4 cm.

Flaring-Neck Jars: Size Variant B 1.1.3B

Eight vessel fragments from this size variant represent 4.7% of the total collection (figs. 14H, 15K). This category accounts for only 12.7% of the necked jars, which is a decrease in relative popularity from the peak in Late Patibamba I and II. It may be that this variant is breaking up to merge with variants A and C. Four rims provide the following description:

Mouth Diameter
range	14-16cm.
mode	15cm.
mean	15cm.

Wall Angle
range	10-35°
mode	—
mean	21.3°

Wall Profile Mode
primary	A,B
secondary	—

Lip Treatment Mode
primary	A,C,C1,D
secondary	—

Rim Modification Mode
primary	A,E2
secondary	—

Neck Thickness
range	.4-.6cm.
mode	.4cm.
mean	.45cm.

The reduction in the thickness of jar neck walls which becomes obvious when examining necked jars is curious because it does not seem to affect the smallest jars but only those of variant B and larger. The fragments of rims of this group provide little information concerning the height of the jar necks, but it appears that they were 3 cm. or slightly taller.

Flaring-Neck Jars: Size Variant C 1.1.3C

As in Late Patibamba II, this size variant is the most popular in the Illaura Phase (fig. 15AE, AP, AQ, AT). Twenty-two fragmentary jars account for 12.8% of the total sample, or 34.9% of the flaring-neck jars. Nine sherds provide the following description:

Mouth Diameter
range	19-23cm.
mode	—
mean	21.2cm.

Wall Angle
range	5-15°
mode	5°
mean	8.9°

Wall Profile Mode
primary	A
secondary	B,C

Lip Treatment Mode
primary	A,D
secondary	C

Rim Modification Mode
primary	E
secondary	E2

Neck Thickness
range	.5-.7cm.
mode	.6cm.
mean	.59cm.

The most complete collars indicate that the height of the vessel necks ranged from 6 cm. to 7.5 cm.

Flaring-Neck Jars: Size Variant D 1.1.3D

Only three sherds represent jars of this size group (fig. 16E). They account for 1.7% of the total sample and 4.8% of the flaring-neck jars. This low frequency continues the decline in popularity which jars of this size experienced following the Middle Patibamba Phase. Two necks with rims provide the following description:

Mouth Diameter
range	25cm.
mode	25cm.
mean	25cm.

Wall Angle
range	20°
mode	20°
mean	20°

Wall Profile Mode
primary	A
secondary	—

Lip Treatment Mode
primary	A,C
secondary	—

Rim Modification Mode
primary	A,E
secondary	—

Neck Thickness
range	.5cm.
mode	.5cm.
mean	.5cm.

Two relatively complete necks were slightly over 5.5 cm. tall.

Flaring-Neck Jars: Size Variant E 1.1.3E

Fourteen jar fragments belong to this size group and represent 8.1% of the sample (fig. 16O, Q, S). The category has recovered from its popularity decline of Late Patibamba I and II, and the frequency of 22.2% of all necked jars is the greatest which the size variant experiences in the entire sequence. However, it seems likely that its popularity increase is a function of the decrease in frequency of the next larger size category.

Five neck fragments provide this description:

Mouth Diameter
range	30-35cm.
mode	—
mean	32.2cm.

Wall Angle
range	0-15°
mode	10°
mean	9°

Wall Profile Mode
primary	A
secondary	D

Lip Treatment Mode	
primary	C1,D
secondary	C
Rim Modification Mode	
primary	H
secondary	A,D
Neck Thickness	
range	.5-.9cm.
mode	.7cm.
mean	.72cm.

The preserved specimens indicate that the height of these necks was about 10 cm.

Flaring-Neck Jars: Size Variant F 1.1.3F

A single fragment of a body-neck juncture indicates a mouth diameter of about 37 cm. or 38 cm. This specimen represents .6% of the pottery, or 1.6% of the necked jars. The low frequency for the group is consistent with its declining popularity in Middle Patibamba and Late Patibamba I and absence from the Late Patibamba II sample.

Flaring-Neck Jars: Size Variant G 1.1.3G

There are no rim sherds in this category, but five body-neck junctures represent jars which had mouth diameters in excess of 41 cm. These pieces account for 2.9% of the total vessel sample, or 7.9% of the flaring-neck jars. This indicates that these large vessels have regained some of their former popularity following their near disappearance in Late Patibamba II.

CLOSED FORMS 1.2

Six sherds from closed vessels represent 3.5% of the Illaura Phase ceramic sample. This is an increase over previous phases, and since four decorated body sherds from unidentified closed forms were not included, the frequency of this general category was still higher. The rising popularity is a trend which originated in Late Patibamba I and continued into Late Patibamba II and Illaura.

Flasks 1.2.2

A section of a flask-shaped vessel represents .6% of the Illaura pottery sample. The side seam is not preserved, but it was probably rounded or tightly curved since there is no evidence of the angle which is associated with flat side seams. The diameter of the vessel body was at least 20 cm., and the flattened sides bore painted decoration of black bands 1 cm. to 1.6 cm. wide on a matte red slip. The center of the flattened side has a disk of clay patched into a circular opening 3.5 cm. in diameter, which provides a clue about how these vessels were manufactured.

Incurving Vessels 1.2.3

Rim sherds from five incurving vessels represent 2.9% of the Illaura vessels, or 83.3% of all the closed forms (fig. 18G, H, J, M, R). These incurving bowls may be described as follows:

Mouth Diameter	
range	9-30cm.
mode	–
mean	18.8cm.
Wall Angle	
range	(-10)-(-55)°
mode	–
mean	(-34°)
Wall Profile Mode	
primary	D
secondary	E
Lip Treatment Mode	
primary	C
secondary	–
Rim Modification Mode	
primary	A
secondary	–
Wall Thickness	
range	.5cm.
mode	.5cm.
mean	.5cm.

The wide range in mouth diameter found in these vessels makes them more consistent with earlier phases at Jargampata than were the incurving bowls of Late Patibamba II, which were all small. The only vessel with part of the base preserved is a subglobular bowl about 8.5 cm. tall with a slightly flattened bottom (fig. 18R). This same vessel is decorated with a horizontal black band with a wavy orange line and dark red dots which circles the broadest part of the bowl. Another decorated bowl has the diagnostically late single black band with wavy white lines placed just below the rim on the bowl's exterior (fig. 18M).

OPEN BOWL FORMS 1.3

Bowls and cups constitute 39% of the Illaura Phase vessel sample, a total of sixty-seven specimens. This frequency is closer to that found in Early Patibamba than that of any intervening phases.

Plain Bowls 1.3.1

There are twenty-three rim fragments from plain bowls which represent 13.4% of the total vessel sample, or 34.3% of the open bowl forms. This represents an increase in the frequency of plain bowls relative to decorated ones. The sample may be described as follows:

Mouth Diameter	
range	10-30cm.
mode	18cm.
mean	16.1cm.
Wall Angle	
range	(-5)-50°
mode	35°
mean	27°
Wall Profile Mode	
primary	A
secondary	D
Lip Treatment Mode	
primary	D
secondary	A,B,C
Rim Modification Mode	
primary	A
secondary	C

Wall Thickness

range	.4-.8cm.
mode	.5cm.
mean	.5cm.

Although the mean mouth diameter shows a slight reduction in the Illaura Phase, the modal size remains unchanged. The decrease is caused by the near disappearance of oversize plain bowls. Wall angle is interesting: it has a bimodal distribution with a primary mode at $35°$ and a second, slightly less frequent, mode at $0°$. These two modes suggest that the progressive differentiation in shape between interior- and exterior-decorated bowls not only reaches its strongest expression in this phase, but that plain bowls were also manufactured according to the two conceptual categories. Bowls with low wall angles have a gently curving union between the walls and bottoms, while those with more flaring walls have a more tightly curving union.

Regular-Size Plain Bowls 1.3.1.1

Twenty-two rims from regular-size plain bowls account for 12.8% of the Illaura vessel sample and 95.7% of the plain bowls (fig. 19U, AB, AE, AG, AJ, AP, AT, BD). They may be described as follows:

Mouth Diameter

range	10-23cm.
mode	18cm.
mean	15.5cm.

Wall Angle

range	$(-5)-50°$
mode	$30-40°$
mean	$26.6°$

Wall Profile Mode

primary	A
secondary	D

Lip Treatment Mode

primary	D
secondary	A,B C

Rim Modification Mode

primary	A
secondary	C

Wall Thickness

range	.4-.8cm.
mode	.5cm.
mean	.5cm.

Regular-size plain bowls appear to have been differentiating into two separate vessel forms. Both wall angle and mouth diameter have broad ranges which are tending toward bimodal distributions. Flaring walls are associated with large mouth diameters, while nearly vertical walls are found on vessels with smaller diameters. This appears to reflect the influence of interior-decorated and exterior-decorated vessel forms. Vessels with vertical walls are becoming smaller, and there are two examples with mouth diameters under 10 cm. (fig. 36T, U). These have been included with miniature vessels, but it seems likely that the miniature vessel category was merging with the regular-size category, just as oversize vessels may have been.

Bowl heights are comparable to those of Late Patibamba II and range from 5 cm. to 7 cm. The vessels with small mouth diameters and vertical walls are generally shallower. There is no evidence for the bowls 8 cm. to 9 cm. deep

which characterize Late Patibamba I.

Very few bases are preserved, but most of those recovered are gently curved with a continuous curve uniting the vessel walls and bottoms. However, one bowl has a slightly salient bottom (fig. 19U), and another has a flat base.

Oversize Plain Bowls 1.3.1.2

One plain bowl fragment from an oversize bowl represents .6% of the vessel sample, or 4.3% of the plain bowls. This specimen may be described as follows:

Mouth Diameter	30cm.
Wall Angle	$35°$
Wall Profile	A
Lip Treatment	A
Rim Modification	E
Wall Thickness	.4cm.

This single example of an oversize bowl is heavily eroded and may have been redeposited with the Illaura material. The sherd provides no evidence for vessel height or base form.

Decorated Bowls 1.3.2

There are thirty-five fragmentary decorated bowls from the Illaura pottery sample. They represent 20.3% of all the vessels, or 52.2% of the open bowl forms. This is a drop in the popularity of decorated bowls from Late Patibamba II. Only twenty-four vessel fragments have rims sufficiently complete for measurement. They may be described as follows:

Mouth Diameter

range	14-22cm.
mode	17cm.
mean	15.7cm.

Wall Angle

range	$0-35°$
mode	$30°$
mean	$21.5°$

Wall Profile Mode

primary	A
secondary	D

Lip Treatment Mode

primary	A
secondary	B,D

Rim Modification Mode

primary	A
secondary	C

Wall Thickness

range	.3-.6cm.
mode	.5cm.
mean	.48cm.

These figures show a tendency for the mean dimensions of mouth diameter, wall angle, and even wall thickness to decline, although apparently the innovations had not yet altered the modes.

Painted decoration is limited to either the interior or the exterior of bowls. Generally the paint is placed on an orange or yellowish natural surface, but a red-slip background is also common.

As in the preceding three phases, white is the most frequent color, although it does not occur as a mono-

chrome. Its most common use is for decorative elements on areas painted with darker colors. Wavy lines and dots are the most frequent, but white outlines are still common. Another white design element is the Saint Andrew's cross on black disks. There is only a single case in which white was used for the major structural lines of a design.

Second to white, dark red is the most commonly used color. It is found more frequently as a monochrome than during Late Patibamba II but is still usually combined with other colors. Dark red is used for horizontal bands and, less frequently, for vertical bands. Less common uses include dark red bands forming rectangles, wavy lines, structural design lines, and, rarely, fields of color or dots. A significant design theme for which dark red is no longer used is the colored disk with a white Saint Andrew's cross. Dark red was generally used for this disk in Middle Patibamba aand Late Patibamba I. In Late Patibamba II, black was also common, but in the Illaura Phase black disks totally replace the dark red ones.

Black remains only slightly less common than dark red and is the only color which regularly appears as a monochrome. It is used most frequently for horizontal bands and, secondly, for colored disks associated with the Saint Andrew's cross. Other uses for black include design lines, wavy lines, dots, and, occasionally, outlines. One specimen has black used as a field color.

Illaura Phase decorated bowls are monochrome, bichrome, or trichrome. There are no color schemes with more than three colors. Uncommon colors—orange, brown, and the matte crusty black of Late Patibamba II—are absent in Illaura, but gray, yellow, and light red can still be distinguished in low frequencies. Gray is used for vertical bands, dots, the Saint Andrew's cross, and other design elements. In these roles, it sometimes substitutes for black and at other times for white. Yellow occurs in only a single case each of a vertical band and a wavy line. Light red appears only as a horizontal or vertical band, a structural position occupied by dark red.

The transformation of the Jargampata polychrome painting into a trichrome tradition seems to involve a process more complex than the simple disappearance of some of the pigments in the color inventory. Rather, it seems as though certain categories become broader and less precisely defined so that several colors previously distinguished become absorbed into the same class. Orange seems to be in the process of being absorbed by dark red during Late Patibamba II and is nearly absent in the Illaura Phase. Similarly, light red seems to be in the process of becoming absorbed by dark red during the Illaura Phase, and it could be speculated that this color would be absent from post-Illaura pottery. Gray may still be contrastive with both black and white but seems to be identified with these colors. It is very rare for gray to occur in combination with black, and it may be merging with it into a single category.

The most popular color combinations found on Illaura Phase decorated bowls include bichrome combinations black and white, dark red and black, and dark red and white and trichrome combinations dark red, white, and black and dark red, white, and gray. As mentioned above, black and dark red are the only monochromes.

Interior-Decorated Bowls   1.3.2.1

Twenty-one fragmentary interior-decorated bowls from the Illaura Phase account for 12.2% of the total vessel sample, or 60% of the decorated bowls. This figure shows a reduction in the popularity of this class, although its frequency relative to exterior-decorated bowls remains essentially unchanged.

Regular-Size Interior-Decorated Bowls   1.3.2.1.1

Only fourteen of the interior-decorated bowl fragments provide measurements of mouth diameter, and all fall within the range of regular-size vessels. Although this represents only 8.1% of the vessel sample, it seems likely that this size accounted for 100% of the interior-decorated bowls and that the frequency of the class was greater. The oversize interior-decorated bowl had probably disappeared. The regular-size bowls may be described as follows:

Mouth Diameter
range	14-22cm.
mode	17cm.
mean	17.8cm.

Wall Angle
range	20-35°
mode	30°
mean	28.5°

Wall Profile Mode
primary	A
secondary	D

Lip Treatment Mode
primary	A
secondary	B,D

Rim Modification Mode
primary	A
secondary	C

Wall Thickness
range	.4-.6cm.
mode	.5cm.
mean	.49cm.

The height of these interior-decorated bowls ranges from about 5.5 cm. to 7.5 cm. This slight reduction in height from the Late Patibamba I Phase is a trend even more noticeable in plain bowls. Bases are gently curved and are joined to the vessel walls by a very tight curve which approaches an angle in several cases.

Decoration is placed on the bowl interior and not on the rim. Paint may be applied to a natural light surface or on a yellowish or tan slip virtually indistinguishable from the paste. Some examples, however, have a light red slip.

The Saint Andrew's cross on a colored disk is an important and frequent design theme in the Illaura Phase which is derived from earlier phases at Jargampata (fig. 21L, M). However, the colored disks contrast with those of earlier phases because black is the only color used. All crosses are placed diagonally, and most examples have circles painted in the quadrants of the disk. Variants include one example with contrasting-color dots painted on the cross (fig. 21M) and two specimens with multiple dots rather than circles in the quadrants. Both of these variants appear for the first time in Late Patibamba II. Unfortunately, there is no information concerning the presence or absence of the narrow band connecting colored disks on opposite sides of the bowl.

Horizontal-band designs are common on Illaura ceramics, but because of the fragmentary nature of the remains it is difficult to determine how many examples had only single bands. Two examples may have had single, dark red bands just below the rim (fig. 23Q), while a third had a natural band bordered by a dark red band or zone just

below the rim (fig. 23P). All of these horizontal bands are decorated with single or multiple wavy lines, and some have dots as well.

Themes which use two parallel horizontal bands continue to be common on Illaura bowl interiors. Color combinations include black over dark red (fig. 24H; plate 13C), dark red over yellow (fig. 24I), and dark red over gray. The bands are decorated with wavy lines or wavy lines with dots, most frequently white.

One bowl has multiple vertical bands from just below the rim to the bottom. The preserved section of the vessel has three bands, with the outer ones gray and the central band dark red. They are outlined with white and have wavy lines and dots as space-filler elements (fig. 22J; plate 12C).

Some design themes common in Late Patibamba I and II are conspicuously absent in Illaura ceramics. Among these are the panel themes, including the panel with horizontal divisions. The zigzag-band theme of Late Patibamba I and II is represented on one or perhaps two Illaura vessel fragments (fig. 26L), although it seems that this theme may have merged with a panel arrangement by the end of Late Patibamba II (fig. 27A, B; plate 12B).

Exterior-Decorated Bowls   1.3.2.2

There are fourteen fragments of exterior-decorated bowls. These represent 8.1% of the entire sample, or 40% of the decorated bowls. These bowls have decreased in popularity within the total complex, but they remain at approximately the same frequency relative to interior-decorated bowls that was found in the immediately preceding phases. Only ten vessel fragments provide mouth diameter measurements.

Regular-Size Exterior-Decorated Bowls   1.3.2.2.1

All of the exterior-decorated bowls which could be measured fall within the range of regular-size bowls, although often at the lower end of the range. Only ten vessels were represented by sections large enough for measurement. This accounts for 5.8% of the total vessel sample, but it seems likely that this frequency should be higher since the four unmeasurable fragments were probably from the same size group. The sample may be described as follows:

Mouth Diameter	
range	10-17cm.
mode	12cm.
mean	12.8cm.
Wall Angle	
range	0-20°
mode	15°
mean	11.5°
Wall Profile Mode	
primary	A
secondary	D
Lip Treatment Mode	
primary	B,D
secondary	A,C
Rim Modification Mode	
primary	A
secondary	E1,E2
Wall Thickness	
range	.3-.5cm.
mode	.4cm.
mean	.47cm.

The long, progressive differentiation of exterior-decorated and interior-decorated bowl forms reaches its maximum expression in this phase. When plotted for both mouth diameter and wall angle, these form categories do not overlap at all and, as indicated above, the complementary groups have begun to influence plain bowls, creating a continuous but bimodal distribution.

Exterior-decorated bowls range from slightly more than 4 cm. to nearly 7.5 cm. in height. They are generally smaller than previous examples, and some approach the upper ranges of miniature vessels from previous phases. Bottoms are slightly curved and are joined to vessel walls by continuous open curves. Small tripod tab feet are frequent additions to the bases and help establish continuity with Late Patibamba I and II.

Decoration is limited to painting on the exterior surface of the bowls. As on interior-decorated bowls, the rim is not deliberately decorated in this phase, although the casual application of paint frequently results in designs which run onto the rim.

Design themes are derived from those of earlier phases of the Patibamba style. Horizontal-band themes predominate, although vertical bands and rectangles also appear.

The two-horizontal-band theme is absent from Illaura exterior-decorated bowls, but the previously very popular three-band theme is represented (fig. 29I). As on earlier examples, the bands are black over dark red over black and are decorated with white elements such as wavy lines and dots. Circular space-filler elements do not appear. Several examples are quite eroded, and their indistinguishability from examples of Late Patibamba I and II makes for some question concerning the validity of the association. However, there is no doubt that they were included in the Illaura period strata C and C1, so until more evidence is available they will be treated as a component of the Illaura pottery.

The single black band just below the rim—a theme common to interior-decorated bowls of Late Patibamba II—has become common on exterior-decorated bowls and especially the smallest specimens (fig. 28F). It appears as though this theme lacked elaboration with space-filler elements, though one variant has a thin horizontal gray band with pendent lines of the same color.

Two bowls have dark red bands forming rectangles. Both are placed diagonally to the vessel rim, so they might be best described as diamonds (fig. 28N). One diamond is outlined with white lines and has white circle space fillers.

Vertical-band themes are reasonably popular and include both multiple-band groups with alternating colors (fig. 30G) and isolated or single bands arranged about the bowl (fig. 30I; plate 14C). Space fillers on these bands are generally white and include wavy lines, wavy lines with dots, and, in one example, circles with central dots.

Tripod Bowls   1.3.3

The large tripod supports of Late Patibamba II—both solid and hollow—are absent from the Illaura pottery sample. The only tripods represented are small tripod tab feet of the kind which originated in Late Patibamba I (figs. 28F, 30G, I). There are seven examples of bowls with these supports which represent 4.1% of the vessels. In spite of the disappearance of the large tripods, this is still the highest frequency for tripod supports during any phase at Jargampata.

The tripod-tab-foot bowls of the Illaura Phase have a greater size range than those of the earlier phases, with

mouth diameters ranging from 10 cm. to 17 cm. and heights from about 4 cm. to 7 cm.

Pedestal Bowls   1.3.5

There are four fragments of pedestal bowls which account for 2.3% of the Illaura Phase vessel sample (fig. 34C, E, L; plate 15). This represents only a very modest increase from Late Patibamba II. The bowls may be described as follows:

Mouth Diameter
range	16-22cm.
mode	–
mean	19cm.

Wall Angle
range	30-40°
mode	30°
mean	32.5°

Wall Profile Mode
primary	A
secondary	–

Lip Treatment Mode
primary	A,D
secondary	–

Rim Modification Mode
primary	E2
secondary	D

Wall Thickness
range	.4-.6cm.
mode	.6cm.
mean	.53cm.

One pedestal bowl from this phase was nearly complete (fig. 34L; plate 15A), which seems to demonstrate the association of these vessels with the Illaura reoccupation. The diameter of the solid base is 14.5 cm., and the vessel height is 12.5 cm.

Like earlier examples, Illaura pedestal bowls have coarse paste and a rough, unpolished surface finish lacking any colored slip or decoration.

Lyre-Shaped Cups   1.3.6

Two sherds from lyre-shaped cups represent 1.2% of the Illaura Phase vessels (fig. 35G, H). However, these rims have nearly straight wall profiles, suggesting that the distinction between straight-sided tall cups and true lyre-shaped vessels may be obscured and that the shape categories were merging. The two vessels most resembling lyre-shaped cups may be described as follows:

Mouth Diameter
range	7-8cm.
mode	–
mean	7.5cm.

Wall Angle
range	0-5°
mode	–
mean	2.5°

Wall Profile Mode
primary	A,E
secondary	–

Lip Treatment Mode
primary	A,C1
secondary	–

Rim Modification Mode
primary	E,E2
secondary	–

Wall Thickness
range	.4-.5cm.
mode	–
mean	.45cm.

These figures indicate a reduction in mouth diameter, but there is no information concerning vessel height. Neither of the examples has a handle or any decoration.

Straight-Sided Tall Cups   1.3.7

A single vessel representing .6% of the Illaura sample comes from what is best identified as a straight-sided tall cup (fig. 35C). It may be described as follows:

Mouth Diameter	9cm.
Wall Angle	0°
Wall Profile	A
Lip Treatment	A
Rim Modification	E2
Wall Thickness	.4cm.

The decoration on this specimen consists of a dark red band with white wavy line and dots around the lower part of the cup. Dark red vertical lines and white dots run from the band to the rim, creating what may be a panel division. The original height of the vessel must have been about 12 cm.

MINIATURE VESSELS   1.4

Three bowls, representing 1.7% of the Illaura sample, may be classed as miniature vessels (fig. 36S-U). They may be described as follows:

Mouth Diameter
range	8-9cm.
mode	9cm.
mean	8.6cm.

Wall Angle
range	10-40°
mode	–
mean	21.6°

Wall Profile Mode
primary	D
secondary	A

Lip Treatment Mode
primary	A
secondary	B

Rim Modification Mode
primary	A
secondary	–

Wall Thickness
range	.4cm.
mode	.4cm.
mean	.4cm.

The separation of miniature vessels from regular-size vessels is not clear in the Illaura Phase. It seems likely that both oversize vessels and miniatures had merged or were merging with regular-size vessels by this time. The bowls placed in this class may simply belong to the lower end of the variation among regular-size bowls.

None of the miniatures are decorated, but in keeping with the developing shape distinctions between interior- and exterior-decorated bowls, it is clear that one (fig. 36S) belongs to the former while two (fig. 36T, U) belong to the latter.

The height of these small bowls probably ranged from 3 cm. to about 5 cm.

SPOONS 1.5

Spoons show a peculiar temporal distribution at Jargampata. There are several examples, including both small and large specimens from the Early Patibamba Phase samples (fig. 27I, J, L) and others from the gravel fill dumped into the House Group which apparently contained Early Patibamba material from the surface (fig. 27G, H). With the exception of imported Cajamarca-style specimens from the House Group (plate 18B-D), spoons are not represented in any intervening samples until the Illaura Phase. This is particularly interesting considering the general similarity in frequency of the major vessel shape categories between these two phases.

The Illaura ceramic sample includes one fragment of a spoon which represents .6% of the collection (fig. 27K). The fragment is small but shows that the spoon had a flat prismatic handle and a more or less circular bowl much like most of the Early Patibamba examples and unlike the single-piece scoop shape characteristic of the Cajamarca imports and the one Early Patibamba example (fig. 27L).

PRESS MOLDS 1.7

There are no press molds in the Illaura ceramic sample, but a small fragment of a face—probably human—was produced by pushing clay into a slightly concave mold. This suggests that press molds were still part of the ceramic inventory at this time.

SCRAPER-POLISHERS 1.9

Three flat ceramic objects may be classed as scraper-polishers. Together they constitute 1.7% of the ceramics. Two of these are clearly manufactured from sherds, probably by use abrasion (plate 15P, R). Although they are not so well finished as earlier examples, they are very similar and probably had the same function. The third specimen is distinct in that it is a well-finished elliptical plaque (fig. 36F; plate 15Q). The shape is reminiscent of a similar plaque from Late Patibamba II (fig. 36E), and it seems likely that these two specimens belong to a category of objects distinct from other scraper-polishers. There is, however, an essential difference between the two because the Illaura piece was manufactured by abrasion from a larger piece of pottery, while the Late Patibamba II specimen was modeled in its final form.

EXOTIC VESSELS 1.10

The ceramic remains at Jargampata document a process of progressive intensification of elite Wari influence at the rural Jargampata site. The quantity of imported elite pottery goes up through the first three phases and is seemingly related to the presence of outside authority manifest in the construction of the North Unit. Late Patibamba II represents a slightly later time period in which the Wari empire was collapsing and both sites were experiencing depopulation. As would be expected, the quantity of elite imported pottery drops off sharply.

The Illaura Phase postdates Middle Horizon unity under Wari. It represents a poorly known time late in the Middle Horizon or during the Late Intermediate Period when there were few integrative influences and local regionalism was probably very strong. Consistent with this image is a total lack of any foreign pottery in the Illaura ceramic sample. All pieces in the collection have paste, surface finish, and colors typical of Jargampata.

There can be no doubt that Illaura pottery represents a continuation of the Patibamba-style ceramic tradition. Furthermore, it seems unlikely that there was any marked foreign influence between Late Patibamba II and the Illaura Phase. The differences between the two phases can be accounted for by patterns or trends already obvious in Late Patibamba II or by deletions and simplifications. There are no new vessel shapes, design themes, design elements, decorative colors, or rules for combinations which could be attributed to external introductions. It seems clear that following the Late Patibamba II abandonment, Jargampata lay in ruins for a considerable time until reoccupied by a small group descendant from the original occupants. Between the abandonment and reoccupation, the Jargampata area remained extremely isolated. No foreign armies or peasant masses surged into the power vacuum at the heart of the Wari state. Local populations at Jargampata were not replaced. There appears to have been simply an extreme depopulation and an emaciation of culture content affecting a vast area but perhaps most extreme in the old Wari center.

Literature Cited

Benavides, Mario
1965 Estudio de la Cerámica Decorada de Qonchopata. Bachelor's thesis in anthropological sciences, Universidad Nacional de San Cristóbal de Huamanga, Ayacucho, Peru.

Bennett, Wendell C.
1934 *Excavations at Tiahuanaco*. Anthropological Papers of the American Museum of Natural History, 34(3). American Museum of Natural History, New York.
1953 *Excavations at Wari, Ayacucho, Peru*. Yale University Publications in Anthropology, no. 49. Yale University Press, New Haven.

Bennett, Wendell C., and Junius B. Bird
1964 *Andean Culture History*. Natural History Press, Garden City, N.Y.

Berger, R.
1970 Ancient Egyptian Radiocarbon Chronology. *Philosophical Transactions of the Royal Society of London*, series A, 269:23-36.

Bird, Robert
1967 La Agricultura en la Visita de Ortiz. In *Visita de la Provincia de León de Huánuco en 1562*, I, Iñigo Ortiz de Zúñiga, 356-67. Universidad Nacional Hermilio Valdizán, Huánuco, Peru.

Bonaviva, Duccio
1967- Investigaciones Arqueológicas en el Mantaro
68   Medio. *Revista del Museo Nacional*, 35:211-94.

Bushnell, G.H.S.
1957 *Peru*. Praeger, New York.

Carter, William E.
1968 Secular Reinforcement in Aymara Death Ritual. *American Anthropologist*, 70:238-63.

Casafranca, José
1960 Los Nuevos Sitios Arqueológicos Chavinoides en el Departamento de Ayacucho. In *Antiguo Peru: Espacio y Tiempo*, 325-34. Liberia-Editorial Mejia Baca, Lima.

Cieza de Leon, Pedro de
n.d. La Crónica del Perú. In *Crónicas de la Conquista del Perú*, edited by J. Le Riverend, 127-497. Editorial Nueva España, Mexico City.

Deetz, James
1965 *The Dynamics of Stylistic Change in Arikara Ceramics*. University of Illinois Press, Urbana.

Donnan, Christopher B.
1968 An Association of Middle Horizon Epoch 2A Specimens from the Chicama Valley, Peru. *Nawpa Pacha*, 6:15-18. Institute of Andean Studies, Berkeley.
1972 Moche-Huari Murals from Northern Peru. *Archaeology*, 25 (2):85-95.

Fallers, L. A.
1967 Are African Cultivators to be Called "Peasants"? In *Peasant Society: A Reader*, edited by J. M. Potter, M. N. Diaz, and G. M. Foster, 35-41. Little, Brown and Co, Boston.

Flores Espinoza, Isabel
1959 El Sitio Arqueológio de Wari Willca, Huancayo. *Actas y Trabajos del II Congreso Nacional de Historia del Perú*, 1:177-86. Centro de Estudios Histórico-Militares del Perú, Lima.

Gonzáles, J. Enrique
1966 *Investigacion Arqueológica en Ñawinpukia*. Consejo General de Investigaciones, Universidad Nacional de San Cristóbal de Huamanga, Ayacucho, Peru.
1967 Período Intermedio Temprano, Arqueología de Ayacucho. *Wamani*, 2 (1):96-108. Organo de la Asociación Peruana de Anthropólogos, Filial, Ayacucho, Peru.

Hardoy, Jorge
1968 *Urban Planning in Pre-Columbian America*. George Braziller, New York.

Harth-Terre, Emilio
1959 Piki-Llacta, cuidad de pósitos y bastimentos. *Revista del Museo e Instituto Arqueológico*, 9(18):41-56. Universidad Nacional del Cuzco, Cuzco, Peru.

Isbell, Billie Jean
1972 Migrants' Adaptation of Traditional Andean Symbolic Systems to the Urban Environment of Lima. Paper presented at the Seventy-first Annual Meeting of the American Anthropological Association, Toronto.

Isbell, William H.
1968 The Interpretation of Prehistoric Site Locations in Terms of a Modern Folk Model. Paper presented at the Sixty-seventh Annual Meeting of the American Anthropological Association, Seattle, Wash.
1970a Las Culturas Intermedias de la Sierra Central: 200 AC-600 DC. *El Serrano*, 19(248):16-20.
1970b El Horizonte Medio o la Unificación de los Andes Centrales. *El Serrano*, 19(249):16-20.
1971 Un Pueblo Rural Ayacuchano Durante el Imperio Huari. *Actas y Memorias del 39th Congreso International de Americanistas*, 3:89-105. Cerro de Pasco Corp., Lima.
1972 Quechua Speakers and the Cultivation of Steep Hillsides. Paper presented at the Thirty-seventh Annual Meeting of the Society for American Archaeology, Miami, Fla.

Izumi, Seiichi, and Toshihko Sono
1963 *Andes 2: Excavations at Kotosh, Peru*. Kadokawa Publishing Co., Tokyo.

Kosok, Paul
1965 *Life, Land and Water in Ancient Peru*. Long

Island University Press, Brooklyn, N.Y.

Kroeber, Alfred L.
1930 *Archaeological Explorations in Peru: Part II, The Northern Coast*. Field Museum of Natural History, Anthropology Memoirs, 2(2). Field Museum of Natural History, Chicago.
1944 *Peruvian Archaeology in 1942*. Viking Fund Publications in Anthropology, no. 4. Wenner-Gren Foundation, New York.

Kroeber, Alfred L., and William D. Strong
1924 *The Uhle Collections from Chincha*. University of California Publications in American Archaeology and Ethnology, 28 (2). University of California Press, Berkeley.

Lanning, Edward P.
1967 *Peru before the Incas*. Prentice-Hall, Englewood Cliffs, N.J.

Lara, Jesus
1967 *Inkallajta Inkaraqay*. Editorial los Amigos del Libro, La Paz, Bolivia.

Larco Hoyle, Rafael
1948 *Cronología Arqueológica del Norte del Perú*. Sociedad Geográfica Americana, Buenos Aires, Argentina.
1963 *Las Epocas Peruanas*. Museo Arqueológico Rafael Larco Herrera, Lima.

Lathrap, Donald W.
1962 Yarinacocha: Stratigraphic Excavations in the Peruvian Montaña. Ph.D. dissertation, Harvard University.
1964 An Alternative Seriation of the Mabaruma Phase, Northwestern British Guiana. *American Antiquity*, 29(3):353-59.
1966 The Mabaruma Phase: A Return to the More Probable Interpretation. *American Antiquity*, 31 (4):558-66.
1970 *The Upper Amazon*. Praeger, New York.

Lumbreras, Luis G.
1959 Esquema Arqueológico de la Sierra Central Del Perú. *Revista del Museo Nacional*, 28:63-117.
1960 La Cultura de Wari, Ayacucho. *Etnología y Arqueología, Publicación del Instituto de Etnología y Arqueología*, 1(1):130-227.
1969 *De Los Pueblos, Las Culturas y Las Artes Del Antiquo Peru*. Francisco Moncloa, Editores, Lima.

MacNeish, Richard S.
1971 Early Man in the Andes. *Scientific American*, 224(4):36-46.

Matos Mendieta, Ramiro
1970 El Período Formativo en la Sierra Central. *El Serrano*, 19(246):14-17.

McCown, Theodore Doney
1945 *Pre-Incaic Huamachuco: Survey and Excavations in the Region of Huamachuco and Cajabamba*. University of California Publications in American Archaeology and Ethnology, 39(4):223-400. University of California Press, Berkeley.

Menzel, Dorothy
1964 Style and Time in the Middle Horizon. *Nawpa Pacha*, 2:1-105. Institute of Andean Studies, Berkeley.
1968a New Data on the Huari Empire in Middle Horizon Epoch 2A. *Nawpa Pacha* 6:47-114. Institute of Andean Studies, Berkeley.

1968b *La Cultura Huari*. Compañía de Seguros y Reaseguros Peruano Suiza, Lima.

Menzel, Dorothy, John H. Rowe, and Lawrence E. Dawson
1964 *The Paracas Pottery of Ica: A Study in Style and Time*. University of California Publications in American Archaeology and Ethnology, 50. University of California Press, Berkeley.

Mishkin, Bernard
1963 The Contemporary Quechua. In *Handbook of South American Indians*, edited by Julian H. Steward, 2:411-70. Cooper Square, New York.

Morris, Craig
1966 El Tampu Real de Tunsucancha. *Cuadernos de Investigación, Numero 1, Antropología*, 95-107. Universidad Nacional Hermilio Valdizán, Huánuco, Peru.
1967 Storage in Tawantisuyu. Ph.D. dissertation, University of Chicago.

Morris, Craig, and Donald E. Thompson
1970 Huánuco Viejo: An Inca Administrative Center. *American Antiquity*, 35(3):344-62.

Murra, John V.
1956 The Economic Organization of the Inca State. Ph.D. dissertation, University of Chicago.
1960 Rite and Crop in the Inca State. In *Culture in History*, edited by Stanley Diamond, 393-407. Columbia University Press, New York.
1966 El Instituto de Investigaciones Andinas y sus Estudios en Huánuco, 1963-66. *Cuadernos de Investigación, Numero 1, Antropología*, 7-21. Universidad Nacional Hermilio Valdizán, Huánuco, Peru.
1967 La Visita de los Chupachu como Fuente Etnológica. In *Visita de la Provincia de León de Huánuco en 1562*, I, Iñigo Ortiz de Zúñiga, 381-406. Universidad Nacional Hermilio Valdizán, Huánuco, Peru.
1972 El "Control Vertical" de un Máximo de Pisos Ecológicos en la Economia de las Sociedades Andinas. In *Visita de la Provincia de Léon de Huánuco en 1562*, II, Iñigo Ortiz de Zúñiga, 429-76. Universidad Nacional Hermilio Valdizán, Huánuco, Peru.

Nordenskiold, Erland
1930 *L'Archeologie du Bassin de L'Amazone*. Editions G. Van Oest, Paris.

O'Neal, Lila M., and Alfred L. Kroeber
1930 *Textile Periods in Ancient Peru*. University of California Publications in American Archaeology and Ethnology, 21(1). University of California Press, Berkeley.

Oppenheim, A. Leo
1964 *Ancient Mesopotamia: Portrait of a Dead Civilization*. University of Chicago Press, Chicago.

Ortiz de Zúñiga, Iñigo
1967 *Visita de la Provincia Léon de Huánuco en 1562*, I. Universidad Nacional Hermilio Valdizán, Huánuco, Peru.
1972 *Visita de la Provincia León de Huánuco en 1562*, II. Universidad Nacional Hermilio Valdizán, Huánuco, Peru.

Pardo, Luis A.
1957 *Historia y Arqueología del Cuzco*, I, II. Cuzco, Peru.

Parker, Gary John
  1969   *Ayacucho Quechua Grammar and Dictionary*. Janua Linguarum, Series Practica, 82. Mouton, The Hague.
Parsons, Jeffrey R.
  1968   An Estimate of Size and Population for Middle Horizon Tiahuanaco, Bolivia. *American Antiquity*, 33(2):243-45.
Paulsen, Allison C.
  1965   Pottery from Huaca del Loro, South Coast of Peru. Manuscript.
  1974   The Thorny Oyster and the Voice of God: Spondylus and Strombus in Andean Prehistory. *American Antiquity*, 39(4, pt. 1):597-607.
Polanyi, Karl, Conrad M. Arensberg, and Harry W. Pearson
  1957   *Trade and Market in the Early Empires: Economies in History and Theory*. Free Press, Glencoe, Ill.
Poma de Ayala, Felipe Guaman
  1936   *Nueva Coronica y Buen Gobierno*. Institut D'Etnologie, Paris.
Ponce Sangines, Carlos
  1969a La Ciudad Tiwanaku. *Arte y Arqueología*, no. 1:5-32. Universidad Mayor de San Andres, La Paz, Bolivia.
  1969b *Descripción Sumaria del Templete Semisubterráneo*. 4th ed. Los Amigos del Libro, La Paz, Bolivia.
  1970   *Las Culturas Wankarani y Chiripa y su Relación con Tiwanaku*. Publication Number 25. Academia Nacional de Ciencias de Bolivia, La Paz, Bolivia.
Ponce Sangines, Carlos, and Gerardo Mogrovejo Terrazas.
  1970   *Acerca de la Procedencia del Material Lítico de los Monumentos de Tiwanaku*. Publication Number 21. Academia Nacional de Ciencias de Bolivia, La Paz, Bolivia.
Ravines, Rogger
  1968   Un Deposito De Ofrendas Del Horizonte Medio En La Sierra Central Del Perú. *Nawpa Pacha*, 6:19-46. Institute of Andean Studies, Berkeley.
  1970a Panorama Arqueológico de la Sierra Central: Primera Parte. *El Serrano*, 19(244):16-19.
  1970b Panorama Arqueológico de la Sierra Central: Segunda Parte. *El Serrano*, 19(245):18-22.
Reichlen, Henri
  1970   Reconocimientos Arqueológicos en los Andes de Cajamarca. In *100 Años de Arqueología en el Peru*, edited by Rogger Ravines, 463-502. Fuentes e Investigaciones para la Historia del Perú, 3. Instituto de Estudios Peruanos, Lima.
Rouse, Irving
  1939   *Prehistory of Haiti: A Study of Method*. Yale University Publications in Anthropology, no. 21. Yale University Press, New Haven.
Rowe, John H.
  1944   *An Introduction to the Archaeology of Cuzco*. Papers of the Peabody Museum of American Archaeology and Ethnology, 27(2). Yale University Press, New Haven.
  1956   Archaeological Explorations in Southern Peru, 1954-1955. *American Antiquity*, 22(2):135-51.
  1961   Stratigraphy and Seriation. *American Antiquity*, 26(3, pt. 1):324-30.
  1962   Stages and Periods in Archaeological Interpretation. *Southwestern Journal of Anthropology*, 18(1):40-54.
  1963   Urban Settlements in Ancient Peru. *Nawpa Pacha* 1:1-28. Institute of Andean Studies, Berkeley.
  1967   An Interpretation of Radiocarbon Measurements on Archaeological Samples from Peru. In *Peruvian Archaeology*, edited by J. H. Rowe and Dorothy Menzel, 16-30. Peek Publications, Palo Alto, Calif.
  1970   La Arqueología del Cuzco como Historia Cultural. In *100 Años de Arqueología en el Perú*, edited by Rogger Ravines, 549-64. Fuentes e Investigaciones para la Historia del Perú, 3. Instituto de Estudios Peruanos, Lima.
Rowe, John H., Donald Collier, and Gordon R. Willey
  1950   Reconnaissance Notes on the Site of Huari, near Ayacucho, Peru. *American Antiquity*, 16(2):120-37.
Schaedel, Richard P.
  1948   Monolithic Sculpture of the Southern Andes. *Archaeology*, 1(2):66-73.
  1951   Major Ceremonial and Population Centers in Northern Peru. In *Civilizations of Ancient America: Selected Papers of the 29th International Congress of Americanists*, 232-43. University of Chicago Press, Chicago.
  1957   *Arqueología Chilena*. Centro de Estudios Antropológicos, Universidad de Chile, Santiago.
  1966   Incipient Urbanization and Secularization in Tiahuanacoid Peru. *American Antiquity*, 31(3):338-44.
Schmidt, Max
  1929   *Kunst und Kultur von Peru*. Propylaen Verlag, Berlin.
Sestieri, P. C.
  1964   Excavations at Cajamarquilla, Peru. *Archaeology*, 17(1):12-17.
Shepard, Anna O.
  1965   *Ceramics for the Archaeologist*. Publication 609. Carnegie Institute of Washington, Washington, D.C.
Stumer, Louis M.
  1956   Development of Peruvian Coastal Tiahuanacoid Styles. *American Antiquity*, 22(1):59-69.
Tello, Julio C.
  1939   Origen y Desarrollo de las Civilizaciones Prehistóricas Andinas. *Actas y Trabajos Científicos del 27th Congreso Internacional de Americanistas*, 1:589-714. Librería e Imprenta Gil, S.A., Lima.
  1956   *Arqueología del Valle de Casma, Culturas: Chavín, Santa o Huaylas Yunga y Sub-Chimu*. Publicacion Anthropológica del Archivo "Julio C. Tello," 1. Universidad Nacional Major de San Marcos, Lima.
  1970   Las Ruinas de Huari. In *100 Años de Arqueología en el Perú*, edited by Rogger Ravines, 519-25. Fuentes e Investigaciones para la Historia del Perú, 3. Instituto de Estudios Peruanos, Lima.
Thompson, Donald E.
  1967   Investigaciones Arqueológicas en las Aldeas Chupachu de Ichu y Auquimarca. In *Visita de la Provincia de León de Huánuco en 1562*, I, Iñigo Ortiz de Zúñiga, 357-62. Universidad Nacional Hermilio Valdizán, Huánuco, Peru.

1970a Habitantes del Período Intermedio Tardio en la Sierra Central del Perú. *El Serrano,* 19(250): 16-20.

1970b La Ocupación Incaica en la Sierra Central del Perú. *El Serrano,* 19(251):16-21.

Tosi, Joseph A.

1960 *Zonas de Vida Natural en el Perú: Memoria Explicativa Sobre el Mapa Ecológico del Perú.* Technical bulletin no. 5. Instituto Inter-americano de Ciencias Agrícolas de la Organización de Estados Americanos, Zona Andina, Lima.

Towle, Margaret A.

1961 *The Ethnobotany of Pre-Columbian Peru.* Aldine Publishing Co., Chicago.

Uhle, Max

1903a Ancient South-American Civilization. *Harpers Monthly Magazine,* October, 1903, 780-86.

1903b Pachacamac. *Report of the William Pepper, M.D.L.L.D., Peruvian Expedition of 1896.* Department of Archaeology, University of Pennsylvania, Philadelphia.

Wallace, Dwight T.

1957 The Tiahuanaco Horizon Styles in the Peruvian and Bolivian Highlands. Ph.D. dissertation, University of California, Berkeley.

Weberbauer, August

1945 *El Mundo Vegetal de Los Andes Peruanos: Estudio Fitogeográfico.* Estacion Experimental Agrícola de la Molina, Dirección de Agricultura, Ministerio de Agricultura, Lima.

Willey, Gordon R.

1953 *Prehistoric Settlement Patterns in the Virú Valley, Peru.* Bulletin 155. Bureau of American Ethnology, Washington, D.C.

Willey, Gordon R., and Philip Phillips

1958 *Method and Theory in American Archaeology.* University of Chicago Press, Chicago.

Wolf, Eric

1955 Types of Latin American Peasantry. *American Anthropologist,* 57:452-71.

1966 *Peasants.* Prentice-Hall, Englewood Cliffs, N.J.

Yacovleff, Eugenio, and F. L. Herrera

1934- El Mundo Vegetal de los Antiguos Peruanos. 35 *Revista del Museo Nacional,* 3:243-322, 4:31-102.

Zuidema, R. Tom, and Ulpiano Quispe

1968 A Visit to God: A Religious Experience in the Peruvian Community Choque-Huarcaya. *Bijdragen,* 124(124):22-39.

Index